HEALTH LAW AND MEDICAL ETHICS IN SINGAPORE

This book encompasses two inter-related disciplines of health law and medical ethics applicable to Singapore. Apart from Singapore legal materials, it draws upon relevant case precedents and statutory developments from other common law countries and incorporates recommendations and reports by health-related bodies, agencies and committees.

The book is written in an accessible manner suitable for tertiary students. It should also serve as a useful resource for medico-legal practitioners, academics and healthcare professionals who wish to keep abreast of the evolving legal and ethical developments concerning health and medicine.

Gary Chan Kok Yew is Professor of Law at Singapore Management University.

"Prof Gary Chan's *Health Law and Medical Ethics in Singapore* not only provides thorough, deft coverage of the major topics in health law and ethics, but uniquely does so with insight and detailed exposition from an Asian and particularly Singaporean perspective. Indeed, topics such as Confucianism and alternative and complementary medicine, not to mention laws such as Singapore's landmark Human Biomedical Research Act, are given comprehensive examination alongside more traditional health law topics such as consent to treatment, confidentiality, reproduction, and medical negligence. This textbook makes for a most welcome addition to the field. Students and academics alike will benefit from its astute analysis and clear composition".

– Edward S. Dove, Lecturer in Health Law and Regulation, Director of Ethics and Integrity, School of Law, University of Edinburgh

HEALTH LAW AND MEDICAL ETHICS IN SINGAPORE

Gary Chan Kok Yew

LONDON AND NEW YORK

First published 2021
by Routledge
2 Park Square, Milton Park, Abingdon, Oxon OX14 4RN

and by Routledge
52 Vanderbilt Avenue, New York, NY 10017

Routledge is an imprint of the Taylor & Francis Group, an informa business

© 2021 Gary Chan Kok Yew

The right of Gary Chan Kok Yew to be identified as the author of this work has been asserted in accordance with sections 77 and 78 of the Copyright, Designs and Patents Act 1988.

All rights reserved. No part of this book may be reprinted or reproduced or utilised in any form or by any electronic, mechanical, or other means, now known or hereafter invented, including photocopying and recording, or in any information storage or retrieval system, without permission in writing from the publishers.

Trademark notice: Product or corporate names may be trademarks or registered trademarks, and are used only for identification and explanation without intent to infringe.

British Library Cataloguing-in-Publication Data
A catalogue record for this book is available from the British Library

Library of Congress Cataloging-in-Publication Data
A catalog record has been requested for this book

ISBN: 978-0-367-42880-8 (hbk)
ISBN: 978-0-367-42935-5 (pbk)
ISBN: 978-1-003-00022-8 (ebk)

Typeset in Interstate
by codeMantra

Visit the eResources: www.routledge.com/9780367429355

Printed in the United Kingdom
by Henry Ling Limited

To my parents, wife and children

CONTENTS

Table of cases   *xii*
Table of legislation   *xxv*
Preface   *xxix*
Acknowledgements   *xxxi*

1 Introduction to the healthcare system, health laws and regulations   1
   1.1 Introduction   *1*
   1.2 Meaning and scope of health, disease and well-being   *2*
   1.3 Healthcare system in Singapore   *4*
      1.3.1 Healthcare costs and insurance   *5*
      1.3.2 Education and training of healthcare professionals and medical research   *7*
   1.4 Health-related laws and regulations   *8*
      1.4.1 Healthcare professionals   *8*
      1.4.2 Healthcare institutions and practices   *11*
      1.4.3 Medical bodies and institutions   *13*
      1.4.4 Disciplinary process for medical practitioners   *14*
      1.4.5 Legal liabilities of medical practitioners   *22*
   1.5 Conclusion   *24*

2 Introduction to medical ethics   26
   2.1 Introduction   *26*
   2.2 Ethical theories   *27*
      2.2.1 Consequentialism   *27*
      2.2.2 Deontology   *29*
      2.2.3 Virtue ethics   *30*
      2.2.4 Confucianism   *31*
      2.2.5 Care ethics   *31*
      2.2.6 Justice and fairness   *32*
      2.2.7 Capabilities approach   *33*
      2.2.8 Moral and cultural relativism   *34*
   2.3 Biomedical ethics: principlism   *34*
      2.3.1 Autonomy   *35*
      2.3.2 Non-maleficence   *37*
      2.3.3 Beneficence   *38*
      2.3.4 Justice   *38*

	2.4 Other ethical considerations and concepts	39
	2.4.1 Personhood, moral status and rights	39
	2.4.2 Human dignity	40
	2.4.3 Right to life, sanctity and quality of life	41
	2.4.4 Right to health and healthcare	41
	2.4.5 Doctrine of double effect	42
	2.5 Medical ethics in Singapore	43
	2.5.1 The SMC Ethical Code and Ethical Guidelines 2016 (ECEG 2016)	44
	2.6 Conclusion	46
3	**Medical negligence (part 1)**	**49**
	3.1 Introduction	49
	3.2 Duty of care	49
	3.2.1 The judicial formulation and development of duty of care	50
	3.2.2 Duty of care in medical contexts	51
	3.3. Standard of care	59
	3.3.1 General principles	59
	3.3.2 The Bolam and Bolitho tests: diagnosis and treatment	61
	3.3.3 Hii Chii Kok: medical advice	64
	3.3.4 Hospital systemic negligence	66
	3.3.5 Emergency services and situations	67
	3.3.6 Joint duty and team-based healthcare	68
	3.4 Res ipsa loquitur	69
	3.5 Conclusion	71
4	**Medical negligence (part 2)**	**72**
	4.1 Introduction	72
	4.2 Causation of damage	72
	4.2.1 Factual causation	72
	4.2.2 Legal causation	76
	4.3 Remoteness of damage and egg-shell skull rule	78
	4.4 Scope of duty	80
	4.5 Loss of chance	80
	4.6 Defences	83
	4.6.1 Ex turpi causa	83
	4.6.2 Volenti non fit injuria	83
	4.6.3 Contributory negligence	84
	4.6.4 No exemption of doctor's liability under UCTA for negligence resulting in personal injury or death	86
	4.7 Remedies: damages	86
	4.7.1 Special damages	87
	4.7.2 General damages	87
	4.7.3 Provisional damages	88
	4.8 Liability of hospitals and clinics for the acts of third parties: vicarious liability and non-delegable duties	88
	4.9 Procedural matters	90
	4.9.1 The medical negligence protocols	90
	4.9.2 Limitation periods	91
	4.10 Conclusion	92

5 Consent to treatment — 94
- 5.1 Introduction — 94
- 5.2 Meaning and scope of consent to treatment — 94
    - 5.2.1 Voluntariness — 96
    - 5.2.2 Content of information — 97
    - 5.2.3 Understanding the information — 97
    - 5.2.4 Scope of consent — 98
- 5.3 Mental capacity — 98
    - 5.3.1 Decisions on treatment for mentally incapacitated persons — 100
    - 5.3.2 When patient is mentally incapable: best interests test — 101
    - 5.3.3 When patient is mentally incapable: defence of necessity — 103
- 5.4 Refusal of treatment — 103
- 5.5 Withdrawal of consent to treatment — 107
- 5.6 ECEG 2016 and disciplinary cases — 108
    - 5.6.1 Consent and patient autonomy — 108
    - 5.6.2 Treatment of patients with diminished mental capacity — 109
- 5.7 Conclusion — 110
- Annex A — 110

6 Mental health — 113
- 6.1 Introduction — 113
- 6.2 Meaning and scope of mental disorder, incapacity and health — 114
- 6.3 Care and treatment of persons with mental disorder — 116
- 6.4 Proxy decision-making on behalf of mentally incapacitated persons and their rights under the Mental Capacity Act — 118
    - 6.4.1 Lasting powers of attorney — 119
    - 6.4.2 Appointment of court deputies — 119
    - 6.4.3 Statutory developments — 120
    - 6.4.4 Protections for mentally incapacitated persons under MCA and other statutes — 120
- 6.5 Criminal liabilities — 122
    - 6.5.1 Unsoundness of mind — 122
    - 6.5.2 Defence of intoxication — 124
    - 6.5.3 Diminished responsibility — 125
    - 6.5.4 Sentencing for accused persons with mental disorder or intellectual disability — 127
- 6.6 Tort liabilities — 130
    - 6.6.1 Tort liabilities of persons with mental disorder — 130
    - 6.6.2 Tort liabilities of doctors and healthcare professionals — 134
- 6.7 Conclusion — 137

7 Confidentiality — 139
- 7.1 Introduction — 139
- 7.2 The equitable doctrine of breach of confidence — 141
- 7.3 Privacy interests and the tort of misuse of private information — 144
- 7.4 Statutory obligations of confidentiality — 146
    - 7.4.1 Statutory duties of public office-holders, hospitals, clinics and doctors — 146

x   Contents

		7.4.2 Duty of organisations under the PDPA	149
	7.5	Access to and ownership of patient information	154
	7.6	Disclosure of patient's genetic information	155
	7.7	Medical ethics and disciplinary cases	157
	7.8	Procedural matters	161
	7.9	Conclusion	162
8	**Complementary and alternative medicine**		**164**
	8.1	Introduction	164
	8.2	Traditional Chinese medicine	166
		8.2.1 Laws and regulations governing the practice of TCM	167
		8.2.2 Ethical Code and Guidelines for TCM practitioners	170
		8.2.3 Criminal liabilities	173
		8.2.4 Civil liabilities	175
		8.2.5 Disciplinary cases	178
		8.2.6 Regulation of Chinese proprietary medicines	180
	8.3	Traditional Malay medicine	181
		8.3.1 Introduction to Malay jamu medicine	181
		8.3.2 Regulation	182
	8.4	Traditional Indian medicine	182
		8.4.1 Introduction to Ayurvedic medicine	182
		8.4.2 Regulation	183
	8.5	Conclusion	183
9	**Reproduction**		**185**
	9.1	Introduction	185
	9.2	Contraceptives and sterilisation	185
	9.3	Abortion	188
		9.3.1 The law on abortion	188
		9.3.2 The ethics of abortion	190
	9.4	Assisted reproduction	192
	9.5	Surrogacy	196
		9.5.1 Surrogacy arrangements and adoption of child	197
		9.5.2 Claim for surrogacy expenses	198
	9.6	Reproductive genetics	199
		9.6.1 Selection of sex and genetic traits	200
		9.6.2 Human cloning and human stem cell research	201
		9.6.3 Genetic defects, mix-ups and inadequate advice	203
	9.7	Conclusion	207
10	**End of life**		**209**
	10.1	Introduction	209
	10.2	Definition of death	210
	10.3	Advanced medical directives	213
	10.4	Withholding, refusal of life-sustaining treatment and death	217
		10.4.1 Patient autonomy	217
		10.4.2 Patient's best interests	218
	10.5	Physician-assisted euthanasia	224
		10.5.1 The Singapore position	224
		10.5.2 Other jurisdictions	225
		10.5.3 Specific Issues on euthanasia	228
	10.6	Conclusion	231

11	**Human organs, tissues and biological materials**	**233**
	11.1 Introduction	233
	11.2 The human tissues regulatory framework	233
	11.2.1 Consent requirements	234
	11.2.2 Restrictions relating to human tissues	235
	11.2.3 Tissue donation from deceased persons	236
	11.2.4 Prohibition of commercial trading of human tissues	236
	11.3 Human Organ Transplant Act	238
	11.3.1 Organ removal from donors upon death for transplant	239
	11.3.2 Donation of organs by living persons	240
	11.3.3 Prohibition of sale and supply of organs and blood	240
	11.4 Medical (Therapy, Education and Research) Act	243
	11.5 Whither property rights in human body or parts	244
	11.5.1 Common law developments	245
	11.5.2 Legal claims and rights	247
	11.6 Bioprinting of human tissues and organs	252
	11.7 Conclusion	252
12	**Human biomedical research, medical innovations and information technologies in healthcare**	**254**
	12.1 Introduction	254
	12.2 Laws and regulations on human biomedical research	256
	12.2.1 Definition of human biomedical research	256
	12.2.2 Consent requirements	258
	12.2.3 Regulation of human biomedical research	260
	12.2.4 Clinical trials of medicinal and therapeutic products	261
	12.3 Ethical guidelines for human biomedical research	264
	12.3.1 Ethics governance	267
	12.3.2 Consent to participation	267
	12.3.3 Personal information	267
	12.3.4 Biobanking and research involving human biological materials	268
	12.3.5 Human genetic research	268
	12.4 Medical innovations and information technologies in healthcare	268
	12.4.1 Innovative treatments and untested practices	269
	12.4.2 Telemedicine and telehealth products	272
	12.4.3 Electronic health records and big data	275
	12.4.4 Robotics and artificial intelligence	276
	12.5 Conclusion	279

Index   281

TABLE OF CASES

Australia

Australian Competition and Consumer Commission v Nuera Health Pty Ltd [2007]
   FCA 695 178
Bawden v Marin [1990] SASC (2 July 1990) (unreported) 176
Bazley v Wesley Monash IVF [2011] 2 Qd R 207 251
Breen v Williams [1996] 138 ALR 359 154
Brightwater Care Group (Inc) v Rossiter (2009) 40 WAR 84 217
Brown v The Mount Barker Soldiers' Hospital Incorporated [1934] SASR 128
   (Supreme Court of South Australia) 57
Carrier v Bonham (2001) QCA 234 131
Cattanach v Melchior [2003] 215 CLR 1 204-5
Doodeward v Spence (1908) 6 CLR 406 245
Giller v Procopets [2008] VSCA 236 144
Graham v Voigt (1989) 95 Fed LR 146; (1989) ACTR 11 (Supreme Court
   of the Australian Capital Territory) 248
Harriton v Stephens (2006) 226 CLR 52 207
McHale v Watson (1966) 115 CLR 199 133
Noone (Director of Consumer Affairs Victoria) v Operation Smile
   (Aust) Inc [2012] VSCA 91 178
Pillai v Messiter (No 2) (1989) 16 NSWLR 197 18
R v MBO, ex parte Attorney-General of Queensland [2012] QCA 202 129
R v Thomas Sam [2009] NSWSC 1003 174
Secretary, Department of Health and Community Services v JWB (1992) 66
   ALJR 300 96
Shorey v PT Ltd (2003) 77 ALJR 1104 79
State of Queensland v Nolan [2001] QSC 174 221
Tabet v Gett (2010) 240 CLR 537 81
Thomas Sam v R [2011] NSWCCA 36 174
Waller v James (2006) 226 CLR 136 207
White v Pile 68 WN (NSW) 176 (1950) 131

Canada

Brushett v Cowan (1990) 69 DLR (4th) 743 (Newfoundland Court of Appeal) 85
Carter v Canada 2015 SCC 5 226
Ciarlariello v Schacter (1993) 100 DLR (4th) 609 107
Crossman v Stewart (1997) 82 DLR (3d) 677 84
Dickson v Pinder [2010] ABQB 269 64
Dumais v Hamilton 1998 ABCA 218 84
Halushka v University of Saskatchewan (1965) 53 DLR (2d) 436 .... 139, 260
Hopkins v Kay 2014 ONSC 321, 237 ACWS (3d) 362, 119 OR (3d) 251 146
Jones v Tsige 2012 ONCA 32, 108 OR (3d) 241 146
Ladas v Apple Inc 2014 BCSC 1821 146
Malette v Shulman 67 DLR (4th) 321, 72 OR (2d) 417 (1990)
    (Ontario Court of Appeal) 106-7
Mason v Westside Cemeteries Ltd (1996) 135 DLR (4th) 361
    (Ontario Court, General Division) 248
McInerney v MacDonald [1992] 2 SCR 138 .... 139, 154
Murrin v Janes [1949] 4 DLR 403 (Newfoundland Supreme Court) 84
Non-marine, Underwriters, Lloyd's of London v Scalera [2000] 1 SCR 551 96
Norberg v Wynrib [1992] 2 SCR 226 .... 94, 96
Reibl v Hughes [1980] 2 SCR 880 95-6
Saadati v Moorhead [2017] 1 SCR 543 54
Sheridan v Ontario 2014 ONSC 4970 146
Slattery v Haley [1923] 3 DLR 156 131
Thomson v Toorenburgh (1973) BCJ No 821 77
Walker Estate v York Finch General Hospital [2001] 1 SCR 647 243
Winnipeg Child and Family Services (Northwest Area) v G 3 BHRC 611 191
Zhang v Kan [2003] BCSC 5; (2003) 15 CCLT (3d) 1 85

New Zealand

Auckland Area Health Board v Attorney General [1993] 1 NZLR 235 .... 212, 220
Bradley v Wingnut Films Ltd [1993] 1 NZLR 415 146
C v Holland [2012] 3 NZLR 672 146
Donaghy v Brennan (1900) 19 NZLR 289 (Court of Appeal of New Zealand) 133
Furniss v Fitchett [1958] NZLR 396 (Supreme Court of New Zealand) 57
Hosking v Runting [2005] 1 NZLR 1 146
L v G [2002] DCR 234 146
Martin v Director of Proceedings [2010] NZAR 333 18
P v D [2000] 2 NZLR 591 146
Rogers v Television New Zealand Ltd [2007] NZSC 91 146
Stephenson v Waite Tileman Ltd [1973] 1 NZLR 153 79
Tucker v News Media Ownership Ltd [1986] 2 NZLR 716 146

Singapore

Case	Pages
A Karthik v PP [2018] 5 SLR 1289	128
ACB v Thomson Medical Centre [2017] 1 SLR 918	86, 205
Ang Leng Hock v Leo Ee Ah [2004] 2 SLR(R) 361	88
Ang Pek San Lawrence v Singapore Medical Council [2015] 1 SLR 436	17, 19
Ang Pek San Lawrence v SMC [2015] 2 SLR 1179	17, 19-20
Ang Peng Tiam v SMC [2017] 5 SLR 356	18, 21
Ang Tiong Seng v Goh Huan Chir [1968-1970] SLR(R) 778	175
Anwar Patrick Adrian v Ng Chong & Hue LLC [2014] 3 SLR 761	50
Armstrong, Carol Ann (executrix of the estate of Peter Traynor, deceased and on behalf of the dependents of Peter Traynor, deceased) v Quest Laboratories Pte Ltd and another [2018] SGHC 66	82
Armstrong, Carol Ann (executrix of the estate of Peter Traynor, deceased and on behalf of the dependents of Peter Traynor, deceased) v Quest Laboratories Pte Ltd and another and other appeals [2020] 1 SLR 133	62, 73, 83
BHR and Another v BHS [2013] SGDC 149	122
BUV v BUU [2019] SGHCF 15	99-100, 119
CGX v Public Prosecutor [2019] 3 SLR 1325	130
Chai Kang Wei Samuel v Shaw Linda Gillian [2010] 3 SLR 587	87-8
Cheong Ghim Fah v Murugian s/o Rangasamy [2004] 1 SLR(R) 628	86
Chew Swee Hiang v Attorney-General [1990] 2 SLR(R) 215	75
Chia Foong Lin v Singapore Medical Council [2017] 5 SLR 334	18
Chia Peng Siang v Attorney-General [2011] SGDC 311	91
Chiarapurk Jack v Haw Par Brothers International Ltd [1993] 2 SLR(R) 620	141
Chow Khai Hong v Tham Sek Khow [1991] 2 SLR(R) 670	88
Clark Jonathan Michael v Lee Khee Chung [2010] 1 SLR 209	87
D'Conceicao Jeanie Doris v Tong Ming Chuan [2011] SGHC 193	61-2, 74, 175
Denis Matthew Harte v Dr Tan Hun Hoe [2000] SGHC 248	70, 89
Dorsey James Michael v World Sport Group Pte Ltd [2014] 2 SLR 208	161
F v Chan Tanny [2003] 4 SLR(R) 231	70
Foo Chee Boon Edward v SMC [2020] SGHC 24	19
Freely Pte Ltd v Ong Kaili [2010] 2 SLR 1065	178
Gan Keng Seng Eric v SMC [2011] 1 SLR 745	17
Gobinathan Devathasan v SMC [2010] 2 SLR 926	19, 179-80, 270
Goh Guan Sin (by her litigation representative Chiam Yu Zhu v Yeo Tseng Tsai and National University Hospital (Singapore) Pte Ltd [2019] SGHC 274	68, 90, 211, 220
Grace Electrical Engineering Pte Ltd v Te Deum Engineering Pte Ltd [2018] 1 SLR 76	70
Hii Chii Kok v Ooi Peng Jin London Lucien [2016] 2 SLR 544	89
Hii Chii Kok v Ooi Peng Jin London Lucien [2017] 2 SLR 492	63-4, 107-8, 135, 175, 187, 277

Huang Danmin v TCMPB [2010] 3 SLR 1108 178-80
I-Admin (Singapore) Pte Ltd v Hong Ying Ting and others [2020] SGCA 32 .... 141, 144
In the Matter of Dr AAT [2009] SMCDC 8 271
In the Matter of Dr ABO [2010] SMCDC 12 271
In the Matter of Dr ABU [2011] SMCDC 2 272
In the matter of Dr ADP [2010] SMCDC 13 271
In the matter of Dr Chan Heang Kng Calvin [2017] SMCDT 6 272
In the Matter of Dr Singh Tregon Randhawa [2011] SMCDC 2017 160
Intas Pharmaceuticals Ltd v DealStreetAsia Pte Ltd [2017] 4 SLR 684 161
Invenpro (M) Sdn Bhd v JCS Automation Pte Ltd [2014] 2 SLR 1045 141-2
Iskandar bin Rahmat v Public Prosecutor and other matters [2017] 1 SLR 505 126
JU v See Tho Kai Yin [2005] 4 SLR(R) 96 206
Khoo James v Gunapathy d/o Muniandy [2002] 1 SLR(R) 1024 62
Koh Chai Kwang v Teo Ai Ling [2011] 3 SLR 610 87-8
Lam Kwok Tai Leslie v SMC [2017] 5 SLR 1168 .... 16, 108, 160
Lee Ngiap Hoon v Teo Sin [1991] 2 SLR(R) 131 87
Lee Wei Kong v Ng Siok Tong [2012] 2 SLR 85 87-8
Leow Li Yoon v Liu Jiu Chang [2016] 1 SLR 595 98
Lian Kok Hong v Ow Wah Foong [2008] 4 SLR(R) 165 91
Lily Pai v Yeo Peng Hock Henry [2001] 1 SLR(R) 517 91
Lim Ghim Peow v PP [2014] 4 SLR 1287 127
Lim Hock Hin Kelvin v PP [1998] 1 SLR(R) 37 128
Lim Meng Suang and another v Attorney-General and another appeal
and another matter [2015] 1 SLR 26 145
Lim Mey Lee Susan v Singapore Medical Council [2013] 3 SLR 900 .... 17-18, 43
Lim Poh Eng v PP [1999] 1 SLR(R) 428 .... 22, 173-4
Loh Chia Mei v Koh Kok Han [2009] SGHC 181 88
Loh Siew Keng v Seng Huat Construction Pte Ltd [1998] SGHC 197 69
Low Chai Lin v SMC [2013] 1 SLR 83 270
Low Cze Hong v Singapore Medical Council [2008] 3 SLR(R) 612 .... 17, 44
Low Swee Tong v Liew Machinery (Pte) Ltd [1993] 2 SLR(R) 10 88
Low Yoke Ying v Sim Kok Lee [1990] 2 SLR(R) 713 87
Mah Kiat Seng v Attorney-General and others [2020] SLR 918 118
Man Mohan Singh s/o Jothirambal Singh v Zurich Insurance
(Singapore) Pte Ltd [2008] 3 SLR(R) 735 .... 78, 199
Management Corporation Strata Title Plan No 3322 v Tiong Aik
Construction Pte Ltd [2016] 4 SLR 521 89-90
Mohammad Shah Jahan Bhanu v Shimizu Corp [2013] SGDC 152 75
Murgan s/o Ramasamy v Public Prosecutor [1994] SGCA 30 211
My Digital Lock Pte Ltd [2018] SGPDPC 3 .... 146, 153
Nagaenthran a/l K Dharmalingam v Public Prosecutor and another
appeal [2019] 2 SLR 216 126-7
Ng Huat Seng v Munib Mohammad Madni and another [2017] 2 SLR 1074 89

xvi Table of cases

Ng Keng Yong v Public Prosecutor [2004] 4 SLR(R) 89 174
Ngiam Kong Seng v Lim Chiew Hock [2008] 3 SLR(R) 674 .... 55-7, 249
Noor Azlin bte Abdul Rahman v Changi General Hospital Pte Ltd
 and others [2019] 1 SLR 834 .... 64, 66-7, 88
Ong Pang Siew v PP [2011] 1 SLR 606 100
Pang Ah San v Singapore Medical Council [2014] 1 SLR 1094 270-1
Pang Koi Fa v Lim Djoe Phing [1993] 2 SLR(R) 366 54-6
Parno v SC Marine Pte Ltd [1999] 3 SLR(R) 377 86
PlanAssure PAC v Gaelic Inns Pte Ltd [2007] 4 SLR(R) 513 76
Poh Huat Heng Corp Pte Ltd v Hafizul Islam Kofil Uddin [2012] 3 SLR 1003 87
PP v Aniza bte Essa [2009] 3 SLR(R) 327 .... 127, 129
Public Prosecutor v ASR [2019] 1 SLR 941 128-9
Public Prosecutor v Chan Lie Sian [2017] SGHC 205 211
PP v Chong Hou En [2015] 3 SLR 222 .... 115, 128
PP v Goh Lee Yin [2008] 1 SLR (R) 824 127-8
PP v Khwan-On Nathaphon [2001] SGHC 313 100
PP v Kong Peng Yee [2018] 2 SLR 295 127
PP v Law Aik Meng [2007] 2 SLR(R) 814 20
Public Prosecutor v Low Ji Qing [2019] 5 SLR 769 128
PP v Mohammad Al-Ansari bin Basri [2008] 1 SLR(R) 449 128
Public Prosecutor v Kong Tong Hong [2017] SGDC 218 173
PP v Othman bin Hussain & Anor [1991] SGHC 168 212
Public Prosecutor v Sulaiman Damanik and Another [2008] SGDC 175 241
Public Prosecutor v Tang Wee Sung [2008] SGDC 26 241
PP v Zhong Zhi Li [2007] SGDC 126 173
QB Net Co Ltd v Earnson Management (S) Pte Ltd [2007] 1 SLR(R) 1 141
Rathanamalah d/o Shunmugam v Chia Kok Hoong [2018] 4 SLR 159 .... 70, 272, 277
Ramesh s/o Krishnan v AXA Life Insurance Singapore Pte Ltd [2015] 4 SLR 1 58
Re BKR [2015] 4 SLR 81 .... 99, 100, 116
Re GAV [2014] SGDC 215 99
Re LP (adult patient: medical treatment) [2006] 2 SLR(R) 13 104-5
Re Singapore Medical Association – Guidelines on Fees [2010] SGCCS 6 6
Re Social Metric Pte Ltd [2017] SGPDPC 17 152
Re The Cellar Door Pte Ltd and Global Interactive Works Pte Ltd [2016] SGPDPC 22 152
Re UKM [2018] SGFC 20 197
Re WTS Automotive Services [2018] SGPDPC 26 152
Salcon Ltd v United Cement Pte Ltd [2004] 4 SLR(R) 353 77
Sek Kim Wah v PP [1987] SLR(R) 371 126
Shorvon Simon v Singapore Medical Council [2006] 1 SLR(R) 182 254
Singapore Health Services Pte Ltd and others [2019] SGPDPC 3 153
SMC v BXR [2019] SGHC 20 20
Singapore Medical Council v Dr Mohd Syamsul Alam bin Ismail [2019] SGHC 58 20
Singapore Medical Council v Dr Leo Kah Woon [2018] SMCDT 12 160
Singapore Medical Council v Dr Lim Lian Arn [2018] SMCDT 9 .... 65, 108

Singapore Medical Council v Dr Soo Shuenn Chiang [2018] SMCDT 11 158
Singapore Medical Council v Kwan Kah Yee [2015] 5 SLR 201 20
Singapore Medical Council v Lim Lian Arn [2019] SGHC 172 ....18-19, 108-9
Singapore Medical Council v Looi Kok Poh and another matter [2019] SGHC 134 19
SMC v Soo Shuenn Chiang [2020] 3 SLR 1129 158-9
Singapore Medical Council v Wong Him Choon [2016] 4 SLR 1086 17-19
Skandinaviska Enskilda Banken AB (Publ), Singapore Branch v Asia Pacific Breweries (Singapore) Pte Ltd [2011] 3 SLR 540 89
Spandeck Engineering (S) Pte Ltd v Defence Science & Technology Agency [2007] 4 SLR(R) 100 50
Stephanie Tang Swan Lee and others v Tan Su San (the personal representative of the deceased Tan Seng Huat) [2018] SGDC 218 132-3
Sunny Metal & Engineering Pte Ltd v Ng Khim Ming Eric [2007] 3 SLR(R) 782 73
Surender Singh s/o Jagdish Singh v Li Man Kay [2010] 1 SLR 428 76
Tan Harry v Teo Chee Yeow Aloysius [2004] 1 SLR(R) 513 86
Tan Hun Hoe v Harte Denis Mathew [2001] 3 SLR(R) 414 ....85, 88
TCZ v TDA; TDB v TDC [2015] SGFC 6 122
TEB v TEC [2015] SGFC 54 119
Teddy, Thomas v Teacly (S) Pte Ltd [2014] SGHC 226 88
Teng Ah Kow v Ho Sek Chiu [1993] 3 SLR(R) 43 69
Teo Sing Keng v Sim Ban Kiat [1994] 1 SLR(R) 340 88
Tesa Tape Asia Pacific Pte Ltd v Wing Seng Logistics Pte Ltd [2006] 3 SLR(R) 116 69
Tong Seok May Joanne v Yau Hok Man Gordon [2013] 2 SLR 18 ....68, 70, 73-4
TV Media Pte Ltd v De Cruz Andrea Heidi [2004] 3 SLR 543 ....60-1, 76, 87, 186, 278
UKM v AG [2018] SGHCF 18 ....196, 198
Vasuhi d/o Ramasamypillai v Tan Tock Seng Hospital Pte Ltd [2001] 1 SLR(R) 303 73
Vestwin Trading Pte Ltd v Obegi Melissa [2006] 3 SLR(R) 573 141
Wang Chin Sing v Public Prosecutor [2009] 1 SLR(R) 870 241
Wang Wenfeng v Public Prosecutor [2012] 4 SLR 590 211
Whang Sung Lin v Public Prosecutor [2010] 2 SLR 958 241
Wong Meng Cheong and another v Ling Ai Wah and another [2011] SGHC 233 119
Wong Meng Hang v Singapore Medical Council and other matters [2018] SGHC 253; [2019] 3 SLR 526 20-2
X Pte Ltd v CDE [1992] 2 SLR(R) 575 141
Yeo Peng Hock Henry v Pai Lily [2001] 3 SLR(R) 555 74
Yip Man Hing Kevin v SMC [2019] SGHC 102 19
Yong Thiam Look Peter v Singapore Medical Council [2017] SGHC 10; [2017] 4 SLR 66 ....94, 108, 160

United Kingdom

A v B plc [2003] QB 195 142
A v Hoare [2008] 1 AC 844 131

xviii Table of cases

A Local Authority v Mrs A and Mr A [2011] 2 WLR 878 186
A NHS Trust v X [2014] EWCOP 35 99
A Trust v H (An Adult) [2006] 2 FLR 958 187
AAA v Associated Newspapers Ltd [2012] EWHC 2103 144
Abbott v R [1976] 3 All ER 140 (PC) 220
ABC v St Georges' Health NHS [2017] PIQR P15 155-6
ABC v St George's Healthcare NHS Trust & Ors [2020] EWHC 455 (QB) 156
Aintree University Hospitals NHS Foundation Trust v James [2013]
    3 WLR 1299 103
Airedale NHS Trust v Bland [1993] AC 789 .... 206, 212, 219-20, 229
Albert v Strange (1849) 1 Mac & G 25; 41 ER 1171 145
Alcock v Chief Constable of South Yorkshire Police [1992] 1 AC 310 55-6
Allied Maples Group Ltd v Simmons & Simmons (a firm) [1995] 1 WLR 1602 82
Anns v Merton London Borough Council [1978] AC 728 51
Appleton v Garrett [1996] PIQR P1 .... 86, 96
Archer v Williams [2003] EWHC 1670 142
Argyll v Argyll [1967] Ch 302 145
Ashworth Security Hospital v MGN Ltd [2002] 1 WLR 2033 161
Attorney-General v Blake [1998] Ch 439 144
Attorney General v Guardian Newspapers Ltd (No 2) [1990] 1 AC 109 .... 142, 144
Attorney-General's Reference (No 3 of 1994) [1998] AC 245 191
Bailey v Ministry of Defence [2009] 1 WLR 1052 74-5
Baker v T E Hopkins & Son Ltd [1959] 1 WLR 966 84
Barker v Corus (UK) Ltd [2006] 2 AC 572 75
Barnett v Chelsea and Kensington Hospital Management Committee [1969] 1 QB 428 73
Barrett v Ministry of Defence [1995] 1 WLR 1217 53
Barrymore v News Group Newspapers Ltd [1997] IP&T Digest 49 142
Blyth v Birmingham Waterworks Co (1856) 11 Exch 781 59
Bolam v Friern Hospital Management Committee [1957] 1 WLR 582 .... 61, 134, 175, 187
Bolitho v City and Hackney Health Authority [1998] AC 232 .... 62, 76, 134, 175, 187
Bolton v Stone [1951] AC 850 60
Bonnington Castings Ltd v Wardlaw [1956] AC 613 74-5
Brice v Brown [1984] 1 All ER 997 79
Campbell v Mirror Group Newspapers Ltd [2004] 1 AC 457 .... 142, 144-5
Caparo Industries plc v Dickman [1990] 2 AC 605 51
Capital and Counties v Hampshire County Council [1997] QB 1004 53
Cassidy v Ministry of Health [1951] 2 KB 343 .... 70, 88-9
Chatterton v Gerson [1981] QB 432 96-7
Chaudhry v Prabhakar [1989] 1 WLR 29 52
Chester v Afshar [2005] 1 AC 134 74
Clunis v Camden and Islington Health Authority [1998] QB 978 .... 83, 137
Coco v AN Clark (Engineers) Ltd [1969] RPC 41 141-2
Collins v Wilcock [1984] 1 WLR 1172 95

Table of cases xix

Cornelius v De Taranto [2001] EMLR 329 144
Corr v IBC Vehicles Ltd [2008] 1 AC 884 85
D v East Berkshire Community Health NHS Trust [2005] 2 AC 373 57
Darnley v Croydon Health Services NHS Trust [2018] 3 WLR 1153 .... 59, 67-8
Dobbie v Medway Health Authority [1994] 1 WLR 1234 91
Dobson v North Tyneside Health Authority [1997] 1 WLR 598 246
Dryden v Johnson Mathey Plc [2018] 2 WLR 1109 54
Dunnage v Randall [2016] QB 639 .... 130-1, 135
Ecila Henderson (A Protected Party, by her litigation friend,
    The Official Solicitor) v Dorset Healthcare University NHS Foundation
    Trust [2018] EWCA Civ 1841 83
Emeh v Kensington and Chelsea and Westminster Area Health Authority
    [1985] QB 1012 77
Evans v Amicus Healthcare Ltd (2004) 2 FLR 766 193
Eyre v Measday [1986] 1 All ER 488 52
Fairchild v Glenhaven Funeral Services Ltd [2003] 1 AC 32 75
Farraj v King's Healthcare NHS Trust [2010] 1 WLR 2139 89
Fish v Kelly (1864) 17 CB NS 194; 144 ER 78 52
Freeman v Home Office (No 2) [1984] QB 524 95
Frenchay Healthcare National Health Service Trust v S [1994] 1 WLR 601 219
Gillick v West Norfolk & Wisbech Area Health Authority [1986] AC 112 .... 97, 139, 186
Gold v Essex County Council [1942] 2 KB 293 88
Gray v Thames Trains Ltd [2009] 1 AC 1339 83
Gregg v Scott [2005] 2 AC 176 81-3
Group B Plaintiffs v Medical Research Council [2000] Lloyd's Rep Med 161 54
H (A Healthcare Worker) v Associated Newspapers Ltd and N
    (A Health Authority) [2002] Lloyd's Rep Med 210 143
HE v A Hospital NHS Trust [2003] EWHC 1017 (Fam) 107
H West & Son Ltd v Shephard [1964] AC 326 87
Hall v Simons [2002] 1 AC 615 66
Hedley Byrne & Co Ltd v Heller & Partners Ltd [1964] AC 465 51-2
Henderson v Merrett Syndicates Ltd [1995] 2 AC 145 52
Hepworth v Kerr [1995] 6 Med LR 139 .... 63, 277
Hills v Potter [1984] 1 WLR 641; [1983] 3 All ER 716 96
Hogan v Bentinck West Hartley Collieries (Owners) Ltd [1948] 1 All ER 129 77
Holtby v Brigham & Cowan (Hull) Ltd [2000] 3 All ER 421 75
Home Department v Robb [1995] Fam 127 107
Hotson v East Berkshire Area Health Authority [1987] AC 750 81
Hucks v Cole [1993] 4 Med LR 393 63
Hughes v Lord Advocate [1963] AC 837 78
Hunter v Hanley 1955 SLT 213 .... 62, 272
Hunter v Mann [1974] QB 767 140
Imerman v Tchenguiz and others [2011] 2 WLR 592 143

xx Table of cases

Janaway v Salford Area Health Authority [1989] AC 537 190
JD v East Berkshire Community NHS Trust [2005] 2 WLR 993 57
Jobling v Associated Dairies Ltd [1982] AC 794 77-8
Jones v Livox Quarries Ld [1952] 2 QB 608 85
Jones v Manchester Corporation [1952] 2 All ER 125 60
Kent v Griffiths [2001] QB 36 53
Khan v MNX [2018] EWCA Civ 2609 80
Kralj and Another v McGrath and Another [1986] 1 All ER 54 78
L Teaching Hospital NHS Trust v A [2003] EWHC 259 (QB) 195
Landall v Dennis Faulkner & Alsop [1994] 5 Med LR 268 (QBD) 58
Leigh v Gladstone (1909) 26 TLR 139 107
Lim Poh Choo v Camden and Islington Area Health Authority [1980] AC 174 87
Lion Laboratories Ltd v Evans [1984] 2 All ER 417 143
Love v Port of London Authority [1959] 2 Lloyd's Rep 541 78
Lumley v Gye [1853] 2 E & B 216; 118 ER 749 142
Mahon v Osborne [1939] 2 KB 14 70
M'Alister (or Donoghue) v Stevenson [1932] AC 562 .... 50, 186
Mansfield v Weetabix [1998] 1 WLR 1263 132
Marriott v West Midland HA [1999] Lloyd's Rep Med 23 63
McFarlane v Tayside Health Board [2000] 2 AC 59 .... 188, 204
McGhee v National Coal Board [1973] 1 WLR 1 75
McKay v Essex Area Health Authority [1982] QB 1166 206
McKennit v Ash [2008] QB 73 145
McKew v Holland & Hannen & Cubitts (Scotland) Ltd [1969] 3 All ER 1621 77
McLoughlin v O'Brian [1983] 1 AC 410 55
Moeliker v A Reyrolle & Co Ltd [1977] 1 WLR 132 88
Montgomery v Lanarkshire Health Board [2015] 2 WLR 768 65
Morriss v Marsden [1952] 1 All ER 925 131
Mosley v News Group Newspapers Ltd [2008] All ER (D) 322 142
Muller v King's College Hospital NHS Foundation Trust [2017] 2 WLR 159 64
North Glamorgan NHS Trust v Walters [2002] EWCA Civ 1792 56
Norwich Pharmacal v Customs and Excise Commissioners [1974] AC 133 161
OBG Ltd v Allan [2008] 1 AC 1 145
Overseas Tankship (UK) Ltd v Morts Dock & Engineering Co Ltd
(The Wagon Mound) [1961] AC 388 78
Overseas Tankship (UK) Ltd v The Miller Steamship Co Pty [1967] 1 AC 617 60
Owens v Liverpool Corp [1939] 1 KB 394 248
Palmer v Tees Health Authority [2000] PIQR 1 .... 136, 156
Paris v Stepney Borough Council [1951] AC 367 60
Parkinson v St James and Seacroft University Hospital NHS Trust [2002] QB 266 204
Penney v East Kent Health Authority [2000] PNLR 323 63-4
Phelps v Hillingdon London Borough Council [2000] 2 AC 619 .... 54, 57
Pidgeon v Doncaster Health Authority [2002] Lloyd's Rep Med 130 84

Powell v Boladz (1997) 39 BMLR 35 56
*R (on the application of Sue Axon) v Secretary of State for Health
and the Family Planning Association* [2006] EWHC 37 140
R v Bentham [2005] 1 WLR 1057 244
R v Bournewood Community and Mental Health NHS Trust, ex parte L [1999] 1 AC 458   103
Regina v Byrne [1960] 2 QB 396 126
R v Cambridge HA Ex p. B [1995] 1 WLR 898 39
R v Cox (1992) 12 BMLR 38 221
R v Croydon HA [1997] PIQR P444 78
R v Department of Health, exp Source Informatics Ltd [2000] 1 All ER 786 .... 140, 154
R v Dudley and Stephens (1884) 14 QBD 273 223
R v General Medical Council [2006] EWHC 3277 17
R v Kelly [1999] QB 621 246
Regina v Gordon Laxton [2010] EWCA Crim 2538 129
*R v Mid Glamorgan Family Health Services Authority and Another
ex p Martin* [1995] 1 WLR 110 154
R v M'Naghten (1843) 10 Cl and Fin 200; 8 ER 718 122-3
Regina v Myles Williams [2013] EWCA Crim 933 129
R v Rowland Jack Forster Hodgson (1968) 52 Cr App R 113 129
R v Sean Peter C [2001] EWCA Crim 125 122
R (Nicklinson) v Ministry of Justice [2014] 3 WLR 200 228
R (Pretty) v Director of Public Prosecutions [2002] 1 AC 800 227
R (Purdy) v DPP [2010] 1 AC 345 228
R (Quintavalle) v Human Fertilisation and Embryology Authority
[2005] 2 AC 561 200
Ratcliffe v Plymouth and Torbay Health Authority [1998] PIQR P170 70
Re (on the Application of Burke) v General Medical Council [2005] 3 FCR 169 214
Re A (A Child) [2015] EWHC 443 212
Re A (children) (conjoined twins: surgical separation) [2001] Fam 147 .... 103, 221-3
Re B (A Minor) [1987] 2 FLR 314 187
Re B (Consent to Treatment: Capacity) [2002] EWHC 429 (Fam) 217
Re C [1994] 1 WLR 290 105
Re F (mental patient: sterilisation) [1990] 2 AC 1 .... 95, 103
Re J (a minor) (wardship: medical treatment) [1991] Fam 33 218
Re MB (Medical Treatment) [1997] 2 FLR 426; 2 FCR 54 .... 104, 191
Re Organ Retention Litigation [2005] QB 506 (also known as
A and B v Leeds Teaching Hospitals NHS Trust; Cardiff and Vale NHS Trust) 246, 248-9
Re S (Adult Patient) [2001] Fam 15 187
Re Sharpe (1856-1857) Dears and B 160 244
Re T (adult: refusal of treatment) [1993] Fam 95 .... 97, 104, 217
Rees v Darlington Memorial Hospital NHS Trust [2004] 1 AC 309 204
Reeves v Commissioner of Police for the Metropolis [2000] 1 AC 360 84-6
Richardson v LRC Products [2000] L1 Med Rep 280 186

Table of cases

Case	Page
Roberts v Ramsbottom [1980] 1 WLR 823	132
Robinson v Post Office [1974] 1 WLR 1176	79
Roe v Minister of Health [1954] 2 QB 66	60, 78
Rose and another v Secretary of State for Health and another (2003) 69 BMLR 83	157
Rothwell v Chemical & Insulating Co Ltd [2008] 1 AC 281	54-5, 80
S v Lothian Health Board [2009] CSOH 9; 2009 SLT 689	90
Sabri-Tabrizi v Lothian Health Board (1998) 43 BMLR 190 at 195 (Scottish Court of Session, Outer House)	77
Saha v the GMC [2009] All ER (D) 306	15
St George's Healthcare NHS Trust v S [1999] Fam 26	104, 191
Saltman Engineering v Campbell [1948] 65 RPC 203	141, 144
Scott v The London and St Katherine Docks Co (1865) 3 H & C 596; 159 ER 665	69
Shakoor v Situ [2001] 1 WLR 410	60, 176
Sharpe v Southend Health Authority (1997) 8 Med LR 299	62
Simmons v British Steel plc [2004] UKHL 20	79
Sion v Hampstead HA [1994] Lexis Citation 3939	56
Smith v Leech Brain & Co Ltd [1962] 2 QB 405	79
South Australian Asset Management Corporation v York Montague Ltd [1997] AC 191	80
Spring v Guardian Assurance plc [1995] 2 AC 296	58
Stephens v Avery [1988] Ch 449	142
Stone v South East Strategic Health Authority [2006] EWHC 1668	140
Stovin v Wise [1996] AC 923	52
Thake v Maurice [1986] 1 All ER 479; 2 WLR 337	52, 187
Thomas v Curley [2013] 131 BMLR 111	70
Tredget & Tredget v Bexley Health Authority [1994] 5 Med LR 178	56
Vaughan v Menlove 3 Bing NC 468	132
W v Egdell [1990] Ch 359	143
W v L [1974] QB 711	2
Wainwright v Home Office [2004] 2 AC 406	95
Walker v Northumberland County Council [1995] 1 All ER 737	60
Ward v Leeds Teaching Hospitals NHS Trust [2004] EWHC 2106	56
Watt v Hertfordshire County Council [1954] 1 WLR 835	60
Webb v Barclay Bank plc and Portsmouth Hospitals [2002] PIQR P8; [2001] EWCA Civ 1141	76-7
Whittington Hospital NHS Trust v XX [2020] UKSC 14	198-9
Williams v Williams (1882) 20 Ch D 659	244
Wilsher v Essex Area HA [1986] 3 All ER 801; [1987] QB 730	60, 174
Wilsher v Essex Area Health Authority [1988] AC 1074	75
Wizniewski v Central Manchester Health Authority [1998] PIQR P324	78
Woolgar v Chief Constable of Sussex Police [1999] Lloyd's Rep Med 335	143
Woodland v Swimming Teachers Association [2014] AC 537	89
Wright v Cambridge Medical Group [2013] QB 312	76
WXY v Gewanter [2013] EWHC 589	144

X v Bedfordshire County Council [1995] 2 AC 633 57
X Health Authority v Y [1988] 2 All ER 648 144
Yearworth v North Bristol NHS Trust [2010] QB 1; [2009] 3 WLR 118 .... 54, 244, 246-7
York City Council v C [2014] 2 WLR 1 98

United States

Anderson v St Francis-St George Hospital 671 NE 2d 225 (Ohio 1996) 216
Breunig v American Family Insurance Company 173 NW2d 619 (Wisc 1970)....................131-2
Cruzan v Director, Missouri Department of Health 110 S Ct 2841 (1990) 226
Diamond v Chakrabarty (1980) 447 US 303 249
Doctors Hospital of Augusta, LLC v Alicea 788 SE 2d 392 (Ga 2016)..................................... 216
Gloria Ochoa et al v The Superior Court of Santa Clara County 39
   Cal 3d 159; 216 Cal Rptr 661; 703 P 2d 1 (Supreme Court of California) 55
Greenberg v Miami Children's Hosp Research Inst, Inc, 264 F Supp 2d
   1064 (SD Fla 2003) 250
Hecht v Superior Court for Los Angeles County (1993) 20 Cal Rptr 2d 275 251
Herskovits v Group Health Co-op of Puget Sound 664 P2d 474 (Wash 1983) 82
Kirschner v Keller 70 Ohio App 111 178
Koerner v Bhatt No L-002983-13 (NJ Super Ct Law Div, Morris Cty 2017) 216
Matsuyama v Birbaum (2008) 890 NE (2d) 819 82
Moore v Regents of the University of California (1990) 793 P 2d 479 249-51
Re Baby M, 537 Am 2d 1227, 109 NJ 396 (NJ 1988) 196
Re Quinlan 70 NJ 10, 355, A 2d 647 (1976) 225
Roe v Wade 410 US 113 (1973) 189
Resiner v Regents of the University of California (1995) 37 Cal Rptr 2d 518..........................156
Safer v Pack (1996) 677 A 2d 1188 (Sup Ct App Div) 156
Schiavo ex rel Schindler v Schiavo, 403 F 3d 1223 (11th Cir 2005) 218
Schneider v Revici 817 F 2d 987 (2nd Cir 1987) 177
Schloendorff v Society of New York Hospital (1914) 105 NE 92 .... 95, 217, 244
Tarasoff v Regents of the University of California (1976) 551 P 2d 334........................ 136, 156
Taylor v Muncie Medical Investors 727 NE 2d 466 (Ind Ct App 2000).....................................216
Tucker's Administrator v Lower Ct Law & Eq., Richmond, Virginia, 25 May
   1972 No 2831 212
Turpin v Sortini 182 Cal Rptr 337 (1982) 207
Vacco v Quill 521 US 793 (1997); 117 S Ct 2293 (1997) 226
Wash Univ v Catalona, 490 F3d 667 (8th Cir 2007) 250
Washington v Glucksberg 521 US 702; 117 S Ct 2258 (1997).. 226
Weisman v Maryland General Hospital (Docket Proceedings at 3,
Entry No. 73/0, Weisman, No 24-C-16-004199)... 216
Williams v Hays 38 NE 449 (NY 1894) 133
Wright v Johns Hopkins Health Systems Corp 28 A 2d 166 (Md 1999) 216

Others

Abdul Rahman bin Abdul Karim v Abdul Wahab bin Abdul Hamid [1996]
    4 MLJ 623 175
Baker v Kaye [1997] IRLR 219 58
Chin Keow v Government of Malaysia [1967] 1 WLR 813 63
Dr Hari Krishnan & Anor v Megat Noor Ishak bin Megat Ibrahim &
    Anor and another appeal [2018] 3 MLJ 281 90
Dr Kok Choong Seng and Sunway Medical Centre Berhad v Soo Cheng
    Lin [2018] 1 MLJ 685 89
Gross v Switzerland (2014) 58 EHRR 7 227
Haas v Switzerland (2011) 53 EHRR 33 227
Ho Ying Wai v Keliston Marine (Far East) Ltd [2002] HKCFI 543 57
Koch v Germany (2013) 56 EHRR 6 227
Pretty v United Kingdom [2002] 35 EHRR 1 227
Schoonheim, Netherlands Jurisprudentie 1985, no 106 227

TABLE OF LEGISLATION

Australia

Civil Law (Wrongs) Act 2002 (ACT) 53
Civil Liability Act 1936 (SA) 53
Civil Liability Act 2002 (NSW) 53, 205
Civil Liability Act 2002 (Tas) 53
Civil Liability Act 2002 (WA) 53
Civil Liability Act 2003 (Qld) 53, 205
Commonwealth Volunteers Protection Act 2003 (Cth) 53
Personal Injuries (Liability and Damages) Act 2003 (NT) 53
Trade Practices Act 1974 (Cth) 178
Volunteers Protection Act 2001 (SA) 53
Volunteers and Food and other Donors (Protection from Liability) Act 2002 (WA) 53
Wrongs Act 1958 (Vic) 53

Canada

An Act to amend the Criminal Code and to make related amendments to other Acts (medical assistance in dying) SC 2016 c 3 227
Canadian Charter of Rights and Freedoms (Constitution Act, 1982) 226
Criminal Code RSC 1985, C-46 226
Good Samaritans Act [RSBC 1996] Chapter 172 53
Good Samaritan Act 2002 (Ontario) 53

Malaysia

Traditional and Complementary Medicine Act 2016 165

Netherlands

The Termination of Life on Request and Assisted Suicide (Review Procedures) Act 227

Singapore

Adoption of Children Act (Cap 4, 2012 Rev Ed)	197
Advance Medical Directive Act (Cap. 4A, 1997 Rev Ed)	101, 147, 213-5, 224
Allied Health Professions Act (Cap 6B, 2013 Rev Ed)	10
Biological Agents and Toxins Act (Cap 24A, 2006 Rev Ed)	12
Civil Law Act (Cap 43, 1999 Rev Ed)	87
Computer Misuse Act (Cap 50A, 2007 Rev Ed)	159
Constitution of the Republic of Singapore	13
Consumer Protection (Fair Trading) Act (Cap 52A, 2009 Rev Ed)	178
Contributory Negligence and Personal Injuries Act (Cap 54, 2002 Rev Ed)	84-5
Coroner's Act (Cap 63A, 2012 Rev Ed)	210, 213, 245
Criminal Justice Reform Act 2018 (No 19 of 2018)	122
Criminal Procedure Code (Cap 68, 2012 Rev Ed)	122, 124, 128-30, 149
Criminal Procedure Code (Reformative Training) Regulations 2018, No S 723	128
Dental Registration Act (DRA) (Cap 76, 2009 Rev Ed)	9, 22, 121
Employment of Foreign Manpower Act (Cap 91A, 2009 Rev Ed)	189
Health Products Act (Cap 122D, 2008 Rev Ed)	12, 262
Health Products (Clinical Trials) Regulations 2016	262
Health Products (Medical Devices) Regulations 2010 (No S436)	12
Health Products (Therapeutic Products) Regulations 2016 (No S 329)	12
Health Products (Therapeutic Products as Clinical Research Materials) Regulations	264
Human Biomedical Research Act (HBRA) (No 29 of 2015)	139, 233-8, 251, 256-61
Human Biomedical Research Regulations 2017 (No S 621)	260-1
Human Biomedical Research (Requirements for Appropriate Consent – Exemption) Regulations 2019	235
Human Biomedical Research (Tissue Banking) Regulations 2019	234
Human Cloning and Other Prohibited Practices Act (HCOPPA) (Cap 131B, Rev Ed 2005)	202-3, 255
Human Organ Transplant Act (HOTA) (Cap 131A, 2012 Rev Ed)	210, 238-42
Infectious Diseases Act (Cap 137, 2003 Rev Ed)	12, 147, 242
Infectious Diseases (COVID-19 – Stay Orders) Regulations 2020	13
Infectious Diseases (Measures to Prevent Spread of COVID-19) Regulations 2020	13
Interpretation (Amendment) Act 1998 (Act 22 of 1998)	210-1
Interpretation (Determination and Certification of Death) Regulations (Rg 1, GN No S505/1998)	211
Limitation Act (Cap 163, 1996 Rev Ed)	91-2
Medical Registration Act (MRA)(Cap 174, 2014 Rev Ed)	7, 9, 13-17, 19, 108, 158
Medical (Therapy, Education and Research) Act (Cap 175, 2014 Rev Ed)	212, 243-4
Medicines Act (Cap 176, 1985 Rev Ed)	12, 147, 181-2, 255, 262
Medicines (Clinical Trials) Regulations (Cap 176, Rg 3, 2000 Rev Ed)	255
Medicines (Clinical Trials) Regulations 2016 (No S 335)	262

Table of legislation   xxvii

Medicines (Labelling) Regulations (Cap 176, Rg 5, 2000 Rev Ed) 182
Medicines (Labelling of Chinese Proprietary Medicines) Regulations
(Cap 176, Rg 13, 2005 Rev Ed) 181
Medicines (Licensing, Standard Provisions and Fees) Regulations
(Cap 176, Rg 6, 2000 Rev Ed) 181
Medicines (Medical Advertisements) Regulations (Cap 176, Rg 2, 2000 Rev Ed) 181-2
Medicines (Traditional Medicines, Homeopathic Medicines and other Substances) (Exemption) Order (Cap 176, O 6, 2005 Rev Ed) 181
Medicines (Medicinal Products as Clinical Research Materials) Regulations 264
Mental Capacity Act (Cap 177A, 2010 Rev Ed) 98-102, 118-22, 215, 219
Mental Capacity Regulations 2010 (No S105) 120
Mental Capacity (Registration of Professional Deputies) Regulations 2018 (No S 529) 120
Mental Disorders and Treatment Act (MDTA) (Cap 178, 1985 Rev Ed) 118
Mental Health (Care and Treatment) Act (MHCTA) (Cap 178A, 2012 Rev Ed) 116-9
Misuse of Drugs Act (Cap 185, 2008 Rev Ed) 126
National Registry of Diseases Act (Cap 210B, 2008 Rev Ed) 148
Nursing and Midwives Act (Cap 209, 2012 Rev Ed) 10
Nurses and Midwives Regulations (GN No S 220/2000, 2002 Rev Ed, Reg 1) 10
Optometrists and Opticians Act (Cap 213A, 2008 Rev Ed) 10
Penal Code (Cap 224, 2008 Rev Ed) 22-3, 34, 122, 124-5, 127-8, 149, 173, 197, 224-5
Personal Data Protection Act (Act 26 of 2012) 149-54
Pharmacists Registration Act (Cap 230, 2008 Rev Ed)   10, 121
Poisons Act (Cap 234, 1999 Rev Ed) 12, 181
Private Hospitals and Medical Clinics Act (Cap 248, 1999 Rev Ed) 146
Probation of Offenders Act (Cap 252, 1985 Rev Ed) 129
Protection from Harassment Act (Cap 256A, 2015 Rev Ed) 122, 153
Registry of Births and Deaths Act (Cap 267, 1985 Rev Ed) 210
Rules of Court, O 24 r 6(5) and O 26A r 1(5) 161
Status of Children (Assisted Reproduction Technology)
Act (Cap 317A, 2015 Rev Ed) 194-5
Supreme Court of Judicature Act (Cap 322, 2007 Rev Ed) 19-20
Termination of Pregnancy Act (Cap 324, 1985 Rev Ed) 149, 188-90
Termination of Pregnancy Regulations (Cap 324, Rg 1) 148, 189-90
Tobacco (Control of Advertisements and Sale) Act (Cap 309, 2011 Rev Ed) 12
Traditional Chinese Medicine Practitioners Act (Cap 333A, 2001 Rev Ed) 10, 167-71, 173
Traditional Chinese Medicine Practitioners (Practice, Conduct and Ethics) Regulations 170
Traditional Chinese Medicine Practitioners (Registration of
Acupuncturists) Regulations 167
Traditional Chinese Medicine Practitioners (Registration of
Traditional Chinese Medicine Physicians) Regulations 167
Traditional Chinese Medicine Practitioners (Prescribed
Practices of Chinese Medicine) (Consolidated Order) 168
Trust Companies Act (Cap 336, 2006 Rev Ed) 120

Unfair Contract Terms Act (Cap 396, 1994 Rev Ed) 86
Women's Charter (Cap 353, 2009 Rev Ed) 197
Voluntary Sterilization Act (Cap 347, 2013 Rev Ed) 98, 186-7
Vulnerable Adults Act (No 27 of 2018) 121

United Kingdom

Access to Health Records Act 1990 154
Chancery Amendment Act 1858 (c 27) 144
Data Protection Act 1984 154
Human Fertilisation and Embryology Act 1990 195
Human Fertilisation and Embryology (Mitochondrial Donation) Regulations 200
Suicide Act 1961 CHAPTER 60 9 and 10 Eliz 2 227-8

United States

Death with Dignity Act (as amended by Senate Bill 579, passed by the 2019 Oregon legislative assembly) 225
National Research Act (Pub L 93-348) 1974 265
Revised Uniform Anatomical Gift Act (amended in 2008) 243

Others

Constitution of WHO adopted by the International Health Conference, New York, 19 June – 22 July 1946, signed on 22 July 1946 and entered into force on 7 April 1948 2
Convention on Human Rights and Biomedicine, Council of Europe, 13 ETS No 164, Oviedo, 4 April 1997 and entered into force on 1 December 1999 40
Convention on the Rights of Persons with Disabilities (2006), adopted on 13 December 2006 and entered into force on 3 May 2008 ....42, 114
European Convention of Human Rights 227-8
International Covenant on Economic, Social and Cultural Rights (ICESCR), New York, 16 December 1966, entered into force on 3 January 1976 42
United Nations Convention on Rights of the Child 197

PREFACE

When the publishers approached me about writing a book, I was in the midst of working out the reading list and detailed syllabus of a course entitled "Health Law and Medical Ethics". This module is offered as part of the Health Economics and Management major open to students at Singapore Management University. I was excited by the prospect of teaching the course and delivering the complex content in an accessible and methodical form to students. Health law and medical ethics represents an extension of my interests in both the law of torts and ethics – subjects which I have taught and researched on for several years. In addition to torts (covering topics such as medical negligence, consent to treatment and privacy interests), health law also delves into criminal law, regulatory frameworks, medical disciplinary processes, data protection law and others. Furthermore, medical ethics offers rich resources in the field of applied ethics involving the philosophical examination of concepts such as personhood, autonomy, beneficence, sanctity and quality of life as well as the surveys and recommendations of expert committees and ethicists.

Another reason I had for writing this book was the lack of a single textbook focusing on the topics of health law and medical ethics in the Singapore context, which I would like to cover for the course. An author's choice of the precise topics may be influenced in part by personal interests and judgement. I thought that the book should, as far as possible, cover core issues impacting on modern healthcare systems such as in Singapore and be relevant to the work and challenges faced by medical practitioners, healthcare professionals and students interested in pursuing a career in the healthcare sector. In writing the book, I have benefited immensely from the many important local textbooks, monographs, journal publications, court judgements and expert recommendations and reports relating to specific aspects of health law and medical ethics some of which I have cited in this book.

To ease the reader into the substantive topics beginning from Chapter 3, I have devoted two introductory chapters on the healthcare system: laws and regulations in Singapore (Chapter 1) and medical ethics (Chapter 2). The substantive areas range from the more traditional general topics (medical negligence, confidentiality and consent to treatment) to the specific topics (reproduction, end of life, human tissues, organs and biological materials, and human biomedical research) to those less commonly found in medical law and ethics texts (mental health, complementary and alternative medicine, and technological innovations in healthcare).

I have learnt as much writing about health law and medical ethics as I have in teaching it. I thank the students for their ideas and interactions during and outside of the seminars. I am also grateful to fellow academics whom I have had the opportunity to share and discuss health law issues. Apart from tertiary students, I hope that this book will also be useful to members of the legal and healthcare professions and academics who are involved and/or interested in legal and ethical issues relating to health and medicine.

Gary Chan
July 2020

ACKNOWLEDGEMENTS

I would like to gratefully acknowledge the research assistance of Ms Rennie Whang Yixuan (JD graduate from Singapore Management University) as well as Mr Wan Ding Yao and Ms Brenda Khoo Yu Qing who are both LLB students from Singapore Management University, for specific chapters of the book. I also appreciate Mr Javier Han Zong Tao, who was my teaching assistant for the course on "Health Law and Medical Ethics", for his ideas on various hypothetical issues relating to the course content. Finally, I would also like to thank Ms Lam Yong Ling, Ms Payal Bharti and Ms Samantha Phua and the production team at Routledge for their kind assistance and guidance throughout the publication process.

1 Introduction to the healthcare system, health laws and regulations

1.1 Introduction

By global standards, Singapore has been performing well on certain key health barometers. Life expectancy has increased significantly over the last few decades standing at 85.7 and 81.4 years for females and males, respectively, as at 2019.[1] The average span of living in good health was 74.2 years based on 2017 figures.[2] The newborn mortality rate per 1,000 live births in Singapore and the infant mortality rate (the probability of dying in the first year per 1,000 live births) have declined, whilst cancer survival rates have increased since the 1970s (Haseltine 2013, at chapter 2). In the Bloomberg Global Health Index 2019, Singapore was amongst the ten healthiest countries in the world based on a number of factors including health risks (tobacco use, high blood pressure, obesity), availability of clean water, life expectancy, malnutrition and causes of death.[3]

In the early years post independence, the focus was on public health programmes (such as proper sanitation procedures and control of infectious diseases through vaccinations against measles and polio). Public health issues continue to be paramount in Singapore in the new millennium with major outbreaks of the Severe Acute Respiratory Syndrome (SARS) in 2003, the Influenza (H1N1) or Swine Flu in 2009[4] and virus SARS-CoV-2 in 2019 (COVID-19). In recent decades, more attention has been paid to health promotion and healthy lifestyles in view of the increased incidence of chronic illnesses, diabetes and hypertension amongst Singaporeans as well as severe dementia in an ageing population. The ageing demographic is exacerbated by declining total fertility rates (with the birth rate of about 1.2 well below the replacement level of 2.1)[5] as parents are postponing giving birth and choosing to have fewer children.

---

1 https://www.singstat.gov.sg/find-data/search-by-theme/population/death-and-life-expectancy/latest-data.
2 https://www.todayonline.com/singapore/singaporeans-living-longer-spending-greater-proportion-time-ill-health-study.
3 https://worldpopulationreview.com/countries/healthiest-countries/.
4 Lim (2010, at pp. 857–861).
5 The total fertility rate was 1.14 as of 2019: https://www.singstat.gov.sg/modules/infographics/total-fertility-rate.

2   *Healthcare system, laws and regulations*

This chapter gives an overview of the general state of the healthcare system in Singapore with a focus on health costs, insurance, medical education, training and research. This is followed by a range of health law and regulatory issues relating to the registration and supervision of healthcare professionals, the establishment and operations of medical clinics and hospitals, public health, health products and medical institutions and bodies in Singapore, the regulation of medical practitioners through the Singapore Medical Council's (SMC) disciplinary processes as well as civil and criminal law sanctions against errant medical practitioners.

1.2 Meaning and scope of health, disease and well-being

Before we discuss Singapore's healthcare system, let us begin with some brief thoughts about some fundamental terms and concepts. What is the meaning of "health" in the first place? Does it refer to "well-being" or merely an absence of illness or disease? What counts as a "disease", "illness" or positive well-being?

The World Health Organization (WHO) – a specialised agency of the United Nations concerned with global health – defined 'health' broadly as a state of complete physical, mental, and social wellÐbeing and not merely the absence of disease or infirmity.[6] This expansive definition of "health" would encompass not only treatments for common diseases such as cancer and diabetes but also certain health services such as aesthetic surgery and traditional and complementary medicine.[7] It may, however, surprise some to learn that infertility has been classified by the WHO as a disease – specifically "a *disease* of the reproductive system defined by the failure to achieve a clinical pregnancy after 12 months or more of regular unprotected sexual intercourse".[8]

Reiss and Ankeny (2016) noted that the term "disease" generally refers to "any condition that literally causes 'dis-ease' or 'lack of ease' in an area of the body or the body as a whole". On the other hand, "illness" typically describes the "more non-objective features of a condition, such as subjective feelings of pain and discomfort", and the "behavioral changes which are judged as undesirable and unwanted within a particular culture, and hence lead members of that culture to seek help" from health professionals. Illness may also relieve a person from certain social responsibilities (*eg*, to take time off work or to avoid family responsibilities) – the social aspect of illness.

The naturalist basis for disease involves the abnormal functioning of system(s) of the human body. It is an objectivist empirical assessment as to what is biologically natural and normal functioning for human beings. For Boorse (2007), a disease is either an impairment of normal functional ability (which is based on biostatistical theory) or a limitation of functional ability caused by environmental agents; thus, health is the absence of disease.

An alternative view is constructivism which emphasises the human interests and values involved in assessing whether a disease exists. This theory is normative in nature.[9] For

---

6   Preamble to the Constitution of WHO adopted by the International Health Conference, New York, 19 June – 22 July 1946; signed on 22 July 1946 and entered into force on 7 April 1948.

7   WHO Global Report on Traditional and Complementary Medicine 2019 at https://www.who.int/activities/implementation-of-the-WHO-traditional-medicine-strategy-2014-2023.

8   WHO website at https://www.who.int/reproductivehealth/topics/infertility/definitions/en/.

9   Murphy (2015). Lawton LJ in *W v L* [1974] QB 711 had suggested that the term "mental illness" should be based on how the ordinary sensible person would construe it.

example, Nordenfelt (2007) regarded health for a person as the ability, given standard circumstances, to reach his or her vital goals. Thus, according to this value-laden approach, a disease represents a divergence from social norms and depends on culture that varies according to place and time. For example, homosexuality was at one time considered a disease due to the social mores against the practice of homosexuality. One problem, however, in constructivism is that it may not be capable of distinguishing between what is socially undesirable (*eg*, alcoholism) and a disease (Reiss and Ankeny 2016).

A hybrid approach is to consider a disease as comprising two features: (i) the abnormal functioning of some bodily system and (ii) the resulting abnormality is harmful. Thus, the existence of a biological dysfunction is not sufficient; it must manifest in tangible harm to the person as a member of society. One proponent of this hybrid approach is Wakefield (2007) who, in relation to the assessment of psychiatric condition, regarded mental disorders as "harmful" dysfunctions.

Instead of a binary categorisation between health/disease and absence of health/disease, it is plausible to regard the concept of "health" as one that lies in a continuum from illness to wellness. Under this approach, health is an aspirational goal of positive well-being. This is consistent with the WHO definition of "health" in 1948 and the idea of health promotion for members of public who may not suffer from any biological diseases. This approach also raises the problem of the subjectivity in the measurement of this expanded scope of health to the extent that the related assessment of well-being is dependent on a person's socio-economic conditions, upbringing, spirituality and outlook and not merely concerned with a biological dysfunction. Where do we draw the line between health and concepts such as happiness or life-satisfaction? Yet the adoption of a purely biological account of health runs the risk of divorcing health assessment from reality. For the individual person or patient, he would probably wish to know how his state of health or otherwise affects his capacity to cope with living in the physical and social environment he is exposed to.[10]

Box 1.1 – The meaning of health and the impact on medical profession and medicine

How would the meaning of "health" impact on our conception of the doctor-patient relationship and the responsibilities of medical profession and health institutions? Is the doctor's duty to improve or optimise health outcomes and well-being or merely to eliminate or reduce the effects of a disease? Should the study and/or practice of medicine aim to contribute to people's well-being (or what it means to live a good life)?

---

10 Canguilhem (1978) stated that health is that which confers a survival value, particularly adaptability within a set of environmental conditions: "to be in good health is being able to fall sick and recover; it is a biological luxury"; on the other hand, disease is characterised by "a reduction in the margin of tolerance for the environment's inconstancies" (p. 116).

1.3 Healthcare system in Singapore

Singapore practises a mixed healthcare delivery model in which (i) the private sector providers dominate the primary care sector (where the patient would typically have the first contact with doctors for common cold, flu, urinary tract infection, skin problems and so on), (ii) the public sector provides the majority of secondary or tertiary hospital facilities (such as specialist care, advanced medical investigation and treatment) and (iii) the care sector (nursing homes and hospices) are mainly provided by the private sector and voluntary welfare organisations funded by the government.[11] The public hospitals are restructured as government-owned corporations held by MOH Holdings Pte Ltd. Each restructured hospital has a board of directors with representation by the Ministry of Health (MOH). Public healthcare is organised into two clusters to enable integration and sharing of resources – the National Healthcare Group (NHG) and the Singapore Health Services (SingHealth) – with each cluster led by a Group CEO.

Singapore implements a regional health system in the North, East, West and Central regions[12] with acute hospitals and healthcare providers (including primary care providers, nursing homes, community hospitals and hospices) located in each geographical region to ensure patient-centric care is accessible, affordable and provided seamlessly throughout the country. In addition, particular areas of expertise to provide clinical services are concentrated in National Specialty Centres (including National Skin Centre, National Heart Centre, National Cancer Centre, National Dental Centre and National Neuroscience Institute).

The Agency for Integrated Care (AIC)[13] – which is constituted as an independent corporate entity under MOH Holdings – is responsible for primary integrated long-term care and community mental health in Singapore. As the "National Care Integrator", the agency interacts with and caters to the needs of the elderly and caregivers. The Silver Generation Office (formerly the Pioneer Generation Office) – which shares information with Singaporean elderly on government schemes, active ageing activities, and healthcare services – merged with AIC in 2018.

The Committee on Ageing has identified three "pillars" to improve the quality of life for the elderly through participation, improved health, and security. The Community Functional Screening Programme for the elderly aged 60 years and above helps the seniors to detect early signs of functional decline and promote health screening relating to aspects such as oral health, hearing, vision, and physical function. The Singapore Programme for Integrated Care for the Elderly (SPICE) supports the elderly in rehabilitation centres and day care

---

11 Thomas et al. (2016, at p. 47).
12 The six regional systems are National Healthcare Group, National University Health System, Alexandra Health, SingHealth, Eastern Health Alliance and Jurong Health System.
13 See https://www.aic.sg/Resources/What%20We%20Do. AIC began as the Care Liaison Services (CLS) under Ministry of Health in 1992 to "coordinate and facilitate the placement of elderly sick to nursing homes and chronic sick units", became the Integrated Care Services (ICS) in 2001 with an expanded role to "discharge planning and facilitate the transition of patients from hospitals to the community" and took on its current name in 2008.

centres. In addition to government initiatives, there are also private organisations such as the Tsao Foundation with a focus on the needs of the elderly.

1.3.1 Healthcare costs and insurance

The slogan "Health is Wealth" has a ring of truth to it in that serious ill health can put significant pressure on one's financial resources. Healthcare costs have been and remain a major issue for Singapore's healthcare system. The Ministry of Health's White Paper on Affordable Health Care (1993) aimed to achieve both efficiency and affordability of the healthcare system to be made accessible to the citizens. The Government sought to regulate healthcare by preventing an over-supply of medical services (by regulating the number of doctors, specialists and the different classes of hospital beds) and reducing demand. The financing model combines Government means-tested subsidies for the healthcare costs of Singapore residents based on household income criteria with the individual responsibility of patients who have to shoulder part of the costs of medical services.

Financing is based on what is known as the 3M model (MediSave, MediShield and MediFund) with "multiple layers of protection" (Lim 2013, at p. 34). Patients may draw from their own accounts under the MediSave scheme that started in 1984 – a compulsory medical care savings under the Central Provident Fund (CPF) scheme – to pay for medical bills. MediSave can also be drawn for approved medical expenses of immediate family members. From 2020, MediSave withdrawals of $200 per month would be allowed for the long-term care of severely disabled Singapore citizens.[14]

The amounts in MediSave may not be sufficient where catastrophic or chronic illnesses occur requiring long hospital stays or treatment. This is where MediShield – a voluntary opt-out medical insurance system – steps in to alleviate the financial burden of the patient or family members subject to certain limits for claims. Patients have to pay a fraction of the medical bill and the medical insurance will pay the remainder ("co-insurance"). The MediSave account can be used to pay for the annual premiums under MediShield which operates on a commercial basis. In addition, MediSave can be drawn upon to pay the premiums for certain approved private insurance plans for enhanced coverage (known as Integrated Shield Plans). A long-term disability insurance scheme for the elderly (known as ElderShield) makes monthly payouts for up to six years to take care of the elderly who cannot undertake basic daily activities such as feeding or washing.

The MediFund – a government endowment fund – is utilised to pay the healthcare costs of the financially needy. It is the "last resort" for the poorest patients (Singapore citizens) who are unable to afford the hospital bills despite government subsidies, and payments via cash, MediSave and MediShield. With a view to contain health costs, the Government had proposed a basic medical care package without frills that is available to all citizens with the costs partially subsidised by the Government. Portions of MediFund are set aside for elderly aged 65 and above (MediFund Silver) and the young (MediFund Junior).

---

14 https://www.moh.gov.sg/careshieldlife/long-term-care-financing/enhancements-(2020).

6 Healthcare system, laws and regulations

More recently, a compulsory long-term care insurance scheme (known as CareShield Life)[15] has been implemented for Singaporeans between 30 and 40 years of age. It is optional for those above 40 years old. The scheme will cover severe disabilities in situations where the insured would require assistance in at least three activities of daily living (such as washing, dressing and feeding, toileting, and walking or moving around) with no cap on the payout duration. Essentially, CareShield Life mandates self-reliance for the future needs of these relatively young members of the cohort who will become old in the future. The ElderFund, which has also taken effect recently in 2020, caters to lower-income Singapore citizens aged 30 years and above who are severely disabled and need financial support for long-term care. In recognition of the importance of caregivers' role for disabled persons, the Home Caregiving Grant (HCG) defrays the costs of caregiving expenses. Subsidies given under the Seniors' Mobility and Enabling Fund offset the costs of assistive devices and home healthcare items.[16]

Primary care is subsidised through the private general practitioners (GP) clinics (with subsidies available under the Community Health Assist Scheme (CHAS) for lower-income and disabled elderly Singaporeans) and government polyclinics (where the medical bills of Singapore citizens are subsidised by the government). Subsidies for selected dental services are also applicable at the private participating dental clinics. It has been noted that significant costs can be saved if patients were to be managed by a good primary care physician as opposed to a number of specialists from a primary care referral (Lee and Satku 2016, at p. 378). It is arguably about "right-siting" patient care to cater to his or her needs. Subsidised medication deemed to be essential and cost-effective in the Standard Drugs List is provided by the government, whilst more costly medication is partially subsidised on a means-tested basis under the Medication Assistance Fund (Lim 2013, at pp. 131-136). It should also be highlighted that a child development account is set up for every Singaporean child and can be used to pay for the child's medical expenses (and others such as education expenses). Most childhood vaccinations are free of charge.

The conscious efforts[17] to boost medical tourism ("SingaporeMedicine") and foreign patient numbers at the start of the new millennium which have scaled down had raised fundamental questions, amongst others, about the core mission of public hospitals to provide affordable healthcare (Lim 2013, at p. 145). One related concern of healthcare costs is the level of consumer protection and education on medical fees. To enhance "price transparency", the MOH has[18]:

(i) required all private medical clinics to display their common charges (ie, pricing transparency for consultations);

---

15 https://www.moh.gov.sg/careshieldlife/about-careshield-life.
16 https://www.moh.gov.sg/cost-financing/healthcare-schemes-subsidies/caregiver-grants-subsidies.
17 See the Healthcare Services Working Group and joint efforts of Singapore Tourism Board, Economic Development Board and International Enterprise Singapore.
18 The Competition Commission of Singapore, Statement of Decision in *Re Singapore Medical Association - Guidelines on Fees* [2010] SGCCS 6 at [28] and [146].

(ii) published individual hospital bill sizes on the MOH's website and requiring hospitals to provide financial counselling to patients (*ie*, price transparency before admissions to hospitals); and

(iii) required medical bills given to patients to be itemised.

It has also published in 2018 the Fee Benchmarks for Private Sector Surgeons Fees with respect to a list of surgical procedures.[19]

1.3.2 Education and training of healthcare professionals and medical research

Education for medical doctors is served by three medical schools in Singapore: (i) the Yong Loo Lin Faculty of Medicine at the National University of Singapore (NUS); (ii) the Lee Kong Chian School of Medicine at Nanyang Technological University (NTU) which offers, in collaboration with Imperial College, medicine as an undergraduate degree; and (iii) the Duke-NUS School of Medicine which caters to graduates from various disciplines.

In addition to the local universities approved under the Medical Registration Act (MRA),[20] medical degrees from a list of approved foreign universities[21] are recognised for the purpose of medical practice in Singapore. Graduates with these approved foreign medical degrees and in active clinical practice will have to undergo a period of supervised practice in a medical institution with their performance monitored and assessed by an SMC-approved healthcare institution (conditional registration) before being formally registered as medical practitioners in Singapore. In addition, the Faculty of Dentistry is housed at NUS. Specialisations in dentistry training in Endodontics, Oral and Maxillofacial Surgery, Orthodontics, Periodontics and Prosthodontics are offered in Singapore. The Government heavily subsidies the costs of studies of medical and dentistry students who are required to serve out a service obligation in the government for a number of years upon graduation.

Diploma programmes in nursing are offered in Nanyang Polytechnic and Ngee Ann Polytechnic, and undergraduate and postgraduate degree programmes are administered by the NUS Alice Lee School of Nursing. There are also academic programmes relating to the fields of allied healthcare such as the Masters in Psychology (Clinical) in NUS, diploma programmes in physiotherapy in polytechnics and degree programmes at the Singapore Institute of Technology and the Oral Health Therapist diploma programme in Nanyang Polytechnic. Other healthcare-related programmes and majors include the Health Economics and Management major in Singapore Management University.

Continuing Medical Education has been made compulsory for medical practitioners since 2003[22] and, for dentists and oral health therapists, compulsory Continuing Professional Education since 2007[23] for the renewal of their practising certificates in order to maintain their competence and knowledge.

---

19 https://www.moh.gov.sg/docs/librariesprovider5/default-document-library/fee-benchmarks-for-private-sector-surgeon-fees-(for-download)_13nov2018.pdf.
20 First Schedule.
21 Second Schedule.
22 https://www.healthprofessionals.gov.sg/smc/continuing-medical-education-(cme)-for-doctors.
23 https://www.healthprofessionals.gov.sg/sdc/continuing-professional-education.

> **Box 1.2 - Assessing the healthcare system**
>
> What do you think are the appropriate criteria to assess a healthcare system? How do you assess the success or failure of a healthcare system? How may the criteria and assessment be applied to Singapore?

Biomedical research was perceived as offering significant opportunities to increase economic growth and attract foreign talent. Notwithstanding the control on the number of medical students, the setting up of Duke-NUS Faculty of Medicine with its focus on biomedical research and training for clinician-scientists was justifiable on those bases. The Saw Swee Hock School of Public Health at NUS was established to investigate healthcare spending and health policy in South and Southeast Asia. The Initiative to Improve Health in Asia (NIHA) – formed through collaborations amongst NUS Global Asia Institute, Yong Loo Lin Faculty of Medicine, NUS Business School and LKY School of Public Policy – focuses on health policy in Asia. The Agency for Science, Technology and Research (or A*Star) includes within its fold the Biomedical Research Council (translational research in medicine) and several biomedical institutes (eg, Bioinformatics Institute, Genome Institute of Singapore, Institute of Bioengineering and Nanotechnology). The MOH's National Medical Research Council funds medical research. Several global pharmaceutical and medical technology companies[24] involved in biomedical research and development have located their manufacturing operations in Singapore.

1.4 Health-related laws and regulations

This section introduces the basic framework relating to one of two core areas of the entire book namely Health Law in Singapore.[25] It considers a broad range of legal and regulatory matters pertaining to the following:

- healthcare professionals
- healthcare institutions and practices
- medical bodies and institutions
- the disciplinary process for medical practitioners
- civil and criminal liabilities of healthcare professionals.

Due to the introductory nature and breadth of the issues covered, the discussion in this chapter will necessarily be non-exhaustive and brief. Further details on health laws and their applications would be examined in the ensuing chapters covering specific topics.

1.4.1 Healthcare professionals

Healthcare professionals include medical practitioners, dentists, nurses and midwives, pharmacists, allied healthcare professionals and traditional Chinese Medicine practitioners governed by the respective statutes and regulations.

---

24 *Eg*, Novartis, Abbott, MSD, Medtronic and GlaxoSmithKline.
25 The other core area – Medical Ethics in Singapore – will be examined in Chapter 2.

A person is entitled to practise as a medical practitioner only if he is registered under the MRA and has a valid practising certificate.[26] An unauthorised person who practises medicine, or advertises or holds himself out as a medical practitioner is guilty of an offence.[27] To obtain a valid practising certificate, the medical practitioner has to, as mentioned, comply with continuing medical education requirements and maintain insurance for indemnity against losses arising from claims for civil liability incurred by the practitioner in the course of his medical practice.[28]

The SMC is a statutory board set up under the MRA to ensure the competence of medical practitioners and uphold professional standards. The Specialist Accreditation Board (SAB) comprising not less than eight medical practitioners appointed by the Minister under the MRA[29] oversees the accreditation, training and continuing medical education of medical specialists[30] based on their overseas and local training in various specialisations (such as cardiology, dermatology, diagnostic radiology, geriatric medicine, psychiatry and neurosurgery). General practitioners may be accredited as Family Physicians by the Family Physicians Accreditation Board[31] under MRA. The SMC's Ethical Code and Ethical Guidelines (2016)[32] is an important guide to professional practice and conduct (Chapter 2).

The Dental Registration Act (DRA)[33] established the Singapore Dental Council (SDC) to oversee the registration of dentists and oral health therapists,[34] make recommendations pertaining to dental education and training as well as regulate the conduct and ethics of dentists and oral health therapists. A person who practises dentistry in Singapore without a valid practising certificate of a registered dentist would be guilty of an offence.[35] The SDC has issued a separate Ethical Code and Ethical Guidelines (2018) for dentists[36] as well as guidelines for aesthetic facial procedures in 2020.[37]

---

26 Section 13.
27 Section 17.
28 Section 36. The Medical Protection Society of Singapore is the main indemnifier; annual subscription rates vary according to the risks involved in a doctor's particular practice (Haseltine 2013, at p. 70).
29 Section 34.
30 Section 35.
31 Section 35A and B.
32 https://www.healthprofessionals.gov.sg/smc/guidelines/smc-ethical-code-and-ethical-guidelines-(2002-and-2016-editions)-and-handbook-on-medical-ethics-(2016-edition).
33 (Cap 76, 2009 Rev Ed).
34 Oral Health Therapists practise dentistry under the supervision of a registered dentist. Approved qualifications include a diploma in dental hygiene and therapy from the Nanyang Polytechnic, a certificate of dental therapy from the Ministry of Health or the Dental Board or a qualification in dental hygiene that is approved by the Dental Council: section 21A.
35 Section 22.
36 Updated in April 2019 at https://www.healthprofessionals.gov.sg/docs/librariesprovider11/default-document-library/sdc-eceg-2018---updated-15-april-2019108d468283c14e15b40f36d0ef057467.pdf.
37 https://www.healthprofessionals.gov.sg/docs/librariesprovider11/default-document-library/guidelines-on-aesthetic-facial-procedures-for-dental-practitioners-(2020)fd3cd63f5646485c89e8a19a3599deda.pdf.

10 *Healthcare system, laws and regulations*

The Singapore Nursing Board (SNB) regulates nursing education and practices in accordance with the Nursing and Midwives Act[38] and regulations.[39] The statute recognises the role of the Advanced Practice Nurse[40] to manage patients with complex health issues. The Code for Nurses and Midwives (2018)[41] issued by the SNB supplements the statutory requirements with ten ethical principles and accompanying practice statements spanning four areas (Nurses/Midwives and People, Nurses/Midwives and their practice, Nurses/Midwives and their profession, and Nurses/Midwives and co-workers).

The Singapore Pharmacy Council (SPC) manages the registration and practicing certificates of pharmacists, training and education and their conduct and ethics in Singapore under the Pharmacists Registration Act,[42] whilst the SAB for Pharmacy decides on the requirements for specialist registration.[43]

The Allied Health Professions Council (AHPC) set up in 2011 under the Allied Health Professions Act[44] is responsible for the registration, issuance of practicing certificates, conduct, ethics and practices of allied healthcare professionals who work alongside the doctors to deliver healthcare services. The statutory list of allied health professionals comprises audiologists, occupational therapists, physiotherapists, speech therapists, radiographers, radiation therapists, clinical psychologists, dieticians, podiatrists and prosthetists/orthotists.[45]

Traditional Chinese Medicine complement the conventional medicine practised in Singapore. The Traditional Chinese Medicine Practitioners Act[46] was passed in 2000 to, amongst others, set up the TCM Practitioners Board which registers TCM acupuncturists and physicians, regulates the professional conduct of registered TCM practitioners and accredits schools and courses on TCM (Chapter 8).

The Secretariat of healthcare Professional Boards (SPB)[47] was recently formed on 1 January 2020 to support the secretariat and operational functions of 11 healthcare councils and boards (SMC, SDC, SNB, SPC, TCMPB, AHPC, Optometrists & Opticians Board,[48] Specialists Accreditation Board, Dental Specialists Accreditation Board, Pharmacy Specialists Accreditation Board and Family Physicians Accreditation Board).

---

38 (Cap 209, 2012 Rev Ed).
39 Nurses and Midwives Regulations (GN No S 220/2000, 2002 Rev Ed, Reg 1).
40 This requires qualifications or special knowledge, and experience in a specialised branch of nursing: section 32.
41 https://www.healthprofessionals.gov.sg/docs/librariesprovider4/publications/code-for-nurses-and-midwives-april-2018.pdf.
42 (Cap 230, 2008 Rev Ed), section 5.
43 Sections 36 and 37.
44 (Cap 6B, 2013 Rev Ed), section 7.
45 Schedule 1.
46 (Cap 333A, 2001 Rev Ed).
47 https://www.healthprofessionals.gov.sg/snb.
48 Optometrists and Opticians Act (Cap 213A, 2008 Rev Ed).

1.4.2 Healthcare institutions and practices

The Private Hospitals and Medical Clinic Act ("PHMCA") was enacted in 1980 to provide a regulatory framework for the licensing of private hospitals (which also included nursing homes) and medical clinics by MOH. The public sector hospitals and polyclinics, after they had undergone corporatisation and restructuring in the 1980s and 1990s, were brought under PHMCA. The purpose of the licensing requirements was to ensure adherence to minimum standards in the provision of healthcare services. As part of the licensing requirements, all hospitals were required to implement quality assurance programmes to review the quality of services, practices and procedures carried out. Guidelines were duly issued to facilitate the work of hospital quality assurance committees in dealing with unexpected occurrences involving death, permanent loss of function or serious injuries associated with the treatment of patients.[49]

The Healthcare Services Bill[50] was introduced for the first time in Parliament in November 2019 and is expected to be passed by Parliament to replace the PHMCA in 2020 with implementation in phases from years 2021 to 2022. First, the Healthcare Services Act ("HCSA") if enacted is likely to broaden the current regulatory scope in PHMCA to include healthcare services, allied health and nursing services, traditional medicine, and complementary and alternative medicine (though MOH will not be licensing allied health services, nursing services and traditional medicine and complementary and alternative medicine which will continue to be regulated under the existing statutes). Second, the intended statute seeks to regulate the provision of healthcare services through the licensing of healthcare providers based on the type of services (such as hospital service, ambulatory care services and long-term residential care service) they provide[51] rather than according to physical premises as in the existing PHMCA. Third, there will be greater oversight of the quality assurance committees for the licensed healthcare services. Moreover, new committees such as Service Review Committees for certain services that are higher-risk, more complex or of greater public interest and Service Ethics Committees for selected licensees to review the ethicality of complex and high-risk medical treatment are envisaged. Other features include MOH's powers to gather data on patients to prevent public health emergencies, implement transitional measures to prevent abrupt discontinuation of residential care services and employment restrictions for certain healthcare services that cater to vulnerable segments of the population.

Apart from the wide scope in PHMCA and the forthcoming HCSA, the regulation of healthcare institutions and practices involve a plethora of functions and measures by ministries, government agencies, boards and the Director of Medical Services whether to license selected activities, approve dealings in certain health products, control infectious diseases, ensure compliance with health laws or regulations or to promote or incentivise desirable healthy activities. Apart from the MOH and its agencies, the health-related responsibilities

---

49 Guidelines for Review of Sentinel Events by Hospital Quality Assurance Committees 2004 (Ministry of Health); see also discussion of quality assurance systems in Kuah (2004).
50 Bill N. 37/2019.
51 See description of expected changes under new law at https://www.moh.gov.sg/hcsa/about-hcsa# Timelines.

of the Ministry of the Environment and Water Resources[52] (sanitation, food safety, water resources and environmental public health) and the Ministry of Manpower (MOM) (occupational health and safety of workers) should be noted (Phua 2018, at p. 18).

The Health Sciences Authority (HSA) administers the licensing and approval processes for the manufacture,[53] importing,[54] and supply by wholesale[55] of health products under the Health Products Act ("HPA").[56] The statute covers medical devices, cosmetic products, therapeutic products and oral dental gum.[57] These laws are implemented via regulations: The Health Products (Medical Devices) Regulations 2010[58] and the Health Products (Therapeutic Product) Regulations 2016[59] which are further supplemented by industry standards and practices.[60] Other laws and regulations under HSA's purview include the Medicines Act[61] (to control the sale, supply, import and manufacture of medicinal products and advertisements[62]), Poisons Act[63] (to regulate the importation, possession, manufacture, compounding, storage, transport and sale of poisons[64]) and the Tobacco (Control of Advertisements and Sale) Act[65] (to prohibit advertisements relating to any tobacco product or its use, and the sale, packaging and trade description of tobacco products). Electronic cigarettes are banned in Singapore whether for purposes of importation, distribution, sale, purchase, use or possession.[66] The HSA is also in charge of blood service and forensic science testing.

With respect to public health, the Biological Agents and Toxins Act[67] under the Director of Medical Services' purview regulates the possession, use and transportation of biological agents (such as the Ebola and smallpox viruses) and toxins to ensure safety in the handling of such agents and toxins. The Director is also responsible together with other agencies to control and prevent infectious diseases under the Infectious Diseases Act[68] and

---

52 This Ministry has recently been renamed as "Ministry of Sustainability and the Environment".
53 Section 12.
54 Section 13.
55 Section 14.
56 (Cap 122D, 2008 Rev Ed).
57 Schedule 1.
58 No S 436.
59 No S 329.
60 *Eg*, the Good Distribution Practice for Medical Devices Requirements (TS01) and the Singapore Standard for Good Distribution Practice for Medical Devices – Requirements (SS 620).
61 (Cap 176, 1985 Rev Ed).
62 Part VI of the statute.
63 (Cap 234, 1999 Rev Ed).
64 See Poisons List in the Schedule.
65 (Cap 309, 2011 Rev Ed). Singapore is a signatory to the WHO's Framework Cooperation on Tobacco Control.
66 Section 16, Tobacco (Control of Advertisements and Sale) Act.
67 (Cap 24A, 2006 Rev Ed).
68 (Cap 137, 2003 Rev Ed).

accompanying regulations including measures restricting individual liberties during the COVID-19 pandemic.[69]

The MOH's law enforcement unit conducts investigations, surveillance and enforcement operations in cooperation with the Singapore Police Force, Singapore Customs, HSA and MOM and investigates offences relating to illegal health-related practices, defaults and breaches of treatment orders.

For public health promotion through increasing public awareness and encouraging healthy behaviour as well as disease prevention, the Health Promotion Board set up in 2001 implements campaigns (eg, the National Healthy Lifestyle campaign), programmes on weight management, healthy eating and encouraging people to quit smoking which are communicated through various media platforms. It should be pointed out that the task of health promotion is not strictly about biological and physical health but is also heavily dependent on social and environmental factors. In this respect, as WHO had indicated, "health literacy"[70] is an important aspect of health promotion. The Healthy Living Master Plan[71] aims to achieve "healthy living as accessible, natural, and effortless for all Singaporeans". There are three prongs to the Master Plan: (a) Place – a conducive environment for healthy living, (b) People – a socially inclusive community for healthy living, and (c) Price – affordable options for healthy living. The focus is on designing programmes or incentives to encourage or "nudge" people to change their lifestyles, behaviours, and habits. Furthermore, the MOH and HPB are working on implementing mandatory requirements for nutrition labels for sugar sweetened beverages and advertising bans on certain unhealthy beverages.

1.4.3 Medical bodies and institutions

As mentioned above, the SMC, as an important medical institution in Singapore, is responsible for, amongst others, the registration of medical practitioners (including specialists[72] and family physicians[73]), their training and education, conduct and ethics, standards of practice and competence as well as making recommendations on the courses and examinations leading to the medical degrees in Singapore.[74] It comprises the Director of Medical Services, 2 registered medical practitioners from each medical school in Singapore, 12 elected registered

---

69 *Eg*, Infectious Diseases (COVID-19 – Stay Orders) Regulations 2020 and Infectious Diseases (Measures to Prevent Spread of COVID-19) Regulations 2020. Article 13(2) of the Singapore Constitution states: "Subject to any law relating to the security of Singapore or any part thereof, public order, *public health* or the punishment of offenders, every citizen of Singapore has the right to move freely throughout Singapore and to reside in any part thereof" (emphasis added).

70 It has been defined as the "cognitive and social skills which determine the motivation and ability of individuals to gain access to, understand and use information in ways which promote and maintain good health": see World Health Organization, 'Health Promotion': https://www.who.int/healthpromotion/conferences/7gchp/track2/en/.

71 https://www.moh.gov.sg/docs/librariesprovider5/resources-statistics/reports/moh_healthy-living-master-plan_inside-page_8d.pdf.

72 Section 22, MRA.

73 Section 22A, MRA.

74 Section 5, MRA.

medical practitioners resident in Singapore, and 8 registered medical practitioners resident in Singapore appointed by the Minister.[75] The President of SMC is elected by its members.[76] A person is disqualified from membership in SMC if he: (a) is a non-citizen and non-permanent resident of Singapore; (b) has less than ten years' experience in the practice of medicine; (c) is an undischarged bankrupt; (d) is a person convicted in Singapore or elsewhere of fraud, dishonesty or moral turpitude or implying a defect of character which makes him unfit for his profession; (e) is a person found guilty of improper act or conduct which brings disrepute to his profession; (f) is a person found guilty of professional misconduct; or (g) his fitness to practise as medical practitioner is impaired due to his physical or mental condition.[77]

Other significant medical bodies include the Academy of Medicine, Singapore (AMS), the College of Family Physicians, Singapore (CFPS) and Singapore Medical Association (SMA). The AMS is a professional institution of medical and dental specialists responsible for postgraduate specialist training, continuous professional development and dissemination of information and knowledge to the public on matters related to health. The CFPS seeks to promote the values and ideals of family medicine. The SMA is the national medical organisation representing the majority of medical practitioners in both the public and private sectors that conducts training on medical ethics and publishes and disseminates medical knowledge.

1.4.4 Disciplinary process for medical practitioners

The disciplinary process is typically initiated by an aggrieved patient who is entitled to lodge a complaint in writing supported by a statutory declaration concerning the medical practitioner to the SMC in relation to any one of the matters specified in section 39(1) of MRA.[78] The SMC may make a complaint or refer information to its Complaints Panel[79] on its own motion[80] in relation to the abovementioned matters in section 39(1).

To deal with the complaints, the SMC sets up a Complaints Panel comprising SMC members, medical practitioners and laypersons.[81] The Complaints Panel is empowered to refer the complaint to a Complaints Committee. The members of the Complaints Committee are appointed from the Complaints Panel[82] to conduct an inquiry into the complaint. The Complaints Committee is required to complete its inquiry within three months from the date of the complaint[83] unless extension of time is granted by the Complaints Panel. The Complaints

---

75 Section 4, MRA.
76 Section 7, MRA.
77 Section 8, MRA.
78 Section 39 refers to (a) complaints touching on the conduct of the medical practitioner in his professional capacity or on his improper act or conduct which brings disrepute to his profession; (b) information on the conviction of a medical practitioner of any offence implying a defect in character which makes him unfit to practice as a medical practitioner; (c) complaint that the professional services provided by the medical practitioner are not of the quality which is reasonable to expect of him; or (d) information touching on the physical or mental fitness to practice of the medical practitioner.
79 This is set up under section 38, MRA.
80 Section 39(3).
81 Section 38.
82 Section 40.
83 Section 42(1).

Committee may decide to dismiss the matter if the complaint is "frivolous, vexatious, misconceived, or lacking in substance",[84] issue a letter of advice to the medical practitioner or refer the matter for mediation[85] or direct investigations into the matter.[86] The investigators[87] notify the medical practitioner to answer the allegations made against him[88] and submit its investigations to the Complaints Committee.[89] The Complaints Committee may decide that a formal inquiry before the Disciplinary Tribunal (DT) is not necessary and make other orders (such as to issue a letter of warning or advice to the medical practitioner or for the latter to undergo further education or training).[90] The complainant, medical practitioner or SMC may appeal to the Minister if they are dissatisfied with the decision of the Complaints Committee.[91]

Should the Complaints Committee determine that a formal inquiry is necessary, it will order an inquiry to be held by a DT[92] which comprises a chairman,[93] and at least two registered medical practitioners of not less than ten years' standing. The DT panel should not consist entirely of medical practitioners; should the chairman be a medical practitioner, a layperson or a former judge or judicial commissioner, advocate or solicitor or legal officer may be appointed as an observer (with no voting power).[94]

The SMC appoints members of Health Committees to determine if a medical practitioner's fitness to practise is "impaired by reason of physical or mental condition". If this is the case, the Health Committee has the power to order suspension for a period not exceeding 12 months, change the registration from that of a fully registered medical practitioner to that of medical practitioner with conditional registration, impose conditions on the registration of the medical practitioner, recommend to the SMC the removal of the medical practitioner from the register and for the medical practitioner to pay costs to the SMC.[95]

---

84 Section 42(4)(a).
85 Sections 42(4)(b) and 43.
86 Section 42(4)(c).
87 The investigator may be a member or employee of SMC or a public officer: section 60A. The powers of the investigator includes the power to enter, inspect and search premises of medical practitioner and to require a person to attend and furnish information in connection with the investigation: section 60A(2).
88 Section 44.
89 Section 48.
90 Section 49(1).
91 Section 49(10), (11) and (12).
92 Section 49(2).
93 Section 50(1) states the chairman of the panel shall be (i) a registered medical practitioner of not less than 20 years' standing; (ii) a former Judge or Judicial Commissioner; (iii) an advocate and solicitor of not less than 15 years' standing; or (iv) a Singapore Legal Service officer of not less than 15 years of full-time employment in Singapore Legal Service.
94 Section 50(1)(c).
95 Section 58(1). See *Saha v the GMC* [2009] All ER (D) 306 where the English court held, in upholding the prior decision of the GMC's Fitness to Practice Panel, that a doctor, who suffered from hepatitis B, failed in his medical professional conduct to provide this information to his former employers; and the doctor's name was removed from the register.

1.4.4.1 DT proceedings

During the DT proceedings which are quasi-criminal in nature, the SMC bears the burden of proving its case beyond a reasonable doubt. Where there are two competing and equally plausible versions of the material facts, that burden is not discharged.[96] The totality of the evidence must be considered to determine if the burden of proof has been discharged.[97] The medical practitioner may appear in person or be represented by counsel,[98] and the SMC may appoint an advocate and solicitor.[99]

The types of conduct which can result in disciplinary sanctions include circumstances where the registered medical practitioner[100]:

(a) has been convicted in Singapore or elsewhere of any offence involving fraud or dishonesty;
(b) has been convicted in Singapore or elsewhere of any offence implying a defect in character which makes him unfit for his profession;
(c) has been guilty of such improper act or conduct which, in the opinion of the DT, brings disrepute to his profession;
(d) has been guilty of professional misconduct; or
(e) failed to provide professional services of the quality which is reasonable to expect of him.

If the medical practitioner has been convicted or is guilty of one of the above, the DT is empowered to make one or more of the following orders[101]:

- remove the name of the registered medical practitioner from the register;
- suspend the registration of medical practitioner for a period of not less than three months and not more than three years;
- change the registration from that of a fully registered medical practitioner to that of medical practitioner with conditional registration;
- impose conditions on the registration of the medical practitioner;
- impose on medical practitioner a penalty not exceeding S$100,000;
- censure the doctor in writing;
- require the medical practitioner to give an undertaking to abstain in future from the conduct complained of;

---

96 *Lam Kwok Tai Leslie v SMC* [2017] 5 SLR 1168 at [38].
97 *Lam Kwok Tai Leslie v SMC* [2017] 5 SLR 1168 at [34]-[35] (where undue weight had been placed on the fact that the medical doctor had not kept contemporaneous records for the taking of consent without giving weight to other evidence with respect to the charge of failing to obtain informed consent from the patient).
98 Section 51(3).
99 Section 59I.
100 Section 53(1).
101 Section 53(2).

- make costs orders (including requiring the medical practitioner to pay costs and expenses incidental to proceeding inclusive of costs to the solicitor appointed by the SMC and reasonable expenses paid by SMC to witnesses[102] and/or cost orders against the SMC).[103]

Conversely, the DT may dismiss the complaint or matter if the medical practitioner is not convicted or guilty of any of the abovementioned conduct.

1.4.4.2 Professional misconduct

A common charge against medical practitioners is that of professional misconduct under section 53(1)(d) of MRA. Allegations of "professional misconduct" under the statute have included research misconduct,[104] failure to obtain informed consent prior to surgery or intervention, and wilful neglect of duties and gross mismanagement of post-operative treatment.[105] The charge of professional misconduct against the medical practitioner may be established under either of the two limbs in *Low Cze Hong v Singapore Medical Council*[106]:

(a) intentional, deliberate departure from standards observed or approved by members of the profession of good repute and competency;
(b) serious negligence that it objectively portrays an abuse of the privileges which accompany registration as a medical practitioner.

If the doctor was not aware of the applicable standard, the charge based on the first limb will not be made out against him; nonetheless, such lack of awareness of the applicable standard may not prevent him from being charged under the second limb of serious negligence.[107] In addition to the two limbs, professional misconduct can extend to breaches of other ethical obligations.[108] The DT will have to determine the following in respect of the two limbs[109]:

---

102 Section 53(5) to (8) on costs orders.
103 This is an implied ancillary power under the MRA to order costs against the SMC if the DT dismisses the charges brought by the SMC: *Ang Pek San Lawrence v SMC* [2015] 2 SLR 1179 at [30]. It was also stated that if the SMC had absolute immunity from an adverse costs order in such circumstances, the medical practitioner would face the real risk of suffering not only professional embarrassment but also financial prejudice to defend what might eventually turn out to be an unmeritorious complaint: [2015] 2 SLR 1179 at [27]-[29].
104 *Eg*, the SMC Inquiry on the professional misconduct by Professor Simon Shorvon, former director of National Neuroscience Institute, Singapore, for obtaining confidential patient information for research without the patients' consent; but see English High Court decision in *R v General Medical Council* [2006] EWHC 3277 which endorsed the UK GMC's decision to stop investigations into the alleged improprieties of Professor Shorvon.
105 *Gan Keng Seng Eric v SMC* [2011] 1 SLR 745.
106 [2008] 3 SLR(R) 612 at [37].
107 *Singapore Medical Council v Wong Him Choon* [2016] 4 SLR 1086 at [90].
108 *Eg*, the doctor's breach of the ethical obligation to charge a fair and reasonable fee for the services rendered to his patient: see *Lim Mey Lee Susan v Singapore Medical Council* [2013] 3 SLR 900 at [44].
109 *Ang Pek San Lawrence v Singapore Medical Council* [2015] 1 SLR 436.

First limb:
(i) what the applicable standard of conduct was amongst members of the medical profession of good standing and repute in relation to the actions that the allegation of misconduct referred to;
(ii) whether the applicable standard of conduct required the doctor to do something and, if so, at what point in time such duty crystallised; and
(iii) whether the doctor's conduct constituted an intentional and deliberate departure from the applicable standard of conduct.

Second limb:
(i) whether there was serious negligence on the party of the doctor; and
(ii) whether such negligence objectively constituted an abuse of the privileges of being registered as a medical practitioner.

As stated by the High Court in *Singapore Medical Council v Lim Lian Arn*,[110] "not every departure from the acceptable standards of conduct would necessarily amount to professional misconduct". The misconduct must be "more than a mere technical breach of the relevant standards".[111] As stated in SMC's ECEG 2016, "serious disregard or persistent failure to meet the standards" set out under the ECEG (2016) can "potentially lead to harm to patients or bring disrepute to the profession with loss of confidence in the healthcare system and consequently may lead to disciplinary proceedings". There is a "strong presumption that a doctor had knowledge of the matters contained" in the ECEG issued by the SMC as this "represented so fundamentally *the most basic aspects of clinical practice*".[112]

Cases under the first limb would include the making of representations intentionally for which the doctor was not able to provide a reasonable basis,[113] and where the medical practitioner was found to have falsely represented the fees of third-party doctors in her bills to her patient.[114]

With respect to the second limb on serious negligence, it has to be misconduct that goes beyond mere carelessness.[115] Relevant broad factors include the nature and extent of misconduct, the gravity of the foreseeable consequences of the doctor's failure and the public interest in pursuing disciplinary sanctions.[116] Case precedents indicate that gross negligence and indifference to the patients' welfare[117] may amount to professional misconduct under the second limb. On the other hand, a one-off failure by the doctor in the course of a routine procedure in which no harm was intended or caused would not fall foul of the second limb.[118]

---

110 [2019] SGHC 172 at [30]-[32], citing *Martin v Director of Proceedings* [2010] NZAR 333.
111 [2019] SGHC 172 at [30].
112 *SMC v Wong Him Choon* [2016] 4 SLR 1086 at [82].
113 *Ang Peng Tiam v SMC* [2017] 5 SLR 356 at [70].
114 *Lim Mey Lee Susan v Singapore Medical Council* [2013] 3 SLR 900. The doctor had added a significant and undisclosed markup to the actual fees of those third-party doctors: at [133]-[134].
115 *Singapore Medical Council v Lim Lian Arn* [2019] SGHC 172 at [36] citing *Pillai v Messiter (No 2)* (1989) 16 NSWLR 197 (NSW Court of Appeal).
116 *Singapore Medical Council v Lim Lian Arn* [2019] SGHC 172 at [38].
117 *Chia Foong Lin v Singapore Medical Council* [2017] 5 SLR 334 at [61]-[62].
118 *Singapore Medical Council v Lim Lian Arn* [2019] SGHC 172 at [38].

Healthcare system, laws and regulations 19

The DT will rely on expert evidence to ascertain the applicable standards and whether the departure from the applicable standards would amount to professional misconduct. The expert evidence should provide the reasons supporting its conclusions so as to allow the DT (and High Court) to evaluate the opinion.[119]

1.4.4.3 Scope of High Court intervention

The medical practitioner is entitled to appeal against the DT's decision to the High Court.[120] The complainant who is dissatisfied with the DT's decision may apply to a Review Committee set up under MRA to direct the SMC to file an appeal.[121]

The appeal will be heard by three Judges of the High Court. The DT's findings as to any issue of medical ethics or standards of professional conduct shall be treated as final and conclusive unless such finding is "in the opinion of the High Court unsafe, unreasonable or contrary to the evidence".[122] The High Court may interfere with the DT decision if[123]:

(a) there was something clearly wrong either:

   (i) in the conduct of the disciplinary proceedings; and/or
   (ii) in the legal principles applied; and/or

(b) the findings of the DT were sufficiently out of tune with the evidence to indicate with reasonable certainty that the evidence had been misread.

The High Court has the power to quash the convictions meted out by the DT where there is a "miscarriage of justice". This can arise in exceptional circumstances where the doctor had pleaded guilty to a charge of professional misconduct before the DT, but the facts themselves do not support the charge.[124] Like the DT, the High Court also has the power to award costs against SMC.[125]

---

119 *Singapore Medical Council v Lim Lian Arn* [2019] SGHC 172 at [43].
120 Section 55(1), MRA.
121 Section 55(2). The Review Committee comprising 3 members under section 55(3) and (4) shall decide by unanimous opinion (s 55(6)) and give the SMC and medical practitioner reasonable opportunity to make written representations as to why the Review Committee should not direct the SMC to file an appeal to the High Court (section 55(7)).
122 Section 55(11). See *Gobinathan Devathasan v SMC* [2010] 2 SLR 926 (the DC had exceeded the scope of the charge of professional misconduct in the use of therapeutic ultrasound as an inappropriate treatment for the patient by (i) referencing a separate treatment not mentioned in the charge, (ii) requiring proof that therapeutic ultrasound was safe for patients in general, and (iii) convicting on the ground of safety when it was not part of the charge).
123 *Singapore Medical Council v Wong Him Choon* [2016] 4 SLR 1086 at [39], citing *Ang Pek San Lawrence v Singapore Medical Council* [2015] 1 SLR 436 at [32]; *Yip Man Hing Kevin v SMC* [2019] SGHC 102 at [48]; *Singapore Medical Council v Looi Kok Poh and another matter* [2019] SGHC 134 at [31].
124 *Singapore Medical Council v Lim Lian Arn* [2019] SGHC 172; *Foo Chee Boon Edward v SMC* [2020] SGHC 24.
125 This power was an implied ancillary power of the High Court to hear and determine appeals from a DT under section 46(7): *Ang Pek San Lawrence v SMC* [2015] 2 SLR 1179 at [31]. In addition, the High Court, in the exercise of its appellate civil jurisdiction under s 20(c) of the Supreme Court of

1.4.4.4 Sentencing

Sanctions in medical disciplinary proceedings aim to uphold the standing of the medical profession as well as to deter the medical practitioner from future transgressions.[126] Deterrence comprises general deterrence which aims to "deter other like-minded members of the general public by making an example of a particular offender"[127] whilst specific deterrence is targeted at the specific offender's experiences and punishment. Factors justifying specific deterrence include the premeditated nature of the respondent's acts and his propensity to repeat his wrongful acts. The ultimate objective of sanctions in medical disciplinary proceedings is to protect the public interest.

Where the sentence meted out by the Disciplinary Tribunal is "manifestly excessive or inadequate", the appellate court may intervene.[128] The decision in sentencing errant medical practitioners is based on the following steps discussed in *Wong Meng Hang v SMC*[129]:

(a) identify the harm to the patient and society and the culpability (or degree of blameworthiness) of the medical practitioner.
(b) identify the applicable indicative sentencing range. The High Court provided a table showing the indicative sentencing ranges which are dependent on the extent of harm (slight, moderate and severe) and the level of culpability (low, medium and high). A fine or other punishment not amounting to suspension from practice is indicated where the harm is slight and culpability low. In contrast, a suspension of a maximum of three years or striking off is indicated where the harm is severe and the level of culpability is high.[130]
(c) identify the appropriate starting point within the indicative sentencing range (by reference to the level of harm caused by the misconduct, the level of culpability, and how the case at hand compares with other analogous cases with broadly similar circumstances).
(d) make adjustments to the starting point to take account of offender-specific factors (whether of an aggravating or mitigating nature).

When analysing the four steps, the court should have regard to the abovementioned sentencing objectives and public interest considerations.

With respect to the decision to strike the medical practitioner off the register, the misconduct of the medical practitioner must be so serious that it renders the doctor unfit to remain as a member of the medical profession.[131] The relevant factors for striking off the medical register include the flagrant abuse of privileges accompanying registration as a medical practitioner, where the medical practitioner's misconduct caused grave harm, culpability, where

---

Judicature Act (SCJA) "may make such order as to the whole or any part of the costs of appeal or in the court below": section 38 read with section 22 of the SCJA. See *Ang Pek San Lawrence v SMC* [2015] 2 SLR 1179 at [32]-[35]; and *SMC v BXR* [2019] SGHC 20.
126 *Singapore Medical Council v Kwan Kah Yee* [2015] 5 SLR 201 at [50].
127 *PP v Law Aik Meng* [2007] 2 SLR(R) 814 at [24].
128 *Singapore Medical Council v Kwan Kah Yee* [2015] 5 SLR 201 at [1], [23] and [28].
129 [2019] 3 SLR 526.
130 Where the culpability was high and harm "moderate", a significantly longer suspension was warranted: *Singapore Medical Council v Dr Mohd Syamsul Alam bin Ismail* [2019] SGHC 58.
131 *Wong Meng Hang v Singapore Medical Council and other matters* [2018] SGHC 253 at [66].

the misconduct evinces a serious defect of character, and the dishonesty of the medical practitioner. Where any of the above factors exist, the additional consideration of whether there was a persistent lack of insight into the seriousness and consequences of the medical practitioner's misconduct[132] should be taken into account. In a case where dishonesty of the medical practitioners discloses a character defect such that the errant doctor is unsuitable for the profession, the presumptive position is to strike him off the register.

The offender's eminence and seniority is an aggravating factor due to the greater negative impact on public confidence in the integrity of the profession.[133] On the other hand, the offender's general good character, or his past contributions to society (such as volunteer work and contributions to charities) could not be regarded as a mitigating factor insofar as it reflects the moral worth of the offender.[134] But evidence of an offender's "long and unblemished record" may be regarded as a mitigating factor of modest weight if, and to the extent, such evidence fairly allows the court to infer that the offender's actions in committing the offence were "out of character" and that therefore, he is unlikely to re-offend.[135] Such mitigating weight to be placed may, however, be readily displaced if the court is satisfied that there are other overriding sentencing considerations such as general deterrence.[136]

The sentencing may be discounted where the delay by the SMC was inordinate, the offender was not responsible for the delay, and the delay had resulted in real injustice or prejudice to the offender.[137]

There are two final points on the disciplinary process. First, the Workgroup To Review The Taking of Informed Consent and SMC Disciplinary Processes had recommended in its November 2019 report[138] reforms to the structure (eg, instituting a Disciplinary Commission to professionalise and preserve the independence of the DT), processes and procedures (eg, imposing strict timelines to control the overall length of time a complaint takes to be resolved), role of mediation in the disciplinary process (eg, to empower the SMC to direct the complainant and doctors to participate in mediation upon receiving the complaint), enhancing training and streamlining and increasing transparency in the appeal process. The proposals were based on what the Workgroup considered to be important features of an effective regulatory system

---

132 *Wong Meng Hang v Singapore Medical Council and other matters* [2018] SGHC 253 at [67].
133 *Ang Peng Tiam* [2017] 5 SLR 356 at [93].
134 *Ang Peng Tiam* [2017] 5 SLR 356 at [101]
   First, it is not the place of the court to judge the moral worth of those who are before it. Second, such considerations will generally have no relevance to the offender's culpability or the harm that he has caused by the commission of the offence for which he is being sentenced. Third, ..., treating contributions to society as mitigating may be perceived as unfairly favouring the privileged who will often be more likely to be able to make such contributions because of their station in life, than will be the case with less privileged offenders.
135 *Ang Peng Tiam* [2017] 5 SLR 356 at [102].
136 *Ang Peng Tiam* [2017] 5 SLR 356 at [103].
137 *Ang Peng Tiam v SMC* [2017] 5 SLR 356. Though there was inordinate delay on the part of the SMC in instituting and prosecuting the proceedings against the doctor, and the delay could not be attributed to him, caused him great anxiety and distress, there was no evidence that he had suffered other prejudice beyond that. The High Court halved the period of suspension from 16 to 8 months.
138 https://www.moh.gov.sg/docs/librariesprovider5/default-document-library/wg-report.pdf.

ie, "independent, expeditious, consistent, fair and proportionate, and outcome-oriented". The MOH has accepted the recommendations and proceeded to introduce a bill in Parliament to amend the Medical Registration Act.[139]

Second, disciplinary processes have also been put in place for the other healthcare professions such as dentists, pharmacists, allied health professionals and TCM practitioners (Chapter 8). Under the DRA,[140] a complaint concerning a dentist may be referred by the Complaints Committee to the Disciplinary Committee (DC) if a formal inquiry is necessary,[141] or referred by the SDC to the DC where the dentist has been the convicted of an offence involving fraud or dishonesty.[142] The DC may make orders including to remove the name of the registered dentist from the register, suspend the dentist's registration for a period from three months to three years, restrict the practice for a period not more than three years, impose a fine not exceeding $50,000 and to censure the dentist.[143]

1.4.5 Legal liabilities of medical practitioners

This sub-section considers briefly potential criminal and civil (in particular tort) liabilities of medical doctors.

1.4.5.1 Criminal liabilities

Medical doctors and healthcare professionals are subject to criminal liability as any person for acts and omissions amounting to offences. Due to their scope of work involving close physical contact with and confidential information of patients, medical doctors and healthcare professionals may be susceptible to complaints and criminal investigations concerning serious injury or death caused to patients, sexual offences against patients and breaches of patient confidentiality. One potential criminal charge is for causing death by rash or negligent act under s 304A Penal Code.[144] A provision with less serious consequences is that of causing hurt and grievous hurt through rash and negligent act under s 337 and s 338 of the Penal Code, respectively. In *Lim Poh Eng v PP*,[145] the TCM practitioner was convicted under s 338 and sentenced to ten months' imprisonment. He was found negligent in prescribing colonic washouts without proper training in the procedure and use of the equipment, and without appreciation of the risks and complications involved. The High Court hearing a disciplinary case may refer a matter to the prosecution concerning possible criminal offences that may have been committed by a medical doctor including that of causing death by rash or negligent act under s 304A of the Penal Code.[146]

Medical doctors and healthcare professionals charged with offences may raise defences under the Penal Code. Examples include cases where there is no intention to cause death to

---

139 See Medical Registration (Amendment) Bill No 30/2020 (3 September 2020).
140 Part V on Disciplinary Proceedings.
141 Section 36.
142 Section 34(3).
143 Section 41.
144 (Cap 224, 2008 Rev Ed).
145 [1999] 1 SLR(R) 428.
146 *Wong Meng Hang v Singapore Medical Council and other matters* [2018] SGHC 253 at [114].

the patient if the act is done in good faith to benefit the patient who has given consent to suffer the harm or assume the risk of harm,[147] and emergency situations where it is impossible to obtain consent from the patient or guardian.[148]

In addition to the Penal Code, there are criminal offences incorporated in more specific health-related statutes and regulations applicable to clinical practice and biomedical research. These include the disclosure of patients' confidential information contrary to statute (Chapter 7), assisting in a patient's suicide (Chapter 10), removal and use of human tissues and organs contrary to statute (Chapter 11), failures of research institutions and researchers to comply with certain statutory preconditions and procedures in carrying out clinical trials and biomedical research (Chapter 12).

1.4.5.2 Civil liabilities

The primary legal causes of action are the tort of battery and the tort of negligence. Unlike for medical disciplinary cases, proof of a cause of action under tort law is on a balance of probabilities. In the first cause of action, the plaintiff typically alleges that the doctor had *intentionally* given a treatment or performed a procedure or surgery without the consent of the plaintiff. In such cases, the plaintiff may not have been properly informed of the broad nature of the treatment or surgery or may have made a decision refusing medical treatment that was not respected by the doctors (Chapter 5).

Alternatively, the plaintiff may seek compensation for their personal injuries that have been *negligently* inflicted by the medical practitioner whether in diagnosis, treatment, medical advice or post-operative care as well as for breach of contract where there is a doctor-patient relationship. The tort of negligence requires proof of a legal duty owed by the doctor to the plaintiff, breach of the duty, causation of and foreseeability of damage. The medical doctor is entitled to raise legal defences to defeat the claim or to reduce the amount of damages payable (Chapters 3 and 4).

Doctors may also be liable under the *equitable action* of breach of confidence and/or the *tort* of misuse of private information if they disclose plaintiff's confidential data thereby resulting in the latter suffering damage or losses. There is also a possible action based on *breach of statutory duty* under the Personal Data Protection Act (Chapter 7).

In civil litigation, parties may be referred to third-party mediation to settle the dispute instead of going through the entire court proceedings. The mediator seeks a resolution of the medical dispute based on the agreement of the parties without imposing a binding ruling on the litigants. The Healthcare Mediation Scheme[149] promotes the use of mediation to resolve disputes between patients and healthcare institutions. It is administered by MOH Holdings Pte Ltd through its Mediation Unit with the support of the Singapore Mediation Centre.

---

147 Section 88.
148 Section 92.
149 https://www.mohh.com.sg/hms/Pages/healthcare-mediation-scheme.aspx.

1.5 Conclusion

Singapore's healthcare expenditure is amongst the lowest when compared to the high-income countries assessed in per capita terms and as a percentage of Gross Domestic Product. Issues relating to healthcare costs, the extent of government financial support for health expenses and long-term care and the perceived ethos of self-reliance on the people for health expenses will likely continue to be debated in Singapore. Yet it is clear that the healthcare system has experienced tremendous progress since independence. To maintain its high standing, the education and training of medical doctors, dentists and other healthcare professionals whether for general practitioners and specialists will have to continue apace. Medical innovations and information technology including the nationwide implementation of Electronic Medical Records and artificial intelligence should be further deployed to enhance efficiency in the delivery of medical services as the government continues to actively support biomedical research relevant to clinical practice. With the overarching HCSA in the pipeline, Singapore should remain nimble and adaptable in its implementation of the wide range of existing health laws and regulations concerning the establishment, functions and processes of the myriad healthcare professions and bodies, the rights and duties of healthcare professionals, and the various legal and regulatory measures to license, control and encourage health-related activities and products. Making improvements to the disciplinary process for medical practitioners so as to deter errant doctors, maintain the strong reputation of the medical profession and protect patient welfare in an efficient and fair manner will remain important for the near future. Such objectives will also be advanced by the development of sound laws pertaining to the potential criminal and civil liabilities of doctors and healthcare professionals.

References

Boorse, C. (1977). "Health as a Theoretical Concept" 44 *Philosophy of Science* 542-573.
Canguilhem, G. (1978). "Disease, Cure, Health" in Canguilhem, G. (ed) *On The Normal and the Pathological*, Studies in the History of Modern Science, vol. 3 (Springer: Dordrecht), pp. 105-118.
Haseltine, W.A. (2013). *Affordable Excellence: The Singapore Health System* (Washington, DC: Brookings Institution Press with the National University of Singapore Press: Washington, DC).
Lee, C.E. & Satku, K. (2016). (eds), *Singapore's Health Care System: What 50 Years Have Achieved*, World Scientific Series on Singapore's 50 Years of Nation-Building (World Scientific: New Jersey).
Lim, C. (2010). "Life and Death: A Decade of Biomedical Law Making 2000-2010" 22 *SAcLJ* 850.
Lim, J. (2013). *Myth or Magic: The Singapore Healthcare System* (Select Publishing: Singapore).
Kaan, T. (2004). "Professional Regulation", chapter 8 in Yeo, K.Q. et al. (eds) *Essentials of Medical Law* (Sweet & Maxwell: Singapore), pp. 289-310.
Kuah, B.T. (2004). "Disclosures of Medical Errors, Risk Management and Quality Assurance in Health Care", chapter 3 in Yeo, K.Q. et al. (eds) *Essentials of Medical Law* (Sweet & Maxwell: Singapore), pp. 67-93.
Murphy, D. (2015). "Concepts of Disease and Health", 2008 (revised 2015) at https://plato.stanford.edu/entries/health-disease/.
Nordenfelt, L. (2007). "The Concepts of Health and Illness Revisited" 10(5) *Medicine, Health Care and Philosophy* 10.
Phua, K.H. (2018). *Healthcare* (Singapore: Straits Times Press Pte Ltd, Institute of Policy Studies: Singapore).
Reiss, J. & Ankeny, R.A. (2016). "Philosophy of Medicine" at https://plato.stanford.edu/entries/medicine/.

Tan, S.Y. (2016). *Halsbury's Laws of Singapore: Medical Negligence and Professional Misconduct*, vol. 14(4) (Butterworths Asia: Singapore).
The Ministry of Health (1993). *White Paper on Affordable Health Care* (Cmd 16 of 1993).
Thomas, J.S., Ong, S.E., Chia, K.S. et al. (2016). "A Brief History of Public Health in Singapore" in Lee, C.E. & Satku, K. (eds), *Singapore's Health Care System: What 50 Years Have Achieved*, World Scientific Series on Singapore's 50 Years of Nation-Building, (World Scientific: New Jersey), pp. 33-56.
Wakefield, J. (2007). "The Concept of Mental Disorder: Diagnostic Implications of the Harmful Dysfunction Analysis" 6(3) *World Psychiatry* 149-156.
Workgroup To Review the Taking of Informed Consent and SMC Disciplinary Process (2019). at https://www.moh.gov.sg/docs/librariesprovider5/default-document-library/wg-report.pdf.

2 Introduction to medical ethics

2.1 Introduction

The field of applied ethics in biomedicine continues to expand and develop as traditional medical practices are being applied in different contexts and medical innovations throw up new conundrums or demand a re-examination of basic concepts. These applications cut across both clinical practice and biomedical research and their intersections. Clinical bioethics refers to ethical decision-making encountered within a hospital or clinic setting that impact on the functions and operations of hospitals and clinics, individual doctors and patients and the doctor-patient relationship generally. In policy-making, ethics can highlight and illuminate issues that affect society or the community as a whole. Matters relating to the appropriate resources to be devoted to a particular field of medicine or healthcare, the potential effect of a legal reform on the medical profession generally and access to healthcare will be relevant here.

The discussion of medical ethics is also intimately connected to the first chapter on health law and regulations. The study of ethics can inform us as to what the law should be and thereby act as an impetus to legal reforms. It can also provide us with justifications for our actions and guide our present and future interactions with each other. Consistency and integrity in the application of ethical principles and values are also important features underlying the rule of law.

This chapter will discuss a number of important ethical theories that may be applied to healthcare, biomedicine and clinical practice generally followed by a few philosophical concepts that are commonly referred to in biomedical ethics. The ethical theories and concepts originate from the US, China, the UK and other parts of the world. The final substantive section will briefly discuss professional medical ethics in Singapore with a focus on the latest edition of the Singapore Medical Council's Ethical Code and Ethical Guidelines (2016).

In addition to the Singapore Medical Council, we should also mention a few institutions, bodies and committees in Singapore that are engaged in the work of understanding, developing and/or providing training on medical ethics that are relevant to healthcare professionals and/or healthcare institutions whether for clinical practice or biomedical research. The National Medical Ethics Committee (NMEC) was formed as an advisory arm of the Ministry for Health on medical ethics in 1994. The Bioethics Advisory Committee (BAC) comprising amongst others philosophers, medical doctors, judges, senior legal service officers and lawyers was established in 2000 to examine the ethical, legal and social issues arising from biomedical research and development in Singapore, and to recommend policies to the Ministerial Committee for Life Sciences on those issues. Teaching and research in bioethics has been the focus of the Centre for Biomedical Ethics (CBmE) at the National University of Singapore (NUS) since 2006. More recently, the National Ethics Capability Committee (NECC) was set up in 2014 with representatives from the various professional boards and councils, the NMEC, professional associations and medical schools. The Singapore Medical Association's Centre for Medical Ethics and Professionalism has been conducting training for medical practitioners including ethics programmes. There are also various ethics committees at the hospital level.

2.2 Ethical theories

At the core of ethical theories lies human decision-making which is a mix of both reason and emotions. Reasoning requires logic and conscious deliberations based on perceptions of events and circumstances. It is normally based on certain rules, principles or values that are meant be applied consistently or at least non-arbitrarily unless the specific circumstances call for more tailored outcomes. Impartiality in according similar weight to certain values in similar circumstances is also a hallmark of ethical reasoning. On the other hand, the affective (emotional) aspects of decision-making tend to be more automatic, intuitive and less conscious. In this context, the approach to decision-making is more subjective and arbitrary depending on how the moral agent responds to the situation or the affected persons.[1]

Singer's statement – "if emotion without reason is blind, then reason without emotion is impotent" (Singer 2000, at p. xix) – emphasises the dual significance of cognitive and affective capacities in ethical decision-making. It is hard work indeed demanding empathy for the affected persons, the capacity for rational and objective assessment and also a subjective appreciation of the impact of one's decision on the specific interests or preferences of the affected persons. Medical decisions may have both tangible and direct (objectively ascertained monetary loss or damage to property or body) or more intangible (psychological or emotional) effects on patients and their family members not to mention the medical doctors themselves. Medical doctors have been known to agonise over difficult clinical decisions, for example, whether to carry out a novel surgical procedure or to withdraw life support from a patient.

What follow are brief descriptions of a few influential ethical theories[2] that may be applied to healthcare and medicine.

2.2.1 Consequentialism

As the name implies, the ethicality of an act is based on the consequences that the act produces whether negative or positive. An act is ethical under Consequentialism to the extent it generates more positive than negative consequences.

---

1 See Chan and Shenoy (2016, at pp. 6-10).
2 See Chan and Shenoy (2016, chapter 2).

Utilitarianism is one version of Consequentialism that is based on the sum of human happiness arising from actions. They key principle is that of promoting the greatest happiness for the greatest number. Jeremy Bentham, in *Introduction to the Principles of Morals and Legislation*, focuses on the "hedonic calculus" utilising factors such as the intensity, duration, certainty, purity, propinquity of the pleasures and pains respectively and the extent (*ie*, the number of people affected) in order to assess the level of happiness and pains generated by a particular decision or course of action.

John Stuart Mill in his book *Utilitarianism* advocated the Greatest Happiness principle based on the aggregate of pleasures over pains that extends to the "whole sentient creation" which would presumably include humans and animals capable of feeling pleasures and pains.[3] One difference from Bentham is that Mill (1987) distinguished higher and lower pleasures. In contrast to the enjoyment of the more basic and lower pleasures (such as the need for food and shelter for survival) which we share with animals, the higher pleasures can only be appreciated by the nobler sentiments of humans with the capacity to reason. The love for music and virtues, for example, are treated by Mill as higher pleasures. Health is also regarded by Mill as a higher pleasure. Mill oft-quoted aphorism ("It is better to be a human being dissatisfied than a pig satisfied; better to be Socrates dissatisfied than a fool satisfied") shows his inclination for intellectual pursuits as a higher calling. But the premise of the statement must be that Socrates is able to appreciate what it is like to be a fool and to indulge in simpler pleasures in order to conclude that the enjoyment of intellectual pleasures is indeed superior. Such an assumption is not necessarily true (Singer 2000, at p. 144).

Another version is preference utilitarianism which is premised on the preferences or desires of the individual moral agent rather than the pleasures and pains generated by the decision. For preferences or desires, we assume that the moral agent knows what he subjectively desires and when such desires are fulfilled. A patient suffering from a broken leg may desire a prosthetic leg for greater independence in moving around and when it is properly installed, his desire would be fulfilled. Pleasures and pains are based on subjective experiences such as when an opiate drug gives one a positive uplifting sensation or mental alertness. Desires and pleasures can certainly overlap. Mill's view in *Utilitarianism* is that people *desire happiness* (which is equated with pleasure and absence of pain) as an end in itself. However, they may diverge in other instances. A patient desiring rapid recovery may be willing to undergo a surgical procedure that will cause significant pain.

Under Utilitarianism, the moral agent has to accord the same weight to the interests of others as his own interests. He must view the situation from the standpoint of a "disinterested and benevolent spectator". To prioritise one's own interest at the expense of others would be to act egoistically. Mill believed that humans would endeavour to adhere to the Greatest Happiness principle instead of egoism due to internal pressures (*eg*, a guilty conscience) and external sanctions (such as disapprovals from the community and God) flowing from non-compliance.

One drawback of Consequentialism is that it may not be possible or even practicable at times to make accurate predictions of the consequences flowing from an action though

---

[3] Query whether Mill would include foetuses in his sentient creation and the interests of future generations yet to be born.

humans will naturally make predictions by learning from past experiences. The effects may be short, medium or long term (such as research and development in biomedicine) which could affect the certainty of predictions. We should also allow time for people to react and respond to external events and influences. Further, it is difficult to weigh intangible values such as the quality of human life, the significance of fair outcomes or processes or the extent of personal or collective guilt arising from an action along the consequentialist scale.

What we have been describing thus far is Act Utilitarianism which requires an assessment of the overall utility for each act. This scenario can be quite bewildering for a moral actor seeking guidance on moral conduct if he has to consider afresh the proper decisions to be made on a daily basis. For reasons of practicality, moral agents may fall back on some general rules of thumb as to appropriate conduct that are in accordance with Utilitarianism. Rule Utilitarianism allows for a set of general rules that will, by and large, promote greatest happiness for the greatest number in the long term. For example, truth-telling or prohibition against killing, to the extent that it promotes more benefits than harms generally, can constitute such a rule of thumb in accordance with Rule Utilitarianism. Another example might be for doctors to prioritise the interests of their own patients to ensure the latter are looked after (Hare 1993, at pp. 54-55).

2.2.2 Deontology

Deontological theories are not based on consequences. Instead, it is about moral duties based on the universal features of human beings as both rational and equal.

Immanuel Kant argued that humans who are rational and equal will conceive of certain fixed rules known as Categorical Imperatives which everyone has to adhere to. The first is that of Universalisation of Maxims (that one must only adopt maxims which can be universalised). Kant's formula is to "act only on that maxim through which you can at the same time will that it should become a universal law". This means that what one adopts as a moral principle for himself should be similarly extended to others (or, more precisely, the entire universe!). For example, giving false promises as a maxim would entail the universalisation of lying which would result in the meaningless concept of promises and the futility on relying on any promise made (Kant 1996, at p. 57).

The second Categorical Imperative is to respect a human as an end in itself (the Principle of Humanity). You must not treat a person (whether yourself or another individual) as a means *only* but also as an end. This relates to notions of personhood, personal autonomy and human dignity which are core concepts in medical ethics. Essentially, we must recognise the intrinsic nature of humanity and not exploit another human being merely as a tool or conduit to achieve our own objectives.

From the two Categorical Imperatives, Kant derived a few moral duties. Committing suicide, Kant argued, would run contrary to self-love and the preservation of life and the Principle of Humanity (that is, the use of one's own person as a means only). Would voluntary euthanasia for a patient undergoing significant physical and mental pain and suffering from a terminal illness violate such a moral duty? Two ideas which Kant held dear namely personal autonomy and preservation of life seem to sit uncomfortably in such a scenario.

Kant's notion of moral duty encourages the development of one's talents and capacities as the end of a rational human being. This is closely connected to the increasingly influential Capabilities approach to bioethics (discussed below). Another moral duty – to show benevolence to others – seeks to advance the interest of others based on the notion of reciprocity.

One material difference between Mill and Kant lies in their approach to the issue of lying. Mill stated in *Utilitarianism* (p. 34) that lying weakens the trustworthiness of human assertions and inhibits the development of civilisation. Lying is therefore wrong as a general rule. Kant, on the other hand, would regard lying as an absolute wrong in all situations. He would not condone lying even if it is to save a life of a fugitive fleeing from a murderer (Kant 1996, at p. 611).

2.2.3 Virtue ethics

Virtue ethics is essentially focused on building human character and traits to promote human flourishing (Eudaimonia). Aristotle in *Nicomachean Ethics* succinctly described the core of virtue ethics as not finding out "what goodness is, but how to be good men". The latter is attained through constant practice and cultivation in daily activities. The moral agent should seek to avoid extremes of excess (*eg*, rashness) and deficiency (*eg*, timidity) and aim for the Mean (*eg*, courage), learn from past errors and guard against pleasures. Virtue, for Aristotle, refers to a "purposive disposition, lying in a mean that is relative to us and determined by a rational principle". Happiness for Aristotle is to be assessed over a complete lifetime rather than based on fleeting sensations.

Thus, Aristotle's version of virtue ethics combines both objective and subjective elements. Though pegged to rationality, virtue theory allows room for the subjective and cultural viewpoints of the moral agent. Each agent's assessment of what counts as excessive pleasure or pains may depend on his upbringing and environment. Quite unlike Utilitarianism and Kantianism, Virtue ethics does not provide any universal moral principles to deal with ethical dilemmas and situations. Instead, what the moral agent has to deal with a problem is based on self-cultivation in accordance with the Mean and a list of desirable virtues or values to promote human flourishing. Furthermore, in contrast to a focus on rule compliance, in the process of self-cultivation, virtue ethics holds great potential to inspire the moral agent to perform supererogatory acts that go beyond what are required.

The virtues of a good doctor should take account the "proper goals of medicine as a *practice*" and what would count as appropriate doctor-patient relationships (Oakley and Cocking 2001, at p. 75). One proper goal would be health which the doctor can seek to fulfil by healing the sick and preventing ill-health. Virtues ethics can incorporate professional integrity as a value in accordance with the specific role responsibility of a doctor. Hence, a doctor may argue in line with such professional integrity that he has a right to conscientiously object to assist in euthanasia or to withhold life-sustaining treatment based on an advance medical directive. Other virtues may include compassion for patients, truthfulness, trustworthiness and humility (Oakley and Cocking 2001, at p. 93). It is not surprising that ethical guidelines, laws and regulations governing the medical profession would exclude from the profession persons who have been found to suffer from defect of character or have been convicted of fraud or dishonesty.

2.2.4 Confucianism

One Asian counterpart of Western Virtue Ethics is Confucianism. Moral cultivation based on *ren* (humaneness or benevolence), *li* (ritual), *yi* (integrity), *xin* (trust) is highly prized in Confucianism. Though largely an approach to virtue ethics, Confucianism also relies on the deontological golden rule: "Do not do unto others what you do not want others to do".

At the same time, it emphasises social relationships and the role of a person in the context of society. This secular and humanist philosophy recognises the hierarchy of relationships ranging from parent-child, siblings and so on. There is a preference given to familial relations as opposed to Mill's idea of the disinterested and benevolent spectator. In Confucianism, benevolence to others is demonstrated not universally (such as under the Kantian approach) but with some partiality for kin relations.

Another material difference from Western ethics is that the notion of individual human rights in terms of a claim-right is absent in Confucianism. Nonetheless, Confucian ethics is intimately concerned with human dignity and respect.

With regard to the concept of autonomy, the dominant Western model of informed consent is individual-directed rather than family-oriented. This means that the individual possesses the sole decision-making authority in biomedical matters independently of his family. In the East Asian family-oriented model, however, the tendency is for the individual patient to make decisions in biomedical matters as part of a family network which may entail some sacrifice of his own interests for the sake of promoting the interests of other family members even as the latter assesses the situation and provides financial and moral support for the patient's benefit. This calls for the doctor to "recognise the family as a fundamental unit for making medical decisions for the patient" (Fan 2015, at p. 12). Fan (2015, at p. 16) argued that the family-oriented model is not the same as "family-paternalism" in which family members impose their views of what is good upon the patient contrary to the latter's values and preferences. In Confucian virtue ethics, the family has a moral obligation to protect the interests of its members by being actively involved in the decision-making process for the benefit of its members.

In practice, family members may request the doctor to withhold from the patient information of his or her terminal illnesses, a request that may be well-intentioned but indirectly cause the doctor to disregard patient autonomy (Chapter 10).

2.2.5 Care ethics

Care ethics was originally associated with feminist ethics starting from Carol Gilligan's book *In a Different Voice* which challenged the psychologist Kohlberg's inclination for abstract reasoning based on universal moral rules as the expression of the highest level of ethical development in adults. This, Gilligan claimed, was male-centric and that more emphasis should be placed on concrete relationships between people.

Thus the focus of care ethics is the relationship between the caregiver and care recipient. In tandem with the focus on relationships are the notions of interdependence and vulnerability. Persons are after all relational and interdependent not individualistic autonomous rational agents (Held 2007, at p. 72). Applied to healthcare, it is clear that the health and

32 Medical ethics

well-being of patients as vulnerable people depend on the caring of others including professionals and informal caregivers. Care ethics is arguably connected to "our own personhood and the personhood of the vulnerable other" (Vanlaere and Gastmans 2011).

The approach to care ethics is particularly useful for understanding the bases for nursing care provided to patients and vulnerable segments of the population. Tronto (1993) usefully analysed Care Ethics in its moral constituents of care: attentiveness to the needs of others; responsibility (to assume the task of caring for others); competence (in terms of acquiring the skills to give care); and responsiveness (of the care receiver to the care to guide the caregiver in caring). The last element is about reciprocity – a reminder that "[c]aring is a relation in which carer and cared-for share an interest in their mutual well-being" (Held 2007, at pp. 34–35).

2.2.6 Justice and fairness

Justice manifests in various forms: *retributive* (to punish someone who has done wrong based on the principle of "an eye for an eye"), *compensatory or rectificatory* (to demand a person who has done wrong to compensate you for what you have lost or suffered as a result of the wrong) and *distributive* (to allocate goods, advantages and burdens to persons within a society or community according to a fair process or to ensure fair outcomes).

John Rawls (1972) sought to find in *A Theory of Justice* a set of just and fair principles for society as a whole. He focused on procedural mechanisms – namely the concept of a rational person in the hypothetical Original Position – to derive principles of equal liberty and the just allocation of socio-economic goods and resources. In the Original Position, the self-interested and rational person does not know in advance his position or status in society, his abilities, intelligence, strengths and assets (Veil of Ignorance). Societal principles fashioned by rational persons under such a Veil of Ignorance would, he contended, be based on procedural fairness, a concept which he further developed in *Justice as Fairness* (Rawls 2001). Two Principles of Justice derived from this fair process would guide the society:

1. Each person is to have an equal right to the most extensive total system of basic liberties compatible with a similar system of liberty for all.
2. Social and economic inequalities are to be arranged so that they are both
   (a) To the greatest benefit of the least advantaged; and
   (b) Attached to offices and positions open to all under conditions of fair equality of opportunity.

The allocation of socio-economic resources is important in clinical settings as well as in cases where the government has to make a decision as to the resources to be devoted to a particular area of biomedical research. Harris (1999) thought that each person should be entitled to an equal opportunity to benefit from the public healthcare system and that such entitlement should not be tied to the size of his or her chance of benefitting from the healthcare system, nor the quality of the benefit nor the length of lifetime remaining in which the person may enjoy the benefit. Further, the benefit is to be seen from the patient's perspective and not that of the public health funders who may be driven by concerns of cost-effectiveness.

> **Box 2.1 – Who gets the ventilator?**
>
> During the COVID-19 pandemic, there was a shortage of ventilators for the victims. How should we allocate resources in such times of scarcity? Should we do so based on egalitarianism or according to need? Or should we allocate based on an assessment of net utility (costs and benefits) to the victims? Are there other ethical considerations? (See Savulescu et al. (2020).)

Daniels (2007) developed a Rawlsian account of just access to healthcare and the social determinants of health. He linked health to opportunity and noted that the social determinants of health (which may include the distribution of income in society, social exclusion, and workplace stress) can reduce health inequalities[4] if they conform to theories of justice. He was of the view that Rawls' theory of justice as fairness would be able to regulate the social determinants of health. For Daniels, a healthcare system should seek to prevent diseases and disabilities that inhibit or reduce the range of opportunities available to individuals to achieve their basic goals in life based on fair equality of opportunity (Beauchamp and Childress 2019, at p. 273).

At the global level, in order to deal with the problem of access and affordability of medicines to the poor in developing countries, Pogge (2012) proposed a Health Impact Fund (HIF) that is to be financed by governments and created by an international treaty. Participants in the HIF who offer new pharmaceutical products would receive an amount annually from the HIF proportionate to its contributed share of the assessed health impact of all HIF-registered products. The new products would have to be made available worldwide at the lowest feasible cost of manufacture.

2.2.7 Capabilities approach

Sen is against the utilitarian model which does not take account of distributional inequalities. Furthermore, according to him, Rawls does not appreciate the diversity of human beings in terms of their needs. Instead of attaching importance to primary social goods as in Rawls' theory, Sen preferred to focus on what humans are actually able to do *ie*, to achieve "functionings" in living; this also constitutes a significant part of human freedoms.

Under the Capabilities Approach, humans should be given the freedom to choose a type of living to achieve such "functionings". It is recognised that the choice may be conditioned by the specific culture and context or environment in which the person finds himself. In this regard, health may be seen as a "functioning" or a set of "functionings". The quality of life is to be "assessed in terms of the capability to achieve valuable functionings" (Sen 1993). Nussbaum (2006, at p. 175) proposed ten core capabilities[5] for human flourishing. She stated that the ten "plural and diverse ends" are "minimum requirements of justice". Law and Widdows (2008) regarded health as the capability to cope with life's demands, and supported the Capabilities approach not least because of its flexibility in accommodating different goals and needs

---

4 Such inequalities can arise, for example, between different socio-economic groups, gender or races.
5 They are: life; bodily health; bodily integrity; senses, imagination and thought; emotions; practical reason; affiliation; other species; play; and control over one's environment.

and types of functionings. For example, in their view, deafness may be regarded as a loss of capability (or disability) by some, but a matter of culture by others (such as the case of a deaf lesbian couple who decided to have a baby from a sperm donor who was deaf) (Levy 2002).[6] This brings us to the enquiry on the validity and implications of moral and cultural relativism.

2.2.8 Moral and cultural relativism

Relativism is the notion that morality may differ from place to place and in different historical periods. For example, slavery was permissible in 17th-century United States but frowned upon in modern societies. Such evidence of variations in morality do not prove the correctness of moral relativism (that is, the view that there is no moral right or wrong). In addition, the fact that two persons or cultures disagree on a moral issue does not in itself prove moral relativism. We will have to investigate further the nature of the disagreement and enquire whether there are underlying facts, reasons or common values which can resolve the disagreement.

Moral relativism refers to the idea that there is no moral truth or principle that people ought to adhere to and that each society or person is free to subscribe to or adopt his or her own moral position. The extent to which a person may adopt moral relativism is issue-dependent. One may be a moral relativist for some intractable issues but not others.

There are important implications if one subscribes to pure moral relativism. A pure moral relativist cannot make a judgement against any societal or cultural practice (*eg*, that infanticide is wrong).[7] Strictly speaking, he or she cannot even make the claim that everyone has a moral right to live if it runs counter to another person's or society's morality which allows killing of a human being without justification. Moreover, moral relativists cannot make statements concerning the moral progress of a person or society since they do not accept the idea of what would count as morally good or bad.[8]

2.3 Biomedical ethics: principlism

Let us now examine an ethical approach specially catered to aid ethical decision-making in biomedicine – Principlism. This approach advocated by Tom Beauchamp and James Childress in their book *Principles of Biomedical Ethics* (2019) consists of four norms:

- Autonomy (a norm of respecting and supporting autonomous decisions)
- Non-maleficence (a norm of avoiding the causation of harm)
- Beneficence (a group of norms pertaining to relieving, lessening, or preventing harm and providing benefits against risks and costs)
- Justice (a group of norms for fairly distributing benefits, risks and costs).[9]

---

6 But see BAC (2005), para 4.45 (that "the functioning of this child within society at large would be severely impaired due to the imposed disability. Therefore, such deliberate restriction of the autonomy of the child is not considered justifiable").
7 In Singapore, infanticide by the mother is an offence under section 310 of Penal Code (Cap 224, 2008 Rev Ed) and also gives rise to a partial defence in Exception 6 to section 300.
8 See Chan and Shenoy (2016, pp. 78-82).
9 Beauchamp and Childress (2019, at pp. 12-13).

Non-maleficence and beneficence have had a long history in medical ethics. Autonomy and justice have emerged as important considerations more recently.

Principlism is partially linked to the basic ethical theories we have encountered above. Beneficence (benefits) and non-maleficence (harms) feature in the Utilitarian calculus. The notion of autonomy may be supported by Kantian deontology. Beauchamp and Childress (2019, at chapter 2) referred to the virtues of compassion, discernment, trustworthiness, integrity and conscientiousness of a doctor who abides by Principlism.

Yet there is potential for conflict amongst the four norms. Allowing the patient to select a drug that relieves him of pain temporarily but which causes material side effects that worsen his physical condition might promote personal autonomy but run contrary to non-maleficence. Following W D Ross, the four principles are to be treated as *prima facie* obligations rather than actual obligations. A *prima facie* obligation must be carried out unless it conflicts with an equal or stronger obligation (Beauchamp and Childress 2019, at p. 15). To aid in the resolution of potential conflicts and balancing amongst the different principles, Beauchamp and Childress (2019, at p. 23) proposed six conditions as follows:

1. Good reasons are offered to act on the overriding norm rather than the infringed norm.
2. The moral objective justifying the infringement has a realistic prospect of achievement.
3. No morally preferable alternative actions are available.
4. The lowest level of infringement, commensurate with achieving the primary goal of the action, has been selected.
5. All negative effects of the infringement have been minimised.
6. All affected parties have been treated impartially.

Beauchamp and Childress gave the example of serious infectious diseases outbreaks such as the severe acquired respiratory syndrome (SARS) and the responses by governments and professionals to control the problem. In order to override respect for the autonomy of individual persons (the infringed norm), recourse has to be made to the measures that may be undertaken to prevent actual and potential harms resulting from the infectious diseases based on the above conditions 4-6.

2.3.1 Autonomy

According to Beauchamp and Childress (2019), there are three conditions of autonomy with respect to actions undertaken by a moral agent:

- intentionality (whether the agent intended his act or not)
- understanding (whether the agent had a substantial degree of understanding of his act)
- non-control (whether the agent is free of external and internal influences with respect to the act; and voluntariness in this regard is a matter of degree).

This is based largely on the Western notion of individualism and liberalism, that is, each individual must be respected as an independent moral agent with the right or freedom to choose how to live his or her own life. Mill in his book *On Liberty* opined that the sole purpose for exercising any power over any person in society is to prevent harm to others. Each mature person is the "proper guardian of his own health, whether bodily or mental and spiritual" and that respecting mankind's autonomy to make decisions to "live as seems good to themselves" will conduce to the greater good of the greatest number (Mill 2003, at p. 83; van Zyl 2000, at p. 158). The notion of autonomy is inextricably linked to the duty-based justification for ethical conduct in Kantianism especially the second Categorical Imperative on Respect for Humanity. It is also arguably connected to virtue theory in the form of a virtue of respectfulness (Van Zyl 2000).

Further, respect to autonomy is consistent with and reinforces certain basic tenets applicable to medical and other contexts: telling the truth; respecting the privacy of others; protecting confidential information; obtaining consent for interventions with patients; when asked, helping others to make important decisions (Beauchamp and Childress 2019, at p. 105).

The autonomy to make decisions is typically limited to those with mental capacity to make decisions and who choose to act based on decisions. For example, a patient's advance medical directive should be respected as a principle based on autonomy. In line with autonomy, the general position in the Mental Capacity Act (MCA) is to assume that an individual has mental capacity to decide for himself unless it is shown otherwise. Those who are mentally incapable will continue to have rights protected in MCA via proxy decision-makers.

Patient autonomy is sometimes contrasted with paternalism which, in the medical context, is often associated with the idea that "the doctor knows best". Paternalism may be used to justify decisions made on behalf of patients who are young children or mentally incapable of making decisions with regard to their health or well-being. For competent adult patients, the current trend is towards patient autonomy and active participation in decision-making in cooperation with the medical doctor and healthcare professional about his or her health.

Coggon (2007) referred to three types of autonomy: (i) current desire autonomy (based on a person's immediate inclinations), (ii) best desire autonomy (in accordance with personal values), and (iii) ideal desire autonomy (by reference to a universal standard of values comparable with Kantianism). If we allow a patient to make a decision for any reason whether rational or irrational, we are appealing to the concept of current desire autonomy. This basic level of "current desire" autonomy would conceivably allow for decisions to consume excessive foods that harm one's health or to commit suicide. The second type of autonomy is not only concerned with making a choice, but *how* the choice is made with reference to one's values and preferences. The personal values and preferences under "best desire" autonomy are based on subjective assessments as opposed to the objective values and rationality underlying "ideal desire" autonomy. A desire to commit suicide would not fulfil the more stringent requirements of "ideal desire" autonomy in the strict Kantian sense but might pass muster as "current desire" autonomy or arguably, "best desire" autonomy (where the desire is consistent with the patient's personal values and preferences to avoid intolerable suffering in the face of impending death).

Autonomy need not be framed exclusively as an individualistic concept. It is argued that there is room for "relational" autonomy (MacKenzie and Stoljar 2000). The decisions of autonomous individuals are often made with the awareness of their potential effects on family members or loved ones, healthcare professionals or other members of society. The patient's decision may be conditioned by a reluctance to burden his family members about his condition whether in physical or financial terms. In more extreme circumstances, the decision of an individual patient to end his or her life in order to stop the pain from a long-drawn illness clearly affects the immediate family members or the healthcare professional who is requested to administer euthanasia. Another scenario is where a person's autonomy to safeguard the confidentiality of his own genetic information conflicts with a family member's interest to protect herself from the harmful effects of a predictive genetic disease.

One's autonomy can also be constrained by personal and social circumstances as well as power relations. The choices by patients are often made in a state of personal discomfort or pain with attendant anxieties. This can affect the patient's ability to make rational choices. Laws and policies that limit access of certain groups to specific forms of healthcare (*eg*, assisted reproduction) indirectly restrict choices. Furthermore, the contexts in which the decisions of surrogate mothers in developing countries are made can be exploitative and oppressive of the women at the social level even if the individual perceives the renting of her womb as an opportunity to eke out a living for her family and desires to enter into surrogacy arrangements with full awareness of the consequences. Here it seems that the "capabilities" or their absence might be relevant for assessing the autonomy of the person to make genuine choices.

> **Box 2.2 – The medical practitioner and patient autonomy**
>
> In your view, should a medical practitioner be entitled from the perspective of ethics to reject a patient's choice and to take a decision or action that is contrary to the patient's choice? If so, in what circumstances?

2.3.2 Non-maleficence

The principle of non-maleficence (together with beneficence) is evident in the Hippocratic Oath which states that "I will use treatment to help the sick according to my ability and judgment, but I will never use it to injure or wrong them".

"Harm" refers to a "thwarting, defeating, or setting back of some party's interests" (Beauchamp and Childress 2019, at p. 158). This would include but is not limited to physical and mental harms to the patient. Some harms may be justified depending on the circumstances. The pain derived from certain injections and medications may, for example, be justified by the potential and overriding health benefits from the treatment.

An important issue is whether the medical doctor ought to provide treatment to his patient to prevent impending harm. The obligation to treat a patient may be subject to circumstances where the treatment would be regarded as futile or the burdens of treatment outweigh the benefits (Beauchamp and Childress 2019, at pp. 171-174). Quality-of-life assessments are also relevant in making such decisions.

Where the patient is suffering from severe and continuous pain, and requests the medical doctor to terminate his life, should the doctor render assistance (physician-assisted euthanasia)? It involves not only the doctor's *prima facie* duty of non-maleficence to prevent either of two competing harms (patient's death versus severe pain) but also patient autonomy and the background considerations of providing benefits through palliative care and again, quality-of-life assessments.

2.3.3 Beneficence

The principle of beneficence goes beyond non-maleficence of harm prevention ("negative prohibitions") and instead call for "positive requirements of action" (Beauchamp and Childress 2019, at p. 219). It demands that medical professionals act to benefit their patients with whom they have a special relationship and to advance patient welfare. In cases where the patients are not mentally capable of making a healthcare decision, doctors have to act in the patient's best interests. The principle of beneficence as *prima facie* obligation can also apply to medical research that generates potential benefits and enables access to improved drugs and treatments. The principle is also intimately connected with Utilitarianism which focuses on net positive benefits justifying an agent's actions.

The notion of paternalistic beneficence (that the doctor knows what is best for the patient) can conflict with patient autonomy. This happens when a medical doctor withholds material medical information requested by the patient, gives treatment contrary to the patient's clear and express refusal with sound knowledge of the consequences and restrains or restricts the patient's physical movements or actions. Medical beneficence may, however, be justified by interventions that prevent grave risks of harm to the patient or the securing of significant benefits that outweigh the infringements of the autonomy interests of the patient provided there is no better alternative to the infringement of autonomy interests and the doctor adopts the least autonomy-restrictive alternative (Beauchamp and Childress 2019, at pp. 238-239).

The benefits may have to be balanced against the risks of harm and costs to be incurred. The decision to introduce new medical technology or devices brings to fore the need for such a balancing exercise. Where the risks from the new technology or devices are not fully known or uncertain based on the state of medical knowledge, but has potential benefits for patients, should they be implemented nonetheless? Application of the precautionary principle in such an instance might prevent the implementation until the risks may be mitigated with reasonable certainty. Taken to its extreme, the principle can impede innovations. Instead of a blanket ban, a more nuanced approach might be to ascertain the appropriate level of precaution needed in a particular case. One possible rubric is that the greater the uncertainty and the extent of harm should the risk materialise, the higher the costs of precaution that are needed to prevent potential harms before any decision to implement the novel treatment or innovation.

2.3.4 Justice

We have already discussed above a few justice concepts and theories including the Capabilities approach. One threshold factor to ensure justice in the healthcare system is to cater to the needs of individuals. Persons with fundamental needs for healthcare that are not catered for can result in significant harms not only to the person but adversely affect the legitimacy of the national healthcare system if such neglect is pervasive.

Another major issue is the allocation of health resources which depends first and foremost on the availability of resources. Courts may be asked at times to intervene in public health decision-making affecting such allocations. In *R v Cambridge HA Ex p. B*,[10] the health authority refused to fund experimental research for a patient suffering from acute myeloid leukaemia. The English Court of Appeal held that it was for the authority to decide on the allocation of its limited budget to the "maximum advantage of the maximum number of patients".[11] This seems to support a utilitarian approach of maximising total welfare without considering the question of fairness as between persons.

Some fairness considerations might be based on the relative extent of need of two or more patients for a particular type of treatment in which resources are limited. Otherwise, a general default position might be to apply the "first come first serve" rule. As a matter of public policy, governments may also consider, in the allocation of healthcare, the status (such as citizenship or residence requirements) of the individuals requiring healthcare.

2.4 Other ethical considerations and concepts

In addition to the ethical theories and Principlism, there are other overlapping but sufficiently distinct ethical considerations and concepts that are commonly discussed in medical ethics.

2.4.1 Personhood, moral status and rights

Foremost amongst the ethical concepts discussed is that of "personhood". What is meant by a "person" in medical ethics? What are the necessary and sufficient attributes of a "person"? According to Kant, one key feature is rationality. A person has a plan or a set of goals in life and is able to consider the means by which the goals may be achieved. Presumably, the ability to reason means that human beings are able to consider and reflect on the moral implications of their actions and not act based merely on instinct or impulse. In this regard, human beings as "persons" have a higher moral status than "non-persons". Humans have rights which a piece of property, for example, does not. Moreover, humans have basic interests that deserve protection which an object such as a chair does not possess.

One problem arising from the focus on rationality is the status of mentally impaired humans and young children who have yet to acquire the ability to think rationally. One way to circumvent the problem is to consider a "person" as a being who is born as a member of the human species (Scanlon 1998, at p. 185). The problem with adopting a "species" approach to the question of moral status or rights, however, is its anthropocentric bias. Why should humans have automatic moral status by virtue of being a human? Stating the question in this fashion exposes immediately the circularity of the reasoning process. An alternative process might be to examine the basic features that make up or contribute to the purported moral status.

We have already mentioned one feature which is the capacity to reason that is characteristic of humans. Such a feature may be a *sufficient* basis for moral status, but it may not

---

10 [1995] 1 WLR 898.
11 [1995] 1 WLR 898 at 906, *per* Sir Thomas Bingham MR.

be a *necessary* condition for conferring moral status. Animals can experience sensations and feelings, pleasures and pains (sentience) and therefore have certain basic interests. To the extent that pains are bad, it may be argued that inflicting pain on an animal is to commit a moral wrong against them (Beauchamp and Childress 2019, at p. 76). In this way, we can take into account sentience as a sufficient feature of moral status and thereby depart from the purely "species" approach.

2.4.2 Human dignity

One intrinsic aspect of human personhood is human dignity. Mill argued in *Utilitarianism* that humans have a greater capacity to appreciate higher pleasures due to the human being's "sense of dignity" and his environment. We have also seen in Kantianism and Confucianism the notion of respect for humanity. Beyleveld (2015, at p. 93) opined that "only creatures that have dignity in the requisite sense have a moral status, on the basis of which those who are capable of discharging duties have obligations to show them moral respect". He recognised that the concept of dignity has been used in discourse in two ways: (i) as empowerment of persons to act or choose as they wish which are intimately connected with personal autonomy, liberty and human rights; and (ii) to constrain autonomous actions. In medical contexts, a mentally capable patient is empowered to refuse treatment. On the other hand, we may restrict transactions in body parts between willing buyers and sellers on the ground that they are contrary to human dignity.

The concept of human dignity has received acknowledgement in international instruments such as the Preamble to the Universal Declaration on Human Rights of 1948 (UDHR).[12] The Council of Europe's Convention on Human Rights and Biomedicine,[13] recognising that the potential "misuse of biology and medicine may lead to acts endangering human dignity", states that member States are to "protect the dignity and identity of all human beings and guarantee everyone, without discrimination, respect for their integrity and other rights and fundamental freedoms with regard to the application of biology and medicine" (Article 1). Apart from informed consent and privacy protections, the Convention specifically prohibits "discrimination against a person on grounds of his or her genetic heritage" (Article 11). The UNESCO's Declaration on Human Rights and the Human Genome[14] advocates respect for everyone's "dignity and for their rights regardless of their genetic characteristics" and that the "dignity makes it imperative not to reduce individuals to their genetic characteristics and to respect their uniqueness and diversity" (Article 2).

---

12 The UDHR Preamble referred to "the inherent dignity and of the equal and inalienable rights of all members of the human family" and "dignity and worth of the human person".
13 ETS No 164, Oviedo, 4 April 1997 and entered into force on 1 December 1999 at https://www.coe.int/en/web/conventions/full-list/-/conventions/treaty/164.
14 Adopted unanimously and by acclamation at UNESCO's 29th General Conference on 11 November 1997, and endorsed by the United Nations General Assembly in 1998 at http://portal.unesco.org/en/ev.php-URL_ID=13177&URL_DO=DO_TOPIC&URL_SECTION=201.html.

2.4.3 Right to life, sanctity and quality of life

According to theistic religions, a human life possesses intrinsic value and is a gift from God. Notwithstanding the religious roots, sanctity of life has also been recognised as part of secular ethics. There are two notions concerning the preservation of life: (i) vitalism (which argues that the preservation of life is absolute and must be protected in all situations); and (ii) sanctity of life (which is not an absolute value in that it allows for killing in certain exceptional circumstances such as in self-defence).

If one adopts the sanctity of life approach, no one has an absolute right to life. But are there any preconditions for enjoying such a right to life? We referred above to features of personhood such as sentience and rationality. Tooley (1972, at p. 49) argued that a being has a right to life if it can conceive of itself as a distinct entity (or person) over time with the desire to continue as such a distinct entity. As a newborn infant could not conceive of itself as a distinct entity and is incapable of the desire to continue as such an entity, he concluded that the infant does not have a right to life.[15]

Human life may be assessed by reference to its intrinsic or instrumental worth (*ie*, as a means to an end). It may also be benchmarked against certain qualities of what it means to be "human" (such as self-awareness, self-control, sense of the future, sense of the past and capacity to relate to others, showing concern for others and communications) (Fletcher 1974).

Quality of life may be assessed based on three theories: hedonist, preference satisfaction (or desire fulfilment), and ideal theories of a good life. The hedonist theory is premised on the balance of pleasures and pains experienced by a person. Preference satisfaction theories, on the other hand, focus on the satisfaction of peoples' desires or preferences rather than the conscious experience of pleasures or pains. A person may, for example, be misinformed or misled by others about his desires for better health from eating certain health supplements. Hedonist and preference theories are both subjective as the notion of Good for a particular person depends on "what in fact makes that person happy or what that person in fact (with appropriate corrections) desires" (Brock 1993). Ideal theories are objective as the basis of a good life for a person is "objectively determined by the correct or justified ideals of the good life" and does not depend on subjective desires or subjectively felt pleasures. Quality-of-life assessments are particularly crucial in end-of-life decisions as to whether a terminally ill patient should continue to be kept on life support and cases where the disabled baby claims that it would have been better if it had not come into existence.

2.4.4 Right to health and healthcare

The intersection between human rights and bioethics was starkly illustrated by the Doctors' Trials in Nuremberg for horrific crimes perpetrated in human experimentations conducted during World War II which gave birth to the Nuremberg Code on ethical principles

---

15 Query whether such a criterion would also disqualify adults who suffer from severe memory loss albeit fluctuating.

for biomedical research involving human subjects. One of these human rights is the right to health. The UNDR explicitly states that "[e]veryone has the right to a standard of living adequate for the *health and well-being* of himself and of his family, including food, clothing, housing and *medical care* … …" (Art 25). The International Covenant on Economic, Social and Cultural Rights (ICESCR)[16] recognises the "right of everyone to the enjoyment of the highest attainable standard of physical and mental health" and the steps to be taken to "achieve the full realization of this right" (Article 12). The General Comment No 14 issued by the UN Committee on Economic, Social and Cultural Rights on Art 12[17] calls upon States to respect, protect and fulfil the right to health[18]:

(i) … obligation to *respect* the right to health by, inter alia, refraining from denying or limiting equal access for all persons …; and abstaining from imposing discriminatory practices as State policy …
(ii) Obligations to *protect* include, inter alia, the duties of States to adopt legislation or to take other measures to ensure equal access to healthcare and health-related services provided by third parties …
(iii) The obligation to *fulfill* requires State parties, inter alia, to give sufficient recognition to the right of health in the national political and legal systems, preferably by way of legislative implementation, and to adopt a national health policy with a detailed plan for realizing the right to health. States must ensure provision of healthcare, including immunization programs against the major infectious diseases and ensure equal access for all to the underlying determinants of health, such as nutritiously safe food and potable drinking water, basic sanitation and adequate housing and living conditions … provide for sexual and reproductive health services.

Furthermore, the Convention on the Rights of Persons with Disabilities (2006)[19] states that people with disabilities have "the right to the enjoyment of the highest attainable standard of health without discrimination" and outlines the attendant obligations of member states (Article 25). The right to health does not mean a guarantee of health by the State or an unconditional right to be healthy.

2.4.5 Doctrine of double effect

Thomas Aquinas in *Summa Theologica* discussed the doctrine of double effect to determine the ethicality of self-defence. The act of self-defence may have two effects: (i) the saving of one's life and (ii) the killing of the aggressor; and that the intention to save one's own life is

---

16 New York, 16 December 1966, entered into force on 3 January 1976 at https://treaties.un.org/Pages/ViewDetails.aspx?src=IND&mtdsg_no=IV-3&chapter=4&clang=_en.
17 Adopted at the Twenty-second Session of the Committee on Economic, Social and Cultural Rights, on 11 August 2000 at https://www.refworld.org/pdfid/4538838d0.pdf.
18 Paras 34-36.
19 Adopted on 13 December 2006 and entered into force on 3 May 2008 at https://www.un.org/development/desa/disabilities/convention-on-the-rights-of-persons-with-disabilities.html#Fulltext.

not unlawful. He argued that an act that generates negative effects may be justified if four requirements are fulfilled:

- the nature of the act is in itself good or morally neutral
- the agent intends the good effects and not the bad
- the good effects are produced by the act not from the bad effects
- the good effect outweighs the bad effect.

With respect to healthcare, take the example of a doctor who intends to relieve the grave and continuous pain experienced by the patient (*ie*, the primary intended effect) and provides medication. This medication may indirectly hasten the patient's death (*ie*, the unintended secondary effect). The doctor can argue that his act is justified under this doctrine as he did not intend to cause the patient's death (Beauchamp and Childress 2019, at p. 167). Intentionality imports the idea of a *goal or objective (ends)* which the agent seeks to achieve by his actions or the *means* (*ie*, the medication) by which the agent utilises to achieve the end. Secondary effects that are merely foreseen by the agent do not amount to proof of intentionality with respect to the actions. Another illustration in the medical context is provided by McIntyre (2018):

> A doctor who believed that abortion was wrong, even in order to save the mother's life, might nevertheless consistently believe that it would be permissible to perform a hysterectomy on a pregnant woman with cancer. In carrying out the hysterectomy, the doctor would aim to save the woman's life while merely foreseeing the death of the fetus. Performing an abortion, by contrast, would involve intending to kill the fetus as a means to saving the mother.

2.5 Medical ethics in Singapore

The High Court emphasised the importance of trust and confidence in the asymmetric doctor-patient relationship in a disciplinary case involving overcharging of fees as follows[20]:

> This proposition – viz, that the relationship between a professional and his or her client is founded on trust and confidence – is so basic as to underpin every professional relationship and, indeed, applies with arguably greater force to medical practitioners, given the particular vulnerability of those who seek out medical services and the high stakes involved in many medical decisions. The especial vulnerability of patients and their dependence on health care professionals are heightened by the reality that information is (in the nature of things) distributed unequally in the medical setting, with a doctor invariably possessing far more information than his or her patient regarding the medical options and services available, where they may be found and how they should be priced… …

It held that there is an ethical obligation on the part of all doctors who practise medicine in Singapore, to charge a fair and reasonable fee for their services[21] even if there is no specific

---

20 *Lim Mey Lee Susan v Singapore Medical Council* [2013] 3 SLR 900 at [44].
21 *Lim Mey Lee Susan v Singapore Medical Council* [2013] 3 SLR 900 at [28].

provision for this. Thus, not all medical ethical guidelines applicable to doctors are required to be specifically enumerated in the ECEG.

Ethical values are embedded in the SMC Physician's Pledge based on the Declaration of Geneva[22] which had been drawn from the 2,500-year-old Hippocratic Oath. Since 1995, every registered medical practitioner upon being admitted to practice has to make the following pledge:

> I solemnly pledge to:
> dedicate my life to the service of humanity;
> give due respect and gratitude to my teachers;
> practise my profession with conscience and dignity;
> make the health of my patient my first consideration;
> respect the secrets which are confided in me;
> uphold the honour and noble traditions of the medical profession;
> respect my colleagues as my professional brothers and sisters;
> not allow the consideration of race, religion, nationality or social standing to intervene between my duty and my patient;
> maintain due respect for human life;
> use my medical knowledge in accordance with the laws of humanity;
> comply with the provisions of the Ethical Code; and
> constantly strive to add to my knowledge and skill.
> I make these promises solemnly, freely and upon my honour.

2.5.1 The SMC Ethical Code and Ethical Guidelines 2016 (ECEG 2016)

Ethical values undergird the SMC ECEG 2016 and its predecessor. The High Court has stated in *Low Cze Hong v SMC*[23] that the ECEG (the 2002 version) provides an "ethical 'compass' to guide doctors on what the acceptable standards are from which a departure may constitute professional misconduct". Further, it is "imperative for doctors to internalise the ethical responsibilities under the SMC Ethical Code and to duly perform them not just in letter, but in accordance with its spirit and intent".[24]

The current version (ECEG 2016)[25] has been updated with the following principles in mind[26]:

- Relevance to modern medical practice
- Adapting to the complexities and variations of medical practice
- Protecting patients' best interests while being fair to doctors

---

22 World Medical Association, declaration adopted by the 2nd General Assembly in Geneva in 1947.
23 [2008] 3 SLR(R) 612 at [37].
24 [2008] 3 SLR(R) 612 at [86].
25 Published on 13 September 2016 and took effect on 1 January 2017 at https://www.healthprofessionals.gov.sg/docs/librariesprovider2/guidelines/2016-smc-ethical-code-and-ethical-guidelines---(13sep16).pdf.
26 The Explanatory Notes to the ECEG 2016 at https://www.healthprofessionals.gov.sg/docs/librariesprovider2/guidelines/explanatory-notes-on-2016-eceg-and-hme-(13sep16).pdf, at para 5.

Medical ethics   45

- Maintaining the values important to society and to the medical profession
- Regulating behaviour rather than imposing blanket prohibitions
- Upholding the principle of professional self-regulation.

The ECEG 2016 is accompanied by the SMC Handbook on Medical Ethics[27] which examines the rationale underlying the ethical guidelines in the ECEG, their meaning and applicability and the possible improvements in medical practice to achieve the expected standards.

There are two phrases that are commonly used in ECEG 2016. The phrase "you must" indicates that the ethical guideline in question is an overriding duty and the principles stated must be upheld unless circumstances prevent it. It does not mean that implementation is mandatory regardless of any circumstances.[28] On the other hand, the phrase "you should" in the ECEG 2016 indicates advice on a variety of best practices. Failure to abide by all the "best" practices indicated by the phrase "you should" does not automatically render doctors in breach of the ECEG 2016.[29]

The core content of the general guidelines for medical doctors in the ECEG (2016) incorporates the norms in Principlism and more. To ensure non-maleficence and beneficence, doctors must show respect for human life, uphold patient welfare, keep abreast of medical knowledge and ensure that clinical and technical skills are current. With respect to autonomy, doctors are enjoined to treat patients with "honesty, dignity, respect and consideration", keep them adequately informed, maintain confidentiality of their medical information and to be "open, truthful, factual and professionally modest in communications" with other members of the profession, patients and the public at large. They should uphold justice by providing access to medical care and treat patients "without unfair discrimination, prejudice or personal bias against any characteristic of patients", and not allow "moral bias or prejudices made on account of patients' habits or lifestyles" to influence the doctor's treatment towards them. The ECEG also state that doctors should "strive to use resources efficiently and balance your duty of care to patients with your duty of care to the community and wider population (distributive justice)". This suggests that the duty to act in the patient's best interests may have to be sacrificed in some circumstances.

The main sections in ECEG 2016 cover the following topics:

A   Good clinical care
B   Good medical practice
C   Relationships with patients
D   Relationships with colleagues
E   Maintaining health and fitness to practice
F   Probity[30]
G   Advertising

---

27   See https://www.healthprofessionals.gov.sg/smc/guidelines/smc-ethical-code-and-ethical-guidelines-(2002-and-2016-editions)-and-handbook-on-medical-ethics-(2016-edition).
28   Explanatory Notes, at para 9.
29   Explanatory Notes, at para 10.
30   *Eg*, being open and honest in formal inquiries about the doctor's practice and acting competently, being objective and impartial when giving expert opinion as an expert witness in court.

46 *Medical ethics*

H   Finances in medical practice
I   Doctors in business relationships.

We will refer to specific ethical principles in ECEG 2016 in the ensuing chapters. On the issue of charging of fees to patients mentioned above, the ECEG 2016 state that doctors can only charge patients for fees paid to third-party administrators (TPAs) who provide intermediary services in processing insurance claims and employer medical benefits. The amounts paid must reflect the actual work provided by the TPAs and are not contingent on the services provided by the doctor or the amount of fees collected from the patients.[31] The Explanatory Notes explain particular ethical restrictions such as the restriction of medical practitioners to only SMC approved modalities of complementary and alternative medicine based on "safety and efficacy" and explain why SMC should have jurisdiction over SMC-registered doctors for cross-border medicine such as telemedicine to protect the "reputation of Singapore doctors" even if the event in question may take place outside of Singapore.[32] Furthermore, outside of ECEG, we should also note ethical guidelines on certain medical practices (*eg*, the Guidelines on Aesthetic Practices for Doctors (2016 Edition)[33] on the applicability of non-maleficence and beneficence principles in aesthetic treatments).

Though the ECEG 2016 do not have the force of law and direct legal sanctions, the non-compliance of the ethical guidelines are relevant in assessing professional misconduct in medical disciplinary cases and negligence under tort law. The Explanatory Notes[34] highlight that the ECEG "derives its authority from the consensus of the medical profession". Where there is a conflict between the law and ECEG 2016, the law will still take precedence.[35]

2.6 Conclusion

The study of ethics and ethical decision-making involves a complex blend of reason and emotions with a judicious dose of impartiality and integrity. Ethical theories possess descriptive and explanatory power and aid in problem-solving even if there may not be a definitive answer to all ethical dilemmas and conundrums. The chapter began with an examination of basic ethical theories that have been influential in the West (Consequentialism, Deontology and Virtue Ethics) and East (Confucianism) with their distinctive focus on outcomes, duties and rights, building human character and cultivation. Principlism consisting of four norms (autonomy, non-maleficence, beneficence and justice) and their interactions are applicable in many biomedical encounters involving privacy, public interest and end-of-life issues. These theories are further supplemented by a few important ethical consideration and concepts widely discussed in medical ethics (including personhood, sanctity and quality of life, and human dignity) and which will also feature prominently in our discussions in subsequent chapters. Finally, the SMC ECEG 2016 has a strong ethical ethos that permeates the general

---

31   ECEG 2016, H3(7).
32   Para 19.
33   See   https://www.healthprofessionals.gov.sg/smc/guidelines/guidelines-on-aesthetic-practices-for-doctors-(2016-edition), at para 6.
34   Para 3(b).
35   The Explanatory Notes, at para 12.

and specific guidelines spanning many areas of medical interactions. Set within the context of this book, the study of the medical ethics also holds important lessons as we examine (and re-examine) our existing health laws and regulations and seek further legal improvements and reforms.

References

BAC. (2005). *Genetic Testing and Genetic Research*: A Report from the Bioethics Advisory Committee, Singapore (November).
Beauchamp, T.L. & Childress, J.F. (2019). *Principles of Biomedical Ethics*, 8th edition (Oxford University Press: New York).
Beyleveld, D. (2015). "Making Sense of Human Dignity", chapter 9 in Coggon, J., Chan, S., Holm, S. et al. (eds), *From Reason to Practice in Bioethics: An Anthology Dedicated to the Works of John Harris* (Manchester University Press: Manchester), pp. 92-101.
Brock, D. (1993). "Quality of Life Measures in Health Care and Medical Ethics", in Nussbaum, M. & Sen, A. (eds) *The Quality of Life* (Oxford Clarendon Press: Oxford), pp. 95-132.
Centre for Biomedical Ethics (2014 and 2017). *Caring for Older People in an Ageing Society and Making Difficult Decisions with Patients and Families: A Singapore Bioethics Casebook* (Volume 1, 2014 and Volume 2, 2017) at http://www.bioethicscasebook.sg.
Chan, G.K.Y. & Shenoy, G.T.L. (2016). (eds) *Ethics and Social Responsibility: Asian and Western Perspectives*, Third Edition (McGraw-Hill: New York).
Coggon, J. (2007). "Varied and Principled Understandings of Autonomy in English Law: Justifiable Inconsistency or Blinkered Moralism?" 15 *Health Care Analysis* 235-255.
Daniels, N. (2007). *Just Health: Meeting Health Needs Fairly* (Cambridge University Press: New York).
Fan, R. (2015). *Family-Oriented Informed Consent: East Asian and American Perspectives* (Springer: Cham).
Fletcher, J.F. (1974). "Four Indicators of Humanhood: The Enquiry Matures" 4(6) *The Hastings Center Report* 4-7.
Hare, R.M. (1993). *Essays on Bioethics* (Oxford Clarendon Press: Oxford).
Harris, J. (1999). "Justice and Equal Opportunities in Health Care" 13(5) *Bioethics* 392-404.
Held, V. (2007). *The Ethics of Care* (Oxford University Press: Oxford).
Kant, I. (1996). *Practical Philosophy* (edited and translated by Mary J Gregor) (Cambridge University Press: New York).
Law, I. & Widdows, H. (2008). "Conceptualising Health: Insights from the Capability Approach" 16 *Health Care Analysis* 303-314.
Levy, N. (2002). "Deafness, Culture and Choice" 28(5) *Journal of Medical Ethics* 284-285.
MacKenzie, C. & Stoljar, N. (2000). (eds) *Relational Autonomy: Feminist Perspectives on Autonomy, Agency, and the Social Self* (Oxford University Press: Oxford).
McIntyre, A. (2018). "Doctrine of Double Effect" *Stanford Encyclopedia of Philosophy* at https://plato.stanford.edu/entries/double-effect/.
Mill, J.S. (1987). *Utilitarianism* (Prometheus Books: New York).
Mill, J.S. (2003). "On Liberty" in Bromwich, D. & Kateb, G. (eds), *On Liberty* (Yale University Press: New Haven, CT), pp. 69-175.
Nussbaum, M. (2006). *Frontiers of Justice: Disability, Nationality, Species Membership* (Harvard University Press: Cambridge, MA).
Oakley, J. & Cocking, D. (2001). *Virtue Ethics and Professional Roles* (Cambridge University Press: Cambridge).
Pogge, T. (2012). "The Health Impact Fund: Enhancing Justice and Efficiency in Global Health" 13(4) *Journal of Human Development and Capabilities* 537-559.
Rawls, J. (1972). *A Theory of Justice* (Oxford University Press: New York).
Rawls, J. (2001). *Justice as Fairness: A Restatement* (Harvard University Press: Cambridge, MA).
Savulescu, J., Cameron, J., & Wilkinson, D. (2020). "Equality or Utility? Ethics and Law of Rationing Ventilators" 125(1) *British Journal of Anaesthesia* 10-15.
Scanlon, T.M. (1998). *What We Owe to Each Other* (Harvard University Press: Cambridge, MA).

Sen, A. (1993). "Capability and Well-being" in Nussbaum, M. & Sen, A. (eds) *The Quality of Life* (Oxford Clarendon Press: Oxford).
Singer, P. (2000). *Writings on an Ethical Life* (The Ecco Press: New York).
Tooley, M. (1972). "Abortion and Infanticide" 2(1) *Philosophy and Public Affairs* 37–65.
Tronto, J. (1993). *Moral Boundaries: A Political Argument for an Ethic of Care* (Routledge: New York).
Vanlaere, L. & Gastmans, C. (2011). "A Personalist Approach to Care Ethics" 18(2) *Nursing Ethics* 161–173.
van Zyl, L.L. (2000). *Death and Compassion: A Virtue-based Approach to Euthanasia* (Ashgate: Aldershot).

3 Medical negligence (part 1)

3.1 Introduction

This chapter and the next will discuss the substantive tort of negligence as applied to medical doctors, healthcare professionals and the hospitals. Essentially, we will be examining circumstances in which the careless conduct of doctors and healthcare professionals that result in the patient's injuries give rise to liability under tort law. Not every case of careless conduct of a doctor or hospital would attract liability. The tort of negligence requires the proof of the following criteria:

- Duty of care owed by defendant to the plaintiff
- Breach of the defendant's duty (*ie*, falling below the standard of care expected of the defendant
- That the breach caused the damage suffered by the plaintiff
- The damage is not too remote.

The main remedy in medical negligence, if established, is the recovery of monetary damages for the losses and injuries suffered by the aggrieved party. Even if the abovementioned requirements are proved by the plaintiff, the defendant may raise defences (such as assumption of risks, *ex turpi causa*, exemption of liability by defendant, contributory negligence by the plaintiff) to either defeat the claim or to reduce the damages payable.

This chapter will focus on duty of care and breach of duty as well as the doctrine of *res ipsa loquitur* on inferences that the defendant's negligence had caused the accident that led to the plaintiff's damage. Chapter 4 will cover the remaining requirements (causation and remoteness), the legal defences, the doctrines of vicarious liability and non-delegable duties, remedies available to the plaintiff and procedural matters relating to medical negligence litigation.

3.2 Duty of care

Before we can ascertain if the defendant (doctor) has breached his duty to the patient, we need to consider if there is a duty of care in the first place. The legal duty of care acts as a filter against unmeritorious claims in the eyes of the law (Chan 2016). Would a doctor owe a duty to a passer-by who may have suffered a health problem or an injury? Does a doctor engaged by an employer to conduct medical examination of its employee owe a duty to the employee? Does the doctor owe a duty to patients or their relatives not to cause psychiatric harm when disclosing information about the patients' adverse health conditions? We explore these and other related questions in this section.

3.2.1 The judicial formulation and development of duty of care

In *Spandeck Engineering (S) Pte Ltd v Defence Science & Technology Agency*,[1] the Singapore Court of Appeal formulated a single, two-stage framework to determine the existence of a duty of care based on (a) proximity and (b) policy considerations, with a threshold requirement of factual foreseeability. This framework applies regardless of the nature of the damage caused.

At the first stage, sufficient *legal* proximity between the plaintiff and defendant is required for establishing a duty of care. The closeness of the relationship between the parties depends on finding physical, circumstantial and causal proximity supported by the twin concepts of voluntary assumption of responsibility by the defendant and reliance by the plaintiff on the defendant. Other factors include the defendant's control over the risks of harm to the plaintiff,[2] the vulnerability of the plaintiff,[3] and the knowledge of the parties in a transaction as to the other party's vulnerable position.

If both the threshold of factual foreseeability *and* proximity are satisfied, a *prima facie* duty of care arises. Policy considerations are then applied at the second stage to determine whether this *prima facie* duty should be limited or negated. Policy considerations refer to broad social welfare goals and the weighing of competing moral claims.[4] The *Spandeck* framework is to be applied incrementally by reference to prior cases in analogous situations.

The concept of duty of care was developed in England several decades ago. In *M'Alister (or Donoghue) v Stevenson*,[5] a claim for personal injury under the tort of negligence was successfully brought by the ultimate consumer of the ginger beer against the manufacturer on the basis of the "neighbour" principle which Lord Atkin described as follows[6]:

> You must take reasonable care to avoid *acts or omissions* which you can *reasonably foresee* would be likely to injure your *neighbour* ... *persons who are so closely and directly affected by my act that I ought reasonably to have them in contemplation as being so affected* when I am directing my mind to the acts and omissions which are called in question. [emphasis added]

---

1 [2007] 4 SLR(R) 100.
2 *Anwar Patrick Adrian v Ng Chong & Hue LLC* [2014] 3 SLR 761 at [152].
3 *Anwar Patrick Adrian v Ng Chong & Hue LLC* [2014] 3 SLR 761 at [154].
4 *Spandeck Engineering (S) Pte Ltd v Defence Science & Technology Agency* [2007] 4 SLR(R) 100 at [85].
5 [1932] AC 562.
6 *M'Alister (or Donoghue) v Stevenson* [1932] AC 562 at 580.

This principle was subsequently extended to apply to claims for financial losses arising from negligent misstatements in *Hedley Byrne & Co Ltd v Heller & Partners Ltd*.[7] This led to a two-stage test in *Anns v Merton London Borough Council*[8] ("*Anns*") which also involved a claim for financial losses[9]:

> [I]n order to establish that a duty of care arises in a particular situation, it is *not necessary to bring the facts of that situation within those of previous situations in which a duty of care has been held to exist*. Rather the question has to be approached in two stages. First one has to ask whether, as between the alleged wrongdoer and the person who has suffered damage there is a *sufficient relationship of proximity or neighbourhood* such that, in the *reasonable contemplation* of the former, carelessness on his part may be likely to cause damage to the latter – in which case a *prima facie* duty of care arises. Secondly, if the first question is answered affirmatively, it is necessary to consider whether there are *any considerations which ought to negative, or to reduce or limit the scope of the duty or the class of person to whom it is owed or the damages* to which a breach of it may give rise … [emphasis added]

In 1990, the House of Lords in *Caparo Industries plc v Dickman*[10] ("*Caparo*") formulated a three-part test to determine if there is a duty owed. Lord Bridge in *Caparo* stated[11]:

> What emerges is that, in addition to the *foreseeability of damage*, necessary ingredients in any situation giving rise to a duty of care are that there should exist between the party owing the duty and the party to whom it is owed a relationship characterised by the law as one of *'proximity' or 'neighbourhood'* and that the situation should be one in which the court considers it *fair, just and reasonable* that the law should impose a duty of a given scope upon the one party for the benefit of the other. [emphasis added]

The House of Lords preferred an incremental approach to develop new categories of negligence by analogy to the established categories instead of the general and broad formula of Lord Wilberforce in *Anns*.

3.2.2 Duty of care in medical contexts

In the medical context, the duty-of-care issue does not give rise to controversy in the typical cases. Where the patient consults the doctor in his clinic on his or health condition to find out the nature of the health problem, seek treatment or advice, the doctor will normally owe a duty of care to the patient in respect of one or more of these aspects. The following subsections discuss the existence and scope of duty of care in specific scenarios.

---

7 [1964] AC 465.
8 [1978] AC 728.
9 *Anns v Merton London Borough Council* [1978] AC 728 at 751-752.
10 [1990] 2 AC 605.
11 *Caparo Industries plc v Dickman* [1990] 2 AC 605 at 617-618.

3.2.2.1 Contractual and tortious duties[12]

A contractual duty arises when the doctor agrees to provide medical services to a patient in exchange for consideration (usually in the form of monetary payment for services by the patient). The contract can be formed orally in a typical consultation at the clinic between the patient and medical doctor without any written agreement.

The law recognises the general rule of concurrent liability in both contract and tort.[13] That is, a contracting party can choose to sue another in contract and/or tort law provided he can establish the requisite elements for each cause of action. There is an implied term of contract to exercise reasonable care and skill in carry out the scope of work whether it is to diagnose the illness, give treatment or to advise the patient.[14] The medical doctor does not normally guarantee a particular medical outcome under the law unless words to that effect are expressly given in clear and unequivocal terms.[15]

Where the medical services or advice are provided by the medical doctor to a person without consideration, no contractual duty arises but there might nevertheless be a tortious duty of care. The existence of a tortious duty would depend on whether the advice was provided with the expectation of some indirect reward or purely out of goodwill, and whether the relationship is a professional relationship or merely casual.[16] A merely casual relationship is unlikely to give rise to a duty of care though one should examine carefully whether the circumstances and context import an assumption of responsibility by the doctor or reasonable reliance by the person to whom the medical advice or services was supplied.[17]

3.2.2.2 Rescue or assistance during emergencies

The general position in tort law is that a passer-by is not liable for the omission to rescue a victim in need. There is a distinction between "making things worse" which is culpable and "failing to make things better"[18] (as in the case of a pure omission to rescue) which is not. We should not ordinarily place on a person the legal responsibility of preventing harm to (or conferring a benefit on)[19] others with whom he has no prior relationship or knowledge. The concern here is that imposing a legal duty in such a circumstance might unjustifiably inter-

---

12   See Mulheron (2017).
13   *Henderson v Merrett Syndicates Ltd* [1995] 2 AC 145.
14   *Eyre v Measday* [1986] 1 All ER 488 at 495.
15   *Thake v Maurice* [1986] 1 All ER 479 (CA) (consultation with doctor for vasectomy for husband; no contractual guarantee of husband's sterility); *Eyre v Measday* [1986] 1 All ER 488 at 495 (no implied term or unqualified collateral warranty that the expected result *ie*, sterilisation would actually be achieved).
16   *Hedley Byrne & Co Ltd v Heller & Partners Ltd* [1964] AC 465 at 529, *per* Lord Devlin.
17   *Fish v Kelly* (1864) 17 CB NS 194; 144 ER 78 (casual relationship between lawyer and plaintiff and therefore no duty of care as to advice given); *Chaudhry v Prabhakar* [1989] 1 WLR 29 (expert on motor cars found to have assumed responsibility to a friend who wanted to purchase a car in misrepresenting that car was accident-free).
18   Lunney and Oliphant (2008, at p. 465).
19   See *Stovin v Wise* [1996] AC 923 at 930, *per* Lord Nicholls.

fere with one's freedom of action or autonomy. This general position is subject to certain exceptions such as when the person had assumed a responsibility by his words or conduct towards the victim in need.

The following case – albeit in a non-medical context – illustrates the principle. In *Barrett v Ministry of Defence*,[20] a naval airman indulged in heavy drinking at a shore-based naval establishment. When he became unconscious, he was placed in his bunk in the recovery position. However, he asphyxiated on his vomit and died. There was no duty of care owed by the Ministry of Defence to prevent the deceased abusing alcohol as the latter was a responsible adult and ought to be responsible for his own actions in consuming alcohol. However, a duty of care arose when the defendant assumed responsibility for the health and safety of the deceased who had collapsed.[21] The defendant was found negligent in the act of caring for the deceased.

An ambulance service may be held liable for negligent delay in responding to an emergency call. In *Kent v Griffiths*,[22] the ambulance delayed in transporting the claimant to the hospital. During the journey, the claimant suffered cardiac arrest and permanent brain damage. The specific request for assistance, which was accepted by the ambulance service and relied upon by the claimant, established the duty of care.

A doctor is not legally required to save or rescue a victim (who is not his patient) in a medical emergency at common law.[23] He may do so out of good will or moral duty. Should he decide to assume responsibility to save the victim, he will only be liable, if he is proved to be negligent, for the additional harms if any to the victim that his breach had caused. Beyond this common law negligence standard, there are no Good Samaritan statutes in Singapore to further protect the doctors or healthcare professionals (such as paramedics) who assume such responsibility to save or rescue a stranger in an emergency situation.[24] In other jurisdictions, the good Samaritan would be protected if the attempt to rescue is made in *good faith*[25] or may enjoy immunity from legal liability unless the damage was caused by his or her *gross negligence*.[26]

---

20 [1995] 1 WLR 1217.
21 Bedlam LJ in *Barrett v Ministry of Defence* [1995] 1 WLR 1217 at 1225 noted that the deceased's "lack of self-control in his own interest caused the defendant to have to assume responsibility for him" and therefore reduced the damages payable by the defendant.
22 [2001] QB 36.
23 *Capital and Counties v Hampshire County Council* [1997] QB 1004 at 1035, *per* Stuart-Smith LJ.
24 The issue has been raised in Parliament but each time, the Minister did not see the need for such statute: see Singapore Parliament Reports, Vol 92 (29 May 2014); Vol 88 (14 Feb 2012); and Vol 84 (21 Jan 2008).
25 In Australia, see *Commonwealth Volunteers Protection Act 2003* (Cth) ss 6-7; *Civil Law (Wrongs) Act 2002* (ACT) ss 5, 8-9; *Civil Liability Act 2002* (NSW) ss 57, 61; *Personal Injuries (Liability and Damages) Act 2003* (NT) ss 7, 8; *Civil Liability Act 2003* (Qld) ss 26, 39; *Civil Liability Act 1936* (SA) s 74; *Volunteers Protection Act 2001* (SA) s 4; *Civil Liability Act 2002* (Tas) ss 35B, 47; *Wrongs Act 1958* (Vic) ss 31B, 37; *Civil Liability Act 2002* (WA) s 5AD; *Volunteers and Food and other Donors (Protection from Liability) Act 2002* (WA) ss 6-7.
26 *Eg*, in Canada, see Good Samaritans Act [RSBC 1996] Chapter 172; and Good Samaritan Act 2002 (Ontario), section 2.

> **Box 3.1 – Whither Good Samaritan statutes**
>
> Do you think there should be Good Samaritan statutes to protect healthcare personnel and professionals? If so, how should the statutes be drafted to give such protection? Or would the existing tort of negligence be sufficient?

3.2.2.3 Personal injuries

Personal injury claims are common in medical negligence and do not normally pose any special legal issues for duty of care. In a few special circumstances, however, the nature of the injury or damage sustained has given rise to interesting points of law in litigation.

Damage to a substance generated by a person's body (sperm samples), and which occurred after the substance was removed for purposes of storage (as the claimants were about to undergo chemotherapy), was held not to constitute personal injury.[27] It was treated instead as a special kind of property damage based on the intended use of the sperm for procreation and the inability of the claimants, due to the defendant's breach, to use the sperm for that purpose.

Pleural plaques (*ie*, fibrous thickening of the membrane which surrounds the lungs) upon exposure to asbestos which did not cause any symptoms or increase the plaintiffs' susceptibility to other asbestos-related diseases were not treated as damage.[28] However, platinum salt sensitisation due to exposure to platinum salts, resulting in allergy and impairment of the claimants' bodily capacity for work, amounted to actionable personal injury.[29]

It has also been held that, arising from a psychologist's breach of duty to diagnose a child's dyslexia, the "failure to mitigate the adverse consequences of a congenital defect such as dyslexia was capable of constituting personal injuries".[30]

3.2.2.4 Psychiatric harm

In psychiatric harm cases, the claimant must first prove the existence of a recognisable psychiatric illness[31] to be determined by medical experts. Grief, anxiety or distress *per se* will not suffice.[32]

In the Creutzfeldt-Jakob Disease (CJD) litigation, *Group B Plaintiffs v Medical Research Council*,[33] several young children received a human growth hormone in a clinical trial and developed psychiatric harm when informed subsequently that they were at risk of developing

---

27 *Yearworth v North Bristol NHS Trust* [2010] QB 1.
28 *Rothwell v Chemical & Insulating Co Ltd* [2008] 1 AC 281.
29 *Dryden v Johnson Mathey Plc* [2018] 2 WLR 1109 at [40].
30 *Phelps v Hillingdon London Borough Council* [2000] 2 AC 619, at 664 and 676.
31 But see Canadian Supreme Court decision in *Saadati v Moorhead* [2017] 1 SCR 543 which rejected such a requirement.
32 *Pang Koi Fa v Lim Djoe Phing* [1993] 2 SLR(R) 366 at [62].
33 [2000] Lloyd's Rep Med 161 (QB).

CJD. A duty of care arose due to foreseeability of psychiatric injury and relational proximity between the parties.[34]

In the medical context, psychiatric harm suffered by the patient's family members or relative may arise from the negligence of the healthcare professional in treating or caring for the patient. The doctor's negligence may have caused the patient serious injuries or death. To establish duty of care for psychiatric harm claims by the family member or relative, the following facets of circumstantial, physical and causal proximity (as part of the first stage of the *Spandeck* framework) were applied in the case of *Ngiam Kong Seng*[35]:

- closeness of relationship between the patient and the family members or relatives (claimants)(*circumstantial* proximity)
- proximity of claimants to the accident in space and time (*physical* proximity)
- means by which the shock is caused (*causal* proximity).

The general position in Singapore for psychiatric harm claims requires proof that the damage was shock-induced.[36] However, an exception has been made for medical negligence cases. In *Pang Koi Fa v Lim Djoe Phing*,[37] the defendant's negligence as a neurosurgeon in the operation, diagnosis and treatment of a patient resulted in the death of the patient and the patient's mother suffered psychiatric injury.[38] The period between the negligent operation and the patient's death was about three months. Applying the English decision in *McLoughlin*, the first proximity requirement was clearly satisfied on the basis of a mother-daughter relationship and a "close" bond between them.[39] With respect to the second and third proximity requirements, the court observed that there was no accident or aftermath which was witnessed by the plaintiff, unlike in *McLoughlin*. In the context of medical negligence, family members would normally not be present at the operation and would not be aware if a specific operation was carried out negligently.[40] The Singapore court held that the plaintiff was proximate in both time and space to the tortious event as she had witnessed throughout, the gradual effects of the defendant doctor's negligent diagnosis, operation and post-operative treatment.[41] The plaintiff was consulting as parent with her daughter at the time of the diagnosis, advised her daughter to proceed with the operation, was by her daughter's side when she was discharged and sent home by ambulance and when the daughter returned to the hospital due to her condition becoming precarious. Moreover, she was a "percipient witness

---

34 But see *Rothwell v Chemical & Insulating Co Ltd* [2008] 1 AC 281 (a non-medical negligence case where the plaintiff was held not entitled to recover for psychiatric illness caused by the apprehension that he might, in the future, contract an asbestos-related disease).
35 *Ngiam Kong Seng v Lim Chiew Hock* [2008] 3 SLR(R) 674 at [101]-[103].
36 *McLoughlin v O'Brian* [1983] 1 AC 410; *Alcock v Chief Constable of South Yorkshire Police* [1992] 1 AC 310; and Fordham (2004).
37 [1993] 2 SLR(R) 366.
38 A mood disorder, a depressive illness secondary to grief arising from her daughter's death.
39 *Pang Koi Fa v Lim Djoe Phing* [1993] 2 SLR(R) 366 at [40]-[41].
40 *Pang Koi Fa v Lim Djoe Phing* [1993] 2 SLR(R) 366 at [46].
41 *Pang Koi Fa v Lim Djoe Phing* [1993] 2 SLR(R) 366 at [55], citing *Gloria Ochoa et al v The Superior Court of Santa Clara County* 39 Cal 3d 159; 216 Cal Rptr 661; 703 P 2d 1 (Supreme Court of California).

in terms of the elements of immediacy, closeness of time and space, visual and aural perception" of the events relating to the negligence and death of her daughter,[42] notwithstanding the absence of any sudden shock to the plaintiff. Furthermore, the learned judge was prepared to allow the claim based alternatively on the fact that the defendant's negligence had caused the plaintiff, in subjecting her daughter to an unnecessary operation based on the defendant's misdiagnosis, to blame herself for her daughter's death.[43]

Pang Koi Fa may be contrasted with the English case of *Sion v Hampstead HA*[44] where the claim for psychiatric injury was struck out as the requirement of nervous shock[45] was not fulfilled. The claimant stayed by his son's side for two weeks at the hospital which had negligently failed to diagnose the son's condition and the psychiatric harm arose from the claimant's gradual realisation that his son's condition would eventually lead to his death.[46]

Another set of cases concerned claims of the patient's relatives for psychiatric harm arising from communications made by the doctor or healthcare professional. The Court of Appeal stated in *Ngiam Kong Seng* the general position against such claims in negligence[47]:

> The court should be slow to allow recovery for psychiatric harm arising from the communication of information in cases where no 'malign intention' ... ... on the part of the person communicating the information is present.

The requirement of proof of malign intention is higher than the proof of negligence. The reason for the higher threshold of proof is the policy consideration that doctors and healthcare professionals should be given greater leeway when delivering bad news to the family members and relatives concerning the patient's condition. To establish legal liability, evidence of an intention on the part of the doctor or healthcare professional to harm the plaintiff through the communication of information is required.

It was held that a doctor did not owe a duty of care to a deceased patient's relative who suffered psychiatric harm as a result of the doctor's alleged removal and falsification of medical records concerning the cause of death due to an absence of proximity between the parties.[48] Further, there was no evidence of any intention to injure the relative. Similarly, no duty of care was owed by health authorities to parents claiming damages for alleged psychiatric

---

42 *Pang Koi Fa v Lim Djoe Phing* [1993] 2 SLR(R) 366 at [62]. The learned judge had stated at [56] that what was required to be witnessed was the "calamitous effect of that [negligent] conduct on the primary victim".
43 *Pang Koi Fa v Lim Djoe Phing* [1993] 2 SLR(R) 366 at [68].
44 [1994] Lexis Citation 3939. See also *Ward v Leeds Teaching Hospitals NHS Trust* [2004] EWHC 2106 requirement of shocking event for claim based on PTSD against NHS Trust.
45 *Alcock v Chief Constable of South Yorkshire* [1992] 1 AC 310.
46 See *North Glamorgan NHS Trust v Walters* [2002] EWCA Civ 1792 at [29] and [39]-[40] (claim allowed as the claimant's appreciation of the events from the son's epileptic fit to his death within 36 hours due to hospital's negligence was "sudden" rather than gradual; *Sion* distinguished); and *Tredget & Tredget v Bexley Health Authority* [1994] 5 Med LR 178 (defendant hospital's negligent management of claimant's labour causing baby to be born in a severely asphyxiated state, put in intensive care and die within 48 hours regarded as a single event).
47 *Ngiam Kong Seng v Lim Chiew Hock* [2008] 3 SLR(R) 674 at [140].
48 *Powell v Boladz* (1997) 39 BMLR 35 (CA).

harm which arose as a result of unfounded allegations made by healthcare and child care professionals that the parents had abused their children.[49]

Nonetheless, a remedy for psychiatric harm resulting from the communication of information under the tort of negligence could arise where there was an existing professional relationship between the parties (*eg*, a doctor-patient relationship).[50] By virtue of the special relationship, the doctor would owe a duty of take reasonable care of his patient's health conditions and this would include taking reasonable care in communicating and disclosing information to the patient (this will be further discussed in the section below on Standard of Care in relation to medical advice).

3.2.2.5 Healthcare professionals engaged by third parties

The doctor may be engaged by a company to medically examine patients. The doctor would owe a duty to the company which engaged him to perform the task in accordance with the purpose and scope of the engagement. In such an instance, would the doctor also owe a duty of care to the patient directly? The answer would be "yes" if the elements in the *Spandeck* framework are satisfied. Previously, in *X v Bedfordshire County Council*,[51] a psychiatrist engaged by the local social services to examine a child for suspected sexual abuse was held not to owe a duty of care to the child to avoid psychiatric injury. A duty of care was owed to the local authority instead of to the child. Subsequently, there was a change of position in *Phelps v Hillingdon LBC*[52] that a duty of care should be owed by educational psychologists engaged by local authorities to the school children whom they were instructed to examine for conditions such as dyslexia. The duty was based on the psychologists' assumption of responsibility to the children.[53] The position was later affirmed in *D v East Berkshire Community Health NHS Trust*[54] which held that the health professionals owed the children they examined a duty of care but not to their parents or carers.

Another scenario concerned a doctor who has been referred to by the patient's employer to medically examine the patient, a diver. In a Hong Kong court decision,[55] a doctor carrying out a medical examination on the patient was held to owe a duty of care to both the patient and his employer. The patient had sued the doctor for negligently failing to carry out proper medical examinations which would have disclosed the existence of his medical problems, and/ or should have referred him to a specialist in medicine. The doctor had assured the patient

---

49 *JD v East Berkshire Community NHS Trust* [2005] 2 WLR 993 (that healthcare and other child care professionals should not be subject to conflicting duties to the child and their parents when deciding whether a child might have been abused and what further steps should be taken).
50 *Ngiam Kong Seng v Lim Chiew Hock* [2008] 3 SLR(R) 674 at [141], citing *Brown v The Mount Barker Soldiers' Hospital Incorporated* [1934] SASR 128 (Supreme Court of South Australia decision) and *Furniss v Fitchett* [1958] NZLR 396 (Supreme Court of New Zealand).
51 [1995] 2 AC 633.
52 [2001] 2 AC 619.
53 The defendant local education authority was also vicariously liable for the psychologist's breach.
54 [2005] 2 AC 373.
55 *Ho Ying Wai v Keliston Marine (Far East) Ltd* [2002] HKCFI 543 (Hong Kong).

that he had been properly examined and assessed by a purported expert in that field of occupational medicine, and his state of health and physical fitness allowed him to be employed accordingly. Both employer and employee were aware of the purpose of the examination.

3.2.2.6 Medical report to third parties

The patient requests a doctor to medically examine him and to send the medical report to a third party (such as the patient's employer or insurer). The central issue is whether the doctor owes a duty to the patient if the latter suffers economic loss (*eg*, loss of employment) due to the reliance of the third party on the medical examination negligently conducted.[56] Whether a duty of care is owed to the patient directly would similarly depend on whether the elements of proximity and policy in the *Spandeck* framework are satisfied.

The existence of a duty of care to the patient in such a case may be argued by analogy to *Ramesh s/o Krishnan v AXA Life Insurance Singapore Pte Ltd*[57] involving the preparation of a report by an insurance company concerning its ex-employee that was sent to the ex-employee's prospective hirers. The Singapore High Court found that both causal and circumstantial proximity as well as assumption of responsibility and reliance existed as between the ex-employer and ex-employee,[58] and noted the following similarities with *Spring v Guardian Assurance plc*[59]:

- the employer had special knowledge about the employee
- the employer provided a reference to a third party for the assistance of the employee
- the employer provided a reference with the tacit authority of the employee
- the provision of a reference is a service provided by employers to their employees
- the employee relied on his employer to exercise due skill and care in preparing the reference.

As a result, the ex-employee could recover for loss of job prospects from the ex-employer which prepared the report.

In the case of a doctor, there would likely be physical, circumstantial and causal proximity between him and the patient who requested for the medical report to be sent to his employer. This is based on the following: that the doctor would possess special knowledge about the employee's health condition, the report was to assist the patient in the job application and was provided with the patient's tacit authority, and the patient would have relied on the doctor's skill and care in the medical examination and preparation of report.

3.2.2.7 Doctor as expert witness in court proceedings

A doctor who prepares a report for the purpose of court proceedings in his capacity as an expert witness is immune from liability in a negligence lawsuit by a litigant.[60] This principle

---

56 *Baker v Kaye* [1997] IRLR 219; but see *Kapfunde v Abbey National* (1998) 46 BMLR 176 (CA).
57 [2015] 4 SLR 1.
58 *Ramesh s/o Krishnan v AXA Life Insurance Singapore Pte Ltd* [2015] 4 SLR 1 at [251].
59 [1995] 2 AC 296.
60 *Landall v Dennis Faulkner & Alsop* [1994] 5 Med LR 268 (QBD).

is for ensuring the full and frank disclosure of expert witnesses for the due administration of justice.

3.2.2.8 Hospital administration

The UK Supreme Court in *Darnley v Croydon Health Services NHS Trust*[61] held that a casualty department owes a duty of care to persons presenting themselves complaining of illnesses even before they are treated or received into care in the hospital wards. In this case, the appellant sought medical help at the respondent's A&E department for a head injury he sustained, was accepted into the respondent's system by the attending receptionist and thereby entered into a patient-health service provider relationship. The non-clinical reception staff acted negligently with respect to their duty to provide information about waiting times and failed to assess the appellant for priority triage which eventually resulted in the patient's permanent brain damage.

The above scenarios on duty of care in medical negligence are not exhaustive. Other specific scenarios will be dealt with in subsequent chapters. These include duty-of-care issues involving disclosure of genetic information about the patient's condition to family members and third parties (Chapter 7), claims based on wrongful conception, wrongful birth and wrongful life respectively (Chapter 9), prolongation of life (Chapter 10), the handling and use of human organs and tissues (Chapter 11) and telemedicine encounters (Chapter 12).

3.3. Standard of care

We will begin this section with an examination of the general principles on standard of care expected of doctors and health professionals[62] followed by the specific legal tests and applications to diagnosis and treatment, the giving of medical advice, hospital systemic negligence, emergency situations and the provision of team-based and joint healthcare.

3.3.1 General principles

As stated in *Blyth v Birmingham Waterworks Co*,[63]

> Negligence is the omission to do something which a reasonable man, guided upon those considerations which ordinarily regulate the conduct of human affairs, would do, or doing something which a prudent and reasonable man would not do.

The standard of care is based on the reasonableness of the conduct. As mentioned above, the doctor does not normally guarantee favourable outcomes for the patient but undertakes to use reasonable skill and care vis-à-vis his patients.

The test for standard of care is that of a reasonably competent doctor in the particular field or specialty. Thus, a general practitioner will be judged by the standards of a general

---

61 [2018] 3 WLR 1153.
62 See Havers and Elliot (2017).
63 (1856) 11 Exch 781 at 784, *per* Alderson B.

practitioner and not that of a specialist, whose reference point will be the standard of a reasonably competent specialist within that specialty. A practitioner of alternative and/or complementary medicine (such as traditional Chinese medicine) will be judged according to the standards of the practitioners of such alternative and/or complementary medicine albeit with some modifications as opposed to the standards of orthodox medicine.[64]

The doctor in question who may be inexperienced is nonetheless judged according to the standards of a reasonably competent and experienced doctor.[65] It is an objective standard which does not take into account the subjective characteristics of the individual doctor. The standard of care should be tied to the post which the doctor occupies as opposed to rank or status.[66] Where a doctor is aware that he is not competent to carry out a complex procedure, he should refer the patient to a specialist or seek the advice of more experienced doctors.

The standard of care is based on what would reasonably be expected of the doctor at the time of the alleged breach of duty. We must not judge the acts or omissions of the doctor with the benefit of hindsight. As stated in *Roe v Minister of Health*,[67] we "must not look at the 1947 accident with 1954 spectacles". The standard should be based on the state of medical knowledge at the time of the alleged breach.

The typical factors for assessing standard of care in the tort of negligence generally are foreseeability of risks, magnitude of risks, costs of precautions, and the objective of the defendant's conduct. The factors are considered holistically to determine the standard of care.[68]

There are some general principles regarding the balancing of factors. First, where the likelihood of injury to the plaintiff is extremely low or remote, a high standard of care is not generally required to prevent the injury.[69] Second, the greater the extent of damage, the more precautions should be undertaken by the defendant to prevent the damage.[70] Third, a reasonable man would weigh the risks of injury against the difficulty of eliminating the risk; he may neglect a small risk if it would involve considerable expense to eliminate the risk.[71] Finally, with respect to the purpose of the defendant's conduct, the risk may be balanced against the "end to be achieved" from the activity in question.[72]

Doctors may sometimes rely on an approving authority for a drug which he or she prescribes to a patient. Can the doctor reasonably place reliance on such approving authority? In *TV Media Pte Ltd v De Cruz Andrea Heidi*,[73] a non-medical negligence case, it was held that

---

64 *Shakoor v Situ* [2001] 1 WLR 410. See chapter 8 on Alternative and Complementary Medicine.
65 *Jones v Manchester Corporation* [1952] 2 All ER 125 at 131, per Denning LJ.
66 *Wilsher v Essex Area HA* [1986] 3 All ER 801 at 813, per Mustill LJ.
67 [1954] 2 QB 66. The contamination of the anaesthetic administered to the patient by the defendants which caused the injury was unforeseeable in 1947.
68 *Overseas Tankship (UK) Ltd v The Miller Steamship Co Pty* [1967] 1 AC 617.
69 *Bolton v Stone* [1951] AC 850.
70 *Paris v Stepney Borough Council* [1951] AC 367; *Walker v Northumberland County Council* [1995] 1 All ER 737.
71 *Overseas Tankship (UK) Ltd v The Miller Steamship Co Pty* [1967] 1 AC 617.
72 *Watt v Hertfordshire County Council* [1954] 1 WLR 835.
73 [2004] 3 SLR(R) 543.

the sole distributor of a drug cannot place "unquestioning reliance" on a health approving authority (*ie*, the Health Sciences Authority) for the contaminated pills which had resulted in the plaintiff's personal injuries.[74] The distributor knew of the inexperience of the importers of the drug, and the existence of a contrary test report on the drug for which he should have sought professional advice.[75]

By analogy, a doctor should not rely unquestioningly on the approvals of a health authority to absolve liability in negligence. This may be applicable to, for example, health products and medical devices approved by Health Sciences Authority and used by the doctor. To assess whether the doctor had reasonably relied on the third party, it is suggested that relevant factors should include the reliability of the third party, the approval process and scope of approval, the doctor's knowledge (actual and constructive) of the product or device and any circumstances that may raise suspicion to a reasonable doctor concerning the product or device.

3.3.2 The Bolam and Bolitho tests: diagnosis and treatment

In the assessment of whether the doctor's conduct in diagnosing or treating the patient had been negligent, evidence of medical experts may be adduced by the litigants. Such expert evidence may conflict with each other. Instead of deciding which expert opinion is more persuasive in order to determine whether the doctor had breached his duty, the judge resolves the conflict by reference to two legal tests. McNair J in the landmark English decision in *Bolam v Friern Hospital Management Committee*[76] ("*Bolam*") said:

> [A doctor] is not guilty of negligence if he has acted in accordance with a *practice accepted as proper by a responsible body of medical men skilled in that particular art* ... Putting it the other way around, a man is not negligent, if he is acting in accordance with such a practice, merely because there is a body of opinion who would take a contrary view. [emphasis added]

The *Bolam* test thus defers to the views of the medical profession on the question of a doctor's standard of care. It recognises the importance of relying on medical views about accepted practices in cases where there are genuine differences in medical opinion as to whether the alleged acts or omissions of the doctor are negligent or not. In such instances, courts without medical knowledge and expertise would not be in a good position to decide in favour of one medical opinion over the other. It should also be noted that ethical guidelines for the medical profession may constitute a source of evidence as to the position taken by a reasonable body of medical opinion.[77]

This deference to medical opinion does not mean that the court has no role at all in assessing whether the doctor in question was negligent. A second test was developed in *Bolitho v*

---

74 *TV Media Pte Ltd v De Cruz Andrea Heidi* [2004] 3 SLR(R) 543 at [63], [68], [71] and [73].
75 *TV Media Pte Ltd v De Cruz Andrea Heidi* [2004] 3 SLR(R) 543 at [70].
76 [1957] 1 WLR 582 at 587.
77 *D'Conceicao Jeanie Doris v Tong Ming Chuan*, [2011] SGHC 193 at [130].

City and Hackney Health Authority.[78] Upon the application of the *Bolam* test, the *Bolitho* test demands that the judge hearing the medical negligence case be satisfied that the medical opinion had a "logical" basis *ie*, whether the opinion had weighed the risks against the benefits to reach a "defensible conclusion". This means that the medical opinion about accepted practices under the *Bolam* test is ultimately subject to the court's scrutiny. On the facts, the defendant in *Bolitho* had failed to intubate the patient who was having a cardiac arrest. The expert medical opinion was that intubation was inappropriate. As this expert opinion was not based on illogical grounds, the defendant was held not negligent.

According to the Singapore decision of *Khoo James v Gunapathy d/o Muniandy*,[79] a two-stage inquiry is to be conducted to determine if the expert opinion was based on logic. Under the first stage, the judge should inquire if the expert had directed his mind to the comparative risks and benefits. At the second stage, the court asks if the expert had reached a "defensible conclusion" after balancing the risk and benefits. On the meaning of "defensible conclusion", the two criteria were that (i) the medical opinion had to be internally consistent on its face, and (ii) it should not ignore or controvert known medical facts or advances in medical knowledge.[80] It was held that "the fact that a doctor acknowledges the practice of one group of doctors while stating that he would have opted for a different course does not of itself cause his opinion to become inconsistent".[81]

The *Bolam* and *Bolitho* tests are applied to ascertain the standard of care in diagnosis and treatment but not for the giving of medical advice (to be discussed below). As mentioned, they are applicable where there is "ample scope for genuine differences of opinion" amongst doctors with respect to diagnosis and treatment.[82] In the case of *Armstrong, Carol Ann (executrix of the estate of Peter Traynor, deceased and on behalf of the dependents of Peter Traynor, deceased) v Quest Laboratories Pte Ltd and another and other appeals*,[83] a mole on the patient's back was wrongly diagnosed as non-malignant when it was in fact a malignant melanoma. With respect to the issue of breach, the Court of Appeal noted that as there were no actual differences in opinion amongst the experts and pathologists as to the diagnosis, the *Bolitho* test did not, strictly speaking, apply[84] and that a reasonable and competent pathologist would have diagnosed it as a melanoma.[85]

On *Bolitho* in particular, though the courts have the power to override the expert opinion's conclusion on the ground that it is illogical, this does not occur very often in practice. The

---

78 [1998] AC 232.
79 [2002] 1 SLR(R) 1024; applied in *D'Conceicao Jeanie Doris v Tong Ming Chuan* [2011] SGHC 193 (the cardiothoracic surgeon was *not* negligent in recommending a redo coronary artery bypass graft surgery, in providing information on risks of the surgery as well as alternative options and in performing the surgery).
80 *Khoo James v Gunapathy d/o Muniandy* [2002] 1 SLR(R) 1024 at [65].
81 See *D'Conceicao Jeanie Doris v Tong Ming Chuan* [2011] SGHC 193 at [109], *per* Tay Yong Kwang J; and *Sharpe v Southend Health Authority* (1997) 8 Med LR 299 at 303, *per* Cresswell J.
82 *Hunter v Hanley* 1955 SLT 213, *per* Lord President Clyde.
83 [2020] 1 SLR 133.
84 [2020] 1 SLR 133 at [54].
85 [2020] 1 SLR 133 at [55].

case of *Hucks v Cole*[86] is one exception where *Bolitho* was applied to override the defendant's expert opinion. Sachs LJ opined that:

> When the evidence shows that a lacuna in professional practice exists by which risks of grave danger are knowingly taken, then, however small the risk, the courts must anxiously examine that lacuna – particularly if the risks can be easily and inexpensively avoided. If the court finds, on an analysis of the reasons given for not taking those precautions that, in the light of current professional knowledge, there is no proper basis for the lacuna, and that it is definitely not reasonable that those risks should have been taken, its function is to state that fact and where necessary to state that it constitutes negligence. In such a case the practice will no doubt thereafter be altered to the benefit of patients.

Hence, the *Bolitho* test is applicable to override the views of a responsible body of medical opinion not to admit a patient to the hospital where the risks of injury may be small, but the consequences are grave or fatal for the patient should these risks materialise, and there were available medical facilities in the hospital to deal with the situation.[87] Further, where the patient has a known allergy to a drug administered by the doctor, the latter would be held negligent in not inquiring about the patient's history notwithstanding a difference in medical opinion regarding the need for drug sensitivity tests.[88]

A departure from accepted medical practices can amount to negligence but this is not necessarily the case. Otherwise, the use of novel techniques by doctors some of which may benefit a patient would be automatically denied. At the same time, doctors should not expose patients to excessive risks of a new technique that deviates from accepted practice without any scientific validation of the technique.[89] This issue will be discussed more fully in Chapter 12.

The *Bolam* and *Bolitho* tests are ultimately "heuristics" for the courts to determine the reasonableness or otherwise of the defendant doctor's conduct, as stated by the Court of Appeal in *Hii Chii Kok v Ooi Peng Jin London Lucien*[90] ("*Hii Chii Kok*"). This decision implicitly suggested that courts have the leeway to refer to other factors that are relevant for the assessment of the doctor's standard of care (risks of harm, extent of harm, costs of precautions and so on) in addition to the application of the *Bolam* and *Bolitho* tests in order to make an overall assessment as to whether the doctor was negligent.[91]

A final point to highlight is that the *Bolam* and *Bolitho* tests do not apply to a mere factual inquiry (*eg*, what the slides for screening cervical smears show)[92] as opposed to a question

---

86 [1993] 4 Med LR 393. The doctors were found negligent for failing to treat a patient with penicillin, despite the great risks of puerperal fever which could have been avoided with little difficulty and cost.
87 *Marriott v West Midland HA* [1999] Lloyd's Rep Med 23.
88 *Chin Keow v Government of Malaysia* [1967] 1 WLR 813.
89 *Hepworth v Kerr* [1995] 6 Med LR 139.
90 [2017] 2 SLR 492.
91 See also Kumaralingam (2015).
92 See *Penney v East Kent Health Authority* [2000] PNLR 323.

of standard of care (*ie*, whether the doctor made a diagnosis in accordance with an accepted medical practice or opinion).[93]

3.3.3 Hii Chii Kok: medical advice

Insofar as medical advice is concerned, the *Bolam* and *Bolitho* tests are not applicable. A patient-centric approach is applied to take account of the patient's active role in decision-making concerning his or her own health conditions. The Court of Appeal in *Hii Chii Kok* applied the following three-staged enquiry for medical advice:

1   the nature of information which ought to have been disclosed: (a) information that would be relevant and material to a reasonable patient situated in the particular patient's position; or (b) information that a doctor knew was important to the particular patient in question
2   whether the doctor was in possession of the information
3   to examine the reasons why the doctor chose to withhold the information and enquire whether the doctor was justified in so withholding.

The first enquiry is determined from the patient's perspective by considering the personal circumstances of the patient and what a reasonable person in that position would consider material. The types of information may include the doctor's diagnosis of the condition, prognosis of the condition, nature of the proposed medical treatment, risks associated with medical treatment, the alternatives to the proposed treatment and the attendant risks and benefits.[94] The relevance or materiality of the information to be disclosed is a matter of common sense.[95] Where the information in question concerns risks, what makes the risk sufficiently material will probably depend on the likelihood and severity of harm.[96]

The second enquiry relates to whether there was negligence associated with the diagnosis and treatment which prevented the doctor from obtaining the relevant information. In this regard, the appropriateness of the doctor's conduct in diagnosis and treatment is to be assessed from the doctor's perspective by applying *Bolam* and *Bolitho*.[97]

The third enquiry is to be assessed from the doctor's perspective without reference to *Bolam*.[98] It would be justified for the doctor to withhold the information in the following non-exhaustive scenarios: (a) the patient has waived his or her right to hear the information; (b) emergency situations where there is a serious threat or harm to the patient and the patient is not capable of making a decision; and (c) where the doctor believes that the disclosure of information would cause the patient serious physical or mental harm (therapeutic privilege).

---

[93] In *Noor Azlin bte Abdul Rahman v Changi General Hospital Pte Ltd and others* [2019] 1 SLR 834 at [63]-[64] (referring to *Penney v East Kent Health Authority* [2000] PNLR 323; and *Muller v King's College Hospital NHS Foundation Trust* [2017] 2 WLR 159).
[94] [2017] 2 SLR 492 at [138] citing *Dickson v Pinder* [2010] ABQB 269.
[95] [2017] 2 SLR 492 at [139].
[96] [2017] 2 SLR 492 at [140].
[97] [2017] 2 SLR 492 at [133].
[98] [2017] 2 SLR 492 at [134].

The *Hii Chii Kok* approach is a modified version of *Montgomery v Lanarkshire Health Board*.[99] In *Montgomery*, the obstetrician failed to warn the patient (a pregnant woman of small stature with a history of insulin-dependent diabetes) of the risk of shoulder dystocia and did not offer a caesarian section as an alternative mode of delivery. The mother suffered injury and the baby brain damage. It was held by the UK Supreme Court that the doctor was under a duty to take reasonable care to ensure that the patient was aware of the material risks involved in the procedure. The test of materiality is whether "a reasonable person in the patient's position would be likely to attach significance to the risk, or the doctor is or should reasonably be aware that the particular patient would be likely to attach significance to it". The patient autonomy approach is subject to the doctor's therapeutic privilege to withhold information from the patient if the doctor reasonably considered that disclosure would be seriously detrimental to the patient.

The patient-centric approach to the giving of medical advice is also evident in the SMC's ECEG 2016 (in particular, section C5 on "Patients' right to information and self-determination") which speaks of the patients' entitlement to "accurate and sufficient information to be able to make their own decisions about their medical management", ensuring that they understand the information in order to make "informed choices" and to "understand the consequences of their decisions".

In the aftermath of the *Hii Chii Kok* decision, a Disciplinary Tribunal (DT) decision on informed consent[100] meted out what some felt were harsh sanctions on a doctor who failed to provide information of side effects of a minor procedure. *Hii Chii Kok* and the DT decision have generated some uncertainty and disquiet amongst the doctors. It was reported that in response to the decisions, some doctors have adopted defensive practices, provided voluminous materials, taken a longer time to explain risks and alternatives, focused on giving medical information rather than medical advice and preferred to refer certain patients to specialists instead of dealing with them directly.[101] With regard to the last point, increased costs would likely be borne by the patients.[102] In view of the issues raised, the Workgroup (2019) – which was set up in the wake of the two decisions – recommended a "patient-centric test based on peer professional opinion" as follows[103]:

1   A healthcare professional shall be regarded as having discharged his duty of care in the provision of medical advice to his patient if the medical advice he has provided is supported by a respectable body of medical opinion as competent professional practice in the circumstances ("peer professional opinion").
2   For the purpose of paragraph 1, the respectable body of medical opinion must consider whether the healthcare professional gave to the patient relevant and material information that a patient in those circumstances would reasonably require in order to make

---

99 [2015] 2 WLR 768.
100 *Singapore Medical Council v Dr Lim Lian Arn* [2018] SMCDT 9.
101 See Wong et al. (2020).
102 See Arvind and McMahon (2020) on *Montgomery* and patients' actual needs and empirical realities.
103 Annex E at https://www.moh.gov.sg/docs/librariesprovider5/default-document-library/wg-report.pdf.

informed treatment decision(s), and information that the healthcare professional knows would be relevant and material to the patient.
3   However, peer professional opinion cannot be relied on for the purpose of paragraph 1 if the court determines that the opinion is illogical.
4   The fact that there are differing peer professional opinions by a significant number of respected practitioners in the field concerning a matter does not in itself mean that the peer professional opinion being relied on for the purpose of paragraph 1 should be disregarded as evidence of a respectable body of medical opinion.

In essence, the recommended approach sought to revive the *Bolam* and *Bolitho* tests for medical advice in combination with the test of "material" information reasonably required by a patient. A Parliamentary bill has been introduced seeking to change the standard of care for medical advice by healthcare professionals in line with the Workgroup (2019) recommendations.[104]

> **Box 3.2 – Reflecting on *Hii Chii Kok***
>
> How does the recommended approach in the Workgroup (2019) report on the assessment of a medical doctor's standard of care in the wake of *Hii Chii Kok* and the disciplinary tribunal decision on informed consent compare with the judicial approach? Can the recommended approach overcome or mitigate the problems raised by the medical profession?

3.3.4 Hospital systemic negligence

Systemic negligence is the failure to put in place proper internal controls or measures to manage the patients and their needs. The duty is not to guarantee that patient's needs will be met but to do so with reasonable care and skill given the available resources.[105] In *Noor Azlin bte Abdul Rahman v Changi General Hospital Pte Ltd and others*,[106] the appellant (patient) complained of chest pains and shortness of breath to A&E doctors in October 2007. The X-ray showed opacity in the appellant's chest. The patient was referred to a respiratory specialist physician in November 2007 who called for another set of X-rays and discharged the patient as he erroneously thought the opacity seen on the X-ray had resolved. In 2010, the appellant again went to the A&E department at the hospital. The A&E doctor observed that the presenting symptoms of the appellant on this visit were not related to the opacity and prescribed painkillers for the appellant, discharged her and sent the April 2010 X-ray for reporting. In 2011, the appellant complained to the accident & emergency (A&E) department

---

104 See Civil Law (Amendment) Bill introduced in Parliament on 3 September 2020 at https://sso.agc.gov.sg/Bills-Supp/33-2020/Published/20200903?DocDate=20200903.
105 *Hall v Simons* [2002] 1 AC 615 at 690C, *per* Lord Hoffmann ("The doctor, for example, owes a duty to the individual patient, but he also owes a duty to his other patients which may prevent him from giving one patient the treatment or resources he would ideally prefer").
106 [2019] 1 SLR 834.

of intermittent left lower ribcage pain. The appellant was diagnosed with Stage IIA non-small cell lung cancer in March 2012. The Court of Appeal found that the appellant had lung cancer by July 2011.

The hospital (CGH) was held to be in breach of its duty of care owed to the appellant for failing to have in place a proper system to ensure adequate follow-up of the appellant's case and that this resulted in a delay in diagnosing the appellant with lung cancer. The specific issues flowing from the system were as follows: (i) the X-ray reports were not reviewed by a respiratory physician but by A&E doctors which did not allow for a "comprehensive management of a patient";[107] (ii) the two A&E doctors could review the radiological reports and advise against the radiologist's recommendation for follow-up without recording their reasons; (iii) the patient was seen by only one respiratory specialist over a period of four years; and (iv) notwithstanding the error of the respiratory physician, the system did not alert the other doctors involved in her case and who subsequently saw the chest X-rays to this mistake.[108]

A distinction must be made between the hospital's systemic negligence and a doctor's personal liability. In this case, the respiratory specialist was eventually adjudged not liable in the tort of negligence for the appellant's lung cancer. Though he breached his duty of care in discharging the appellant in 2007 when he was not certain that the suspected infection had completely resolved, it was found that the appellant did not suffer from lung cancer in November 2007 but only in 2011.

3.3.5 Emergency services and situations

The Singapore Court of Appeal in *Noor Azlin*[109] stated that the standard of care of A&E doctors must take account of the working conditions such as the "high volume of patients" involving trauma and life-threatening conditions, the "highly pressurised environment" and "time constraints" the doctors are subject to. As it would be "unreasonable to expect A&E doctors to review cases in as much breadth, depth or specificity as a GP or specialist in an outpatient clinic", Andrew Phang JA opined that an A&E doctor must necessarily adopt a "targeted approach" by prioritising the "diagnosis and treatment of the patient's presenting symptoms and elimination of life-threatening conditions".[110] Furthermore, the A&E doctor who works in shifts and rotations will not normally be expected to follow through on the particular patient.[111]

With respect to receptionists working in an A&E department, in the UK case of *Darnley v Croydon Health Services NHS Trust*[112] discussed in the section on Duty of Care above, it was stated that the expected standard of care is that of an "averagely and well-informed person performing the function of a receptionist at a department providing emergency medical care". On the facts, the information communicated by the reception to the appellant that he

---

107 [2019] 1 SLR 834 at [99].
108 [2019] 1 SLR 834 at [101].
109 [2019] 1 SLR 834 at [68].
110 [2019] 1 SLR 834 at [69].
111 [2019] 1 SLR 834 at [70].
112 [2018] 3 WLR 1153.

68 *Medical negligence (part 1)*

was to wait for up to four or five hours to see a doctor was incomplete and misleading as to the availability of medical assistance. According to standard procedures at the A&E department in the UK, a person complaining of head injury would be informed that he would be seen by a triage nurse within half an hour.[113] It was reasonably foreseeable, according to the court, that the appellant upon receiving the misleading information would decide to leave the hospital without receiving treatment, which led to his damage.

The MOH Standards for Emergency Ambulance Service (2017)[114] stipulate minimum requirements for the providers of emergency ambulance services. They include but are not limited to the engagement of a clinical director to supervise and advise on the patient care, ensuring training, competency and certification of the emergency ambulance service crew, developing written ambulance care protocols for patients transported and ensuring measures and protocols for infection control.[115] Fulfilling these requirements does not automatically absolve the emergency ambulance service provider from negligence liability but these standards are likely to be relevant for assessing the expected standard of care in a negligence lawsuit.

3.3.6 Joint duty and team-based healthcare

A doctor may be under a duty to give medical advice to a patient jointly with another doctor.[116] In such a case, each doctor may have to take steps to provide the relevant explanation to the patient in accordance with his or her field of expertise.[117]

The High Court case of *Goh Guan Sin (by her litigation representative Chiam Yu Zhu v Yeo Tseng Tsai and National University Hospital (Singapore) Pte Ltd*[118] concerned team-based care with one consultant having overall responsibility over the patient together with a team of doctors. Tan J accepted that it was "reasonable for other members of the operating surgeon's team to explain the risks of the proposed treatment and to obtain the patient's consent on the operating surgeon's behalf".[119] The learned judge noted,[120] by reference to the SMC Ethical Code and Ethical Guidelines (SMC ECEG) (2016) and the SMC ECEG (2002),[121] that

---

113 [2018] 3 WLR 1153 at [25].
114 Updated 21 November 2018 at https://www.moh.gov.sg/docs/librariesprovider5/default-document-library/emergencyambulancestandards.pdf.
115 Para 2.2.
116 *Tong Seok May Joanne v Yau Hok Man Gordon*. [2013] 2 SLR 18 (anaesthetist may, together with the primary treating physician, be jointly responsible to the patient in the giving of advice).
117 *Tong Seok May Joanne v Yau Hok Man Gordon* [2013] 2 SLR 18 at [75].
118 [2019] SGHC 274.
119 [2019] SGHC 274 at [50] and [87].
120 [2019] SGHC 274 at [51].
121 See paragraph 4.1.1.4

A doctor may delegate another doctor, nurse, medical student or other healthcare worker to provide treatment or care on his behalf, but this person must be competent to carry out the care or procedure required. A doctor retains responsibility for the overall management of the patient when he delegates care. If the person delegated to is not duly registered as a practitioner, this must be in the

Medical negligence (part 1) 69

the practice of team-based care has been endorsed by the medical profession. The SMC ECEG 2016, in particular, stipulate the follow guidelines on delegation of care and consent-taking:

> If you delegate another person to provide some aspect of care to your patients, you retain overall responsibility for your patients and you must take reasonable care to ensure that the other person is capable of providing care to the required quality and standards.[122]
>
> You must either take consent personally or if it is taken for you by a team member, you must, through education, training and supervision of team members, ensure the quality of the consent taken on your behalf. In any case, you must ensure adequate documentation of the consent taking process where this involves more complex or invasive modalities with higher risks.[123]

3.4 Res ipsa loquitur

It is quite possible that the plaintiff will at times encounter difficulties in adducing direct evidence of the defendant's negligent act or omission (*eg*, where there were no eye witnesses to the incident). In such circumstances, the plaintiff may wish to rely on the doctrine of *res ipsa loquitur* ("the thing speaks for itself") to persuade the court that the defendant was indeed negligent and that the negligence resulted in the incident leading to his injury. The doctrine requires three criteria[124] to be fulfilled:

(a) the defendant must have been in control of the situation or thing which resulted in the accident;
(b) the accident would not have happened, in the ordinary course of things, if proper care had been taken[125]; and
(c) the cause of the accident must be unknown.[126]

Once all the criteria are satisfied, an inference of negligence on the part of the defendant arises. The *legal* burden of proving a *prima facie* case in negligence (*ie*, establishing a duty of care, a breach of that duty and the resultant harm caused) lies with the plaintiff throughout the legal proceedings. The doctrine of *res ipsa loquitur* operates to shift the *evidential* burden to the defendant to rebut the inference.[127] It is insufficient to "merely show that the accident was due to a neutral event" in order to rebut the inference. Instead, the defendant must "show either that (a) this neutral event does not connote negligence on its part (*ie*, the

---

context of a legitimate training programme and the doctor must exercise effective supervision over this person.
122 A4(1).
123 C6(8).
124 *Scott v The London and St Katherine Docks Co* (1865) 3 H & C 596; 159 ER 665, *per* Erle CJ; *Tesa Tape Asia Pacific Pte Ltd v Wing Seng Logistics Pte Ltd* [2006] 3 SLR(R) 116 at [21].
125 *Teng Ah Kow v Ho Sek Chiu* [1993] 3 SLR(R) 43 at [23].
126 *Loh Siew Keng v Seng Huat Construction Pte Ltd* [1998] SGHC 197 at [240].
127 *Teng Ah Kow v Ho Sek Chiu* [1993] 3 SLR(R) 43 (res ipsa loquitur merely a rule of evidence).

70 Medical negligence (part 1)

event was a non-negligent cause of the accident); or (b) it had exercised all reasonable care in relation to that event".[128]

The applicability of *res ipsa loquitur* is limited to specific circumstances. The rule does not apply to prove negligence on the part of doctors arising from the birth of still-born babies or babies who die soon after birth or are born damaged or deformed. Lai Kew Chai J in *F v Chan Tanny*,[129] added that "in the field of professional negligence, there is no liability without proof of fault" which appears to suggest that the *res ipsa loquitur* rule should not apply in all cases of professional negligence, not only medical negligence.[130] However, in *Tong Seok May Joanne v Yau Hok Man Gordon*,[131] a medical negligence case, the High Court did not automatically exclude the application of *res ipsa loquitur*.

Where there are other probable causes apart from the defendant's act or omission for the plaintiff's damage, the principle of *res ipsa loquitur* does not assist the plaintiff.[132] It was held in *Rathanamalah d/o Shunmugam v Chia Kok Hoong*[133] that *res ipsa loquitur* did not apply where the damage suffered by the patient was due to the inherent risks of surgical procedures. Moreover, it was not a case where the accident was unknown as there was "extensive expert evidence on both sides" on the issue of negligence.[134] The High Court also cited *Ratcliffe v Plymouth and Torbay Health Authority* as follows[135]:

> Medical negligence cases are unlikely to give rise to the stark problems encountered in road traffic accident cases where there may be a total dearth of evidence or where one or other side may choose, no doubt for tactical reasons, not to present evidence ... Where expert and factual evidence has been called on both sides at a trial [the] usefulness [of the principle] will normally have long since been exhausted.

Notwithstanding the above, exceptional instances where *res ipsa loquitur* applied to medical negligence include the following: (a) a patient with two stiff fingers ends up after hospital treatment with four stiff fingers,[136] (b) swabs or surgical instruments were left inside a patient after an operation,[137] and (c) a patient wakes up in the course of surgical operation despite general anaesthetic.[138]

---

128 *Grace Electrical Engineering Pte Ltd v Te Deum Engineering Pte Ltd* [2018] 1 SLR 76 at [66].
129 [2003] 4 SLR(R) 231 at [116].
130 *F v Chan Tanny* [2003] 4 SLR(R) 231 at [116].
131 [2013] 2 SLR 18 at [220]-[223].
132 *Denis Matthew Harte v Dr Tan Hun Hoe* [2000] SGHC 248 at [246].
133 [2018] 4 SLR 159 at [113]. See also *Thomas v Curley* [2013] 131 BMLR 111 at [25] (that injury suffered was a recognised non-negligent risk of procedure).
134 [2018] 4 SLR 159 at [109].
135 [1998] PIQR P170 at P189, *per* Hobhouse LJ.
136 *Cassidy v Ministry of Health* [1951] 2 KB 343.
137 *Mahon v Osborne* [1939] 2 KB 14 at 50, *per* Goddard LJ.
138 *Ratcliffe v Plymouth and Torbay HA* [1998] PIQR P170 at P184, *per* Brooke LJ.

3.5 Conclusion

Sound knowledge of medical negligence is crucial for understanding a patient's legal rights in myriad circumstances when doctors or hospitals may have committed errors through careless conduct thereby causing injuries suffered by the patient. Though a duty to take reasonable care with respect to the patient's health condition is generally owed by the doctor, hospital or healthcare professionals to a patient under their direct care unless specified otherwise, it is less clear in other cases involving omissions to passers-by, emergency rescue, the engagement of a doctor's services by third parties, and when the doctor is engaged as an expert witness in litigation. The overall standard of care expected of a doctor and healthcare professional is the objective reasonable person test based on factors such as the risks and extent of harm and level of precautions undertaken. Where there are genuine differences of opinion as to the proper standard for medical diagnosis and treatment, the general judicial approach is to give deference to the opinion of a responsible body of the medical profession provided that opinion is logical and its conclusion defensible. On the other hand, in the giving of medical advice, the caselaw requires that the doctor provides information assessed as "material" from the perspective of a reasonable patient in the particular patient's shoes so that the patient can make an informed decision on his own health. This issue will likely be debated in Parliament. The doctrine of *res ipsa loquitur* aids the aggrieved patient in persuading the court that the doctor, hospital or healthcare professional was indeed responsible for his injuries should the cause of the incident leading to injury be unknown, and the defendant's control over the situation in question is such that, in the ordinary course of events, the incident would not have occurred if the defendant had taken proper care.

References

Arvind, T.T. & McMahon, A.M. (2020). "Responsiveness and the Role of Rights in Medical Law: Lessons from Montgomery" *Medical Law Review* 1-33 at https://academic-oup-com.libproxy.smu.edu.sg/medlaw/advance-article/doi/10.1093/medlaw/fwaa006/5809184

Chan, K.Y.G. (2016). Chapters 3 to 5 on Duty of Care in Chan G.K.Y and Lee P.W. (eds) *The Law of Torts in Singapore* (Academy Publishing: Singapore), pp. 77-225.

Fordham, M. (2014). "Psychiatric Injury, Secondary Victims and the 'Sudden Shock' Requirement" *Sing JLS* 4.

Havers, P.Q.C. & Elliot, J. (2017). "Breach of Duty", chapter 4 in Judith, L. and Jean, M. (eds) *Principles of Medical Law* (Oxford University Press: Oxford), pp. 101-162.

Kumaralingam, A. (2015). "Medical Negligence and Patient Autonomy: Bolam Rules in Singapore and Malaysia – Revisited" 27 *SAcLJ* 666.

Lunney, M. & Oliphant, K. (2008). *Tort Law: Text and Materials*, 3rd Ed (Oxford University Press: Oxford).

Mulheron, R. (2017). "Duties in Contract and Tort", chapter 3 in Judith, L. & Jean, M. (eds) *Principles of Medical Law* (Oxford University Press: Oxford), pp. 163-235.

Tan, S.Y. (2006). *Medical Malpractice: Understanding the Law, Managing the Risk* (World Scientific Publishing: Singapore).

Wong, C. Y., Surajkumar, S., Lee, Y.V. and Tan, T. L. (2020). "A Descriptive Study of the Effect of a Disciplinary Proceeding Decision on Medical Practitioners' Practice Behaviour in the Context of Providing a Hydrocortisone and Ligonocaine Injection" 61(8) *Singapore Medical Journal* 413-418.

Workgroup To Review The Taking of Informed Consent and SMC Disciplinary Process (2019). Report (Nov) at https://www.moh.gov.sg/news-highlights/details/workgroup-proposes-wide-ranging-reforms-on-the-taking-of-informed-consent-and-singapore-medical-council-s-disciplinary-process/

4 Medical negligence (part 2)

4.1 Introduction

This chapter is a continuation from the previous chapter outlining medical negligence and the legal requirements of establishing a legal duty of care owed by doctors, hospitals and healthcare professionals, their standard of care and the doctrine of *res ipsa loquitur*. This chapter covers the remaining requirements of causation and remoteness of damage which are part of the proof of damage suffered by the plaintiff under the tort of negligence. Even if the requirements of duty of care, breach, causation and remoteness of damage are proved by the plaintiff, the defendant may nevertheless raise certain legal defences to defeat the plaintiff's claim or reduce the damages payable (Chan 2016; Goldberg 2017). We will briefly examine the criteria for the legal defences and the remedies available to the plaintiff.

This is followed by a consideration of the circumstances in which a hospital or clinic may be liable for the acts of third parties (under the doctrines of vicarious liability and non-delegable duties) as well as some procedural matters on the litigation process.

4.2 Causation of damage[1]

The requirement of causation in damage refers to the linkage between the specific breach of duty and the damage suffered. It is sufficient if the plaintiff proves on a balance of probabilities that the defendant's breach (more likely than not) caused the damage suffered by the plaintiff. There are two concepts in causation: cause in fact and in law. A breach of duty by the doctor *per se* does not mean that the patient can recover damages. As a general principle, if causation of damage is not established, the patient will be left without a remedy in the tort of negligence. Put in another way, the doctor is not legally responsible for damage which he did not cause. There are, however, exceptions to this general rule which we will discuss below.

4.2.1 Factual causation

This relies essentially on the "but for" test and alternatively, the proof of material contribution to damage. The burden of proof in respect of "but for" causation is on the plaintiff

---

1 See Tong (2004).

alleging negligence liability[2] and this is to be discharged on a balance of probabilities. The test enquires whether, but for the defendant's breach of duty, the damage would not have been suffered by the plaintiff. If the answer is in the affirmative, the "but for" test is satisfied. For example, in the *Noor Azlin* case (in Chapter 3), the hospital's breach in failing to put in place a proper system led to the lung cancer and complications. A referral to a respiratory physician would have been made if there had been a proper system to ensure the appropriate follow-up. It was also stated in the case that but for the delay in diagnosis, the progression of the lung cancer from Stage I to Stage IIA, the growth of the nodule and nodal metastasis (*ie*, spread to the lymph node) would not have occurred.

In another case, a wrong diagnosis by a medical doctor deprived the patient of an opportunity to obtain proper treatment. It must be shown on a balance of probabilities that if the medical doctor had correctly diagnosed the symptoms, the patient would have sought treatment and that the treatment would have cured the patient's illness or prevented the damage or even death.[3] The same case also made important clarifications about the use of statistical evidence in medical negligence claims. When courts decide on whether the defendant's breach had caused the damage on a balance of probabilities, it is based on the "degree of overall strength and credibility attributed by the decision-maker" to the fact probability evidence (which may involve a statistical study).[4] The assessment of causation is not based merely on statistical evidence but may involve the "credibility of the study, its authors, and the reliability of the study". The mere fact that there is a 55% statistical chance, for example, that the pleaded damage was caused by the defendant's conduct does not necessarily mean that the test of causation is satisfied.[5]

The following are examples of medical negligence cases where the "but for" test was not satisfied. Notwithstanding a finding of negligence on the doctor's part, there was ultimately no legal liability in the tort of negligence. In the English case of *Barnett v Chelsea and Kensington Hospital Management Committee*,[6] even if the doctor had examined and treated the plaintiff who was vomiting at the relevant time, the patient would still have died of arsenic poisoning. Moving on to Singapore cases, in *Vasuhi d/o Ramasamypillai v Tan Tock Seng Hospital Pte Ltd*,[7] as the patient had died before the date on which the hospital was expected to arrange for the angiogram, the delay by the hospital did not cause the death. In *Tong Seok May Joanne v Yau Hok Man Gordon*,[8] there was no evidence that the patient would have chosen regional anaesthesia instead of general anaesthesia if she had been informed by the

---

2 *Sunny Metal & Engineering Pte Ltd v Ng Khim Ming Eric* [2007] 3 SLR(R) 782 at [76].
3 *Armstrong, Carol Ann (executrix of the estate of Peter Traynor, deceased and on behalf of the dependents of Peter Traynor, deceased) v Quest Laboratories Pte Ltd and another and other appeals* [2020] 1 SLR 133 at [163], [172] and [190].
4 [2020] 1 SLR 133 at [97]: this term "fact probability" refers to the "piece of probabilistic evidence that speaks to the existence (or non-existence) of a causal connection between the defendant's actions (or omissions) and the pleaded damage".
5 [2020] 1 SLR 133 at [99].
6 [1969] 1 QB 428.
7 [2001] 1 SLR(R) 303 at [52].
8 [2013] 2 SLR 18 at [170].

doctor of the alternatives. She left it to the anaesthetist to make the decision on the type of anaesthesia.

The next case – *Yeo Peng Hock Henry v Pai Lily*[9] – requires more elaboration. The plaintiff complained to a general medical practitioner about fever, cough, cold as well as blurred vision and spots on her left eye. The defendant doctor suspected the plaintiff of having a detached retina and urinary tract infection but did not advise the plaintiff to consult an eye specialist or to go to a hospital immediately. The plaintiff alleged that the doctor was negligent in not advising her to see an eye specialist or go to the hospital immediately, and that as a result, she had lost the chance of an earlier diagnosis by a specialist which would have prevented her from losing her sight. Though the doctor was negligent, the claim failed on causation.

It turned out that the plaintiff did not suffer from a detached retina. The loss of vision was due to a rare infection from klebsiella bacteria that grew at an exponential rate. Whether the plaintiff's eye could have been saved was subject to three variables, namely (a) the correct diagnosis by the doctor at the hospital at the material time, (b) the appropriate treatment administered, and (c) the eye's response to the treatment. In the absence of conclusive evidence, the court concluded that the plaintiff had not proved, on a balance of probabilities, that had the defendant advised her to go to a hospital immediately and had she done as advised, the plaintiff's eye would have been saved.

The issue of the recovery of damages arising from a medical practitioner's failure to warn the patient of the risks of surgery is more contentious. In *Chester v Afshar*,[10] the medical practitioner was held liable for the negligent omission to warn the plaintiff of the risks, even though the plaintiff could not prove that the doctor's failure to warn resulted in the plaintiff proceeding with and suffering the risks of the surgery. The majority judges[11] decided based on the patient's informed consent and right of autonomy and dignity. On the other hand, the Singapore courts were not prepared to make such an exception on causation. The concept of autonomy in *Chester* based on the UK Human Rights Act did not extend to Singapore.[12] In *Tong Seok May Joanne v Yau Hok Man Gordon*,[13] Andrew Ang J stated that the rule in *Chester* should not be used to vindicate the plaintiff's right of autonomy when there has been no provable damage caused.

As an alternative to the "but for" test, the plaintiff may show that the defendant's breach was a material (*ie*, not *de minimis*) contribution to the plaintiff's damage.[14] The defendant's breach is not required to be the sole or even substantial cause of damage. For example, if the severity or extent of the disease suffered by the plaintiff was in proportion to the extent of exposure to toxic dust due to the defendant's breach, and the amount of exposure was not negligible, we can say that the defendant's breach materially contributed to the plaintiff's

---

9 [2001] 3 SLR(R) 555.
10 [2005] 1 AC 134.
11 Lord Steyn, Lord Hope and Lord Walker.
12 *D'Conceicao Jeanie Doris v Tong Ming Chuan* [2011] SGHC 193 at [199].
13 [2013] 2 SLR 18 at [172].
14 *Bailey v Ministry of Defence* [2009] 1 WLR 1052; *Bonnington Castings Ltd v Wardlaw* [1956] AC 613.

damage.[15] In *Bailey v Ministry of Defence*,[16] the first defendant's negligence materially contributed to the weakness of the plaintiff's physical condition which led to her cardiac arrest and hypoxic brain damage. The English court therefore ruled that the first defendant was liable for causing the claimant's brain damage.

Causation could not, however, be proved in the next case of *Wilsher v Essex Area Health Authority*.[17] A premature infant was negligently administered excess oxygen by the doctors that could possibly lead to retrolental fibroplasia ("RLF") causing blindness. There were five possible causes for the RLF and the claimants could not prove on a balance of probabilities that the excess oxygen was the cause whether based on the "but for" test or material contribution to damage. It was also not shown that the excess oxygen would have probably increased the risk of any of the other four possible causes leading to RLF. The doctors were thus not liable.[18]

Apart from material contribution to damage, a less common test is for the plaintiff to show that the defendant's breach materially contributed to the *risk* of damage suffered by the plaintiff.[19] This may be applied in cases where there is some scientific uncertainty as to the alleged causal link between the specific breach and actual damage. In the English cases concerning employees' exposure to toxic dust in *McGhee v National Coal Board*[20] (McGhee) or asbestos (in *Fairchild v Glenhaven Funeral Services Ltd*[21] ("*Fairchild*") and *Barker v Corus (UK) Ltd*[22] ("*Barker*"), the courts allowed the employees compensation for damage from the employers' breach in exposing them to the dust or asbestos. It was clear that exposure to the toxic dust or asbestos would result in the specific diseases (dermatitis and mesothelioma, respectively) suffered by the employees. However, the state of scientific knowledge rendered it impossible to ascertain whether the dust or asbestos that caused the respective diseases had in fact emanated from a specific employer's breach. In the *Fairchild* and *Barker* cases, science could not tell the courts which fibre or strand of the asbestos from the various employers' breaches is in fact *the* cause of the mesothelioma. Hence, insofar as the specific employer's breach is concerned, it could only be said that on a balance of probabilities, it contributed in a non-negligible way to the *risk* of the employee contracting the disease. Notwithstanding that causation of *damage* was *not* in fact established, the English courts allowed recovery of damages as an *exception* to the general rule of causation.

---

15 *Bonnington Castings Ltd v Wardlaw* [1956] AC 613 (joint and several liability of employers). Cf *Holtby v Brigham & Cowan (Hull) Ltd* [2000] 3 All ER 421 (proportionate liability of employers).
16 [2009] 1 WLR 1052.
17 [1988] AC 1074. Applied in *Chew Swee Hiang v Attorney-General* [1990] 2 SLR(R) 215 at [37].
18 *Wilsher* was applied in the District Court decision in *Mohammad Shah Jahan Bhanu v Shimizu Corp* [2013] SGDC 152; and *Chew Swee Hiang v Attorney General and another* [1990] 2 SLR(R) 215 at [37] (surgery by doctor was not a cause of damage to the patient's voice cord due to a number of different factors such as viral infections and post-operative scarring).
19 See Kumaralingam (2007).
20 [1973] 1 WLR 1.
21 [2003] 1 AC 32.
22 [2006] 2 AC 572.

The Singapore High Court in *Surender Singh s/o Jagdish Singh v Li Man Kay*[23] applied *McGhee*[24] to a medical negligence case. The learned judge ruled that the hospital was negligent in failing to monitor the patient after the operation. The issue was whether the hospital's failure to monitor had caused the patient's death from haemorrhage post operation. The haemorrhage occurred due to the slippage of certain clips which were supposed to secure the left renal artery of the patient. However, there was insufficient evidence concerning how the clips had slipped off. Nevertheless, relying on *McGhee*, Lai Siu Chiu J held that, as the hospital's breach of duty increased the *risk* of complications arising from the surgery which culminated in the death, causation was established.[25]

4.2.2 Legal causation

In addition to factual causation, the plaintiff has the burden to show that the defendant's negligence is a cause in law (sometimes referred to as "proximate" or "effective" cause) of the plaintiff's damage. One relevant legal concept is that of *novus actus interveniens* (*ie*, a new intervening act that takes place between the defendant's negligent conduct and the damage). If there is a *novus actus interveniens* which breaks the chain of causation, the defendant's breach would not be regarded as a cause of the plaintiff's damage. The chain of causation is not normally broken unless the intervening act was "wholly unreasonable",[26] a "wholly independent cause" or was reckless or deliberate.[27] In medical negligence cases, the intervening act that is capable of breaking the chain of causation has been described as "grossly negligent" and a "completely inappropriate response" to the injury[28] or was "egregious".[29] If the chain of causation is not broken, however, the defendant remains liable for the injury caused.

The intervening act may be due to the plaintiff, a third party or a natural event. As a preliminary point, we should not take account of the defendant's *own* intervening act. That is, the defendant should not be able to rely on his own subsequent negligence to break the chain of causation that began from his initial negligent conduct in order to absolve himself from liability.[30]

Assuming that the initial negligent act was committed by a defendant (*eg*, employer) and the alleged intervening act is that of a doctor towards his patient, the extent of the doctor's

---

23 [2010] 1 SLR 428.
24 *McGhee v National Coal Board* [1973] 1 WLR 1.
25 *Surender Singh s/o Jagdish Singh v Li Man Kay* [2010] 1 SLR 428 at [240] and [243]–[245].
26 *TV Media Pte Ltd v De Cruz Andrea Heidi* [2004] 3 SLR(R) 543 at [76] (plaintiff's omission to seek medical aid when she experienced certain physical symptoms upon taking pills sold by the sole distributor).
27 *PlanAssure PAC v Gaelic Inns Pte Ltd* [2007] 4 SLR(R) 513 at [100].
28 *Webb v Barclay Bank plc and Portsmouth Hospitals* [2002] PIQR P8.
29 *Wright v Cambridge Medical Group* [2013] QB 312.
30 *Bolitho v City and Hackney Health Authority* [1998] AC 232 at 240, *per* Lord Browne-Wilkinson (doctor's failure to administer intubation amounting to a breach would not have broken the chain of causation arising from the initial negligence).

Medical negligence (part 2)

conduct would be relevant in determining whether it would relieve the original defendant from liability. In *Webb v Barclays Bank plc and Portsmouth Hospitals NHS Trust*,[31] the doctor's conduct in advising amputation was negligent but not so grossly negligent as to break chain of causation flowing from the negligence of the defendant employer who caused the plaintiff to trip and fall. Hence, the employer remained liable for the injury. A different outcome was reached in *Hogan v Bentinck West Hartley Collieries (Owners) Ltd*.[32] The plaintiff suffered injury to his superfluous thumb (a congenital defect) in an accident negligently caused by defendants and consulted a doctor who negligently amputated the superfluous thumb as well as the normal bone of the thumb at a particular joint. The operation by the doctor was regarded as a *novus actus interveniens* that broke the chain of causation arising from the defendant's negligence. Though the extent of the doctor's negligence was not explicit from the holding, it could be explained on the basis that the doctor's act in amputating the normal bone constitutes a wholly independent act from the original negligence.

Assume an alternative scenario where the doctor had been negligent in treating a patient which resulted in a physical injury. Can the patient's subsequent conduct break the chain of causation so as to absolve the doctor's liability? For example, the patient was unreasonable in refusing to accept aid or support to deal with his initial injury or weakened state caused by the defendant such that an additional injury resulted,[33] or was unreasonable in deciding to have intercourse though she knew that she was fertile after the defendant's negligently performed sterilisation operation.[34] In contrast, it would not be unreasonable for a patient to decide not to abort a child subsequent to a negligent operation by the defendant to sterilise the claimant as in *Emeh v Kensington and Chelsea and Westminster Area Health Authority*.[35]

Relatedly, how is causal responsibility assessed in terms of damages where the doctor's negligence caused an injury but a natural and unrelated event occurred subsequently which wiped out the physical effects of the initial injury? Assume that the initial injury resulted in the patient's loss of future earnings or earning capacity. Would the doctor remain liable for such damages for future losses? According to the English decision in *Jobling v Associated Dairies Ltd*[36] ("*Jobling*") albeit not a medical negligence case, the answer would appear to be "No". The principle is that the defendant's liability would cease at the point in time when the natural supervening condition manifested itself. In *Jobling*, the plaintiff suffered an injury caused by the defendant and his earning capacity was

---

31 [2001] EWCA Civ 1141 at [56]-[57] (also, the employer's original negligence had "increased the vulnerability of the claimant and reduced the mobility of the claimant over and above the effect of the amputation"). See also *Thomson v Toorenburgh* (1973) BCJ No 821 at [7] (hospital "failed to provide an actus interveniens that would have saved her life, but that is not the same as committing an actus interveniens that caused [plaintiff's] death").
32 [1948] 1 All ER 129.
33 *McKew v Holland & Hannen & Cubitts (Scotland) Ltd* [1969] 3 All ER 1621.
34 *Sabri-Tabrizi v Lothian Health Board* (1998) 43 BMLR 190 at 195 (Scottish Court of Session, Outer House).
35 [1985] QB 1012.
36 [1982] AC 794. The Singapore Court of Appeal in *Salcon Ltd v United Cement Pte Ltd* [2004] 4 SLR(R) 353 was inclined to the *Jobling* approach.

reduced by 50%. Subsequently, he developed an unrelated condition known as spondylotic myelopathy (disease of the spine) and was rendered totally unfit for work. Treating this supervening event as one that would have occurred naturally as part of the "vicissitudes of life",[37] the House of Lords limited the damages recoverable from the defendant up to the point of the supervening event.

4.3 Remoteness of damage and egg-shell skull rule

The next legal requirement to be proved by the plaintiff in medical negligence is the remoteness of damage (*ie*, whether the type of injury suffered by the plaintiff was reasonably foreseeable). The loss is not too remote where the *type* of damage which actually occurred was reasonably foreseeable, notwithstanding that the precise extent of the damage[38] or the manner in which the damage arose[39] was not foreseeable.[40] Thus, a mother whose new-born baby had died due to the obstetrician's negligence was entitled to recover the costs of a future pregnancy as she had intended to have more children and the financial loss which the mother would suffer in replacing the dead baby was not too remote.[41]

If the type of damage were not reasonably foreseeable by the defendant, the plaintiff cannot recover monetary damages.[42] For example, the costs of fertility treatment incurred by the parents of two children who had died in a car accident due to the defendant's negligence, with the hope of having another child, were held "not reasonably foreseeable".[43] Hence, the damages claim was denied.

In addition to the remoteness of damage, the courts also apply the egg-shell skull rule[44] in cases where the plaintiff suffered from an inherent susceptibility to health risks which

---

37 *Jobling v Associated Dairies Ltd* [1982] AC 794 at 804, per Lord Wilberforce; at 809, per Lord Edmund-Davies; at 815, per Lord Keith.
38 *Overseas Tankship (UK) Ltd v Morts Dock & Engineering Co Ltd (The Wagon Mound)* ("Wagon Mound (No 1)") [1961] AC 388.
39 *Hughes v Lord Advocate* [1963] AC 837; *Wizniewski v Central Manchester Health Authority* [1998] PIQR P324 at P345 (foreseeable that defendants' negligence would lead to plaintiff being born with hypoxia though the defendants could not have foreseen that the plaintiff's hypoxia in fact resulted from strangulation of umbilical cord of plaintiff's neck).
40 See *R v Croydon HA* [1997] PIQR P444 (reasonably foreseeable that the radiologist's failure to diagnose a potentially fatal condition (Primary Pulmonary Hypertension or PPH) in a married woman of the plaintiff's age would result in the plaintiff's pregnancy and the injuries suffered during pregnancy; evidence showed that the plaintiff would not have become pregnant if she had been told that she was suffering from PPH).
41 *Kralj and Another v McGrath and Another* [1986] 1 All ER 54.
42 *Overseas Tankship (UK) Ltd v Morts Dock & Engineering Co Ltd (The Wagon Mound (No 1)* [1961] AC 388 (not a medical negligence case).
43 *Man Mohan Singh s/o Jothirambal Singh v Zurich Insurance (Singapore) Pte Ltd* [2008] 3 SLR(R) 735 at [55]; *Roe v Minister of Health* [1954] 2 QB 66 (defendant could not reasonably foresee the cracks in the sealed glass ampoules that stored the nupercaine, a spinal anaesthetic, in phenol solution, that led to the phenol causing the patient's paralysis).
44 See *Love v Port of London Authority* [1959] 2 Lloyd's Rep 541 (pre-existing heart condition).

resulted in the damage. The rule recognises that the defendant has to take the victim (plaintiff) as he finds him with the latter's inherent susceptibilities.[45] In *Robinson v Post Office*,[46] the plaintiff was injured due to his employer's negligence. He consulted a doctor and was given an anti-tetanus injection and suffered an allergic reaction to the anti-tetanus injection which led to the increased damage (encephalitis) resulting in brain damage and partial disability. The employer was adjudged liable for the damage and disability as it was reasonably foreseeable that the plaintiff would require medical treatment (including the injection) arising from the employer's negligence. Furthermore, the employer had to take the plaintiff as he found him with his allergy and the risks of adverse reaction to the injection.

The egg-shell-skull rule also applies to psychiatric harm. If it was reasonably foreseeable that the plaintiff would suffer psychiatric harm due to the defendant's negligence, the plaintiff would be able to recover for the psychiatric harm suffered regardless of the extent.[47] In *Brice v Brown*,[48] the psychiatric harm ensued due to the plaintiff's pre-existing personality disorder since childhood though she led a normal life with her husband and family albeit with occasional bouts of depression. After the defendant's negligence in driving that resulted in serious injuries to the plaintiff's daughter, the plaintiff was prone to violent displays of temper, attempts at suicide and had to be admitted to hospital. Her mental condition became abnormal requiring constant supervision. In other cases, psychiatric harm suffered by a plaintiff may have flowed from a combination of pre-existing physical and mental conditions of the plaintiff.[49]

Box 4.1 - Is the egg-shell skull rule fair?

Do you think it is fair to make the doctor compensate the patient for additional injuries even if the doctor may not be aware of the patient's inherent weaknesses or susceptibilities to those additional injuries?

---

45 *Smith v Leech Brain & Co Ltd* [1962] 2 QB 405.
46 [1974] 1 WLR 1176.
47 *Brice v Brown* [1984] 1 All ER 997.
48 [1984] 1 All ER 997. See also *Stephenson v Waite Tileman Ltd* [1973] 1 NZLR 153 (vulnerability to neurosis).
49 See *Shorey v PT Ltd* (2003) 77 ALJR 1104 at [41]-[45], *per* Kirby J (appellant suffered physical injuries as a result of the respondent's negligence. The appellant's pre-accident condition - her back disability and her husband's death - rendered her particularly susceptible to developing the bizarre symptoms inherent in a conversion disorder, a persistent psychologically disturbed condition. Kirby J also stated that the "disproportion between cause and effect" did not render the damage unforeseeable and the negligent defendant must take its victim as it finds her); *Simmons v British Steel plc* [2004] UKHL 20 (psychiatric illness resulting from the exacerbation of a physical condition contributed to by anger concerning a past accident).

80 *Medical negligence (part 2)*

4.4 Scope of duty

Assume a doctor negligently failed to diagnose that the patient had a weak knee. If the patient suffered an injury when he went mountaineering which was not related to the weak knee, should the doctor be liable for the injury? The general legal position is that the doctor is not liable as the injury fell outside the scope of the doctor's duty.[50]

This scope of duty test was applied in the English decision of *Khan v MNX*.[51] The respondent (MNX) sought advice on whether she was a carrier of the haemophilia gene. The doctor (appellant) provided negligent advice that she was not a carrier. The respondent gave birth to a child (FGN) with both haemophilia and autism. The English Court of Appeal held that the appellant was liable to compensate for the additional costs associated with the condition of haemophilia. However, the additional costs associated with autism were not recoverable. The Court of Appeal explained as follows[52]:

> The scope of the appellant's duty was not to protect the respondent from all the risks associated with becoming pregnant and continuing with the pregnancy. The appellant had no duty to prevent the birth of FGN, this was a decision that could only be made by the respondent taking into account matters such as her ethical views on abortion, her willingness to accept the risks associated with any pregnancy and was outside [sic] the limits of the advice/treatment which had been sought from the appellant. It has not been any part of the respondent's case that the appellant had a duty to advise more generally in relation to the risks of any future pregnancy. The risk of a child born with autism was not increased by the appellant's advice, the purpose and scope of her duty was to advise and investigate in relation to haemophilia in order to provide the respondent with an opportunity to avoid the risk of a child being born with haemophilia.

4.5 Loss of chance

Typically, in cases where loss of chance is claimed, the plaintiff could not prove the "but for" test of causation or material contribution to damage on a balance of probabilities. Instead, the plaintiff alleges that because of the defendant's breach, the plaintiff would be deprived of a chance of a cure or better medical prospects even if this loss of chance is assessed at less than 50%. The plaintiff claims for a fraction of the total damage suffered based on the extent of the loss of chance.

Insofar as medical negligence is concerned, loss of chance claims have been denied at common law in England and Australia where causation of damage has not been proved. Furthermore, it is trite law that damage is the gist of the action in negligence. It must be proved on a balance of probabilities that the defendant's breach caused the plaintiff to be worse off physically or economically.[53] As will be seen below, the Singapore courts have

---

50 *South Australian Asset Management Corporation v York Montague Ltd* ("SAAMCO") [1997] AC 191, *per* Lord Hoffmann.
51 [2018] EWCA Civ 2609.
52 [2018] EWCA Civ 2609 at [27].
53 *Rothwell v Chemical & Insulating Co Ltd* [2008] 1 AC 281 at 286, *per* Lord Hoffmann.

not made any definitive conclusions on this controversial issue of loss of chance in medical negligence.

The following two English cases have disallowed recovery for lost chances in medical negligence. In *Hotson v East Berkshire Area Health Authority*[54] ("*Hotson*"), the plaintiff fell and sustained an acute traumatic fracture of the left femoral epiphysis. The doctor was negligent in delaying diagnosis and treatment of the injury. If the doctor had properly diagnosed and treated the injury, there was only a 25% chance that the injury would have healed and that the complications of avascular necrosis of the epiphysis would not have developed. At the time of the trial, necrosis had developed. The House of Lords in *Hotson* held that causation was not proved on a balance of probabilities and the defendant was not liable for the "lost" chance that the plaintiff would recover completely from the injury.

In *Gregg v Scott*,[55] there was a negligent delay by the defendant doctor in the diagnosis and treatment of the claimant suffering from cancer. The chances of the claimant surviving for ten years were assessed at 25%. If the claimant had been treated without any delay, he would have had a 42% chance of survival for ten years. Based on the above statistical figures, there was no evidence that the delay would, on a balance of probabilities, cause the premature death. Unlike *Hotson*, the cancer had not materialised at the time of trial or the appeal to the House of Lords. The majority of the law lords[56] held that the plaintiff could not recover damages in respect of the loss of chance of survival caused by the delay.[57] Lord Nicholls, one of the dissenting law lords, was of the view that a doctor's duty included "maximising the patient's recovery prospects",[58] and thus, the claimant should be entitled to claim for the reduced prospects even if they fell short of 50%.

It has been argued that allowing loss of chance claims would represent a radical departure from the traditional rule of causation of damage. The floodgates of claims might result as virtually any claim for a loss of an outcome "could conceivably be reformulated as a claim for a loss of a chance of that outcome" thereby circumventing the traditional rules on causation.[59] In addition, the corollary of allowing loss of chance where the probabilities of a medical outcome are less than even is that it should extend, applying the same logic, to cases where the prospect of a favourable medical outcome in question is more than 50%. If so extended, there would be increased time and costs including that of medical experts giving evidence on the precise probabilities of outcomes in medical negligence litigation. Similar to England, Australian courts have rejected loss of chance claims.[60]

---

54 [1987] AC 750.
55 [2005] 2 AC 176.
56 Lord Nicholls and Lord Hope dissenting.
57 See the Australian High Court decision of *Tabet v Gett* (2010) 240 CLR 537 (a patient cannot recover for the loss of chance for a better medical outcome unless it was shown, on a balance of probabilities, that he or she would have had a better outcome but for the doctor's negligence).
58 *Gregg v Scott* [2005] 2 AC 176 at [42].
59 *Gregg v Scott* [2005] 2 AC 176 at [224]-[226] cited in *ACB* [2017] 1 SLR 918 at [124].
60 *Tabet v Gett* (2010) 240 CLR 537 (negligent delay in ordering a CT scan that caused the patient to lose a chance of avoiding further brain damage).

The US courts have, however, allowed such claims in medical negligence for the following reasons[61]:

- the "all or nothing" rule of tort recovery provides a "blanket release" from liability for doctors as long as there is a less than 50% chance of survival regardless of how flagrant the doctor's negligence.
- the "all or nothing" rule fails to provide the proper incentives to ensure that the care patients receive do not fall below the standard of care and skill of the average member of the profession practising the specialty.
- the rule fails to ensure that victims, who incur the real harm of losing their opportunity for a better outcome, are fairly compensated for their loss.

Furthermore, at common law, lost financial chances are recoverable. Where the outcomes flowing from the defendant's alleged negligent act is dependent on the future conduct of a third party, this is normally treated as a hypothetical event in which financial loss of chance may apply.[62]

One possibility raised by academic commentators is to allow loss of chance claims in narrow circumstances. Norton (2019) argued that loss of chance should be applicable to indeterministic events where a variety of outcomes could materialise in relation to the existence of genuine "objective chances" (see also Reece 1996). Put in another way, lost objective chances should be viewed as actionable damage (Norton 2019, at p. 981). This is to be distinguished from deterministic events ("epistemic" chances) where the outcome had already been decided[63] and may be treated as a past event (such as in *Hotson*).

> **Box 4.2 – Loss of chance claims and the medical profession**
>
> Should a patient who is likely to die from a serious disease be allowed to claim against a medical doctor should the latter's negligence remove that minimal chance of recovery? What do you see as the rightful duty of the doctor towards such a patient? Would there be any repercussions on the medical profession if the doctor has to compensate in such circumstances?

The issue of loss of chance in medical negligence was raised by a Singapore High Court judge in *Armstrong, Carol Ann (executrix of the estate of Peter Traynor, deceased and on behalf of the dependents of Peter Traynor, deceased) v Quest Laboratories Pte Ltd and another*.[64] Choo J preferred the approach of Lord Nicholls in *Gregg v Scott* that the "loss of a chance should constitute actionable damage". On appeal against the decision in *Armstrong*,

---

61 *Matsuyama v Birbaum* (2008) 890 NE (2d) 819. See also *Herskovits v Group Health Co-op of Puget Sound* 664 P.2d 474 (Wash. 1983); and King Jr (1981).
62 *Allied Maples Group Ltd v Simmons & Simmons (a firm)* [1995] 1 WLR 1602.
63 Horton gave the example of a coin flip.
64 [2018] SGHC 66.

the Court of Appeal[65] decided to leave the issue open but provided a brief analysis of *Gregg*. The majority law lords in *Gregg* examined the statistics of persons with similar characteristics who perished ten years from the initial state and noted that 58% died whilst only 42% survived. They then concluded that Gregg would not survive. However, Andrew Phang JA in *Armstrong* observed that the defendant's breach in *Gregg* had "interrupted the usual course of events" such that "Gregg never got to the 10-year mark"; hence, the statistical outcome was not reflective of what actually happened.[66] As a result, it was not apparent which category of persons (whether it is the 58% who perished or the 42% who survived) Gregg would have fallen into.[67]

4.6 Defences

The defences have to be proved on a balance of probabilities by the defendant. Complete defences (such as *ex turpi causa* and *volenti* which will be explained below) prevent any recovery of damages whilst a partial defence (eg, contributory negligence) reduces the amount of monetary damages payable to the plaintiff.

4.6.1 Ex turpi causa

This defence is based on the policy that no action can be founded on a wicked act. The defence can be used to deny recovery of damages against a medical doctor or hospital that arose from the plaintiff's own criminal conduct. In *Clunis v Camden and Islington Health Authority*,[68] the plaintiff claimed against the health authority for its negligent omission to provide him with psychiatric care whose omission resulted in the plaintiff killing a person and his conviction for manslaughter on the basis of diminished responsibility. The defence of *ex turpi causa* was successfully raised to defeat the plaintiff's claim in negligence. This was because the plaintiff's conviction was the outcome of his own criminal act and it was taken that he knew the nature of his criminal act.

As an extension of the legal principle, a claimant cannot recover damages (eg, loss of earnings) that is a consequence of a sentence imposed on him (eg, detention in a hospital) to punish him for a criminal act which he is responsible for.[69]

4.6.2 Volenti non fit injuria

In order to establish the defence, the defendant has to show that the plaintiff had (a) acted freely and voluntarily; (b) acted with full knowledge of the nature and extent of the risks of harm created by the defendant's negligence; and (c) expressly or impliedly consented to the abovementioned risks.

---

65 [2020] 1 SLR 133 at [97] and [98].
66 [2020] 1 SLR 133 at [106].
67 [2020] 1 SLR 133 at [107].
68 [1998] QB 978.
69 *Gray v Thames Trains Ltd* [2009] 1 AC 1339. See appeal pending before the UK Supreme Court against decision of English Court of Appeal [2018] EWCA Civ 1841: *Ecila Henderson (A Protected Party, by her litigation friend, The Official Solicitor) v Dorset Healthcare University NHS Foundation Trust*.

This concept of *volenti* in negligence – which is focused on the plaintiff's consent to the risks arising from negligence with knowledge of the nature and extent of the risks – is distinct from that of *consent* in the tort of battery to the carrying out of a medical procedure or operation (Chapter 5). Due to the high threshold for proof and the very duty of the doctor to prevent such risks to a patient,[70] this *volenti* defence rarely succeeds in medical negligence.

This defence failed in a case where a doctor suffered physical injuries when he attempted to rescue the defendant's employees in a well filled with poisonous gas though he was warned about the noxious fumes. He suffered injury as a result of the rescue and claimed against the defendant in negligence. The *volenti* defence could not be used to negate the claim. The rescue was the natural and probable result of the defendant's negligence. The court also acknowledged that the plaintiff had a professional duty to save lives and exhibited bravery in the rescue.[71]

4.6.3 Contributory negligence[72]

A doctor may require information from the patient about the latter's symptoms and health conditions in order to make an accurate medical diagnosis or to administer proper treatments. If the patient failed to provide the relevant information, which resulted in the doctor misdiagnosing or giving the wrong treatment, the patient may be adjudged contributorily negligent for his injuries. Alternatively, if the patient had negligently failed to follow the doctor's instructions or delayed doing so, and that led to the patient's injuries, he would also not be entitled to claim full damages due to his contributory negligence.[73]

Section 3(1) of Singapore's Contributory Negligence and Personal Injuries Act[74] reads:

> Where any person suffers damage as the result partly of his own fault and partly of the fault of any other person or persons, a claim in respect of that *damage* shall not be defeated by reason of the *fault* of the person suffering the damage, but the *damages* recoverable in respect thereof shall be *reduced* to such extent *as the court thinks just and equitable* having regard to the *claimant's share in the responsibility for the damage*.

---

70 See *Reeves v Commissioner of Police for the Metropolis* [2000] 1 AC 360.
71 In *Baker v T E Hopkins & Son Ltd* [1959] 1 WLR 966 at 976. Morris LJ said that it would not be "rational" to say that the doctor freely and voluntarily agreed to incur the risks.
72 See Herring and Foster (2009).
73 *Pidgeon v Doncaster Health Authority* [2002] Lloyd's Rep Med 130 (patient did not follow doctor's instructions to undergo smear tests for cervical cancer); *Murrin v Janes* [1949] 4 DLR 403 (Newfoundland Supreme Court) (delay in seeing dentist for severe bleeding after tooth extraction); *Dumais v Hamilton* 1998 ABCA 218 at [15]-[17](patient's continued smoking after surgery contrary to surgeon's repeated instructions contributed to his skin necrosis); *Crossman v Stewart* (1997) 82 DLR (3d) 677 at [32]-[34] (patient used drugs from unauthorised sources for prolonged period which resulted in near blindness without consulting the defendant doctor).
74 (Cap 54, 2002 Rev Ed).

Medical negligence (part 2)

The defence of contributory negligence is premised on some "fault" on the part of the plaintiff who suffered "damage" (including "loss of life and personal injury").[75] The term "fault" means "negligence, breach of statutory duty or other act or omission which gives rise to a liability in tort or would, apart from [the statute], give rise to the defence of contributory negligence",[76] and includes deliberate acts of self-harm such as suicide.[77]

Denning LJ in *Jones v Livox Quarries Ld*[78] explained the requirements of contributory negligence as follows:

> ... contributory negligence requires the foreseeability of harm to oneself. A person is guilty of contributory negligence if he ought reasonably to have foreseen that, if he did not act as a reasonable, prudent man, he might be hurt himself; and in his reckonings he must take into account the possibility of others being careless.

The patient may be contributorily negligent in not taking sufficient care of his own personal safety as in *Tan Hun Hoe v Harte Denis Mathew*.[79] The plaintiff had undergone a bilateral varicocelectomy, a fertility operation for low sperm count. Shortly after the operation, the plaintiff fainted and fell whilst in the toilet and this resulted in the contusion of his testes. When the plaintiff consulted the defendant doctor concerning the abnormal swelling of his testes, the doctor was negligent in giving prompt post-operative treatment, failed to warn the plaintiff that there was a risk of atrophy of the testes and that the plaintiff would not be able to father a child. The trial judge awarded the plaintiff damages but discounted the amount by 40% based on his finding that if the defendant had undertaken "prompt intervention" after the surgery, 60% of the plaintiff's testes would have been saved from atrophy. The Court of Appeal decided that the defendant had *caused* the atrophy[80] and that the other cause was the plaintiff's fall (*ie*, contributory negligence).

Other bases for contributory negligence include the patient's omission to ask the doctor for clear instructions about carrying out certain ordinary daily activities without crutches after a medical procedure,[81] or failing to take reasonable steps to prevent risks of harm occurring despite having prior knowledge of such risks and preventive actions.[82] Doctors and medical staff who have been sued for negligent failure to prevent a suicide attempt by a patient

---

75 Section 2.
76 Section 2.
77 *Reeves v Commissioner of Police of the Metropolis* [2000] 1 AC 360 at 369-370, *per* Lord Hoffmann; at 376, *per* Lord Jauncey; *Corr v IBC Vehicles Ltd* [2008] 1 AC 884.
78 [1952] 2 QB 608 at 615.
79 [2001] 3 SLR(R) 414.
80 *Tan Hun Hoe v Harte Denis Mathew* [2001] 3 SLR(R) 414 at [52] (the Court of Appeal took this view despite the fact that it was "not clear" how the trial judge arrived at the conclusion that 60% of the testes would have been saved if the doctor had not been negligent).
81 *Brushett v Cowan* (1990) 69 DLR (4th) 743 (Newfoundland Court of Appeal).
82 *Zhang v Kan* [2003] BCSC 5; (2003) 15 CCLT (3d) 1 (patient's and husband's contributory negligence for failure to arrange for amniocentesis despite knowledge of the need for amniocentesis and risks of child with Down's syndrome.)

may plead contributory negligence where the patient made a deliberate decision to end his own life albeit in a state of depression.[83]

With regard to the "share of responsibility", the courts take into consideration the "causative potency" and the "blameworthiness" of the parties involved.[84] The degree of fault or blameworthiness must depend on the particular facts and circumstances.[85]

4.6.4 No exemption of doctor's liability under UCTA for negligence resulting in personal injury or death

A defendant cannot exclude or restrict its liability for negligence which results in personal injury or death under the Unfair Contract Terms Act.[86] The term "personal injury" includes any disease and any impairment of a person's physical or mental condition.[87] A medical doctor cannot therefore exclude liability in respect of his negligence that resulted in the patient's personal injury or death.

4.7 Remedies: damages

The main form of damages in Singapore is compensatory damages where the main purpose is to *compensate* for losses suffered by the plaintiff (*ie*, to restore the plaintiff as far as possible to the position he or she would have been in if the tort had not been committed). Aggravated damages are awarded where the defendant's conduct "aggravates" the injury to the plaintiff resulting in additional injury to feelings and mental distress. The purpose of an award of aggravated damages is also compensatory in nature.[88] The test is whether there was exceptional or contumelious conduct or motive on the part of the defendant in committing the wrong.[89] Exemplary or punitive damages are awarded in exceptional circumstances where "the totality of the defendant's conduct [was] so outrageous that it warrants punishment, deterrence, and condemnation".[90]

The types of damage commonly suffered by plaintiff in medical negligence claims against medical doctors and healthcare professionals are personal injuries and psychiatric harms. For both physical injury and psychiatric harm, the heads of damages in medical negligence may be classified under (a) *special damages* which are specifically quantifiable (including medical expenses and transport costs which have been incurred and pre-trial loss of earnings); and (b) *general damages* which are not specifically quantifiable as at the date of trial (including pain and suffering, loss of amenities, loss of earnings (future) and/or loss of earning capacity and costs of future medical care).

---

83 *Reeves v Commissioner of Police for the Metropolis* [2000] 1 AC 360.
84 *Cheong Ghim Fah v Murugian s/o Rangasamy* [2004] 1 SLR(R) 628 at [87].
85 *Parno v SC Marine Pte Ltd* [1999] 3 SLR(R) 377 at [64] (Court of Appeal).
86 (Cap 396, 1994 Rev Ed), section 2(1).
87 Section 14.
88 *Appleton v Garrett* [1996] PIQR P1.
89 *Tan Harry v Teo Chee Yeow Aloysius* [2004] 1 SLR(R) 513 at [82] and [83].
90 *ACB v Thomson Medical Centre* [2017] 1 SLR 918.

4.7.1 Special damages

Medical expenses (such as hospitalisation expenses, expenses for medical prescriptions and drugs as well as treatment and consultation expenses) may be claimed provided they were reasonably incurred.[91] The pretrial loss of income of a care-giver to the plaintiff may also be recovered where the care-giver had to give up his job or employment to care for the plaintiff.[92] Pretrial loss of earnings refers to the earnings lost between the date of the accident to the date of the trial.

4.7.2 General damages

Damages for pain and suffering are awarded for both future pain and suffering as well as for what has already been endured by the plaintiff.[93] In order to claim for pain and suffering, the plaintiff had to be conscious at the relevant time of the accident.[94] The quantum of the award would depend on various factors: the plaintiff's awareness of the pain, his capacity for suffering, the extent of the pain, whether the pain was temporary or permanent[95] and the severity of injury. A claim for loss of amenities is premised on the plaintiff's loss of ability to enjoy the qualities of life such as impairment of a person's senses and interference with sexual life, marriage prospects[96] or leisure activities. To make a successful claim for pain and suffering in respect of the loss of expectation of life, it has to be shown, based on medical evidence, that the plaintiff's expectation of life has been reduced as a result of the accident.[97]

Loss of future earnings and loss of earning capacity are separate and distinct heads of damage.[98] Loss of future earnings is assessed from the date of the trial to the end of the plaintiff's prospective working life. The amount claimable is the product of the multiplicand (in dollars) and multiplier (in years or months). The multiplicand is based on the amount of earnings which the plaintiff would have earned if the tort had not occurred. On the other hand, loss of earning capacity is normally awarded where the plaintiff is still in employment at the date of the trial, but the court finds that there is a risk of him losing employment in the future due to his injuries *and* that the plaintiff would be at a disadvantage in the open

---

91 *Clark Jonathan Michael v Lee Khee Chung* [2010] 1 SLR 209 at [40] (on claims for Ayurvedic and osteopathic treatment).
92 *Lee Wei Kong v Ng Siok Tong* [2012] 2 SLR 85 at [61]-[62].
93 *TV Media Pte Ltd v De Cruz Andrea Heidi* [2004] 3 SLR(R) 543 at [166].
94 *Lee Ngiap Hoon v Teo Sin* [1991] 2 SLR(R) 131 at [23]; *Low Yoke Ying v Sim Kok Lee* [1990] 2 SLR(R) 713 at [23].
95 *Lim Poh Choo v Camden and Islington Area Health Authority* [1980] AC 174; *H West & Son Ltd v Shephard* [1964] AC 326.
96 *Poh Huat Heng Corp Pte Ltd v Hafizul Islam Kofil Uddin* [2012] 3 SLR 1003 at [35].
97 Civil Law Act, section 11.
98 *Chai Kang Wei Samuel v Shaw Linda Gillian* [2010] 3 SLR 587; *Koh Chai Kwang v Teo Ai Ling* [2011] 3 SLR 610.

employment market due to the injuries.[99] With regard to the costs of future medical care,[100] the courts have to be satisfied that the medical expenses would be necessary in the future. The average life expectancy is normally used to measure the period of the loss.[101] The courts may use a multiplier-and-multiplicand approach to calculate the loss of future medical care.

4.7.3 Provisional damages

Damages are generally awarded for illnesses or medical conditions that have already occurred to the extent that they were caused by the defendants and not too remote. Where there is uncertainty at the time of the trial whether the plaintiff would develop further illnesses or medical conditions (referred to as a "contingency") subsequent to the trial, he or she may apply for an award of provisional damages based on the Rules of Court. If the award is made by the court, the successful applicant is entitled to apply to the court for reassessment at a later date when the illness or medical conditions (or contingency) materialises.[102]

4.8 Liability of hospitals and clinics for the acts of third parties: vicarious liability and non-delegable duties

Medical doctors or the clinics that they own and operate may be found personally liable for negligent acts which caused harm to the patient or related persons. We have seen that hospitals may also be directly liable in the tort of negligence in respect of systemic negligence[103] or hospital administration. In some cases, clinics and hospitals may be liable even though they are not at fault (*ie*, strict liability) in respect of the tortious acts committed by other parties such as employees (under vicarious liability) or independent contractors (under the doctrine of non-delegable duties).

Hospitals and clinics may be vicariously liable[104] to the plaintiff when three criteria are fulfilled: (i) existence of an employment relationship between the healthcare professional and hospital/clinic; (ii) the healthcare professional committed a tort; and (iii) the tort was committed in the course of employment. Arguments for the doctrine of vicarious liability are that the employer is likely to have deeper pockets, greater capacity to insure the losses and the

---

99 *Chai Kang Wei Samuel v Shaw Linda Gillian* [2010] 3 SLR 587 at [36] (citing *Moeliker v A Reyrolle & Co Ltd* [1977] 1 WLR 132); *Teo Sing Keng v Sim Ban Kiat* [1994] 1 SLR(R) 340; *Loh Chia Mei v Koh Kok Han* [2009] SGHC 181 at [31]; *Low Swee Tong v Liew Machinery (Pte) Ltd* [1993] 2 SLR(R) 10 at [36] (citing *Chow Khai Hong v Tham Sek Khow* [1991] 2 SLR(R) 670); *Lee Wei Kong v Ng Siok Tong* [2012] 2 SLR 85 at [29]; *Teddy, Thomas v Teacly (S) Pte Ltd* [2014] SGHC 226 at [48].
100 *Tan Hun Hoe v Harte Denis Mathew* [2001] 3 SLR(R) 414; *Lee Wei Kong v Ng Siok Tong* [2012] 2 SLR 85 (costs of future psychiatric treatment).
101 *Ang Leng Hock v Leo Ee Ah* [2004] 2 SLR(R) 361 at [59].
102 *Koh Chai Kwang v Teo Ai Ling* [2011] 3 SLR 610 ("contingency" must be capable of being objectively determined).
103 *Noor Azlin bte Abdul Rahman v Changi General Hospital Pte Ltd and others* [2019] 1 SLR 834.
104 *Cassidy v Ministry of Health* [1951] 2 KB 343 (hospital vicariously liable for negligent post-operation treatment by an employee causing harm to the patient); *Gold v Essex County Council* [1942] 2 KB 293 (hospital vicariously liable to a patient for the negligent act of a radiographer it had employed).

ability to control and supervise the employee's scope and reap the benefits from the latter's discharge of work responsibilities.

The existence of an employment relationship between the hospital and medical doctor would depend on the level of control exercised by the hospital over the doctor's provision of medical services,[105] whether the doctor was providing medical services on his own account[106] and the terms of their agreement. In *Denis Matthew Harte v Dr Tan Hun Hoe*,[107] the hospital only supplied facilities and nursing care services to the surgeons who had admitting privileges to perform surgery at a particular hospital; further, the hospital in question did not have control over the surgeons' treatment and management of their own patients and was therefore not vicariously liable.

The employee's commission of tort may cover both negligent as well as intentional tortious acts that harm the plaintiff. The "course of employment" criterion is based on the closeness of the connection between the tort committed and the employment scope taking into account policy considerations such as compensation for innocent victims and deterring future harms by encouraging employers to take steps to mitigate potential harms. Two other factors are relevant: whether it was foreseeable from the defendant's perspective that the tort was likely to be committed by the tortfeasor[108] and whether the defendant has created or significantly enhanced, by virtue of the relationship, the very risk that in fact materialised such that the employer should be held vicariously liable for the tortfeasor's wrongful acts.[109]

In addition, a hospital or clinic *prima facie* owes a non-delegable duty to a patient under its care, supervision or control subject to taking into account fairness and reasonableness in imposing such duties and policy considerations in the local context.[110] If this is established, the hospital or medical doctor remains liable to the patient under their care, custody or supervision notwithstanding that the former may have delegated the function relating to the care of the patient to an independent contractor. Non-delegable duties are personal duties

---

105 *Dr Kok Choong Seng and Sunway Medical Centre Berhad v Soo Cheng Lin* [2018] 1 MLJ 685 at [99] (doctor was not instructed or required by the hospital to perform the operation which was arranged according to the doctor's schedule).
106 *Dr Kok Choong Seng and Sunway Medical Centre Berhad v Soo Cheng Lin* [2018] 1 MLJ 685 at [100] (doctor was free to conduct his own diagnosis and treatment of the patient at his own time, charge fees to the patient without interference from the hospital and did not receive salary from hospital).
107 [2000] SGHC 248 at [440]-[441].
108 *Skandinaviska Enskilda Banken AB (Publ), Singapore Branch v Asia Pacific Breweries (Singapore) Pte Ltd* [2011] 3 SLR 540.
109 *Ng Huat Seng v Munib Mohammad Madni and another* [2017] 2 SLR 1074 at [66].
110 *Management Corporation Strata Title Plan No 3322 v Tiong Aik Construction Pte Ltd* [2016] 4 SLR 521 at [62] (that non-delegable duties apply to cases where the facts (i) fall within one of the established categories including hospital-patient relationships or (ii) possess the five defining features enunciated by Lord Sumption JSC in *Woodland v Swimming Teachers Association* [2014] AC 537 at [23]. For medical negligence cases, see *Hii Chii Kok v Ooi Peng Jin London Lucien* [2016] 2 SLR 544 at [70]; *Cassidy v Ministry of Health* [1951] 2 KB 343; *Farraj v King's Healthcare NHS Trust* [2010] 1 WLR 2139 (no non-delegable duty imposed on hospital as the hospital only provided diagnostic services to claimant who was not a patient and sent claimant's tissue sample to laboratory for testing which was allegedly performed negligently).

90 *Medical negligence (part 2)*

which cannot be discharged by delegation,[111] the breach of which gives rise to primary rather than secondary tortious liability.[112] Thus, a hospital's non-delegable duty owed to a patient, in contrast to systemic negligence, imposes a more stringent duty on the holder to ensure that reasonable individual care is exercised by the independent contractor.

Unlike the concept of duty of care discussed in Chapter 3, a non-delegable duty refers to the duty to ensure that care is taken or to procure the careful performance of the work that has been delegated (Giliker 2017, at p. 110). Whether a non-delegable duty is owed to the patient would first depend on the scope of duty assumed by the hospital in the first place[113] and second, whether such duty was non-delegable. A hospital or doctor may assume a duty to perform or provide a specific medical service but no duty with regard to another aspect of medical services. In *Goh Guan Sin (by her litigation representative Chiam Yu Zhu v Yeo Tseng Tsai and National University Hospital (Singapore) Pte Ltd*,[114] the Singapore High Court found that the lead surgeon did not assume a non-delegable duty of care with respect to the post-operative monitoring of the patient by the medical team. In a hospital which practises team-based care, it would be reasonable for the lead surgeon to rely instead on his colleagues to render post-operative care to the patient. It added that the imposition of such a non-delegable duty would "fracture" the practice of team-based care and would be "excessively onerous", and "disregard the reality" on the ground where a consultant in a public healthcare institution may have to attend to many patients in a single day.[115]

4.9 Procedural matters

There are two procedural matters relating to medical negligence in Singapore that deserve mention. They relate to the preparations and gathering of evidence that potential litigants should undertake before initiating a lawsuit as well as the time limits for doing so under the law.

4.9.1 The medical negligence protocols

The High Court Protocol for Medical Negligence Cases[116] (Appendix J) covers a wide range of rules relating to pre-writ exchange of information[117] with a view to resolving medical negli-

---

111 *Management Corporation Strata Title Plan No 3322 v Tiong Aik Construction Pte Ltd* [2016] 4 SLR 521 at [21].
112 *Management Corporation Strata Title Plan No 3322 v Tiong Aik Construction Pte Ltd* [2016] 4 SLR 521 at [24].
113 *S v Lothian Health Board* [2009] CSOH 97, 2009 SLT 689 (hospital taken to have assumed responsibility for tests conducted as it did not communicate clearly to patient that the test would be undertaken by third party researchers).
114 [2019] SGHC 274.
115 [2019] SGHC 274 at [138]. Cf Malaysian case of *Dr Hari Krishnan & Anor v Megat Noor Ishak bin Megat Ibrahim & Anor and another appeal* [2018] 3 MLJ 281 at [136]-[138] (non-delegable duty as hospital had assumed a positive duty to provide an anaesthetist for the operation to keep the patient anaesthetised throughout the operation – an integral to the assumed positive duty by the hospital).
116 This took effect on 1 July 2017.
117 This includes the application for medical reports and medical records from the healthcare provider.

gence disputes without protracted litigation, arrangements for an early pre-trial conference (PTC) after entry of appearance, PTCs before a Judge after close of pleadings and to explore the possibility of resolving the case by mediation, neutral evaluation or other forms of alternative dispute resolution, the attachment of the claimants' expert reports to statements of claim, and the appointment of medical assessors to assist Judges on "specialised and technical aspects" of the case. The parties' non-compliance with the High Court Protocol may be taken into consideration when the court exercises its discretion in making costs orders or determining the amount of interest payable.

The earlier State Courts pre-action protocol for medical negligence cases which applied from January 2007 only provided for a medical report and medical records to be given, and a without prejudice discussion to be held, before commencement of legal action. The new State Courts Practice Directions 39 (Medical Negligence Claims)[118] is more extensive. Appendix D of the State Courts Practice Directions covers pre-action specific discovery of documents[119] as well as the commencement of suit and pre-trial proceedings.[120] There is, however, no provision for medical assessors for State Courts proceedings. Similar to the High Court Protocol, the State Courts may look to the parties' compliance with the State Courts Protocol when making costs orders or determining the amount of interest payable.

4.9.2 Limitation periods

The limitation periods are imposed by statute to place a time limit for the commencement of lawsuits including the tort of (medical) negligence. The following limitation periods will apply to a claim for damages for personal injuries in medical negligence[121]:

(i) three years from the date on which the cause of action accrued; or
(ii) three years from the earliest date on which the plaintiff has the knowledge required for bringing an action for damages in respect of the relevant injury.

For non-personal injury claims for damages in tort, which would be less common, the relevant periods are (i) six years from the date on which the cause of action accrued; or (ii) three years from the earliest date on which the plaintiff or any person in whom the cause of action was vested before him first had both the knowledge required for bringing an action for damages in respect of the relevant damage and a right to bring such an action.[122]

With respect to (i), the date of accrual of the cause of action refers to the date on which the damage occurred. Under (ii), knowledge includes *actual* and *constructive* knowledge.

---

118 With effect from 1 October 2018.
119 This includes the application for obtaining a medical report and medical records of the patient from the healthcare provider by prescribed form, arranging for a without prejudice discussion, negotiations between parties, and providing a prescribed notice to potential defendants of intention to proceed with a writ.
120 Such as the filing of medical reports and lists of documents, and convening of the first CDR session within two weeks after filing of the memorandum of appearance.
121 24A(2) of the Limitation Act.
122 Section 24A(3).

92   Medical negligence (part 2)

The potential plaintiff may have taken reasonable steps to acquire or obtain the requisite knowledge, whether from facts observable or ascertainable by himself *or* with the help of "appropriate expert advice".[123] Constructive knowledge on the part of the plaintiff does not arise without expert assistance where the plaintiff's affliction was a rare condition; hence, it may be necessary to show that the plaintiff sought an opinion from an expert before it can be said that knowledge has been acquired by him.[124]

The level of knowledge required is constructive knowledge of the "factual essence of his complaint"[125] as opposed to knowledge of comprehensive and detailed facts. The requisite knowledge in the statute refers to knowledge of facts, not law. Knowledge that any act or omission did or did not, as a matter of *law*, involve negligence, nuisance or breach of duty is irrelevant.[126]

The time will only run if the plaintiff possesses knowledge of material facts about the injury or damage which would lead a reasonable person who had suffered such injury or damage to consider it "sufficiently serious" to justify his instituting proceedings for damages against a defendant who did not dispute liability and who was able to satisfy a judgment.[127] The word "sufficiently serious" means that the claim must not be frivolous or without merit.[128]

In the case of a plaintiff under disability (while he is a minor or lacks capacity within the meaning of the Mental Capacity Act to conduct legal proceedings), time runs from the date when the person ceased to be under a disability or died, whichever event occurred first, notwithstanding that the period of limitation has expired.[129]

In exceptional cases, the lawsuit may be time-barred if it exceeds the overriding time period of 15 years from the date of the alleged act or omission which constitutes the negligence and which the injury or damage in question is alleged to be attributable.[130]

4.10 Conclusion

In addition to establishing a legal duty of care owed by doctors and hospitals and their breach of duty, the plaintiff must also prove that the breach had caused the damage whether based on the "but for" test or by materially contributing to the damage. In exceptional circumstances, plaintiff may rely on the test of material contribution to the risk of damage where it is impossible to prove based on current medical knowledge the link between the breach and the damage. The breach must also be a proximate or effective cause of the damage suffered in the absence of a *novus actus interveniens* or a supervening event that breaks the chain

---

123   Section 24A(6).
124   *Lily Pai v Yeo Peng Hock Henry* [2001] 1 SLR(R) 517 at [53].
125   *Lian Kok Hong v Ow Wah Foong* [2008] 4 SLR(R) 165 at [34].
126   Section 24A(5). See *Dobbie v Medway Health Authority* [1994] 1 WLR 1234.
127   Section 24A(4)(d).
128   *Lian Kok Hong v Ow Wah Foong* [2008] 4 SLR(R) 165 at [39].
129   Section 24. See *Chia Peng Siang v Attorney-General* [2011] SGDC 311 (the action was time-barred as more than six years had accrued from the date of the plaintiff's release from the Institute of Mental Health).
130   Section 24B.

of causation. Moreover, the type of damage must be reasonably foreseeable and within the scope of duty. If so, damages would be recoverable even if the defendant did not know that the plaintiff was suffering from inherent weakness or susceptibilities that led to his additional injuries. Outside of a direct negligence claim, hospitals and clinics may nonetheless be strictly liable if their employees have committed a tort in the course of employment. They also remain liable under the scope of positive duties assumed to patients under their care even if they may have delegated an integral function of those duties to an independent contractor whose negligence resulted in the injuries. Finally, legal practitioners should note the statutory limitation periods to commence a lawsuit in medical negligence and the protocols issued by the courts.

References

Chan, K.Y.G. (2016). Chapters 7 to 8 on the "Tort of Negligence: Damage" and "Tort of Negligence: Defences" and Chapter 20 on "Remedies" in Chan, K.Y.G. and Lee, P.W. (eds) *The Law of Torts in Singapore* (Academy Publishing: Singapore), pp. 271-372 and pp. 823-876

Giliker, P. (2017). "Non-Delegable Duties and Institutional Liability for the Negligence of Hospital Staff: Fair, Just and Reasonable?" 33 *Tottel's Journal of Professional Negligence* 109-127.

Goldberg, R. (2017). "Causation and Defences", chapter 6 in Laing, J. & McHale, J. (eds) *Principles of Medical Law* (Oxford University Press: Oxford), pp. 297-370.

Herring, J. and Foster, C. (2009). "Blaming the Patient: Contributory Negligence in Medical Malpractice Litigation" 25(2) *Professional Negligence* 76-90.

King Jr, J.H. (1981). "Causation, Valuation and Chance in Personal Injury Torts Involving Preexisting Conditions and Future Consequences" 90 *Yale Law Journal* 1353-1397.

Kumaralingam, A. (2007). "The Changing Face of the Gist of Negligence" in Neyers, J.W., Chamberlain, E., & Pitel, S.G.A. (eds) *Emerging Issues in Tort Law* (Hart Publishing: Oxford), pp. 469-476.

Norton, J. (2019). "Treating Chance Consistently: Recasting the Approach to Causation and Damage in Negligence" 42(3) *Melbourne University Law Review* 954.

Reece, H. (1996) "Losses of Chances in the Law" 59(2) *Modern Law Review* 188.

Tong, E. (2004). "Causation of Damage", chapter 5 in Quan Y.K., et al. (eds) *Essentials of Medical Law* (Sweet & Maxwell: Singapore), pp. 145-205.

5 Consent to treatment

5.1 Introduction

Consent to treatment is a fundamental issue in healthcare. Without consent, the doctor cannot administer treatment on the patient under the law save in exceptional circumstances. The concept is significant not only in the carrying out of typical clinical activities by doctors and nurses vis-à-vis patients in hospitals and clinics, but also in relation to a variety of biomedical contexts: reproduction (*eg*, abortions and IVF procedures) (Chapter 9), end-of-life decisions (*eg*, advance medical directives, withdrawal of life-sustaining treatment) (Chapter 10), the removal and use of organs or tissues (Chapter 11) and the testing of research subjects and patients in biomedical research (Chapter 12).

Weir (2004) argued that informed consent is premised on patient benefits (such as better patient compliance and participation in treatment and patients' awareness and knowledge of prognosis in order to plan their lives). Informed consent is also important in biomedical research which aims to enhance the store of generalisable knowledge rather than to generate specific patient benefits (Lemmens 2015, at p. 33).

The doctor-patient relationship has been described as a *fiduciary* relationship where the doctor (as fiduciary) is expected to act in the patient's best interests.[1] This implies trust of the patient that the doctor who has superior power and responsibility would exercise that power for the benefit of his patients. The need for consent to treatment is also a fundamental aspect of patient autonomy[2] and intimately connected to the Kantian respect for persons and the focus on preserving relationships in care ethics (Chapter 2).

5.2 Meaning and scope of consent to treatment

In the event that a valid consent has not been obtained from the patient to undergo a medical procedure, the doctor may be liable under the tort of battery (a form of trespass to the

---

1 The characteristics of such a relationship comprise the following: (1) the fiduciary has scope for the exercise of some discretion or power; (2) the fiduciary can unilaterally exercise that power or discretion so as to affect the beneficiary's legal or practical interests; and (3) the beneficiary is peculiarly vulnerable to the fiduciary holding the discretion or power: see McLachlin J (L'Heureux-Dube J. concurring) in *Norberg v Wynrib* [1992] 2 SCR 226.
2 *Yong Thiam Look Peter v Singapore Medical Council* [2017] SGHC 10 at [9].

person) should he administer the procedure. The tort protects one's bodily integrity based on the maxim that "every person's body is inviolate".[3] The elements of the tort are the direct and intentional physical contact with the plaintiff that is unjustified. Touching which exceeds the bounds of acceptable everyday conduct would be considered unjustifiable physical contact.[4] Damages may be claimed from the doctor in battery in respect of injury to feelings, indignity, mental suffering, humiliation or distress. It is not necessary to prove actual damage in an action based on the tort of battery unlike for negligence. Cardozo J in *Schloendorff v Society of New York Hospital* stated[5]:

> Every human being of adult years and sound mind has a right to determine what shall be done with his own body; and a surgeon who performs an operation without his patient's consent commits an assault.

Where consent has been given by the patient for the physical contact (*eg*, medical procedure) by the doctor or healthcare professional, the latter would have a defence against a claim based on battery (Chan 2016; Herring 2018). To distinguish actions of battery from tort of negligence in respect of medical treatment, battery

> should be confined to cases where surgery or treatment has been performed or given to which there has been no consent at all or where, emergency situations aside, surgery or treatment has been performed or given beyond that to which there was consent.[6]

On the other hand, a doctor may be liable for medical negligence if he fails to provide to the patient "material" information of the risks, benefits, complications and alternatives of the treatment or medical procedures (Chapter 3). Where the doctor failed to provide sufficient information to the patient, there is then a potential breach of duty in giving medical advice under the tort of negligence (Monks 1993, at pp. 223-225).

Consent may be oral or written. A consent form signed by a patient would normally constitute *prima facie* evidence of the consent. Notwithstanding the signed form, the validity of the consent can nevertheless be challenged on the grounds that the patient was misled into signing or did not understand the nature of the procedures he was purportedly consenting to.

Consent can be expressly stated or implied from the words or conduct of the person alleged to give consent and the surrounding circumstances. The consent may be tacit in nature or presumed where the patient does not object to a particular medical procedure when specifically asked by the doctor.

The English case of *Freeman v Home Office (No 2)*[7] held that, rather than imposing the burden on the doctor to prove the defence of consent, the plaintiff was required to prove the absence of consent. The case involved a medical officer who injected the plaintiff (a prisoner) with a drug but who could not adduce evidence of consent as he had died before the trial.

---

3 *Collins v Wilcock* [1984] 1 WLR 1172 at 1177.
4 *Re F (mental patient: sterilisation)* [1990] 2 AC 1 at 73; *Wainwright v Home Office* [2004] 2 AC 406 at [9].
5 (1914) 105 NE 92 at 93.
6 *Reibl v Hughes* [1980] 2 SCR 880 at [11].
7 [1984] QB 524.

96 Consent to treatment

This holding may arguably be confined to its exceptional facts as the defendant should ordinarily shoulder the burden to prove consent by the plaintiff.[8]

The concept of consent to treatment can be further explicated by reference to the notions of voluntariness, content or information as to the nature of the treatment, understanding the information, and the scope of consent. The mental competence to consent to treatment will be discussed in the next section.

5.2.1 Voluntariness

The concept of voluntariness in consent implies the existence of a choice. First, the patient must understand the nature of the act he is doing (in this case, the decision with respect to the treatment). For a viable choice to be made, the decision-maker cannot be ignorant of the material circumstances relating to the choice he is making. For example, if the patient is considering whether to undergo an operation to remove a tumour, he should be aware of the illness he is suffering from, the tumour's impact on his health or particular bodily function and how the removal of the tumour would cure the illness or relieve certain symptoms.

Further, he should not be so adversely affected by external factors as to vitiate his ability to make a choice. Consent may be invalidated if it is induced by misrepresentation or fraud.[9] Withholding of material information in bad faith would amount to fraud.[10] For instance, purported consent to a mastectomy based on a doctor's misrepresentation of the patient's condition (eg, that he has cancer which happens to be false) would be invalid.

Voluntariness may also be diminished by certain physical and mental conditions internal to the patient (eg, psychiatric disorders, diseases or addictions) such that he is unable to understand the choice he is making with respect to the specific treatment. In addition to the above factors, as consent is based on a presumption of individual autonomy and free will, it can arguably be vitiated where the doctor has exploited the unequal power relationship and the weaknesses of a vulnerable patient by acting to the latter's detriment instead of using his power in discharge of his professional responsibility to assist the patient.[11]

---

8   See *Non-marine, Underwriters, Lloyd's of London v Scalera* [2000] 1 SCR 551 (defendant, not plaintiff, to prove consent in a case of sexual battery); and *Secretary, Department of Health and Community Services v JWB* (1992) 66 ALJR 300 at 337, per McHugh J (consent to carrying out of surgical procedure to be proven by defendant; "[t]he contrary view is inconsistent with a person's right of bodily integrity. Other persons do not have the right to interfere with an individual's body unless he or she proves lack of consent to the interference").

9   *Appleton v Garrett* [1996] PIQR P; *Reibl v Hughes* [1980] 2 SCR 880.

10 *Chatterton v Gerson* [1981] QB 432 at 443, per Bristow J.

11 In *Norberg v Wynrib* [1992] 2 SCR 226, per La Forest L (Gonthier and Cory JJ concurring). The patient had a drug addiction which the doctor exploited by initiating an exchange of drugs for sex. This is not, strictly speaking, about consent to treatment (but consent to sexual contact). Punitive damages were awarded against the doctor as a deterrence against the doctor whose conduct was "offensive and reprehensible".

5.2.2 Content of information

For the purpose of the tort of battery, the patient is only required to be informed in "broad terms" as to the nature of the medical procedures intended to be performed.[12] For instance, the patient must be aware of the main and general purpose of the brain surgery proposed by the surgeon (*eg*, to remove a tumour diagnosed by the brain scan). The fact that the doctor failed to warn him of a possible side effect from the removal of tumour (*eg*, that the patient may experience intermittent headaches shortly after the surgery) does not negate the consent to the surgery itself.

There is a material difference between the consent requirement in respect of a battery versus an action in negligence. The doctor's failure to warn of a possible side effect might be relevant to an action in negligence provided such information would be regarded as material to a reasonable patient (Chapter 3). Bristow J in *Chatterton v Gerson*[13] stated that,

> in order to vitiate the reality of consent [in the tort of battery] there must be a *greater failure of communication* between doctor and patient than that involved in a breach of duty if the claim is based on negligence.[14] [emphasis added]

The failure to highlight the main and general purpose of the medical procedure would be a major failure of communication as compared to the omission to mention the possible side effect.

5.2.3 Understanding the information

In order to make a viable choice in consenting to treatment, the patient must be able to understand the information given by the medical doctor. The patient's ability to understand is conditioned by (i) his or her mental capacity to understand the information given; and (ii) the doctor's ability to communicate and his mode of communicating the information.

With respect to (i), the House of Lords in *Gillick v West Norfolk & Wisbech Area Health Authority*[15] held that the patient's capacity or competence to consent to medical examination and treatment at common law was based on the level of maturity and intelligence of the patient to understand the nature of the proposed treatment. Young age *per se* is not an automatic barrier to capacity to consent to treatment. The capacity of the patient to give consent or to refuse treatment varies with the gravity of the decision to be made.[16] On the facts, the child under 16 years old possessed the capacity to consent to contraceptive treatment. Great emphasis was placed on the child's personal autonomy and interests. Lord Scarman in *Gillick*[17] stated that "parental rights are derived from parental duty and exist only so long as they are needed for the protection of the person and property of the child".

---

12 *Chatterton v Gerson* [1981] QB 432 at 443. On the facts, the patient was aware of the general nature of the injection given by the medical doctor; thus, the consent was valid. See also *Hills v Potter* [1984] 1 WLR 641; [1983] 3 All ER 716.
13 [1981] QB 432.
14 *Chatterton v Gerson* [1981] QB 432 at 442.
15 [1986] AC 112.
16 *Re T (adult: refusal of treatment)* [1993] Fam 95 at 113, *per* Lord Donaldson.
17 [1986] AC 112 at 183-184.

98 *Consent to treatment*

Outside of common law, there may be specific statutory requirements on consent relating to age and status of the patient. For example, the Voluntary Sterilization Act[18] stipulates that:

> A registered medical practitioner may carry out treatment for sexual sterilization on any person if, and only if, the following conditions are satisfied: ...
> (*c*) ... ... in the case of an unmarried person who is below 21 years of age, if the person, and at least one parent or guardian of the person, both give consent to such treatment;
> (*d*) in the case of a married person who lacks capacity within the meaning of section 4 of the Mental Capacity Act (Cap 177A) to consent to such treatment, if, on the application of the person's spouse, the court makes an order declaring that such treatment is necessary in the best interests of that person...

The patient's mental capacity to understand the information in relation to the requirements of the MCA will be further elaborated on below.

As for the communication of information to the patient, the doctor should be conscious of the patient's level of understanding and seek to communicate the sometimes complex medical or health information to the patient without technical jargon so that the patient can understand the broad nature of the treatment that he will be undergoing. Sometimes, the information may have to be communicated with the aid of family members or via translation to a language or dialect that the patient understands.

5.2.4 Scope of consent

The scope of consent has to be tailored to the treatment sought to be performed or carried out by the doctor on the patient. Consent may be given for a treatment or aspect of the treatment but not another surgical procedure. For example, consent to surgery for the purpose of removing an appendix does not extend to the removal of a fallopian tube.[19]

5.3 Mental capacity

Under the MCA,[20] a mentally incapacitated person is one who is unable to make a decision for himself in relation to a matter due to both clinical and functional inability.[21] The clinical component refers to the "impairment of, or a disturbance in the functioning of, the mind or brain".[22] As for the functional inability component, the statute states that a person is "unable to make a decision for himself" if he is unable to understand the information relevant to the decision, to retain that information, to use or weigh that information as part of the process

---

18 (Cap 347, 2013 Rev Ed), section 3(2).
19 *Eg, Potts v North West Regional Health Authority*, The Guardian, 23 July 1983 (consent to routine postnatal vaccination against rubella but the syringe for the injection contained a contraceptive drug, and defendants liable in battery).
20 (Cap 177A, 2010 Rev Ed).
21 See *Leow Li Yoon v Liu Jiu Chang* [2016] 1 SLR 595 (on mental capacity to execute CPF nomination form).
22 Section 4.

of making the decision, or to communicate his decision.[23] Furthermore, it must be shown that the functional inability to make a decision was caused by the mental impairment.[24] The impairment or disturbance may be permanent or temporary.[25]

The fact that a person suffers from a mental disorder does not necessarily mean he or she is mentally incapable of making decisions.[26] A person may lack capacity to make certain decisions but have capacity for other decisions.[27] Hence, mental capacity is issue-specific.

Factors such as undue influence exerted by a third party on the person can affect his or her mental capacity. Relevant enquiries include (i) whether the person was capable of understanding that a third party was opposed to his interests or if that inability was caused by mental impairment; (ii) whether the person's susceptibility to undue influence was caused by mental impairment; and (iii) whether the person was unable to obtain assistance in making decisions due to undue influence.[28]

It should be stated from the outset that the MCA does not apply to certain matters such as consent to sexual sterilisation, consent to treatment to terminate a pregnancy and the making or revocation of an advance medical directive.[29] In the Voluntary Sterilization Act mentioned above, where an unmarried person undergoing sexual sterilisation lacks mental capacity to consent to treatment, the parent or guardian may apply to the court for a declaration that such treatment is "necessary in the best interests" of the person.[30]

There are a few general principles stipulated in section 3 of the MCA on the presumption of mental capacity:

- A person must be assumed to have capacity unless it is established that he lacks capacity.
- A person is not to be treated as unable to make a decision unless all practicable steps to help him to do so have been taken without success.
- A person is not to be treated as unable to make a decision merely because he makes an unwise decision.

In addition, a person cannot be adjudged to be mentally incapable merely by reference to his age or appearance, or a condition or aspect of his behaviour.[31]

---

23 Section 5.
24 *Re BKR* [2015] 4 SLR 81 at [109]; *York City Council v C* [2014] 2 WLR 1.
25 Section 4(2).
26 *Eg, Re GAV* [2014] SGDC 215 ("existence of a diagnosis of schizophrenia did not in itself mean that P must automatically be determined to lack capacity").
27 *A NHS Trust v X* [2014] EWCOP 35 (patient mentally incapable of understanding her condition of anorexia nervosa, but mentally capable with regard to her alcohol dependence syndrome).
28 *Re BKR* [2015] 4 SLR 81 at [125]-[126]. On the impact of presumed undue influence on mental capacity, see *BUV v BUU* [2019] SGHCF 15; and discussion in Chan (2020).
29 Section 26.
30 Section 3(2)(e).
31 Section 4(3).

100 Consent to treatment

With respect to functional inability to make decisions, the "information relevant to a decision" includes information about the reasonably foreseeable consequences of (i) deciding one way or another; or (ii) failing to make the decision. The patient is

> not to be regarded as unable to understand the information relevant to a decision if he is able to understand an explanation of it given to him in a way that is appropriate to his circumstances (using simple language, visual aids or any other means).[32]

Though this statutory provision is "aimed at helping a person retain her existing decision-making ability", there is nonetheless a need for a base level of decision-making capacity.[33] On the inability to retain information, the "fact that a person is able to retain the information relevant to a decision for a short period only does not prevent him from being regarded as able to make the decision".[34]

The clinical assessment of mental capacity depends on the person's state of mind and possible external factors impacting on the diagnosed mental disorders.[35] Reference may be made to expert evidence and symptoms enumerated in diagnostic manuals.[36] Doctors may also use certain questionnaires and tests[37] to assess mental capacity.

The Singapore Court of Appeal in *Re BKR*[38] stated that evidence would be drawn from medical experts as to the nature of mental impairment and its effect on the person's cognitive abilities. As for the functional aspects to make a decision, this will be primarily assessed by the court rather than by medical experts. The Court of Appeal preferred an inquisitorial approach to assessing mental capacity, and suggested that a more "sensible" approach would be for judges to direct the inquiry with input from an independent medical expert; such an approach can also save time and costs.

5.3.1 Decisions on treatment for mentally incapacitated persons

When the person is assessed to be mentally incapable, the "best interests" test and the "least restrictive" approach are applicable[39]:

- An act done, or a decision made, under the MCA for or on behalf of a person who lacks capacity must be done, or made, in his best interests.

---

32 Section 5(2).
33 *BUV v BUU* [2019] SGHCF 15 at [88].
34 Section 5(3).
35 *Ong Pang Siew v PP* [2011] 1 SLR 606 at [43] and [44] (symptoms of depressive disorder may overlap with other medical conditions and factors such as death of loved one or divorce may lead to depression).
36 The diagnostic criteria listed in the Diagnostic and Statistical Manual of Mental Disorders (4th edition), published by the American Psychiatric Association (DSM-IV); see *PP v Khwan-On Nathaphon* [2001] SGHC 313 at [106] and [111].
37 *Egs*, Mini-Mental State Examination and the Abbreviated Mental test.
38 *Re BKR* [2015] 4 SLR 81 at [134].
39 Section 3, MCA.

- Before the act is done, or the decision is made, regard must be had to whether the purpose for which it is needed can be as effectively achieved in a way that is less restrictive of the person's rights and freedom of action.

The patient (or P) who has attained the age of 21 years may authorise a person (donee) under a lasting power of attorney (LPA) to make decisions as to the patient's personal welfare should he become mentally incapable of making such decisions. Where the LPA has authorised the donee to make decisions about the patient's personal welfare, such authority may extend to giving or refusing consent to the carrying out or continuation of a treatment by a person providing healthcare for P if, and only if, the LPA states so expressly.[40] There are, however, two restrictions on the scope of decisions relating to P's personal welfare. The donee authorised to make decisions about P's personal welfare may not make any decision with respect to the carrying out or continuation of[41]:

(a) life-sustaining treatment on P, whether or not amounting to extraordinary life-sustaining treatment[42]; or
(b) any other treatment on P which a person providing healthcare reasonably believes is necessary to prevent a serious deterioration in P's condition.

Alternatively, if the patient has not made an LPA, the court may, upon application, appoint a deputy to deal with the patient's personal welfare relating to treatment (that has not been excluded by the MCA).

Under the MCA, the proxy decision-maker is immune from battery if he takes reasonable steps to establish whether the person lacks capacity, and reasonably believes, when doing the act (such as administering medical treatment to the patient) that the person lacks capacity and that it will be in his best interests for the act to be done.[43] However, this does not exclude liability arising from negligence in doing the act.[44]

Where a person intends to restrain the mentally incapacitated person, he must, in addition to the above requirements, reasonably believe that it is necessary to do the act in order to prevent harm to the mentally incapacitated person *and* the act is a proportionate response to the likelihood of the mentally incapacitated person suffering harm and the seriousness of the harm.[45]

5.3.2 When patient is mentally incapable: best interests test

Before applying the "best interests" approach, we must consider whether it is likely that the patient would at some point be mentally incapable of making the decision in question and

---

40 Section 13(6) MCA. See also Section 22(1)(d) MCA on the scope of decisions relating to P's "personal welfare".
41 Section 13(8).
42 As defined in section 2 of the Advance Medical Directive Act (Cap. 4A).
43 Section 7.
44 Section 7(3).
45 Section 8.

when he is likely to have capacity,[46] and allow for and encourage his participation in the act done for him and the decisions affecting him as far as reasonably practicable.[47]

To ascertain whether a decision as to the carrying out or continuation of treatment (not excluded by the MCA) is in the best interests of the person, the following considerations would be relevant[48]:

- the person's past and present wishes and feelings (and, in particular, any relevant written statement made by him when he had capacity)
- the beliefs and values that would be likely to influence his decision if he had capacity
- the other factors that he would be likely to consider if he were able to do so.

Furthermore, the views of the following persons must take into account, if it is practicable and appropriate to consult them[49]:

- anyone named by the person as someone to be consulted on the matter in question or on matters of that kind
- anyone engaged in caring for the person or interested in his welfare
- any donee of an LPA granted by the person
- any deputy appointed for the person by the court.

The best interests approach promotes beneficence and welfare for the patient. Moreover, the references to the patient's past and present wishes, beliefs and values go towards enhancing authenticity in the decisions made. In considering the patient's past and present wishes, beliefs and values that would influence the decision if he had capacity, the "best interests" approach in the MCA would appear to incorporate, to some extent, the notion of substituted judgement (Chan 2011, at pp. 122-123). Strictly speaking, the "best interests" approach is focused on the welfare of the patient which is conceptually distinct from making a substituted judgement on behalf of the patient (*ie*, in effect, attempting to make a decision which the patient would have made in the circumstances that may or may not be to promote his best interests). Nonetheless, in considering what the patient would have preferred or desired in the circumstances, the "best interest" approach seeks to promote patient autonomy where possible even in a situation where the patient was mentally incompetent to make the decision.

Box 5.1 - Substituted judgement versus best interests

Are there any material differences between substituted judgement and best interests? To what extent do they respect patient autonomy? Which approach do you prefer?

---

46 Section 6(3).
47 Section 6(4).
48 Section 6(7).
49 Section 6(8).

The case of *Aintree University Hospitals NHS Foundation Trust v James*[50] illustrates the application of the "best interests" approach. The Hospital Trust sought a declaration that the patient (James) lacked capacity to consent to or refuse treatment and that it would be in his best interests for the treatment to be withheld. James was suffering from stroke, cardiac arrest, recurring infections and multiple organ failure. The treatment consisted of: (1) invasive support for circulatory problems (*ie*, drugs to correct low blood pressure); (2) renal replacement therapy; and (3) cardiopulmonary resuscitation. He received assisted nutrition and hydration through a nasogastric tube.

The issue according to the UK Supreme Court was whether it would be in the best interests of the patient to have the treatment rather than whether it was in his best interests to withhold treatment. The court ultimately stated that it was not in the best interests of the patient to be given the treatment. It considered the patient's welfare in the widest sense including the medical, social and psychological aspects.[51] It is based on a subjective test which means that decision-makers should put themselves in the shoes of the individual patient and assess the patient's attitude to the treatment, his or her wishes, feelings, beliefs and values and consult others interested in his welfare and their views of the patient's attitude.[52]

5.3.3 When patient is mentally incapable: defence of necessity

At common law, doctors may rely on the defence of necessity to treat patients in emergency situations where there is imminent threat to life or serious injury. In *Re F (mental patient: sterilisation)*,[53] the defence was justified on the basis of saving the patient's life or to prevent deterioration of the patient's physical or mental health. In *Re A (children) (conjoined twins: surgical separation)*,[54] a common artery allowed J to circulate oxygenated blood for the conjoined twins J and M. A separation surgery would result in J continuing to live and M's death within minutes; however, without the surgery, both will die within 3-6 months. The parents, who were Roman Catholics, refused to consent to separation surgery. The hospital sought a court declaration to perform separation surgery. The English court held it was lawful for the doctors to carry out separation surgery based on necessity and the balancing of interests of both twins (see Chapter 10). The defence of necessity was also applied in *Bournewood*[55] with respect to the treatment and detention of a mentally ill patient.

5.4 Refusal of treatment

With respect to refusal of treatment by patients, the courts will generally consider the following issues: the patient's right or autonomy to decide whether to refuse treatment, the patient's competence to make such a decision, and if the patient was not mentally capable of

---

50 [2013] 3 WLR 1299.
51 [2013] 3 WLR 1299 at [39].
52 [2013] 3 WLR 1299 at [39].
53 [1990] 2 AC 1.
54 [2001] Fam 147.
55 *R v Bournewood Community and Mental Health NHS Trust, ex parte L* [1999] 1 AC 458.

104 Consent to treatment

refusing treatment, the courts will then consider what decision would be in the best interests of the patient.

The English court in *Re T (adult: refusal of medical treatment)*[56] held that a patient's autonomy to refuse medical treatment can be overridden if there is evidence vitiating such a refusal. T, who was 34 weeks pregnant, indicated her refusal of blood transfusion to the doctor and midwife in the presence of her mother, a Jehovah Witness. When her condition became critical, her father and boyfriend applied to the court for a declaration that, notwithstanding T's refusal, it was not unlawful to administer the blood transfusion. The English Court of Appeal stated that patients have the right of autonomy to refuse medical treatment, notwithstanding that the reasons for making the choice might be "rational, irrational, unknown or even non-existent".[57] The court found, however, that T's refusal of blood transfusion was vitiated due to the impairment of the patient's mental capacity arising from her injuries and medication, undue influence from the patient's mother and the misinformation given to her about alternative treatment. The doctor was therefore entitled to treat the patient in accordance with the clinical judgement of what was in the "best interests" of the patient.[58]

A pregnant woman was held to be competent to refuse admission to hospital for induced delivery due to pre-eclampsia which was life-threatening for both mother and unborn child.[59] Further, a pregnant woman, if she is mentally competent, may refuse medical intervention even if the consequence was the death or serious handicap of the foetus, and may refuse anaesthesia knowing that her decision might significantly reduce the chance of her unborn child being born alive.[60]

The Singapore High Court case of *Re LP (adult patient: medical treatment)*[61] is an intriguing case on the extent to which patient autonomy ought to be respected and the application of the "best interests" approach. The patient, a diabetic who complained of pain in both her feet, was told by doctors that her legs had to be amputated. She was "conscious and alert" when she requested her doctors to "save her legs at all costs". Subsequently, the patient went into a coma. The medical condition of the legs became critical and the doctors gave evidence that if the operation to amputate the legs were not carried out, the patient would soon die. The High Court ruled that, despite the patient's abovementioned request to the doctors, there was no clear and express refusal of treatment by the patient. With respect to the patient's request not to amputate her legs, the learned judge observed that the decision was probably made without the benefit of medical advice about imminent death.[62] As such, the correct approach was to act in the best interests of the patient.[63] Choo J explained the approach as follows[64]:

---

56 [1993] Fam 95.
57 *Re T (adult: refusal of medical treatment)* [1993] Fam 95 at 102 and 113, per Lord Donaldson.
58 *Re T (adult: refusal of medical treatment)* [1993] Fam 95 at 115, per Lord Donaldson.
59 *St George's Healthcare NHS Trust v S* [1999] Fam 26.
60 *Re MB* [1997] 2 FLR 426 at [30], [36] and [60] (she was adjudged not mentally competent due to her phobia of the anaesthetist's needle; and the best interests test was applied in favour of the operation).
61 [2006] 2 SLR(R) 13.
62 *Re LP (adult patient: medical treatment)* [2006] 2 SLR(R) 13 at [11].
63 *Re LP (adult patient: medical treatment)* [2006] 2 SLR(R) 13 at [9].
64 *Re LP (adult patient: medical treatment)* [2006] 2 SLR(R) 13 at [9].

if there is clear evidence of consent or refusal to consent to any medical treatment, doctors will have to respect the patient's decision. When it comes to a situation where the patient is incapable of giving her consent, or where such consent (or lack of it) was not made reasonably clear, the doctors would have to treat the patient according to what they think is in the best interests of the patient. The best interests of the patient may not be the best interests of her spouse or parents or children. And likewise, what the patient might think is in her own best interests may not be similarly shared by the doctors. The decision as to what is in a patient's best interests from the point of view of the doctors is strictly a medical one, and one that is expected to be professionally formed.

In this case, the court accepted the medical opinion that the amputation of the legs would be in the patient's best interests.[65]

The case suggests that the threshold for ascertaining the validity of the patient's refusal of treatment is fairly high. The patient had contemplated death as a possibility when she also mentioned to her son that she would "rather die than lose her legs", and expressed a wish that the doctors would not amputate her legs. In this case, unlike in *Re T*, there was no evidence of mental incapacity nor misinformation given to the patient. Yet her request was not sufficiently clear to amount to a refusal of treatment. Three points may be noted here. First, the case was decided before the enactment of the MCA in Singapore and the court did not therefore make reference to the MCA principles on ascertaining mental capacity and the assessment of "best interests" of the patient discussed in the previous section (*eg*, to take account of the patient's preferences and other circumstances rather than a strictly medical decision). Further, the more recent UK decision of *Aintree* suggested that the "best interests" test would require decision-makers to place themselves in the shoes of the patient and is more holistic than a purely medical decision. Second, the judge did not place much emphasis on the patient's request to her doctors to "save her legs at all costs", and her statement to her son that she would "rather die than lose her legs" because the substituted judgement approach in US, according to the learned judge, was not applicable in Singapore. It should be noted that even under the "best interests" approach, the patient's statements, to the extent that they revealed her preferences and values, should remain relevant to the assessment. Third, the judicial outcome in *Re LP* was understandable given that acceding to the patient's request not to amputate her legs would likely result in her death, the urgency of the particular court application where there was "little time for reflection",[66] and that the judge could not take cognisance of the views of family members of the patient who had only one 16-year-old son at that time.

---

65 *Re LP (adult patient: medical treatment)* [2006] 2 SLR(R) 13 at [3]. See analogous fact situation in *Re C* (1994) 1 WLR 290 (surgeon advised treatment by amputation of the leg below the knee which patient refused, and instead received conservative treatment which improved patient's condition; patient successfully obtained injunction to prevent the amputation of his leg by the hospital without his written consent).
66 *Re LP (adult patient: medical treatment)* [2006] 2 SLR(R) 13 at [10].

A comparison may be made with the approach in *Malette v Shulman*[67] where the Canadian court stated that the right of the patient – a Jehovah Witness – to refuse treatment (blood transfusion) should be respected. This is based on the principles of self-determination and individual autonomy. Such freedom of patients to decide would only be "meaningful" if they were given the "right to make choices that accord with their own values, regardless of how unwise or foolish those choices may appear to others".[68] The plaintiff was injured in a motor vehicle accident and taken to a local hospital. She was bleeding profusely. A card was found by nurses in the plaintiff's purse forbidding, under any circumstances, any form of blood transfusion though permitting the use of alternative non-blood therapies. When the patient's condition deteriorated and continued to bleed, the doctor decided to administer blood transfusion notwithstanding the prohibition and the instructions of the daughter of the patient who sought to terminate the transfusion. The patient's claim based on the tort of battery against the doctor for disregarding the prohibition succeeded. General damages were awarded against the doctor notwithstanding the doctor's "honest and even justifiable belief that the treatment was medically essential",[69] and that the medical procedure was performed with proper care. Further, the card was regarded as a valid advance directive from the plaintiff *vis-à-vis* treatment and applied to such an emergency situation[70]:

> Its instructions were clear, precise and unequivocal and manifested a calculated decision to reject a procedure offensive to the patient's religious convictions. The instructions excluded, from potential emergency treatment, a single medical procedure well known to the lay public and within its comprehension. The religious belief of Jehovah's Witnesses, with respect to blood transfusions, was known to the doctor and, indeed, is a matter of common knowledge to providers of health care. The card undoubtedly belonged to and was signed by Mrs. Malette; its authenticity was not questioned by anyone at the hospital and, realistically, could not have been questioned.

Robin JA also opined that a balance has to be struck amongst competing interests. In this case, the "interest in the freedom to reject or refuse to consent to intrusions of her bodily integrity – outweighs the interest of the state in the preservation of life and health and the protection of the integrity of the medical profession".[71]

Box 5.2 – Judicial approaches to refusal of treatment

What in your view are the merits and demerits of the approach in *Re LP* and *Malette*, respectively, on the patient's refusal of treatment?

---

67 67 DLR (4th) 321, 72 OR (2d) 417 (1990) (Ontario Court of Appeal).
68 67 DLR (4th) 321, 72 OR (2d) 417 at [19].
69 67 DLR (4th) 321, 72 OR (2d) 417 at [13].
70 67 DLR (4th) 321, 72 OR (2d) 417 at [44].
71 67 DLR (4th) 321, 72 OR (2d) 417 at [37].

Such advance directives need not be in writing. The court may also take account of a change of religious beliefs which may have the effect of revoking or invalidating a previous directive to refuse blood transfusion.[72]

In certain limited situations, the refusal of treatment (*eg*, the refusal of injections to prevent the spread of an infectious disease) may result in health threats not only to the individual patient but also to others or even the larger community. In *Malette*,[73] despite the significance of an individual's right of self-determination, the judge also acknowledged that the individual right may be overridden in a case where the state may "require that citizens submit to medical procedures in order to eliminate a health threat to the community or it may prohibit citizens from engaging in activities which are inherently dangerous to their lives". The objectives of non-maleficence and beneficence may be relevant here.

With respect to the refusal to receive food and nutrition, the case of *Secretary of State for the Home Department v Robb*[74] suggested that such refusal should be respected. In that case, the prisoner wanted to go on a hunger strike and refused to give consent to receive nutrition. The court declared that it was lawful for prison officers to refrain from providing nutrition to the prisoner on hunger strike since the prisoner made the decision with a sound mind.[75]

5.5 Withdrawal of consent to treatment

The patient should have the right to withdraw his consent to treatment provided the patient is capable of doing so at the relevant time and the expression of his decision to withdraw consent was unambiguous.[76] Upon a valid withdrawal of consent by the patient, the treatment or procedure must be terminated unless the effect of termination of treatment is life threatening or will pose immediate and serious health problems to the patient.[77]

In considering whether to continue with the procedure, the patient may also want to have information from the doctor as to whether there has been a material change of circumstances impacting on the risks and benefits of continuing with the procedure. This should arguably form part of the doctor's duty to give medical advice provided the information on the change of circumstances would be regarded as material from the perspective of a reasonable patient.[78]

---

72 *HE v A Hospital NHS Trust* [2003] EWHC 1017 (Fam) (patient was raised a Muslim, became a Jehovah witness, was subsequently engaged to a Muslim man and had committed to return to Islam a few months before her illness).
73 67 DLR (4th) 321, 72 OR (2d) 417 at [34] (1990).
74 [1995] Fam 127.
75 But see older case of *Leigh v Gladstone* (1909) 26 TLR 139 (force-feeding a prisoner on hunger strike was regarded as lawful).
76 *Ciarlariello v Schacter* (1993) 100 DLR (4th) 609 (SCC).
77 (1993) 100 DLR (4th) 609 at 619, *per* Cory J.
78 *Hii Chii Kok v Ooi Peng Jin London Lucien and another* [2017] 2 SLR 492.

5.6 ECEG 2016 and disciplinary cases

We will examine how the SMC's ethical code and ethical guidelines on consent have been applied in medical disciplinary (and medical negligence) cases and important ethical considerations for medical doctors dealing with patients with diminished mental capacity.

5.6.1 Consent and patient autonomy

Section C6 of ECEG 2016 states that

> [a]n important part of patient autonomy involves ensuring that patients give their valid consent (if they are able to do so) to any treatment or procedure prior to their undergoing such treatment or procedure. This involves the patients making voluntary decisions on their medical care after having known and understood the benefits and risks involved.

It also lists what amounts to "good consent taking" (Annex A).[79] The guidelines cover a myriad of issues including information to be given to patient, scope of consent, emergency situations, refusal of treatment, withdrawal of consent, minors and patients with diminished mental capacity.

Guideline 4.2.2 of the ECEG (2002) on informed consent states that the doctor shall provide information on benefits, risks, possible complications and alternative courses available.[80] This is applicable to the giving of medical advice under the tort of negligence. The ECEG does not, however, impose on doctors an "absolute and unyielding obligation to explain *all* the benefits, risks, complications, and alternative viable treatment options to a patient regardless of the patient's existing knowledge" but only to ensure that the patient is apprised of the relevant information about the various viable treatment options.[81] This duty will be discharged as long as the doctor has reasonable grounds to believe that the patient was already well acquainted with such information.

The Disciplinary Tribunal (DT) in *Singapore Medical Council v Dr Lim Lian Arn*[82] imposed a maximum fine of $100,000 under the law for failing to inform a patient about the risks associated with a relatively simple procedure. The decision was criticised for being harsh on the medical doctor and raised a query why the doctor's conduct amounted to "professional misconduct". The DT's decision was quashed by the High Court.[83] In considering the question of informed consent, the High Court applied the tort of negligence approach in *Hii Chii Kok v Ooi Peng Jin London Lucien and another*[84] that the information to be disclosed must be relevant and material to the patient (see Chapter 3). This is to be assessed from the reasonable patient's perspective as to what he or she regards as significant for the purpose of making a

---

79 Note the Workgroup (2019) Report had recommended in Annex F a shorter list of consent-taking guidelines.
80 *Yong Thiam Look Peter v Singapore Medical Council* [2017] SGHC 10 (the medical doctor was convicted of the charge of professional misconduct under s 53(1)(*d*) of the MRA for failing to comply with Guideline 4.2.2 of ECEG 2002 and was suspended for six months).
81 *Lam Kwok Tai Leslie v Singapore Medical Council* [2017] 5 SLR 1168 at [77].
82 [2018] SMCDT 9.
83 *Singapore Medical Council v Lim Lian Arn* [2019] SGHC 172.
84 [2017] 2 SLR 492.

decision. Where there are a few options available, what is material would depend on the nature and likelihood of any adverse side effects or complications in respect of those options.[85]

5.6.2 Treatment of patients with diminished mental capacity

Section C9 of the ECEG 2016 (on caring for patients with diminished mental capacity) is consistent with the main tenets of the MCA with respect to the presumption of mental capacity where possible, respecting patient autonomy, deciding in the best interests of patient and protecting them from harm, neglect and abuse:

> Caring for patients with diminished mental capacity comes with additional responsibilities. Apart from their increased vulnerability arising from their diminished mental capacity, they may have fluctuating mental capacity (as opposed to an irreversible loss of such capacity) and this needs to be taken into account when decision making is required. Providing good care to patients with diminished mental capacity means:
>
> 1   You must treat patients with diminished mental capacity with respect and recognise their rights, values and preferences.
> 2   You must assess how much patients can understand given that they may have fluctuating or residual cognitive function that may well be sufficient to allow them to participate in decision-making.
> 3   If you determine that patients do not have sufficient cognitive function, you may consider the views of family, carers or those with legal authority to represent them, but in all cases, you must ascertain as best as you can what is in the patients' best interests and decide accordingly.
> 4   You must be aware of the vulnerability of such patients to abuse, neglect or self-harm and if you have reasonable grounds for suspicions, you must either offer assistance to rectify this or report this to the relevant authorities.

The Handbook on Medical Ethics explains that "[p]atients' "best interests" are representative of their right to autonomy". Whilst the MCA as mentioned above refers to "the other factors that [the patient] would be likely to consider if he were able to do so" in applying the "best interests" approach, the Handbook provides a list of "relevant non-exhaustive factors" from the medical doctor's perspective when assessing what would be in the best interests of the patient:

(a)   The benefits expected from the proposed intervention.
(b)   Patients' previously expressed preferences or wishes.
(c)   Patients' personal views, values and beliefs which should be ascertained insofar as the patient is able to shed light on them or has previously expressed.
(d)   The background culture or religion of the patients that may influence the decision in question.

---

85   There was no expert evidence on the gravity and likelihood of adverse side effects or complications of the injection in *Singapore Medical Council v Lim Lian Arn* [2019] SGHC 172 at [50].

110   *Consent to treatment*

(e) The opinions of other healthcare workers, caregivers or immediate family members of the patients, or other professionals involved in the patients' care.
(f) The values of society.
(g) The option which least restricts a patient's future choices in situations where there are multiple appropriate options that may potentially be in patients' best interests.
(h) Resource availability and limitations on the part of both the healthcare provider and patients.

5.7 Conclusion

An individual's bodily integrity is sacrosanct such that the act of making physical contact or touching without his consent offends basic legal and moral norms save in limited situations. To explicate the concept of "consent" to treatment, we need to analyse the voluntariness of the patient purportedly giving consent, the content of information provided to the patient, the patient's understanding the information or lack thereof, and scope of the consent depending on the nature and purpose of treatment. Another important consideration for consent to treatment is of course the clinical and functional assessment of the patient's mental capacity under the MCA in a manner that is respectful of personal autonomy. The best interests approach, which applies should the patient not be mentally capable to make the decision on treatment, is assessed holistically with reference to, amongst others, the patient's preferences, values and beliefs, the evidence of caregivers and family members and the doctor's assessment. A similar approach based on the autonomy and best interests of the patient is applicable to cases involving refusal of treatment and withdrawal of consent. These cases have generated some controversy as to the extent to which the patient's wishes should be respected and what should be involved in assessing the "best interests" of the patient. Finally, in the penultimate section, we note the significance of ethical guidelines for medical doctors on consent-taking and dealing with patients with diminished mental capacity and related medical disciplinary cases that are generally consistent with the statutory framework.

Annex A

ECEG 2016 Section C6

1. Consent must be obtained for all aspects of medical care, whether it is minor interventions with minimal risks or major interventions with significant risks or side effects. For minor tests, treatments or procedures that have low risks, oral consent or implied consent through compliance is sufficient.
2. You must take valid and adequately documented consent from patients for tests, treatments or procedures that are considered complex, invasive or have significant potential for adverse effects.
3. You must ensure that patients are made aware of the purpose of tests, treatments or procedures to be performed on them, as well as the benefits, significant limitations, material risks (including those that would be important to patients in their particular circumstances) and possible complications as well as alternatives available to them.

Consent to treatment

4. You must (to the best of your knowledge) inform patients about the persons who will be performing the tests, treatments or procedures that are invasive and carry higher risks. The more invasive or risky a test, treatment or procedure, the more specific and detailed must be the information about the persons conducting it.
5. If patients consent to you performing any test, treatment or procedure under anaesthesia, you must not engage other persons to carry out the procedures on your behalf, or support your performance in a material way (excepting routine assistant surgeons), without patients' knowledge, unless it is an urgent or emergency situation.
6. You must be clear about the scope of patients' consent. If there are likely to be further tests or treatments that are contingent upon your initial findings, you must explain this to your patients. Advance or anticipatory consent for such further procedures must be obtained if patients are going to be unable to participate in decision-making at the time of your initial findings. You must be clear about the limits to the range of options or alternatives that patients set in their consent.
7. Patients must be made to understand that they may withdraw or modify their consent at any time. Unless you have reasons to believe that their judgement is impaired by illness, anaesthesia or temporary mental incapacity, you must respect patients' decisions to withdraw or change consent.
8. You must either take consent personally or if it is taken for you by a team member, you must, through education, training and supervision of team members, ensure the quality of the consent taken on your behalf. In any case, you must ensure adequate documentation of the consent taking process where this involves more complex or invasive modalities with higher risks.
9. You must ensure that patients understand the information you give for the purpose of consent. If there are language difficulties, you must use interpreters.
10. Except in emergency situations, consent must be taken before a test or treatment, such that patients have sufficient time to think over their decisions and to clarify any doubts.
11. You may proceed with treatment without consent in emergency situations when patients are not capable of giving consent and where you deem treatment is necessary in patients' best interests.
12. If during a procedure you encounter situations in which you want to perform further procedures (that are not reasonable extensions of the procedure within the parameters of the consent) at the same sitting but the patient is unable to consent to it, you may proceed if you deem that the patient's life is at risk unless the further procedure is done immediately.
13. You must respect patients' right to refuse consent for tests, treatments or procedures, except when it is evident that their judgement is impaired or their mental capacity so diminished that they cannot make choices about their own care.
14. Despite it being standard practice that consent for minors is taken from parents or legal guardians, you must give consideration to the opinions of minors who are able to understand and decide for themselves.
15. If there is disagreement about consent between minors with the capacity to consent and their parents or legal guardians, you must, to the best of your ability, provide them with information and explain in a way that helps them to make more informed decisions.

16 If minors who have the capacity to understand ultimately refuse to undergo tests, treatments or procedures consented to by parents or legal guardians, but you have good reasons to believe it is medically imperative for you to proceed, you may do so if it is feasible.
17 If parents or legal guardians object to tests, treatments or procedures that you deem necessary despite your best explanations, you must act in the best interests of the minors and not of the parents. You may then have to take steps (such as going through independent advocates or the courts) in order to prevent harm to the minors.
18 If patients are too young to understand but there are no parents or legal guardians available within reasonable time to give consent, you may proceed according to your best judgement of the patients' best interests.
19 Taking consent from patients with diminished mental capacity must take into account the patients' residual or fluctuating cognitive ability. If patients can demonstrably understand, retain and use your information and explanations to make clear and consistent decisions and communicate them in a coherent manner, you must obtain consent from the patients themselves.
20 If patients have such diminished mental capacity that they cannot give consent, you must obtain consent from persons with the legal authority to make such medical decisions for them unless such persons are not contactable within reasonable time depending on the urgency of the situation. Otherwise, you must proceed according to your best judgement of the patients' best interests.

References

Chan, K.Y.G. (2020). "Assessing Mental Capacity: *BUV v BUU* [2019] SGHCF 15" 32 *SAcLJ* 287.
Chan, K.Y.G. (2016). "Intentional Torts to the Person" in Chan, K.Y.G. and Lee, P.W. (2016). *The Law of Torts in Singapore*, (Academy Publishing: Singapore), in particular pp. 52–58.
Chan, T.E. (2011). "The Elderly Patient and the Healthcare Decision-Making Framework in Singapore" in Chan, W.C. (ed) *Singapore's Ageing Population: Managing Healthcare and End of Life Decisions* (Routledge: London), pp. 113–136.
Herring, J. (2018). "Consent to Treatment", chapter 4 in Herring, J. (ed) *Medical Law and Ethics, 7th Edition* (Oxford University Press: Oxford), pp. 149–227.
Lemmens, T. (2015). "Informed Consent", Chapter 3 in Joly, Y. & Knoppers, B.M. (eds) *Routledge Handbook of Medical Law and Ethics* (Routledge: London), pp. 27–51.
Monks, S.S. (1993). "The Concept of Informed Consent in the United States, Canada, England and Australia: A Comparative Analysis" 17(2) *University of Queensland LJ* 222.
Weir, S. (2004). *Informed Consent: Patient Autonomy and Clinical Beneficence within Health Care*, 2nd Edition (Georgetown University Press: Washington, DC).
Workgroup To Review The Taking of Informed Consent and SMC Disciplinary Process (2019). Report (November) at https://www.moh.gov.sg/news-highlights/details/workgroup-proposes-wide-ranging-reforms-on-the-taking-of-informed-consent-and-singapore-medical-council-s-disciplinary-process/.

6 Mental health

6.1 Introduction

In a 2016 study, it was found that one in seven people in Singapore has experienced a mood, anxiety or alcohol use disorder in their lifetime, and that a significant majority of people (*ie*, more than three-quarters) with a mental disorder in their lifetime did not seek any professional help.[1] Singapore is also facing the acute challenges of an ageing population. In 2012, about 28,000 elderly aged 60 years and above suffered from dementia; this figure is expected to rise to 80,000 by 2030.[2] More Dementia Care Centres and Dementia villages are being built to cater to the increasing needs of the elderly.

Several decades ago, the Institute of Mental Health (IMH), the government mental health hospital, started out as a mental asylum which tended to stigmatise, exclude and isolate its patients from the community. That perception of IMH has changed over time though some stigma relating to mental health sufferers remains. The National Mental Health Blueprint for 2007-2012 signalled a shift from a hospital-based healthcare delivery system to a community-based model of psychiatric care. The Community Mental Health Masterplan subsequently launched in 2017 sought to build on the momentum. Dementia-Friendly Communities were set up to enhance, support networks for those with dementia and their caregivers. Programmes such as the Response, Early Intervention and Assessment in Community Mental Health (REACH) and the Community Health Assessment Team (CHAT) are targeted at persons from different age groups to improve community mental well-being. Community Mental Health Intervention Teams (COMIT) provide access to counselling and psychotherapy services within the community. The Agency for Integrated Care (AIC) is responsible for coordinating care and providing links to healthcare and social service agencies. Voluntary welfare organisations (VWOs) such as the Singapore Association of Mental Health (SAMH) and Simei Care Centre, a psychiatric rehabilitation centre, lend further support to persons with mental health issues.

---

1 The study was spearheaded by Institute of Mental Health (IMH) in collaboration with Ministry for Health (MOH) and Nanyang Technological University (NTU) at https://www.imh.com.sg/uploadedFiles/Newsroom/News_Releases/SMHS%202016_Media%20Release_FINAL_web%20upload.pdf.

2 https://www.channelnewsasia.com/news/commentary/dementia-anguish-and-guilt-plague-caregivers-challenge-12026944

114 *Mental health*

Mental health work in Singapore is performed by a range of healthcare and allied professionals including psychiatrists, psychiatric nurses, clinical psychologists, psychiatric case managers, and medical social workers working in government general hospitals, the IMH, outpatient polyclinics, private psychiatric services and general practitioner (GP) clinics. IMH provides training to GPs to manage patients with mild to moderate mental illness under the Mental Health-General Practitioner Partnership Programme. MOH subsidises operating subvention to IMH, psychiatry units in other Public Healthcare Institutions and intermediate and long-term care facilities to provide subsidised patient care, and funds various programmes under the National Mental Health Blueprint and Community Mental Health Masterplan. The MediShield covers inpatient treatment for psychiatric conditions.[3]

Singapore has in 2013 ratified the United Nations Convention on Rights of Persons with Disabilities.[4] Under the Convention, State parties recognise that persons with disabilities (including those with long-term mental, intellectual or sensory impairments)[5] have the right to the enjoyment of the highest attainable standard of health without discrimination on the basis of disability.[6]

Bearing in mind the general infrastructure for mental healthcare in Singapore, we will begin by examining the meaning and scope of mental disorder, incapacity and health before focusing on more specific legal issues relating to the care and treatment of persons with mental disorder and the extent to which mentally incapable persons are able to make decisions with respect to their personal and financial affairs. Furthermore, how should we assess the responsibilities of persons with mental disorder when a third party is injured by their acts under criminal and tort law?[7] Do medical doctors (especially psychiatrists) and allied healthcare professionals owe a duty of care to persons with mental health issues, and if so, to what extent? These issues are particularly challenging for lawyers and judges familiar with the proverbial mix of logic and experience in the law as they tap on the knowledge and expertise from neuroscience, psychiatry and psychology[8] about the workings of the mind, human behaviour and the symptoms associated with mental abnormalities or disabilities.[9]

6.2 Meaning and scope of mental disorder, incapacity and health

Mental disorder is a dynamic and contested concept that may be based on purely medical assessments, social standards or both. In the past, certain phenomena that have been

---

3 Singapore Parliament Reports, "Care for Persons with Mental Disabilities" (12 November 2012), Vol 89 (The Minister of State for Health Dr Amy Khor Lean Suan).
4 Adopted on 13 December 2006 during the sixty-first session of the General Assembly by resolution A/RES/61/106. It took effect in Singapore on 18 August 2013 with three reservations at https://treaties.un.org/pages/ViewDetails.aspx?src=TREATY&mtdsg_no=IV-15&chapter=4.
5 Article 1.
6 Article 25.
7 See generally Kok et al. (1994).
8 See Gwee (2017).
9 The duties and rights of a mentally disordered person under contract law, law of probate and administration and intestacy, family law and employment law are beyond the scope of this chapter.

regarded or classified as mental illnesses would surprise many people today. These include "drapetomania" (*ie*, the tendency of black slaves to flee from their masters) and homosexuality. Szasz (2001), a professor of psychiatry, argued that so-called mental illnesses were based on what people consider as unacceptable or deviant social behaviour rather than diseases proper. Other theorists (*eg*, Graham 2013)[10] preferred a hybrid model that encompasses both the medical/clinical aspect in terms of a mental incapacity or impairment and assessments of harm (*eg*, to commit suicide) to the person.

One source reference that courts and lawyers look to for information about mental disorders is the Diagnostic and Statistical Manual of Mental Disorders, American Psychiatric Association (DSM-5) which contains a catalogue of the different types of mental disorders. The DSM has undergone a number of iterations.[11] DSM-5 field trials were conducted mainly in the US to evaluate the clinical utility and feasibility of the proposed diagnoses and dimensional measures. DSM-5 was meant to be consistent with the World Health Organization's (WHO) publication of the International Classification of Diseases, 11th edition (ICD-11). The DSM-5's aim is to "create a framework for the evolution of psychiatry to advance clinical practice and facilitate ongoing research of mental disorders" (Scott 2015, at pp. 9-10). Scott (2015, at p. 11) noted that most though not all mental disorders are on a spectrum and that they may overlap with each other and to normality without distinct boundaries. Nonetheless, DSM-5 retained the categorial approach to mental disorders.

Major Depressive Disorder, alcohol abuse and Obsessive-Compulsive Disorder are the more common mental disorders amongst Singaporeans.[12] Other notable mental disorders include schizophrenia, panic disorder, bipolar disorder, post-traumatic stress disorder, addiction, anxiety disorder and dementia.

The DSM-5 states that whilst its diagnostic criteria and text are primarily used to aid clinicians in "clinical assessment, case formulation and treatment planning", it can also assist courts and attorneys in the US in assessing "forensic consequences of mental disorders" and the "legal decision-makers" in making their "determinations" (Scott 2015, at p. 17). The Singapore courts have acknowledged this difference between the clinical and judicial purpose. More specifically, it has been judicially noted that "just because a disorder is stated or described in DSM-5 or ICD-10 does not *automatically* lead to it being a mitigating factor" for the purpose of determining the appropriate sentence for an offender.[13]

---

10 Graham (2013, at p. 28) also referred to two additional elements of a theory of mental order namely that the incapacity or impairment is brought about by an "interactive mix of mental forces" and "a-rational neural mechanisms" that result in "truncated 'logic' or an impaired or compromised rationale".
11 The first edition of The Diagnostic and Statistical Manual, Mental Disorders was published in 1952 followed by subsequent editions: DSM-II (1968); DSM-III (1980); DSM-III-R (1987); DSM-IV (1994).
12 https://www.imh.com.sg/uploadedFiles/Newsroom/News_Releases/SMHS%202016_Media%20Release_FINAL_web%20upload.pdf.
13 *PP v Chong Hou En* [2015] 3 SLR 222 at [58], *per* Chan Seng Onn J.

Case precedents have referred to the diagnostic criteria in the DSM on dementia for the purpose of ascertaining mental capacity under the Mental Capacity Act (MCA).[14] It is sufficient for courts to assess whether a person suffered from "an impairment of, or a disturbance in the functioning of, the mind or brain" within the meaning of s 4(1) of the MCA even if they cannot specifically identify the medical condition.[15] Apart from the clinical assessment of mental impairment, we have also examined the functional aspects of incapacity in terms of making a decision as to treatment or the patient's personal affairs under the MCA (Chapter 5).

Where a person suffers from mental disorder, incapacity or impairment, we may regard him or her as experiencing mental health problems. But mental health is not merely used as a contrast to mental disorder, incapacity or impairment. "Mental Health" is an omnibus term that encompasses mental well-being in the positive sense and not only the absence of mental disorder, illness, incapacity and disability. Going beyond mental disorder, incapacity and disability, the positive sense of mental health embraces efforts to improve our mental well-being in order to cope with the stresses of daily living and interactions with others whether at work, school, home or in public areas.

We will encounter in this chapter different terms and definitions in various statutes denoting an absence or lack of mental health including "mental disorder", "disability of the mind", "mental incapacity" to make a decision, "unsound mind", "abnormality of the mind" and so on. There are substantial overlaps amongst the terms as well as material differences. The fact that a person is mentally disordered or ill does not mean he is always mentally incapable of making any decision. It is also possible to justify the detention of a mentally disordered person who is otherwise mentally capable of making a decision on medical treatment because he poses a serious danger to the public (Herring 2018, at p. 585).

6.3 Care and treatment of persons with mental disorder

The Mental Health (Care and Treatment) Act (MHCTA)[16] provides for the admission, detention, care and treatment of mentally disordered persons in designated psychiatric institutions. The term "mental disorder" has been broadly defined in the statute as "any mental illness or any other disorder or disability of the mind".[17] The decision to admit or to detain a mentally dis-

---

14 *Re BKR* [2015] 4 SLR 81 at [166] (that "The DSM-IV requires at least one of the following: (a) aphasia, which is deterioration in language function, (b) apraxia, which is impaired ability to execute motor activities, (c) agnosia, which is failure to recognise or identify objects despite intact sensory function, and (d) disturbances in executive functioning". Moreover, the memory impairment and the other symptoms "must be severe enough to cause significant impairment in social or occupational functioning", and "must represent a decline from a previous level of functioning").

15 In *Re BKR* [2015] 4 SLR 81 at [172], the court's assessment of P's condition was that it lay somewhere between Mild Cognitive Impairment and dementia on the continuum or scale.

16 (Cap 178A, 2012 Rev Ed). The old Mental Disorders and Treatment Act 1965 was repealed. See *Singapore Parliamentary Debates, Official Report* "Mental Health (Care and Treatment) Bill" (15 September 2008) vol 85, cols 57-107.

17 Section 2.

ordered person is made by a designated medical practitioner at a psychiatric institution who has examined the person and is of the opinion that the person should be treated, or continue to be treated, as an inpatient at the psychiatric institution.[18] The person shall not be detained in a psychiatric institution unless (i) he is suffering from a mental disorder that warrants his detention in a psychiatric institution for treatment; and (ii) the detention is "necessary in the interests of the health or safety of the person or for the protection of other persons".[19] An order for detention for treatment based on the opinion of a designated medical practitioner at a psychiatric institution will be for an initial period of 72 hours, which may be extended to one month by another medical practitioner, and if need be, for a further period not exceeding six months based on the opinions of two medical practitioners at a psychiatric institution (including one psychiatrist).[20] Patients with less severe mental health problems may be treated as outpatients.

Inspections of psychiatric facilities are carried out by a Board of Visitors at least once every three months who will also examine patients and report to the Director of Medical Services.[21] The Visitors may apply to a Magistrate for the person to be detained for up to 12 months.[22]

It is not surprising that a medical practitioner who has under his care a person believed to be mentally disordered or to require psychiatric treatment may refer him to a designated medical practitioner at a psychiatric institution.[23] In addition, the statute provides that a police officer may apprehend any person believed to be dangerous to himself or other persons and such danger is reasonably suspected to be attributable to a mental disorder[24] and bring the person to a medical practitioner or designated medical practitioner at a psychiatric institution.

It is a criminal offence for a medical practitioner, nurse, attendant or other person employed by or rendering service in any psychiatric institution or hospital to "ill-treat" any patient.[25] The scope of ill-treatment is broad. It includes the act of subjecting the patient to physical or sexual abuse, and wilfully or unreasonably doing any act or causing the patient to do any act or neglecting the patient[26] so as to endanger the safety of the patient thereby causing unnecessary physical pain, suffering or injury, emotional injury and injury to health.[27]

---

18 Section 10(1). This is subject to the prohibition in section 11 on medical practitioners who are excluded from making such a decision.
19 Section 10(6).
20 Section 10.
21 Section 5.
22 Section 13.
23 Section 9.
24 Section 7(1). The police officer's reasonable belief that a person is doing or about to do an act which is dangerous to himself is sufficient basis for the police officer's or special police officer's reasonable suspicion that the danger to that person is attributable to a mental disorder: section 7(2).
25 Section 22(1).
26 This includes neglecting to provide adequate food, clothing, medical aid or care for the patient: section 22(3).
27 Section 22(2).

118   *Mental health*

The MHCTA[28] grants immunity to persons (including the medical practitioners) who have done an act under the statute from any civil or criminal liabilities, whether on the ground of want of jurisdiction or on any other ground, unless the person has acted in bad faith or without reasonable care. Persons who have been arrested or detained under the statute will have to seek the court's permission prior to commencing legal action against such persons who have been granted immunity under the statute.[29] Permission will be refused unless there is "substantial ground" for the contention that the person(s) enforcing the statute have acted in bad faith or without reasonable care.[30]

6.4 Proxy decision-making on behalf of mentally incapacitated persons and their rights under the Mental Capacity Act

In Chapter 5, we have already discussed a patient's mental capacity under the MCA for the purpose of assessing whether there is valid consent to treatment, and if the patient is mentally incapable of giving consent to treatment, the application of the "best interests" approach for decision-making.

We will now examine the MCA framework relating to proxy decision-making on behalf of mentally incapacitated persons in relation to their personal welfare and/or financial affairs, the scope of protection and their legal rights. Prior to the MCA, there were already provisions in the Mental Disorders and Treatment Act (MDTA)[31] for the appointment of Committee of Persons and Committee of Estate by the High Court to act on behalf of mentally incapacitated persons in their daily affairs and financial matters respectively. This component of the MDTA has been supplanted by provisions in the MCA for court-appointed deputies to act on behalf of such persons. A new provision in MCA 2008, which was not found in the previous MDTA, introduced the lasting power of attorney (LPA), a legal mechanism allowing those who are still cognitively intact to appoint one or more persons to decide and to act on their behalf if and when they lack mental capacity in the future.

A Mental Capacity Code of Practice[32] has been promulgated to provide guidance and information about how the MCA works in practice. A failure to follow the Code of Practice can be used as evidence in court[33] whether in civil or criminal proceedings.[34] The proxy interacting with a person who lacks mental capacity would have to take note of the Code of Practice.[35]

The demarcation between the MCA and MHCTA should also be noted. Where a person's treatment for mental disorder is regulated by the MHCTA, the MCA does not authorise

---

28 Section 25.
29 Section 25(2) of the MHCTA.
30 See *Mah Kiat Seng v Attorney-General and others* [2020] SLR 918.
31 (Cap 178, 1985 Rev Ed).
32 See https://www.msf.gov.sg/opg/Pages/Home.aspx.
33 See Code of Practice, p. 6 ("For example, the court can use someone's failure to follow the Code as evidence that he has not acted in the best interests of a person lacking capacity").
34 Section 41(6), MCA.
35 Section 41(5), MCA.

anyone to give the person medical treatment for mental disorder, or consent to the person being given medical treatment for a mental disorder.[36]

6.4.1 Lasting powers of attorney

Under the MCA,[37] a person (donor) can choose to appoint another person (the donee) without remuneration under an LPA to make decisions concerning the donor's personal welfare and/or property and financial matters on the donor's behalf should the donor lack mental capacity. An independent certificate issuer is required to explain the terms of the LPA to the individual who wishes to make an LPA, ensure that the individual understands the purpose and scope of authority conferred under the LPA, and that he/she is not induced by fraud and under undue pressure in making the LPA.[38] The prescribed certificate issuers include practising lawyers, psychiatrists and accredited general practitioners. There is a six-week mandatory waiting period before an LPA can be registered during which objections which can be raised. An LPA and/or the powers of the donee(s) can be revoked under certain circumstances (eg, where the donee acted contrary to the donor's best interests,[39] or fraud or undue pressure was used to induce the making of the LPA[40]).

6.4.2 Appointment of court deputies

Where the person has not made an LPA, the court can appoint a deputy without remuneration to make certain decisions on behalf of a person who lacks mental capacity. The relationship between a court deputy and an incapacitated person was regarded as akin to a fiduciary relationship between a trustee and a beneficiary.[41]

A deputy application has to be supported by a doctor's affidavit and medical report attesting to the person's lack of capacity which must comply with the Family Justice Courts Practice Directions.[42] This requires the medical doctor to state his or her opinion on the patient's mental capacity in relation to personal welfare and/or property and affairs depending on what the deputy application covers. The doctor should connect his examination of the patient with the criteria for determining mental capacity in section 4 of MCA (namely the understanding, retention and weighing of information and the communication of decision). In addition, the doctor has to give a prognosis of whether the person will likely regain his mental capacity and whether the person would understand if he were informed of the deputy application. It would be relevant for the lawyer advising on deputy applications to look out for the doctor's statement as to whether the patient's mental incapacity is permanent or temporary; and if

---

36 Section 27, MCA; and section 29, MHCTA. See also Chan (2011) generally on the healthcare decision-making framework.
37 Section 12.
38 First Schedule.
39 Section 17(3)(b) and (4), MCA; *TEB v TEC* [2015] SGFC 54.
40 Section 17(3)(a) and (4), MCA; *BUV v BUU* [2019] SGHCF 15.
41 See Lai Siu Chiu J in *Wong Meng Cheong and another v Ling Ai Wah and another* [2011] SGHC 233.
42 Form 224 of Appendix A.

120 *Mental health*

the latter, to ascertain if the patient would have recovered since the last date of the medical report.[43]

6.4.3 Statutory developments

Statutory amendments in 2016 introduced the concept of "professional donees" and "professional deputies" who are to be remunerated for their services. The MCA enables the elderly, especially those with assets, and who may not have family members or relatives to act as proxies, to have a wider choice of donees and deputies.

Professional donees who provide services for remuneration are classified into two groups: (a) professional deputies who are registered with the Public Guardian[44]; and (b) certain prescribed classes of persons which list thus far includes licensed trust companies[45] in respect of a donor's property and affairs.[46] The professional deputy as an individual must be an eligible professional[47] with five years of practice, and satisfy other requirements including the completion of training courses stated in the regulations.[48] Professional deputies also have to take note of a separate Code of Practice for Professional Deputies on their specific responsibilities.[49]

Based on the statutory amendments, the current position is as follows: where the power under an LPA relates to a person's property and affairs, the person may appoint a donee without remuneration (as mentioned above) or a professional donee who is not related to him by blood or marriage or a non-individual professional donee (licensed trust company); in other cases (*eg*, to take care of personal welfare), he may appoint a donee without remuneration or an individual professional donee.[50]

6.4.4 Protections for mentally incapacitated persons under MCA and other statutes

Under the MCA, acts of ill-treatment and/or wilful neglect towards the person who lacks capacity will be treated as criminal offences; any caregiver, donee or deputy found guilty of

---

43 Lee (2016).
44 Section 25A, MCA.
45 The licensed trust companies are regulated by the Monetary Authority of Singapore (MAS) under the Trust Companies Act (Cap 336, 2006 Rev Ed).
46 Mental Capacity Regulations 2010, Reg 5.
47 Advocate and solicitor, public or chartered accountant, registered medical practitioner, allied health professional, registered nurse, social worker or social service practitioner: Mental Capacity (Registration of Professional Deputies) Regulations 2018 (No S 529), Reg 2 and 4.
48 *Eg*, he must be a Singapore citizen or permanent resident of at least 21 years old, satisfy the requisite credit rating, not be subject to criminal convictions or disciplinary proceedings and pass designated training courses: see Mental Capacity (Registration of Professional Deputies) Regulations 2018 (No S 529), Reg 4.
49 https://www.msf.gov.sg/opg/Pages/About-PDD.aspx.
50 Section 12, MCA.

such an offence can be imprisoned and/or fined.[51] Healthcare workers[52] are immune from liability for reporting suspected cases of ill treatment or wilful neglect of a mentally incapacitated person.[53]

The Office of Public Guardian (OPG) provides a range of functions under the MCA[54] to protect persons who lack capacity including the provision of information to help potential donors understand the importance of planning in advance and making an LPA, setting up and maintaining a register of LPAs and court orders appointing deputies, supervising court-appointed deputies, receiving reports from donees and deputies, and dealing with and investigating complaints relating to how a donee or a deputy is discharging his duty.

The Vulnerable Adults Act[55] protects vulnerable persons *ie*, any adult above 18 years of age who is by reason of mental or physical infirmity, disability or incapacity, incapable of protecting himself or herself from abuse,[56] neglect[57] or self-neglect.[58] The words "neglect" and "self-neglect" encompass situations where the adult suffers from mental health problems or mental illnesses. The Director-General of Social Welfare and designated public officers have the power under the statute to enter into private premises to assess and, if necessary, remove a vulnerable adult in order to protect him or her from abuse, neglect and self-neglect.[59] The

---

51 Section 42, Mental Capacity Act.
52 The term "health care worker" means any registered medical practitioner, dentist registered under the Dental Registration Act (Cap. 76), pharmacist registered under the Pharmacists Registration Act (Cap. 230), therapist, psychologist, social worker, counsellor, nurse, attendant or other person providing healthcare services.
53 Section 43, Mental Capacity Act.
54 Sections 31 and 32.
55 No. 27 of 2018.
56 The term "abuse" means –
    (a) physical abuse;
    (b) emotional or psychological abuse;
    (c) conduct or behaviour by an individual that in any other way controls or dominates another individual and causes the other individual to fear for his or her safety or wellbeing; or
    (d) conduct or behaviour by an individual that unreasonably deprives, or threatens to unreasonably deprive, another individual of that other individual's liberty of movement or wellbeing.
57 The term "neglect" refers to the "lack of provision to the individual of essential care (such as but not limited to food, clothing, medical aid, lodging and other necessities of life), to the extent of causing or being reasonably likely to cause personal injury or physical pain to, or injury to the mental or physical health of, the individual".
58 The term "self-neglect", in relation to an individual, means the failure of the individual to perform essential tasks of daily living (such as but not limited to eating, dressing and seeking medical aid) to care for himself or herself, resulting in the individual –
    (a) living in grossly unsanitary or hazardous conditions;
    (b) suffering from malnutrition or dehydration; or
    (c) suffering from an untreated physical or mental illness or injury.
59 Sections 6, 8 and 10.

122 Mental health

penalties for offences against vulnerable persons have been enhanced under the Protection from Harassment Act[60] (as amended by the 2019 Act) as well as under the Penal Code.[61]

The procurement of sexual activity with a person with mental disability is explicitly proscribed under the Penal Code.[62] Furthermore, the abetment of suicide or attempted suicide of a person who lacks mental capacity is a criminal offence.[63]

In addition, the courts protect the interests of mentally incapacitated persons via the mechanism of statutory wills. Where a person (P) who was suffering from a lack of mental capacity has executed a will against her interests and acted under undue influence, the courts would step into her shoes and attempt to execute a will on her behalf. In this exercise, the court remains guided by P's best interests.[64]

6.5 Criminal liabilities

We examine in this section the Penal Code provisions on unsoundness of mind, intoxication and diminished responsibility, and how they may absolve the accused person of criminal liability or reduce his criminal responsibility, followed by the sentencing approach for persons with mental disorder and intellectual disability.[65]

Apart from substantive provisions on criminal liability, it should be noted that as a matter of procedure, the court may, in the course of criminal proceedings, investigate and ascertain whether the accused is of sound mind and capable of making his defence (*ie*, to assess the accused person's fitness to stand trial).[66] Further, a court-administered panel of psychiatrists has been set up for the purpose of giving expert opinions in criminal proceedings.[67]

6.5.1 Unsoundness of mind

The defence of unsoundness of mind in the Penal Code was derived historically from rules (known as *M'Naghten* Rules) pronounced in an English common law case decided in 1843.[68] The term "unsoundness of mind" in section 84 included forms of mental malfunctioning such

---

60 (Cap 256A, 2015 Rev Ed), section 8A.
61 Section 74A.
62 Section 376F. The term "mental disability" means "an impairment of or a disturbance in the functioning of the mind or brain resulting from any disability or disorder of the mind or brain which impairs the ability to make a proper judgement in the giving of consent to sexual touching".
63 Section 305.
64 Section 6 of MCA. See *TCZ v TDA; TDB v TDC* [2015] SGFC 63; *BHR and Another v BHS* [2013] SGDC 149 at [56] and [63].
65 Criminal responsibility of mentally disordered accused persons may be relevant in other criminal statutes such as the Protection from Harassment Act *eg, R v Sean Peter C* [2001] EWCA Crim 125 (schizophrenic and under influence of strong cannabis convicted of harassment for writing abusive letters to an MP due to compulsive behaviour).
66 Sections 247 and 248, Criminal Procedure Code.
67 Criminal Justice Reform Act 2018 (No 19 of 2018), section 270. See also (Hor 2008, at pp. 671-672).
68 (1843) 10 Cl and Fin 200; 8 ER 718 ("… to establish a defence on the ground of insanity it must be clearly proved that, at the time of committing of the act the party accused was laboring under such

as delirium tremens, substance abuse disorder, and substance-induced psychosis (Yeo et al. 2018, at p. 756). The statutory provision reads:

84. Nothing is an offence which is done by a person who, at the time of doing it, by reason of unsoundness of mind, is –

   (a) incapable of knowing the nature of the act;
   (b) incapable of knowing that what he is doing is wrong (whether wrong by the ordinary standards of reasonable and honest persons or wrong as contrary to law); or
   (c) completely deprived of any power to control his actions.

In order to raise this defence, the accused person has to first show that he was of unsound mind at the time of the alleged offence. He must then prove that the effect of his unsoundness of mind either:

- rendered him incapable of knowing[69] (a) the nature of the act; or (b) that what he is doing is wrong (morally and legally); or
- resulted in him lacking volition over his actions

With respect to the cognitive defects of the accused person, incapacity to know the nature of the act under limb (a) above may refer to the absence of knowledge of only the harmful consequences of the act (Yeo et al. 2018, at p. 763). Under limb (b), the accused person must show that he was incapable of knowing that what he committed was both morally and legally wrong, as shown by the illustration in section 84:

> A, while labouring under a delusion, believes that he has received divine instructions to kill Z and that it is morally right for him to do so. A however knows that it is contrary to law to kill Z. A kills Z. Here, the defence of unsoundness of mind is not available to A as he is capable of knowing that it is contrary to law to kill Z.

Alternatively, based on 2019 statutory amendments, the accused person may show under limb (c) that he lacked the volition (power of control over his actions) to commit the alleged offence at the relevant time by reason of unsoundness of mind.

Though the Penal Code does not explicitly define the meaning of "automatism", it has been argued that the concept should refer to volitional defects as opposed to a lack of consciousness (Yeo 2004). As long as the accused person lacks volition over his actions, he should not be criminally responsible for those actions even if he still retained consciousness at the time of the alleged crime. To put it in another way, proof of a lack of consciousness on the part of the accused person would be sufficient for automatism but is not a necessary requirement. This notion of automatism as volitional defects in terms of a lack of control over one's actions has now been incorporated in the defence of unsoundness of mind under limb (c) above.

---

a defect of reason, from disease of the mind, as not to know the nature and quality of the act he was doing, or, if he did know it, that he did not know he was doing what was wrong").
69 Cf the *M'Naghten* Rules which require an actual lack of knowledge on the part of the accused person.

124 *Mental health*

Where the court is satisfied that the accused has proved the defence of unsoundness of mind, the practical consequence is that he would receive a qualified acquittal[70] and be subject to orders on custody and treatment[71] which means, in effect, indefinite detention.

6.5.2 Defence of intoxication

Proof of intoxication in itself can constitute a defence. Section 85(2) states that:

2   Intoxication is a defence to any criminal charge if by reason of the intoxication the person charged, at the time of the act or omission complained of –

   (a) did not know what he was doing; or
   (b) did not know that such act or omission was wrong (whether wrong by the ordinary standards of reasonable and honest persons or wrong as contrary to law), and the state of intoxication was caused without the knowledge or against the will of the person charged with the offence.

The term "intoxication" includes a state produced by narcotics or drugs.[72] When the defence is proved, the accused person will be acquitted.

First, it must be shown that the intoxicated accused person, at the time of the act or omission complained of, lacked knowledge as to what he was doing or that such act or omission was wrong. The lack of knowledge in s 85(2) refers to an *actual* lack unlike in s 84 (unsoundness of mind) which is based on an incapacity to know. Second, the provision covers only *involuntary* intoxication in which the state of intoxication is caused without the accused's knowledge or is against his will. Prior to the 2019 amendments, it was possible to raise a defence based on self-induced intoxication. The current law prevents the accused person, who had voluntarily or knowingly become intoxicated (prior fault) and thereby committed a criminal act, from exculpating himself.

Intoxication, when proved, may also be used to determine whether the person charged had formed any knowledge or belief, specific or otherwise, in the absence of which he would not be guilty of the offence.[73]

In addition, intoxication associated with unsoundness of mind is a defence under section 85(3) of the Penal Code:

Intoxication is a defence to any criminal charge if by reason of the intoxication the person charged was of unsound mind as determined in accordance with section 84.

The focus here is on intoxication of the accused person who was of unsound mind at the time of the alleged offence. If such intoxication under section 85(3) is proved, section 84 of

---

70 Section 251 Criminal Procedure Code (acquittal on ground of unsound mind).
71 Section 252 Criminal Procedure Code (the court may "order that person to be kept in safe custody in such place and manner as the court thinks fit and shall report the case for the orders of the Minister" and the "Minister may order that person to be confined in a psychiatric institution, prison or other suitable place of safe custody during the President's pleasure").
72 Section 86(3).
73 Section 86(2).

the Penal Code and sections 251 and 252 of the Criminal Procedure Code 2010 (on qualified acquittal and custody orders) shall apply.[74]

6.5.3 Diminished responsibility

Diminished responsibility is applicable as a defence for murder under the Penal Code. It is also considered in certain drug offences with capital charges under the Misuse of Drugs Act, together with the accused person's involvement in the offence, to determine whether the accused should be sentenced to life imprisonment instead of a death sentence.

6.5.3.1 Partial defence for murder

In Singapore, the doctrine of diminished responsibility is applicable to a charge of murder where the accused's abnormality of mind substantially impaired his mental responsibility for the killing. This is a partial defence to murder which, if successfully pleaded, results in the accused being convicted of culpable homicide not amounting to murder. Exception 7 to section 300 (murder) reads:

> Culpable homicide is not murder if at the time of the acts or omissions causing the death concerned, the offender was suffering from such abnormality of mind (whether arising from a condition of arrested or retarded development or any inherent causes or induced by disease or injury) as substantially –
>
> (a) impaired the offender's capacity –
>
>   (i) to know the nature of the acts or omissions in causing the death or in being a party to causing the death; or
>
>   (ii) to know whether such acts or omissions are wrong (whether wrong by the ordinary standards of reasonable and honest persons or wrong as contrary to law); or
>
> (b) impaired the offender's power to control his acts or omissions in causing the death or being a party to causing the death.

Prior to the 2019 amendments, it was stipulated that the accused had to show that the abnormality of mind "substantially impaired his mental responsibility for his acts and omissions" in relation to his offence. There was no mention of the specific nature of substantial impairment of the accused person's mental responsibility. The current provision for substantial impairment refers to either (a) the substantial impairment of the offender's capacity to know; or (b) substantial impairment of the offender's power to control his acts and omissions. The other two requirements (that he was suffering from an abnormality of mind, and the manner in which the abnormality of mind arose or was induced) remain unchanged.

Notwithstanding the amendments, reference may nonetheless be made to judicial pronouncements on the defence of diminished responsibility prior to the amendments. With respect to the requirement of "abnormality of mind", the Court of Appeal had opined that

---

74 Section 86(1).

whether an abnormality of mind has been established depends on whether, having regard to all the facts of a given case, the accused person's state of mind was so different from that of ordinary human beings that the reasonable man would term it abnormal.[75]

The ascertainment of abnormality of mind should be based on all evidence including medical opinion.[76]

On the second requirement relating to the manner in which abnormality of mind arose or was induced, the accused person has to identify which of the prescribed causes is applicable with the help of expert witnesses to diagnose "whether the accused person was suffering from a recognised mental condition, identify which prescribed cause, if any, in their opinion gave rise to the accused's abnormality of mind".[77]

With regard to the requirement of substantial impairment, the Court of Appeal stated that

> substantial impairment does not require total impairment; but nor would trivial or minimal impairment suffice. What is required is an impairment of the mental state that is real and material but which need not rise to the level of amounting to the defence of unsoundness of mind under s 84 of the Penal Code.[78]

It is argued that with respect to the substantial impairment of the offender's capacity to know or power to control his acts or omissions, a similar threshold may be applied.

6.5.3.2 Specific offences under Misuse of Drugs Act (MDA): life sentence for a capital charge

Under section 33B(3)(*b*) of the MDA, an offender convicted on a capital charge for drug trafficking[79] or the importation or exportation of a controlled drug[80] may be sentenced to life imprisonment instead if he was suffering from such abnormality of mind (whether arising from a condition of arrested or retarded development of mind or any inherent causes or induced by disease or injury) as substantially impaired his mental responsibility for his acts and omissions in relation to the offence, and on the basis of his restricted involvement in the offence.[81] Further, the provision does not apply to "offenders suffering from transient or even self-induced illnesses that have no firm basis in an established psychiatric condition that

---

75 *Nagaenthran a/l K Dharmalingam v Public Prosecutor and another appeal* [2019] 2 SLR 216 at [23] and [29] (citing cited *Regina v Byrne* [1960] 2 QB 396 at 403, *per* Lord Parker CJ).
76 *Sek Kim Wah v PP* [1987] SLR(R) 371 at [33].
77 *Iskandar bin Rahmat v Public Prosecutor and other matters* [2017] 1 SLR 505 at [89].
78 *Nagaenthran a/l K Dharmalingam v Public Prosecutor and another appeal* [2019] 2 SLR 216 at [33].
79 MDA, section 5.
80 MDA, section 7.
81 Where the involvement in the offence under section 5(1) or 7 was restricted -
   (i) to transporting, sending or delivering a controlled drug;
   (ii) to offering to transport, send or deliver a controlled drug;
   (iii) to doing or offering to do any act preparatory to or for the purpose of his transporting, sending or delivering a controlled drug; or
   (iv) to any combination of activities in sub-paragraphs (i), (ii) and (iii).

arose from an arrested or retarded development of mind, any inherent root cause, or was induced by disease or injury".[82]

6.5.4 Sentencing for accused persons with mental disorder[83] or intellectual disability

The sentencing of offenders with mental disorder seeks to take account of the offender's legal responsibility for the wrongdoing as well as to balance the interests of the public and the offender.[84] Rehabilitation is generally presumed to be the main sentencing objective for mentally disordered offenders.[85] The welfare, reform and treatment of the individual offender and the public interest in mitigating the risk of recidivism are important considerations in rehabilitation.[86] The objective of rehabilitation may be combined with that of prevention to ensure the offender's access to psychiatric services in a "structured environment" under the supervision of trained staff as well as to "assuage" public concerns about a "potentially dangerous person living in its midst".[87]

This objective of rehabilitation does not imply that the mentally disordered offender will always receive a lighter sentence. The sentencing will also depend on the nature of the offence and the nature and extent of the mental disorder.[88] In balancing the objectives of rehabilitation and protecting others in society, imprisonment may nevertheless be appropriate in certain cases such as those involving culpable homicide not amounting to murder.[89]

A related consideration is whether there is a causal link between the offender's mental disorder and the commission of the offence. The mental disorder may, for example, adversely affect the offender's ability to control his or her actions relevant to the commission of the offence. In this regard, kleptomania was regarded as an impulse control disorder such that it resulted in the offender being unable to control his actions prior to or whilst committing the

---

82 *Nagaenthran a/l K Dharmalingam v Public Prosecutor and another appeal* [2019] 2 SLR 216 at [31].
83 See Chua (2011); Kow (2019).
84 *PP v Goh Lee Yin* [2008] 1 SLR (R) 824 at [2].
85 *Lim Ghim Peow v PP* [2014] 4 SLR 1287 at [37].
86 *Lim Ghim Peow v PP* [2014] 4 SLR 1287 at [37].
87 *PP v Kong Peng Yee* [2018] 2 SLR 295 at [96], [99]-[100].
88 *Lim Ghim Peow v PP* [2014] 4 SLR 1287 at [38]. If the offender's capacity to appreciate the "gravity and significance of his criminal conduct" is not affected by the mental disorder, the objective of general deterrence remains relevant: at [35].
89 *Lim Ghim Peow v PP* [2014] 4 SLR 1287 (20 years' imprisonment for culpable homicide not amounting to murder under s 304(a) of Penal Code for killing ex-lover when suffering from major depressive disorder; offender was able to comprehend actions and wrongfulness of conduct); *PP v Aniza bte Essa* [2009] 3 SLR(R) 327 (nine years' imprisonment for abetting culpable homicide not amounting to murder when suffering from moderate depression); *PP v Kong Peng Yee* [2018] 2 SLR 295 (culpable homicide not amounting to murder for killing wife during psychiatric episode).

offence in one case,[90] whilst certain conditions such as voyeurism[91] and paedophilia[92] did not deprive the offenders of control over their impulses.

The case of *Public Prosecutor v ASR*[93] concerned the sentencing approach for young offenders. The accused suffered from intellectual disability, had an IQ of 61 and a mental age of between eight and ten. He was charged under the Penal Code[94] with one count of aggravated rape and two counts of sexual assault by penetration. He committed the offences when he was 14 years old and pleaded guilty to them after he turned 16. The High Court sentenced him to reformative training. At the time of the appeal to the Court of Appeal, he was 18 years old. The Court of Appeal eventually decided on the order for incarceration at a reformative training centre for up to three years[95] contrary to the Prosecution's appeal for the accused to be imprisoned for 15–18 years and caned. For intellectually disabled young offenders convicted of serious offences, the sentencing approach consisted of a two-step enquiry[96]:

(a) whether rehabilitation remained the dominant sentencing consideration, it being presumptively so in the case of young offenders[97]; and
(b) which is the appropriate sentencing option in the light of the answer at the first step.

Rehabilitation was indeed the dominant sentencing objective in this case. The Court of Appeal took account of the accused's state of mind at the time of the offence. Evidence indicated

---

90 *PP v Goh Yee Lin* [2008] 1 SLR(R) 824; *Public Prosecutor v Low Ji Qing* [2019] 5 SLR 769 (theft of wallets from female victims by offender suffering from fetishistic disorder which is an abnormal sexual preference for smelling women's wallets to get a sense of euphoria and to feel sexually aroused; secondary diagnosis of an adjustment disorder with depressed mood impaired offender's ability to control his desire to act on his fetishism).
91 *PP v Chong Hou En* [2015] 3 SLR 222 at [61] and [66] (deterrence remains relevant to sentencing for offences under section 509 of the Penal Code for insulting the modesty of a woman by intruding upon her privacy).
92 *Lim Hock Hin Kelvin v PP* [1998] 1 SLR(R) 37 at [31] (offence under section 377 of the Penal Code for having carnal intercourse against the order of nature).
93 [2019] 1 SLR 941.
94 (Cap 224, 2008 Rev Ed).
95 See Criminal Procedure Code (Cap 68), section 305 (for offenders between the age of 16 and 21 years at the date of conviction). The sentence requires the Commissioner of Prisons' report on the offender's physical and mental condition, the offender's suitability for the sentence, and the nature of the rehabilitation that is recommended for the offender. The maximum sentence for reformative training including the supervision period is 54 months. See also Criminal Procedure Code (Reformative Training) Regulations 2018, No. S 723.
96 *PP v Mohammad Al-Ansari bin Basri* [2008] 1 SLR(R) 449.
97 The factors underlying the presumption are: (a) young offender's generally lower culpability due to their immaturity; (b) their enhanced prospects for rehabilitation; (c) society's interest in rehabilitating them; and (d) the recognition that the prison environment might have a corrupting influence on young offenders who are more impressionable and subject to bad influence than older offenders: [2019] 1 SLR 941 at [95]. See also *A Karthik v PP* [2018] 5 SLR 1289 at [37]–[42].

that his low cognitive ability (based on his mental age[98]) had significantly reduced his culpability, impaired his impulse control ability, and he only possessed a limited understanding of the nature and consequences of his offences as well as their legal and moral wrongfulness.[99] On the other hand, the objective of deterrence – which presumes "cognitive normalcy" and offender's ability to weigh the consequences of his actions – was less important here.[100] The alternative of probation would not be an adequate sentence in view of the seriousness of the offences and the threat posed to society due to his high risk of recidivism; further, probation would not provide the "structured environment that was necessary to manage and treat that risk".[101] A probation order requires an offender to be supervised by a probation officer for a period from six months to three years with a maximum residence requirement of not more than 12 months.[102]

Other considerations for sentencing include the treatability of the offender's condition,[103] and whether the offender is dangerous and mentally unstable[104] and therefore more likely to commit such offences in the future[105] as distinct from offenders who "suffer from a transient illness who can be rehabilitated and reintegrated into society" for which lesser sentences may be imposed.[106]

In line with the rehabilitation objective, community-based sentences are targeted at certain categories of offenders including persons with specific and minor mental conditions.[107] A Mandatory Treatment Order (MTO)[108] may be appropriate for offenders with mental disorders or intellectual disabilities for prescribed offences that are punishable with imprisonment for a term exceeding three years but not exceeding seven years.[109] The court has the power to issue an MTO, subject to obtaining a report from an appointed psychiatrist,[110] that requires

---

98 Mental age is a "useful heuristic tool" which must take into consideration the "context of the offender's life experiences": [2019] 1 SLR 941 at [50] citing *Regina v Gordon Laxton* [2010] EWCA Crim 2538; *Regina v Myles Williams* [2013] EWCA Crim 933; *R v MBO, ex parte Attorney-General of Queensland* [2012] QCA 202 (cases dealing with offender's mental age).
99 [2019] 1 SLR 941 at [113].
100 [2019] 1 SLR 941 at [115].
101 [2019] 1 SLR 941 at [135]. The residence requirement for probation order is a maximum of 12 months which the Court of Appeal felt was too short in this case: s 5(3A) Probation of Offenders Act.
102 Probation of Offenders Act (Cap 252, 1985 Rev Ed), section 5. During the probation, the offender has to comply with requirements "necessary for securing the good conduct of the offender or for preventing a repetition by him of the same offence or the commission of other offences" and may be required to perform community service.
103 *PP v Aniza bte Essa* [2009] 3 SLR(R) 327 at [40] (life imprisonment not appropriate sentence as accused's condition was treatable).
104 This does not necessarily mean that the offender must suffer from a mental disorder.
105 *R v Rowland Jack Forster Hodgson* (1968) 52 Cr App R 113 at 114 (to justify life imprisonment).
106 *PP v Aniza bte Essa* [2009] 3 SLR(R) 327 at [34].
107 *Singapore Parliamentary Debates, Official Report* (18 May 2010) vol 87 at col 422 (K Shanmugam, Minister for Law and Second Minister for Home Affairs).
108 Sections 339 and 340, Criminal Procedure Code.
109 Section 337(2)(c), Criminal Procedure Code.
110 Section 339(3).

130 Mental health

the offender to undergo psychiatric treatment (which may include a residence requirement in a psychiatric institution) for a specified period not exceeding 36 months.[111] The court has to consider, in making the MTO, the circumstances including the nature of the offence and the character of the offender. The psychiatrist report must state the following:

(a) the offender is suffering from a psychiatric condition which is susceptible to treatment;
(b) the offender is suitable for the treatment; and
(c) the psychiatric condition of the offender is one of the contributing factors for his committing the offence.[112]

6.6 Tort liabilities

We will now turn our attention to the civil (tort) liabilities of persons with mental disorder as well as those of medical doctors and healthcare professionals when dealing with persons with mental disorder under the tort of negligence.

6.6.1 Tort liabilities of persons with mental disorder

Let us consider the case of a mentally disordered person who negligently injured a person. In *Dunnage v Randall*,[113] the claimant (the defendant's nephew) sustained personal injuries due to the act of the defendant, who was suffering from florid paranoid schizophrenia, in igniting petrol and setting both of them on fire. The defendant was insured under a household policy, and the insurer assumed control of the defence. The English Court of Appeal held that first, the defendant's acts were voluntary. Second, the standard of care expected of the defendant was that of a reasonable man notwithstanding his mental illness. In the circumstances, it was held that the defendant had breached his duty of care towards the claimant and was therefore liable in negligence.

On the issue of voluntariness, expert evidence from psychiatrists revealed that in the weeks preceding the incident, Dunnage was in a delusional state and "most unlikely to be capable of forming a rational plan or intention to cause harm".[114] Moreover, he was "most likely beyond meaningful capacity to exercise "free will" such that he felt overwhelmed and compelled to act as he did without benefit of moral or rational thinking to deter him".[115] Yet his irrationality does not necessarily mean he was "deprived of the ability to understand the nature and quality of the act"; and "there is no reason to conclude that he was unable to understand that what he was doing would cause serious and catastrophic harm".[116] Lady Justice Rafferty found that the defendant knew he had the petrol in its can and decided at

---

[111] Section 339(1) and (1A).
[112] *CGX v Public Prosecutor* [2019] 3 SLR 1325 at [76]-[77] and [81] (sufficient for psychiatrist report to state that offender's adjustment disorder had "substantially contributed" to the commission of the offence; unnecessary to state that adjustment disorder caused the offender to commit offence).
[113] [2016] QB 639.
[114] [2016] QB 639 at [26].
[115] [2016] QB 639 at [28].
[116] [2016] QB 639 at [27].

that stage not to use it immediately which implied he possessed "control".[117] Lady Justice Arden observed that the defendant was able to "choose" to bring the petrol and lighter into the claimant's flat.[118]

In an analogous case *Morriss v Marsden*,[119] a schizophrenic who suffered from delusions was held liable for assaulting the manager of a hotel where he was staying. He understood the nature and quality of his act even though he was deluded and did not know that what he was doing was wrong. Knowledge of the nature and quality of the act would suffice for voluntariness of the act which may be considered a threshold element in tort law whether in negligence or intentional assault and battery. Where the defendant's act is adjudged involuntary, he will not be liable in tort.[120]

Voluntariness of the act is to be not equated with acting rationally. Though Dunnage understood the nature and quality of his act, Lady Justice Arden observed that he could not "act rationally" due to his delusions.[121] Rafferty LJ opined that an involuntary act is not the same as an irrational act.[122] Vos LJ stated that "a person can still be acting if he acts irrationally".[123]

Moving on to standard of care, the objective standard in negligence is on one level inconsistent with the notion of the defendant's mental abnormality. In *Carrier v Bonham*,[124] McPherson JA stated that

> "[T]here is no such thing as a 'normal' condition of unsound mind in those who suffer that affliction. It comes in different varieties and different shades or degrees. For that reason it would be impossible to devise a standard by which the tortious liability of such persons could be judged as a class."

Lord Hoffmann in *A v Hoare*[125] also mentioned that it would destroy the word "reasonable" to speak of the "reasonable unintelligent person". A plausible response to these judicial opinions is that when we apply the objective standard of care, the reasonable person is to be put in the defendant's shoes. This would inevitably entail taking into account some personal circumstances and characteristics of the defendant (Goudkamp and Ihuoma 2016, at p. 141). Hence, the general standard of care is not always applied in a purely objective manner without considering any subjective elements.

More specifically, there are a few arguments (and counterarguments) as to whether we should consider the subjective characteristics of mentally disordered defendants in assessing

---

117 [2016] QB 639 at [106].
118 [2016] QB 639 at [148].
119 [1952] 1 All ER 925.
120 *Slattery v Haley* [1923] 3 DLR, per Middleton J; *White v Pile* 68 WN (NSW) 176 (1950); *Breunig v American Family Insurance Company* 173 NW2d 619 (Wisc 1970) (the driver believed that God was controlling her car and that she could "fly like Batman").
121 [2016] QB 639 at [143].
122 [2016] QB 639 at [111] and [112].
123 [2016] QB 639 at [135].
124 (2001) QCA 234 at [35].
125 [2008] 1 AC 844 at [35].

standard of care. First, if we take account of subjective characteristics, mentally ill persons who do not have the capacity to attain the objective reasonable man standard would not be regarded as at fault in the moral sense. As such, it might be unfair to hold them to the objective standard if they are not subjectively capable of avoiding the harm. Moreover, mentally ill defendants will not fully appreciate the rightness or wrongfulness of their acts. Here we encounter a divergence between moral and legal standards.

On the other hand, it may be countered that acting honestly to the best of one's judgement is not a defence for not measuring up to the objective prudent standard.[126] Further, from the compensatory perspective, we should consider that innocent victims who have been hurt by a mentally disordered defendant would have no remedy. A related point is that failing to measure up to the objective standard should not be viewed as a personal failing of the defendant; rather, tort law should be focused on the negligent (or faulty) *conduct* that justifies compensation to an innocent victim (Coleman 1980).

Second, analogies may be drawn from existing cases of defendants acting under a physical disability to support the argument for taking account of the defendant's subjective characteristics. In *Mansfield v Weetabix*,[127] the defendant suffered the onset of a rare form of hypoglycemic attack. He had no prior experience or knowledge of this condition which came on gradually, so that he was not aware of the change in his condition. He was held not liable for injuries and damage caused by his inability to control the vehicle due to the hypoglycemic attack. This suggests that a rigid adherence to the objective reasonable man standard without taking account of the defendant's knowledge of his condition is not tenable. Extending *Mansfield*, in a case where the mental illness reduced the defendant's capacity for knowing whether he was suffering from physical or mental condition which impaired his ability to drive, such lack of knowledge should be taken into consideration in assessing whether he was negligent.[128] It is further suggested that another factor to consider in assessing standard of care is whether the plaintiff, if he is aware of his mental illness, had sought treatment prior to the alleged breach and whether it would be reasonable for him to have done so (Bromberger 2010, at p. 430).

According to another English case *Roberts v Ramsbottom*,[129] however, the defendant would be subject to the objective reasonable driver standard unless he or she had suffered a total loss of consciousness (defence of automatism) at the relevant time.[130] The Singapore District Court in *Stephanie Tang Swan Lee and others v Tan Su San (the personal representative of*

---

126 *Vaughan v Menlove* 3 Bing NC 468 at 474-475, *per* Tindal CJ.
127 [1998] 1 WLR 1263.
128 See *Breunig v American Family Insurance Co* 173 NW 2d 619 (Wis. 1970) at 623 (that question of liability depends on whether there is "an absence of notice or forewarning to the person that he may be suddenly subject to such a type of insanity or mental illness"); and Goldstein (1995, at p. 92) ("mentally ill individuals whose disease is sudden or untreatable cannot *ex ante* prevent the harm and thus should not be found culpable").
129 [1980] 1 WLR 823.
130 As mentioned above in the section on criminal liability, the term "automatism" should refer to volitional defects rather than the lack of consciousness.

the deceased Tan Seng Huat)[131] had decided – in a case involving physical injuries suffered by plaintiffs when a car driven by the defendant who was suffering from a haemorrhage collided into them – that the "objective test as applied in *Roberts* and *Dunnage* is to be preferred over the subjective test in *Mansfield*" based on, amongst others, reasons of public safety and protection of innocent victims.[132]

It is submitted that this notion of total loss of consciousness which eliminates the defendant's responsibility is better analysed as part of the involuntariness rule that applies across tort law generally (Goudkamp and Ihuoma 2016, at pp. 148-149) rather than as a factor to be considered in assessing standard of care for defendants suffering from a physical disability. The purported acts of a person who has totally lost consciousness would clearly be involuntary. There may be other instances of involuntary acts such as where the plaintiff though conscious has lost control over his actions. In this sense, *Roberts v Ramsbottom* is not good authority for dismissing the need to take account of the defendant's subjective characteristics in assessing standard of care.

Third, the law of negligence takes into account the subjective characteristics of a child in assessing the child's standard of care. In *McHale v Watson*,[133] the standard of child defendants is assessed by reference to a reasonable child of similar age, intelligence and experience. This approach was justified as objective in that the child's age is "characteristic of humanity at his stage of development". Kitto J added that "normality is, for children, something different from what normality is for adult".[134] A legitimate question arises as to whether allowance should also be given for those who are mentally disordered. Lord Justice Vos in *Dunnage*, however, opined that "people with physical and mental health problems should not properly be regarded as analogous to children".[135] That is, according to the learned judge, mental disorders unlike age cannot be described as characteristic of humanity at a particular stage of development.

Let us now consider a separate though related issue of a defence of insanity, assuming for the moment that the mentally disordered defendant fell below the objective standard of reasonableness and harmed the claimant as a result. Can insanity "excuse" the defendant's legal liability on the ground that the defendant is not responsible for his acts? At common law, the legal position is that there is no affirmative defence of insanity in tort law[136] in contrast to the statutory defences in criminal law. Insanity *per se* is not a ground for absolving the defendant's tortious liability. The fact that defendant's act is not voluntary which we have already discussed above is separate and independent from the (affirmative) defence of insanity.

---

131 [2018] SGDC 218 at [18].
132 Despite the defendant's haemorrhage on the right side of the body, the judge found that he did not lose total consciousness and had sufficient control of the vehicle at the relevant time to avoid the harm to plaintiffs. As a result, he was found negligent whether based on *Roberts* and *Dunnage* or *Mansfield*: [43]-[44].
133 (1966) 115 CLR 199.
134 (1966) 115 CLR 199.
135 [2016] QB 639 at [130].
136 *Donaghy v Brennan* (1900) 19 NZLR 289 (Court of Appeal of New Zealand) (no defence of insanity to a claim in assault); *Williams v Hays* 38 NE 449 (NY 1894).

134 *Mental health*

The distinction between criminal law and tort law may be explained by their differing goals: punishment versus compensation for losses. Though the award of damages in tort law may be premised on notions of deterrence (through the award of significant amounts of damages and aggravated damages based on the defendant's conduct leading to the commission of tort) and punishment (by imposing punitive damages in limited circumstances), compensation for the plaintiff's loss remains the central objective of damages awards in Singapore.

That said, the compensatory approach does not necessarily mean that there is no role for a defence of insanity. Goudkamp (2011) provides two arguments to explain why insanity should be treated as an affirmative defence: (a) insanity diminishes a person's capacity for self-determination and (b) that tort liability serves as a sanction which would make it unjust to impose it on an insane defendant.

Box 6.1 - Mentally disordered persons in "normal" society

In *Carrier v Bonham* (2001) QCA 234 at [36], McPherson JA noted that with regard to mentally disordered persons,

> [m]ore humane methods of treatment now prevail, under which greater liberty of movement is, for their own perceived good, permitted to patients in this unhappy state. If in the process they take advantage of that liberty to venture, even if briefly, into "normal" society, it seems only proper that, in the event of their doing so, their conduct should be judged according to society's standards including the duty of exercising reasonable foresight and care for the safety of others.

Do you agree? Consider the statutory framework for admission and detention of mentally disordered patients in psychiatric hospitals and the community-based model for psychiatric care. Do you think the current common law position on the liability of mentally disordered persons under the tort of negligence is consistent with the statutory and government policy?

6.6.2 Tort liabilities of doctors and healthcare professionals

Doctors, healthcare professionals and institutions owe a legal duty to take reasonable care towards their patients under their care and custody. The standard of care of a psychiatrist or doctor specialising in the field of psychiatry would be that of a reasonable psychiatrist or doctor professing such skill and knowledge. Insofar as the diagnosis and treatment of mental health patients are concerned, where there are genuine differences of opinion on the expected standard, the courts will look to the *Bolam* test[137] (which defers to a respectable body of medical opinion as to whether the defendant's practice was acceptable),the *Bolitho* addendum[138] (to assess the logic underlying the medical opinion) and possibly other factors as part of a holistic assessment to determine whether the psychiatrist was negligent. After all, though this is not commonly recognised, *Bolam* involved the treatment of a person

---

137 *Bolam v Friern Hospital Management Committee* [1957] 1 WLR 582 at 587.
138 *Bolitho v City and Hackney Health Authority* [1998] AC 232.

suffering from mental health problems (specifically depression) via electro-convulsive therapy without relaxant drugs. With respect to medical advice, the legal test in *Hii Chii Kok*[139] is whether a reasonable person in the shoes of the patient would desire to be informed of his health condition, risks, benefits and alternatives; if so, the doctor is obliged to disclose the material information unless he can justify non-disclosure based on the patient's waiver of his right to know, the urgency of the situation at hand involving imminent peril to life or serious injury to patient and the therapeutic privilege not to disclose lest it result in serious harm to patient (Chapter 3).

With respect to disclosure of diagnosis, to what extent should the doctor reveal to the patient suffering from mental health issues his condition? It is clear that a reasonable patient would desire to be made aware of a serious (mental) health condition which is likely to constitute a material risk or information. This is particularly pertinent where non-disclosure of a patient's diagnosis can potentially harm the patient and others. For example, if the doctor knows that the patient is suffering from severe dementia, and that it would be dangerous for a person with his serious condition to drive on the roads, he should disclose information about such impairments to the patient or indirectly ensure that the patient is prevented from harming himself as well as other road users.

We have discussed in Chapter 3 the standard of care of doctors in giving medical advice according to the approach in *Hii Chii Kok*. How should we adopt the patient autonomy approach if the doctor's standard for giving medical advice is to be determined by what a reasonable patient would want to know? The determination should include an assessment of the severity and the effects of the mental illness on the patient's cognitive ability to understand the information concerning the risks, benefits and complications relating to the treatment as well as the alternatives to the proposed treatment. Where the patient is suffering from a mental disorder, the doctor has to take reasonable steps to ascertain if the patient actually understood the information in order to give consent. In case of doubt, it may be advisable to refer to the assessment of an expert (such as a psychiatrist) as to the patients' ability to give consent. A related concern is whether the psychiatrist would be able to communicate the information in such a way that the patient can understand.

Furthermore, assuming the information is material to the reasonable patient and in the possession of the doctor, another question is whether the doctor may have the therapeutic privilege not to disclose the information of the mental illness on the ground that it would likely cause physical or mental harm to the patient. As mentioned by the Court of Appeal in *Hii Chii Kok*[140]:

> doctors should have a measure of latitude in invoking the therapeutic privilege, and this should extend to cases where although patients have mental capacity, their decision-making capabilities are impaired to an appreciable degree. These will include patients with anxiety disorders (to whom the mere knowledge of a risk may, without more, cause harm) or certain geriatric patients who, as described by the NCCS, may be "easily frightened

---

139 *Hii Chii Kok v Ooi Peng Jin London Lucien* [2017] 2 SLR 492. Note that a parliamentary bill has been introduced on 3 September 2020 with a view to change the legal approach relating to the giving of medical advice by healthcare professionals (Chapter 3).

140 [2017] 2 SLR 492 at [152].

out of having even relatively safe treatments that can drastically improve their quality of life", and whose state of mind, intellectual abilities or education may make it impossible or extremely difficult to explain the true reality to them.

> **Box 6.2 – Dementia patients and the problem of deception**
>
> To illustrate the ethical dilemma associated with disclosures to a dementia patient, an analogy may be drawn to the use of Simulated Presence, a device developed for Alzheimer's patients consisting of an audiotape recording or video of family members concerning his or her memories of the patient. Even if the tape or video is played back repeatedly via a device, the Alzheimer's patient may not realise and continue to regard it as a fresh conversation (see Schermer (2014, at p. 160)). Is this a form of deception to the patient? What if it can promote the patient's emotional well-being? Are there alternatives to Simulated Presence which do not deceive? Should the healthcare professional instead invest time in carrying out real conversations? (See Schermer (2014, at p. 165).)

Apart from legal liability to psychiatric patients for negligent medical diagnosis, treatment or advice, the healthcare professional or institution should also take note of potential legal actions by *third parties* flowing from a breach of duty towards their psychiatric patients. In *Tarasoff v Regents of the University of California*,[141] the Supreme Court of California held that the therapist, upon being told by the patient, who was a paranoid schizophrenic, during therapy of his intention to murder a third party after his release from police custody, had a duty of care to warn the identifiable third party that she was at risk of being murdered. It explained as follows:

> The Defendant therapists cannot escape liability merely because Tatiana herself was not their patient. When a therapist determines, or pursuant to the standards of his profession should determine, that his patient presents a serious danger of violence to another, he incurs an obligation to use reasonable care to protect the intended victim against such danger. The discharge of this duty may require the therapist to take one or more of various steps, depending upon the nature of the case. Thus it may call upon him to warn the intended victim or others likely to appraise the victim of the danger, to notify the police, or to take whatever other steps are reasonably necessary under the circumstances.

In contrast, in *Palmer v Tees Health Authority*,[142] there was no proximity between the defendant (psychiatrist) and the victim who was a young girl, abducted, sexually abused and murdered by the psychiatric patient under the defendant's care. The victim's mother – the claimant – suffered psychiatric injury. The victim was not identified but merely a member of the public who was subject to the risk posed by the psychiatric patient. As these cases involved the doctor disclosing patient information, the actions would arguably breach medical confidentiality unless disclosure is justified on grounds of public interest and law (see Chapter 7).

---

141 (1976) 551 P 2d 334.
142 [2000] PIQR 1.

That said, doctors and healthcare professionals who breach their duty of care towards psychiatric patients under their care may not always be liable for the consequences flowing from the breach. In *Clunis v Camden and Islington Health Authority*,[143] the plaintiff claimed against the healthcare authority for its negligent omission to provide him with psychiatric care. This resulted in the plaintiff killing a person and his conviction for manslaughter. However, the defendant successfully pleaded the defence of *ex turpi causa* (illegality). The plaintiff's conviction was the outcome of his own criminal act and the plaintiff had to be regarded to have known what he was doing. It should be highlighted that the defence is limited to cases of serious wrongdoing on the part of the plaintiff which is substantially connected to the damages suffered by him.

6.7 Conclusion

Mental health is at present a protean and contested concept that does not have fixed boundaries. As we learn more about human brain processes, behaviours, and associated mental abnormalities and disabilities, the law has to constantly adapt to better protect and balance the interests of mentally ill persons, their family members and caregivers as well as members of the public. Mentally disordered persons may be detained in a psychiatric hospital for treatment only where there is a threat of danger to himself or the public as ascertained by medical practitioners in psychiatric institutions and external experts. The MCA provides a framework with built-in legal safeguards to allow a mentally capable person the autonomy to make decisions on his personal welfare and financial matters as far as possible, and should he lose mental capacity, for proxy decision-makers (donees, court deputies and professional deputies) to make such decisions in his best interests with supervision from the Public Guardian and the courts. Psychiatric expertise remains crucial in criminal proceedings involving mentally disordered accused persons relying on Penal Code defences based on unsoundness of mind, intoxication or diminished responsibility. Doctors may be liable not only to the patient for negligent diagnosis, treatment and omission to provide material information on the risks, benefits, complications and alternatives to enable the person with mental illness to make or participate in a decision as to his treatment, but in more exceptional cases, to third parties who have not been warned of physical harm caused by the mentally ill patient.

References

Bromberger, N. (2010). "Negligence and Inherent Unreasonableness" 32 *Sydney Law Review* 411.
Chan, T.E. (2011). "The Elderly Patient and the Healthcare Decision-Making Framework in Singapore" in Chan, W.C. (ed) *Singapore's Ageing Population: Managing Healthcare and End of Life Decisions* (Routledge: London), pp. 113-136.
Chua, H.H.E. (2011). "Sentencing Mentally Disordered Offenders: Lessons from the US and Singapore" 23 *SAcLJ* 434.
Coleman, J. (1980). "Mental Abnormality, Personal Responsibility, and Tort Liability" in Brody, B.A. & Engelhardt Jr, H.T. (eds), *Mental Illness: Law and Public Policy* (Springer: Dordrecht), pp. 107-133.
Graham, G. (2013). *The Disordered Mind*, 2nd Edition (Routledge: London).

---

143 [1998] QB 978.

Goldstein, E.J. (1995). "Asking the Impossible: The Negligence Liability of the Mentally Ill" 12 *Journal of Contemporary Health Law & Policy* 67.
Goudkamp, J. (2011). "Insanity as a Tort Defence" 31(4) *OJLS* 727-754.
Goudkamp, J. & Ihuoma, M. (2016). "A Tour of the Tort of Negligence" 32(2) *Professional Negligence* 137-152.
Gwee, K. (2017). "Psychology and Psychiatry in Singapore Courts: A Baseline Survey of the Mental Health Landscape in the Legal Arena" 52 *International Journal of Law & Psychiatry* 44-54.
Herring, J. (2018). "Mental Health Law", chapter 10 in Herring, J. *Medical Law and Ethics*, 7th Edition (Oxford University Press: Oxford), pp. 585-618.
Hor, M. (2008). "Murder: The Abnormal Mind - Mad or Just Bad", 20 *Singapore Academy of Law Journal* 662-676.
Kok, L.P., Cheang, M., & Chee, K.T. (1994). *Mental Disorders and the Law* (Singapore University Press: Singapore).
Kow, K.S. (2019). *Sentencing Principles in Singapore* (Academy Publishing: Singapore), pp. 630-660.
Lee, H.M. (2016). "Medical Reports Supporting Deputy Applications - Encouraging the Good, Rescuing the Bad" *Singapore Law Gazette* (January 2016), pp. 19-25.
Schermer, M. (2014). "Telling the Truth: The Ethics of Deception and White Lies in Dementia Care" in Foster, C., Herring, J., and Doron I. (eds) *The Law and Ethics of Dementia* (Hart Publishing: Oxford), pp. 159-167.
Scott, C.L. (2015). *DSM-5 and the Law: Changes and Challenges* (Oxford University Press: Oxford).
Szasz, T. (2001). "Mental Illness: Psychiatry's Phlogiston" 27 *Journal of Medical Ethics* 297.
Yeo, S. (2004). "Situating Automatism in the Penal Codes of Malaysia and Singapore" XXXIII(4) *Journal of the Malaysian Bar* 1-31.
Yeo, S., Morgan, N., & Chan, W.C. (2018). *Criminal Law in Malaysia and Singapore*, 3rd Edition (LexisNexis: New York).

7 Confidentiality†

7.1 Introduction

In the Hippocratic Oath, doctors declare "I will respect the secrets which are confided in me, even after the patient has died". More contemporary judicial pronouncements reiterate that the doctor should hold information received from or about a patient in confidence.[1]

This doctor-patient relationship is after all premised on trust. The general doctrine of confidentiality gives the assurance to the patient to provide a full and frank disclosure of his health condition to the doctors so that the doctors can better provide medical diagnosis, treatment and advice to the patient. If doctors are generally entitled to disclose patients' confidential information, this might deter patients from seeking medical assistance. One utilitarian basis for confidentiality is therefore to preserve and enhance the well-being of patients. Another basis (deontological) for maintaining confidentiality is the respect for the patient as a person with dignity and capacity to make autonomous choices, an important corollary being the patient's right to control the use and to prevent the disclosure of private information about himself.

This duty of confidentiality is not only applicable in the clinical context but is also relevant to biomedical research. The relationship between research institutions, researchers and research subjects has been described as a fiduciary relationship at common law,[2] and confidentiality obligations of research institutions and researchers towards research subjects are also governed by statute.[3] The domains of clinical practice and medical research may intersect in that confidential information may sometimes be sought from patients in hospitals for the purpose of medical research.[4] The duty of confidentiality also extends to patients who are minors with sufficient maturity and understanding of the medical treatment.[5]

---

† The author thanks Brenda Khoo Yu Qing, a third-year law student at SMU, for her research assistance.
1 Eg, *McInerney v MacDonald* [1992] 2 SCR 138.
2 *Halushka v University of Saskatchewan* (1965) 53 DLR (2d) 436 (on informed consent).
3 Human Biomedical Research Act (No 29 of 2015) (see Chapter 12).
4 See case of professional misconduct by Professor Simon Shorvon, former director of National Neuroscience Institute, Singapore, who had obtained confidential patient information for medical research without the patients' consent.
5 *Gillick v West Norfolk and Wisbech AHA* [1986] AC 112 (a minor could consent to treatment if she had sufficient maturity and intelligence to comprehend the medical treatment and its potential

Though confidentiality is a fundamental principle, it is not absolute. There are certain circumstances where disclosure of confidential information concerning patients may be legally justified:

1. *Consent and/or agreement*: Disclosure of confidential information with the patient's consent does not amount to a breach of confidentiality. The consent must be validly given absent fraud, misrepresentation or undue influence. The consent may be express, implied or "deemed consent" based on statute (*eg*, Personal Data Protection Act examined below). Patients may, for example, expressly give consent for information of his health condition to be shared with family members. Consent may be implied if the medical doctor shares the patient's confidential information with healthcare professionals in order to seek advice on the appropriate treatment. In some cases, it is possible for the patient to enter into an agreement with the doctor or hospital permitting disclosure of information.
2. *Public interests*: Disclosure of patient information may be justified by overriding public interests[6] such as the avoidance of serious harms posed to others. Such public interests for disclosure must be weighed against the interests of the patient and the public interest to maintain confidentiality.
3. *Legal requirement for disclosure*: A doctor is justified to disclose confidential patient information if he is required by law to do so.[7]
4. *Anonymised information*: Disclosing anonymised medical information would not constitute a breach of confidentiality if the privacy rights of the individual patients are not infringed.[8]

The exceptions to the duty to maintain confidentiality will be discussed in greater detail below. The next three sections will briefly set out the legal positions concerning confidentiality in equity and tort[9] as well as under the various Singapore statutes including the Personal Data Protection Act. This chapter will proceed to discuss specific legal and ethical issues on access to and ownership of patient information, disclosure of patient (genetic) information to family members, medical disciplinary cases relating to breaches of confidentiality and finally, the procedural aspects of obtaining confidential information and sources for the purpose of litigation.

---

consequences); *R (on the application of Sue Axon) v Secretary of State for Health and the Family Planning Association* [2006] EWHC 37 (confidentiality of advice given to patients who are minors should be respected provided the minor's physical and mental health are not adversely affected by non-disclosure to their parents, the minor understands the medical advice given and treatment to be undertaken and the advice or treatment was in the minor's best interests).

6 *Eg, Stone v South East Strategic Health Authority* [2006] EWHC 1668 (privacy of medical information of claimant, a convicted murderer, in a report by an independent inquiry panel which looked into the care, treatment and supervision of the claimant to be published to world at large based on public interest grounds).
7 *Hunter v Mann* [1974] QB 767.
8 *R v Department of Health, exp Source Informatics Ltd* [2000] 1 All ER 786.
9 See generally Herring (2018); Stauch & Wheat (2015); Taylor (2017).

7.2 The equitable doctrine of breach of confidence

In the equitable action of breach of confidence that was originally recognised in Singapore,[10] reference was made to the three legal requirements in *Coco v AN Clark (Engineers) Ltd*[11] as follows:

(a) the information in question was of a confidential nature;
(b) the information was imparted in circumstances imposing an obligation of confidence; and
(c) there was an unauthorised use of the information by the defendant.

In 2020, the Court of Appeal in *I-Admin (Singapore) Pte Ltd v Hong Ying Ting and others* – not a medical law case – considered that the third legal requirement may prevent the claimant from obtaining any remedy in circumstances where the defendants "wrongfully access or acquire confidential information but do not use or disclose the same".[12] As such, it proposed a modified approach for breach of confidence claims[13]:

> Preserving the first two requirements in *Coco*, a court should consider whether the information in question "has the necessary quality of confidence about it" and if it has been "imparted in circumstances importing an obligation of confidence". An obligation of confidence will also be found where confidential information has been accessed or acquired without a plaintiff's knowledge or consent. Upon the satisfaction of these prerequisites, an action for breach of confidence is presumed. This might be displaced where, for instance, the defendant came across the information by accident or was unaware of its confidential nature or believed there to be a strong public interest in disclosing it. Whatever the explanation, the burden will be on *the defendant* to prove that its conscience was unaffected...

In essence, the first two legal requirements (modified to encompass the access and acquisition of confidential information) remained but the third would no longer be applicable for breach of confidence.

With respect to the first requirement, in order for information to have that requisite quality of confidence, it should be relatively secret or inaccessible to the public as compared to information already in the public domain.[14] The oft-used test is whether any special intellectual skill and labour would be required for a member of the public to reproduce the information.[15] It is possible that information which has been assembled from its component parts

---

10 *X Pte Ltd v CDE* [1992] 2 SLR(R) 575 at [21]; *Chiarapurk Jack v Haw Par Brothers International Ltd* [1993] 2 SLR(R) 620; *Vestwin Trading Pte Ltd v Obegi Melissa* [2006] 3 SLR(R) 573 at [34]; and *QB Net Co Ltd v Earnson Management (S) Pte Ltd.* [2007] 1 SLR(R) 1 at [65].
11 [1969] RPC 41.
12 [2020] SGCA 32 at [43].
13 [2020] SGCA 32 at [61].
14 *Invenpro (M) Sdn Bhd v JCS Automation Pte Ltd* [2014] 2 SLR 1045 at [130], per George Wei JC; *Coco v AN Clark (Engineers) Ltd* [1969] RPC 41.
15 *Saltman Engineering v Campbell* [1948] 65 RPC 203 at 215, per Lord Greene MR.

142 Confidentiality

that are available in the public domain may nevertheless remain confidential.[16] It is not necessary for confidential information to exist in any particular form or that it be recorded in some material or permanent form.

Information relating to the sexual conduct of a person has been regarded as confidential.[17] Hence, information pertaining to a patient's sexual conduct which the doctor obtained in the course of medical consultation would likely constitute confidential information. Information that the claimant had undergone cosmetic surgery was also held to be confidential information.[18]

Applying the second legal requirement, a doctor owes an equitable obligation of confidence in circumstances where a reasonable doctor would have known that the information was confidential and imparted to the doctor in confidence. This equitable duty is based on good faith and conscience. Thus, a doctor will owe a duty of confidentiality to his patient with respect to medical information he has diagnosed about the patient's condition. The wording of the second requirement extends even to a case where the doctor has acquired confidential information about an individual who is not a patient as long as any reasonable person would understand the information was imparted in confidence (Aplin et al 2012, at p. 388). By logical extension, a person who submits his blood sample to a laboratory should be owed a duty of confidentiality by the laboratory with respect to the results of the genetic testing (Wei 2002, at p. 73).

The requirement that the obligation of confidentiality had to arise from a pre-existing relationship (such as in an employment or contractual relationship[19]) has been relaxed over time with an increased focus instead on the protection of the information itself (Aplin et al 2012, at p. 4). Lord Goff's *dictum* in *Attorney General v Guardian Newspapers Ltd (No 2)*[20] about a person who came across an obviously confidential document such as a private diary left in a public place and picked up by a passer-by is often cited. Years later, the UK decision of *Campbell v Mirror Group Newspapers Ltd*[21] developed the tort of misuse of private information which did not require such a pre-existing relationship (which will be discussed in the section below).

The original third limb for breach of confidence – that the plaintiff has to prove unauthorised use of the confidential information obtained by the doctor[22] – is no longer required to be proved by the plaintiff. Prior to the *I-Admin (Singapore)* case mentioned above, there were

---

16 *Coco v AN Clark (Engineers) Ltd* [1969] RPC 41 at 47, per Megarry J.
17 *Stephens v Avery* [1988] Ch 449 (information of a lesbian relationship disclosed to the press); *Barrymore v News Group Newspapers Ltd* [1997] IP&T Digest 49 (injunction against disclosing information revealed during a homosexual relationship); *Mosley v News Group Newspapers Ltd* [2008] All ER (D) 322 (information of sexual activities committed by consenting adults on private property).
18 *Archer v Williams* [2003] EWHC 1670 at [74]-[76] (breach of confidentiality by ex-employee in breach of undertaking of confidentiality).
19 This extended to the tortious action against third party recipients of confidential information (*ie*, tort of inducing breach of contract): see *Lumley v Gye* [1853] 2 E & B 216; 118 ER 749.
20 [1990] 1 AC 109 at 281. See also Lord Woolf in *A v B plc* [2003] QB 195.
21 [2004] 1 AC 457.
22 *Invenpro (M) Sdn Bhd v JCS Automation Pte Ltd* [2014] 2 SLR 1045 at [170].

already judicial pronouncements that the third requirement should be relaxed such that the act of looking at documents which the defendant knows to be confidential or "intentionally obtaining [confidential] information, secretly and knowing that the claimant reasonably expects it to be private", would amount to a breach of confidence.[23]

In order to protect patient confidential information under breach of confidence, the prohibition from disclosure may extend to information of related parties. It is possible that the protection of confidential patient information may entail the obligation not to disclose the private information of related persons or entities which are likely to lead to the disclosure of the patients' identities.[24]

As abovementioned, the obligation of confidence is subject to overriding public interests.[25] The defendant has the onus to establish the existence of public interests that justify the unauthorised disclosure. The public interests sought to justify disclosure will have to be balanced against the public interests in maintaining confidentiality and the patient's private interests. Some relevant factors include[26]:

(a) the question whether the information is merely interesting to the public or whether there is a real public interest supporting the disclosure;
(b) the fact that the media have a private interest of their own in publishing in terms of circulation and public interest should not be confused with their own interest;
(c) the fact that the public interest may be best served by giving the information in certain cases to the police and competent authorities rather than to the press;
(d) that the rule that there is no confidence in an iniquity is merely one justification for breaking confidence.

One important public interest to justify disclosure of confidential information is the protection of innocent people against potential violence or dangers. In *W v Egdell*,[27] the defendant psychiatrist had revealed in a report that the plaintiff, who was suffering from paranoid schizophrenia and was detained in a secure hospital after he had killed and injured certain persons, had a long-standing and continuing interest in making bombs. The plaintiff's application for an injunction to prevent the disclosure of the report to a medical officer at the hospital failed. The court was of the view the plaintiff remained a danger to society and the report would be relevant to the medical officer for the treatment of the plaintiff and to determine whether he

---

23 *Imerman v Tchenguiz and others* [2011] 2 WLR 592 at [68], per Lord Neuberger MR.
24 *Eg, H (A Healthcare Worker) v Associated Newspapers Ltd and N (A Health Authority)* [2002] Lloyd's Rep Med 210 (CA) (that private information relating to H, a healthcare worker working at N health authority who was diagnosed HIV positive and the details of his patient, should be protected from disclosure by the press together with information about N based on public interest, and the likelihood that disclosure of N's identity would lead to H's identity being uncovered).
25 *Eg,* disclosure of nurse's statement relating to a patient's death by the police to the regulatory body was justified by reasons of public health or safety: *Woolgar v Chief Constable of Sussex Police* [1999] Lloyd's Rep Med 335.
26 *Lion Laboratories Ltd v Evans* [1984] 2 All ER 417.
27 [1990] Ch 359.

144 *Confidentiality*

should be released from hospital. In another case, *X Health Authority v Y*,[28] the English court ruled against the publication of information by the defendant newspapers concerning two doctors who were diagnosed as HIV positive. The information was obtained from the press by bribing employees of the health authority in breach of confidence. There is public interest in discouraging employees from disclosing confidential information to the newspapers, and to ensure that AIDS sufferers in hospitals would not be subject to their medical condition being made public. These public interests substantially outweighed the public interests to disclose the information relating to the doctors' conditions.

Remedies for breach of confidence include damages, account of profits and injunctions. Injunctions to prevent disclosure of information may not be granted if an award of damages would be adequate.[29] An injunction is not normally granted if the information was already in the public domain. Under an action in breach of confidence, the plaintiff may also have a remedy against the defendant for an account of profits.[30] An award of equitable damages which is a statutory remedy under s 2 of the Chancery Amendment Act 1858[31] is also possible.[32] Damages for injury to the plaintiff's feelings have been awarded in a case[33] in which a consultant psychiatrist disclosed a medico-legal report to the patient's GP and another psychiatrist in breach of confidentiality. Aggravated damages may be awarded to the extent the defendant's conduct has aggravated the plaintiff's injury.[34]

7.3 Privacy interests and the tort of misuse of private information

Privacy refers to the right to control and determine information about oneself being communicated to others.[35] It is generally based on respect for persons[36] and human dignity.[37] Privacy interests are not necessarily concomitant with property interests. The fact that a person does not own a piece of personal information does not mean he cannot assert privacy interests with regard to the information. The Singapore constitution does not contain an explicit right

---

28 [1988] 2 All ER 648.
29 *Saltman Engineering Co Ltd v Campbell Engineering Co Ltd* [1948] 65 RPC 203.
30 *Attorney-General v Blake* [1998] Ch 439; *Attorney-General v Guardian Newspapers Ltd (No 2)* [1990] 1 AC 109.
31 (c 27) (UK).
32 *I-Admin (Singapore) Pte Ltd v Hong Ying Ting and others* [2020] SGCA 32 at [77].
33 *Cornelius v De Taranto* [2001] EMLR 329; *AAA v Associated Newspapers Ltd* [2012] EWHC 2103; and *WXY v Gewanter* [2013] EWHC 589. In Australia, see *Giller v Procopets* [2008] VSCA 236 (damages for mental distress resulting from the breach of confidence).
34 *Campbell v MGN Ltd* [2002] EMLR 30.
35 Westin (1967, at p. 7).
36 *Eg*, Benn (1975).
37 *Campbell v MGN Ltd* [2004] 2 AC 457 at [51], [53] and [56], *per* Lord Hoffmann.

to privacy for citizens,[38] though privacy rights may be protected under the private law of obligations such as equity and tort.[39]

Privacy interests were already protected in older English cases.[40] More recently, the traditional equitable doctrine of breach of confidence in particular the second legal requirement concerning the existence of a pre-existing relationship was thought to be unduly restrictive for protecting privacy interests. The House of Lords' decision in *Campbell v Mirror Group Newspapers Ltd*[41] (*Campbell*) concerned private information relating to a celebrity's treatment for drug addiction. The information included photographs showing Noami Campbell leaving a meeting of Narcotics Anonymous and a newspaper article supplying details of the treatment. Though she had made public statements that she did not take drugs, the details of her drug therapy were nevertheless held to be confidential and private in nature. In fact, the majority law lords were of the view that the information relating to Campbell's health and therapeutic treatment were no different from clinical information relating to the treatment of a patient's medical condition. The relevant test for privacy of information adopted by a majority of the House of Lords[42] was whether a person had a reasonable expectation of privacy from the facts disclosed. Campbell was eventually awarded damages arising from the defendant newspaper's breach of confidence.

Lord Hoffmann in *Campbell* specifically referred to the protection against the misuse of private information based on individual autonomy and dignity and the right to control the dissemination of information about one's private life[43] (as opposed to good faith and conscience in the equitable action in breach of confidence). Following *Campbell*, it was held in *McKennit v Ash*,[44] that a person's health information was clearly private information. Under this newly developed tort of misuse of private information influenced by ECHR jurisprudence, it is not necessary to prove the relationship of confidence. The tort of misuse of private information and the equitable breach of confidence are distinct causes of action and, in some cases, the information in question may be protected under both actions.[45] More clarity would, however, be needed with respect to the legal elements of the tort, possible defences and the range of remedies available (Giliker 2015). With this judicial development, commentators have argued that the underlying basis for breach of confidence is not confined to contract, equity, tort or property but is *sui generis* in character (Aplin et al 2012, at p. 99).

---

38 See *Lim Meng Suang and another v Attorney-General and another appeal and another matter* [2015] 1 SLR 26 at [44] (that the right to privacy and personal autonomy is not part of the "life or personal liberty" in Art 9(1)).
39 [2015] 1 SLR 26 at [49].
40 *Albert v Strange* (1849) 1 Mac & G 25; 41 ER 1171 (injunction against third party to restrain from publishing and printing the claimant's private etchings); *Argyll v Argyll* [1967] Ch 302 (details of private life of spouse revealed to husband in the course of marriage).
41 [2004] 1 AC 457. See Saw and Chan (2005).
42 Lord Nicholls, Baroness Hale and Lord Hope. This required a balancing between the rights in Article 8 (right to private life) and Article 10 (right to freedom of expression) of the ECHR.
43 *Campbell v MGN Ltd* [2004] 2 AC 457 at [51], *per* Lord Hoffmann.
44 [2008] QB 73 at [23].
45 *OBG Ltd v Allan* [2008] 1 AC 1 at [255], *per* Lord Nicholls.

146 *Confidentiality*

Such a tort against the misuse of private information appeared to have been accepted by the Singapore Personal Data Protection Commission (PDPC).[46] It should be highlighted that there is no omnibus or general tort of privacy in Singapore. In contrast, New Zealand courts have recognised a common law tort of privacy.[47] Gault P and Blanchard J in *Hosking v Runting*[48] were of the view that it would be "conducive of clearer analysis" to recognise privacy and breach of confidence as separate causes of action. They referred to the tests of (i) reasonable expectation of privacy and (ii) publicity of the facts that would be considered highly offensive to an objective reasonable person and the defence based on legitimate public concern in the information. However, doubts were later cast in a subsequent judicial decision[49] on the second test. The Ontario court in *Jones v Tsige*[50] has allowed a claim based on intrusion upon seclusion. This is not a general tort of privacy but nonetheless protects privacy interests based on a narrower factual matrix.

7.4 Statutory obligations of confidentiality

Statutory obligations of confidentiality are imposed on public office-holders as well as public and private hospitals, clinics and doctors. The Personal Data Protection Act applies to organisations generally including those providing medical or health-related services.

7.4.1 Statutory duties of public office-holders, hospitals, clinics and doctors

The confidentiality of medical records is imposed under the Private Hospitals and Medical Clinics Act.[51] Subject to specified exceptions,[52] the Director of Medical Services shall not disclose any information which is contained in the medical record, or which relates to the condition,

---

46 *My Digital Lock Pte Ltd* [2018] SGPDPC 3 at [35], [38]-[40] ("a private claimant prosecuting his case in the civil courts can plead both the common law tort to prevent publication of private information as well as pursue a private claim based on breaches of the PDPA").
47 *Hosking v Runting* [2005] 1 NZLR 1; *Tucker v News Media Ownership Ltd* [1986] 2 NZLR 716; *Bradley v Wingnut Films Ltd* [1993] 1 NZLR 415; *P v D* [2000] 2 NZLR 591; and *L v G* [2002] DCR 234.
48 [2005] 1 NZLR 1. See also *C v Holland* [2012] 3 NZLR 672.
49 *Rogers v Television New Zealand Ltd* [2007] NZSC 91, *per* Elias CJ and Anderson J.
50 2012 ONCA 32, 108 OR (3d) 241; applied in *Sheridan v Ontario* 2014 ONSC 4970 at [56]; referred to in *Ladas v Apple Inc* 2014 BCSC 1821 at [83]-[84]; and *Hopkins v Kay* 2014 ONSC 321, 237 ACWS (3d) 362, 119 OR (3d) 251 at [28].
51 (Cap 248, 1999 Rev Ed).
52 Where the disclosure is made –
   (a) under or for the purpose of administering and enforcing –
      (i) [the Private Hospitals and Medical Clinics Act];
      (ii) the Infectious Diseases Act (Cap. 137);
      (iii) the Termination of Pregnancy Act (Cap. 324);
      (iv) the Human Organ Transplant Act (Cap. 131A);
      (v) the Health Products Act (Cap. 122D); or
      (vi) the Medicines Act (Cap. 176);

Confidentiality 147

treatment or diagnosis, of any person, as may have come to his knowledge in the course of carrying out any investigation or performing any duty or function under the statute.[53]

The licensing authority under the Medicines Act,[54] with respect to an application for an innovative medicinal product which contains confidential supporting information, is obliged to desist from disclosing or using the information for a five-year period. This obligation of confidentiality is subject to certain statutory exceptions[55] including instances where it is "necessary to protect the health or safety of members of the public".[56]

Under the Advance Medical Directives (AMD) Act,[57] the register of AMDs shall be kept confidential and shall not be disclosed to any person except the person who made the directive, the Registrar and medical practitioner responsible for the treatment of the person who made the directive. In fact, information relating to the patient's making of a directive, or of the patient's intention to make a directive shall be kept confidential by the medical practitioner and medical worker.[58]

Medical doctors, clinics, hospitals and healthcare institutions may be under statutory duties or permitted in limited situations to disclose confidential information relating to patients. Under the Infectious Diseases Act,[59] every medical practitioner who has "reason to believe or suspect that any person attended or treated by him is suffering from a prescribed infectious disease or is a carrier of that disease" shall notify the Director of Medical Services.[60] A medical practitioner is permitted, subject to certain conditions,[61] to disclose information relating to a person whom he "reasonably believes" is infected with HIV to the spouse,

---

  (b) for the purpose of making a complaint or providing information under Part V of the Dental Registration Act (Cap. 76), Part VII of the Medical Registration Act (Cap. 174) or Part VI of the Pharmacists Registration Act 2007; or
  (c) for any other purpose with the consent of the person to whom the information relates or the representative of such person.
53 Section 13(2).
54 (Cap 176, 1985 Rev Ed), section 19A.
55 See section 19B generally (including disclosure with the consent of the applicant; disclosure to a Government department or statutory body; disclosure to any adviser engaged by the licensing authority to advise on any aspect of the medicinal product to which the confidential supporting information relates; disclosure to World Health Organisation and certain specific agencies).
56 Section 19B(1)(a)(ii).
57 (Cap 4A, 1997 Rev Ed), section 6(3).
58 Section 15(3).
59 (Cap 137, Rev Ed 2003).
60 Infectious Diseases Act, section 6.
61 Section 25A (4) states the three conditions namely that the medical practitioner:
  (a) reasonably believes that it is medically appropriate and that there is a significant risk of infection to the spouse, former spouse or other contact;
  (b) has counselled the infected person regarding the need to notify the spouse, former spouse or other contact and he reasonably believes that the infected person will not inform the spouse, former spouse or other contact; and
  (c) has informed the infected person of his intent to make such disclosure to the spouse, former spouse or other contact.

former spouse or other contact of the infected person or to a Health Officer for the purpose of making the disclosure to the spouse, former spouse or other contact.

The manager of a healthcare institution[62] shall notify the Registrar of the National Registry of Diseases[63] that a person is diagnosed with or undergoes treatment for a reportable disease at the healthcare institution. The Registrar is entitled to require the manager to produce additional information including any medical record, book or document.[64] Nonetheless, patient confidentiality is preserved as the Registrar is prohibited from disclosing the contents of any register or any individually identifiable information which may have come to his knowledge in the course of performing his statutory duty or function.[65] The prohibition does not, however, apply to the disclosure or publication of any information held by the Registry in an anonymised form.[66] The Registrar may, with the approval of the Director of Medical Services, [67] disclose individually identifiable information held by the Registry to any public officer or any other person for the purpose of conducting national public health programmes concerning any reportable disease. The Registrar may also approve disclosure of such information to a medical practitioner[68] or a researcher[69] provided the statutory criteria are satisfied.

Subject to permitted disclosures to specified parties or for limited purposes under the statute,[70] persons responsible for keeping medical records in connection with a treatment to

---

62 "Healthcare institution" means
    (a) any private hospital, medical clinic, clinical laboratory or healthcare establishment licensed under the Private Hospitals and Medical Clinics Act (Cap. 248); or
    (b) any facility, premises or conveyance which is declared by the Minister, by order published in the *Gazette*, to be a healthcare institution for the purposes of this Act.
63 Section 6(1), National Registry of Diseases Act (Cap 210B, 2008 Rev Ed).
64 Section 7(2), National Registry of Diseases Act.
65 Section 8(2), National Registry of Diseases Act.
66 Section 9(1), National Registry of Diseases Act.
67 Section 10, National Registry of Diseases Act.
68 See Section 11, National Registry of Diseases Act. This is provided the Registrar is satisfied that –
    (a) the medical practitioner is responsible for the treatment and care of that person;
    (b) the disclosure is necessary for the proper treatment of that person; and
    (c) the requisite consent has been given for such disclosure.
69 Section 12, National Registry of Diseases Act. This is provided the Registrar is satisfied that –
    (a) the research cannot be carried out with anonymised information;
    (b) the requisite consent has been given for such individually identifiable information to be disclosed to the researcher for the purpose of the research;
    (c) the research may –
        (i) improve the quality of health services provided for patients suffering from any reportable disease in Singapore; or
        (ii) support any national public health policy, initiative or programme concerning any reportable disease; and
    (d) the researcher and the research comply with such conditions as may have been prescribed.
70 Termination of Pregnancy Regulations (Cap 324, Rg 1), Reg 12 with respect to disclosures to *eg*, officer in Ministry of Health and Attorney-General or for the purpose of criminal proceedings and *bona fide* research.

terminate a pregnancy or who participate in such a treatment have the obligation to maintain confidentiality of any facts or information relating to the treatment unless the pregnant woman gives express consent for disclosure.[71] Contravention of the statutory obligation will result in a criminal offence. In addition, the doctor is under a statutory obligation[72] to report to the Police where he is aware of an offence committed against the patient under Part XVI of the Penal Code[73] (Offences against the Human Body) which include sexual offences such as rape and sexual assault involving penetration.[74]

7.4.2 Duty of organisations under the PDPA

The objective of the Personal Data Protection Act (PDPA) is primarily the

> collection, use and disclosure of personal data by organisations in a manner that recognises both the right of *individuals*[75] to protect their personal data and the need of *organisations* to collect, use or disclose personal data for purposes that a reasonable person would consider appropriate in the circumstances.

Personal data refers to data from which the individual may be identified. Two important principles in the PDPA governing the collection, use or disclosure of data are (i) the existence of *consent* of the individual and (ii) the identification and scope of the *purpose(s)* for which the personal data is to be collected, used or disclosed.[76] The statute requires organisations to develop and implement policies and practices that are necessary to meet statutory obligations under PDPA.[77]

An organisation is generally prohibited from collecting, using or disclosing any personal data of an individual unless the individual has given or is deemed to have given his consent for the collection, use or disclosure of the data.[78] The exceptions are discussed below.

At present, an individual is deemed to have given consent in two situations under the PDPA:

(a) where he voluntarily provides his personal data to an organisation for a purpose, and it is reasonable that he would voluntarily provide the data[79]; and
(b) where an individual gives, or is deemed to have given, consent to the disclosure of personal data about the individual by one organisation to another organisation for a

---

71 Termination of Pregnancy Act (Cap 324), 1985 Rev Ed, section 7.
72 Criminal Procedure Code (Cap 68, 2012 Rev Ed), section 424.
73 (Cap 224, 2008 Rev Ed).
74 Sexual penetration of a person under 16 (with or without consent) is an offence: section 376A.
75 This includes both living and deceased individuals: see Advisory Guidelines on Key Concepts in the PDPA (updated 9 Oct 2019), para 4.4. But the PDPA does not apply to personal data about an individual who has been deceased for more than ten years: para 5.19.
76 See Pt IV of the Personal Data Protection Act (Act 26 of 2012).
77 PDPA, section 12(1).
78 PDPA, section 13.
79 PDPA, section 15(1).

particular purpose, the individual is deemed to consent to the collection, use or disclosure of the personal data for that particular purpose by that other organisation.[80]

The PDPC Advisory Guidelines for the Healthcare Sector (revised 28 March 2017)[81] also provide some examples of what would or would not amount to deemed consent with respect to health-related information:

(a) Collecting personal data from patients seeking medical care: Healthcare Institution ABC may wish to use John's personal data for marketing of health products unrelated to John's condition. It is unlikely that John would be deemed to have given his consent for this purpose.[82]

(b) Disclosing personal data in referral cases: During separate consultations with the following patients, a doctor makes the recommendations as follows: (i) for Patient A to consult a specialist; (ii) for Patient B to visit a hospital for further medical tests; and (iii) for Patient C to consider long-term care services at a nursing home. Patients A, B and C each agree (verbally) to the respective recommendations and the doctor proceeds to make the necessary arrangements, for example, by contacting another doctor directly or providing the patient with a referral letter. Since each patient agreed to the recommendation, he would have consented to the doctor disclosing his personal data as required for the referral when contacting the recommended healthcare service provider directly.[83]

(c) Collecting personal data of individuals to respond to an emergency: John takes his father to Clinic ABC. His father has been suffering from a very high fever for a few days. During the doctor's examination, John's father suddenly collapses. Clinic ABC immediately calls an ambulance to transfer him to a hospital. This involves Clinic ABC disclosing John's father's personal data to the hospital and ambulance services. Clinic ABC and the hospital may collect, use and disclose John's father's personal data without consent to respond to an emergency that threatens his life or health.[84]

The organisation may collect,[85] use[86] or disclose[87] personal data about an individual without the consent of the individual in certain circumstances. For the purpose of health and medical data, the most relevant circumstances justifying disclosure of personal data are the following:

(a) the disclosure is necessary for any purpose which is clearly in the interests of the individual, if consent for its disclosure cannot be obtained in a timely way;

(b) the disclosure is necessary to respond to an emergency that threatens the life, health or safety of the individual or another individual;

---

80 PDPA, section 15(2).
81 See PDPC Advisory Guidelines at https://www.pdpc.gov.sg/-/media/Files/PDPC/PDF-Files/Sector-Specific-Advisory/advisoryguidelinesforthehealthcaresector28mar2017.pdf.
82 Pages 5–6.
83 Page 7.
84 Page 11.
85 Second Schedule.
86 Third Schedule.
87 Fourth Schedule.

(c) subject to the conditions in paragraph 2, there are reasonable grounds to believe that the health or safety of the individual or another individual will be seriously affected and consent for the disclosure of the data cannot be obtained in a timely way;

...

(m) the personal data about the current or former patients of a healthcare institution licensed under the Private Hospitals and Medical Clinics Act (Cap. 248) or any other prescribed healthcare body[88] is disclosed to a public agency for the purposes of policy formulation or review ......

...

2. In the case of disclosure under paragraph 1(c), the organisation shall, as soon as may be practicable, notify the individual whose personal data is disclosed of the disclosure and the purposes of the disclosure.

The Ministry of Communications and Information (MCI) and the PDPC are working on the Personal Data Protection (Amendment Bill) 2020 which includes, amongst others, proposals to expand the concept of "deemed consent" and introduce new exceptions to the consent requirement.[89]

Personal data in the possession or under the control of the relevant organisation is subject to correction.[90] An organisation should, upon receipt of a correction request, correct the personal data as soon as practicable and send the corrected personal data to every other organisation to which the personal data was disclosed by the organisation unless the organisation is satisfied on reasonable grounds that the correction should not be made.[91] However, the organisation shall not be required to correct or otherwise alter an opinion, including a professional or an expert opinion.[92] The obligation to make corrections does not extend to "opinion data" kept solely for an evaluative purpose.[93] An organisation shall also take

---

88 The prescribed healthcare bodies mentioned in section 2 of PDPA are:
   1 Agency for Integrated Care Pte. Ltd.
   2 Alexandra Health System Pte. Ltd.
   3 Eastern Health Alliance Pte. Ltd.
   4 Jurong Health Services Pte. Ltd.
   5 National Healthcare Group Pte. Ltd.
   6 National University Health System Pte. Ltd.
   7 Singapore Health Services Pte. Ltd.
   8 An organisation that is an approved provider within the meaning of the Medical and Elderly Care Endowment Schemes Act (Cap. 173A).

   See Personal Data Protection (Prescribed Healthcare Bodies) Notification 2015 which came into force on 1 March 2015.
89 Such as "deemed consent by notification" and the legitimate interests exception: see Public Consultation Paper (14 May 2020) at https://www.mci.gov.sg/public-consultations/public-consultation-items/public-consultation-on-the-draft-personal-data-protection-amendment-bill, pp. 12-14.
90 Personal Data Protection Act (Act 26 of 2012), section 22.
91 Section 22(2).
92 Section 22(6).
93 Sixth Schedule, para 1(a).

152 *Confidentiality*

reasonable steps to ensure that personal data collected by or on behalf of the organisation is accurate and complete.[94]

Two other important statutory obligations should be mentioned. The organisation has to make reasonable security arrangements[95] to prevent unauthorised access, collection, use, disclosure, copying, modification, disposal or similar risks ("protection obligation"),[96] and shall cease to retain its documents containing personal data, or remove the means by which the personal data can be associated with particular individuals, as soon as it is reasonable to assume that the purpose for which that personal data was collected is no longer being served by retention of the personal data; and retention is no longer necessary for legal or business purposes ("retention limit obligation").[97]

The PDPA statutory obligations also extend to third parties who receive confidential patient information. A data intermediary that processes personal data on behalf of and for the purposes of another organisation pursuant to a written contract will be subject only to the protection obligation and retention limitation obligation under the PDPA. For example, a testing laboratory may, in providing blood testing services to a medical clinic's patients, agree that the laboratory will use personal data of the clinic's patients provided by the clinic for the sole purpose of conducting the blood test on behalf of and for the purposes of the clinic.[98]

Where an organisation has outsourced work to an IT vendor, the responsibility for complying with statutory obligations under the PDPA remains with the organisation and cannot be delegated,[99] though in such a case, the organisation would have a supervisory or general role for the protection of the personal data, and the data intermediary assumes a more direct and specific role.[100]

The PDPC has the power to direct organisations to stop collecting, using or disclosing personal data, to destroy personal data collected and to pay a financial penalty.[101] A person is entitled to claim for loss or damage suffered directly as a result of the contravention of specific provisions[102] by an organisation.[103] In this regard, the PDPA protects informational

---

94 Personal Data Protection Act (Act 26 of 2012), section 23.
95 *Re The Cellar Door Pte Ltd and Global Interactive Works Pte Ltd* [2016] SGPDPC 22 at [29] (that IT systems must be sufficiently robust and comprehensive to guard against a possible intrusion or attack).
96 Personal Data Protection Act (Act 26 of 2012), section 24.
97 Section 25.
98 PDPC Advisory Guidelines for the Healthcare Sector (revised 28 March 2017), para 2.18.
99 *Re WTS Automotive Services* [2018] SGPDPC 26 at [23].
100 *Re Social Metric Pte Ltd* [2017] SGPDPC 17 at [16].
101 The aggrieved individual or organisation may appeal against the Personal Data Protection Commission's decision to the Data Protection Appeal Panel (s 34 of the Personal Data Protection Act (Act 26 of 2012)) with the possibility of a further appeal to the High Court (s 35).
102 Provisions found in Pts IV ("Collection, Use and Disclosure of Personal Data"), V ("Access to and Correction of Personal Data") and VI ("Care of Personal Data") of the Personal Data Protection Act (Act 26 of 2012).
103 Section 32 of the PDPA.

privacy.[104] Instead of the statutory tort, an aggrieved party may decide to initiate claims under the tort of misuse of private information or a civil claim under the Protection from Harassment Act.[105] The PDPC is entitled to exercise its discretion to suspend, discontinue or refuse to conduct investigations where the legal actions at common law may be more appropriate.[106]

In 2018, a cyberattack was made on the Singapore Health Services Pte Ltd's (SingHealth) patient database system containing the personal data (names, NRIC numbers, addresses, gender, race, and dates of birth) of nearly 1.5 million patients and the outpatient prescription records of nearly 160,000 patients. Integrated Health Information Systems Pte Ltd ("IHiS") - the central national IT agency for the public healthcare sector in Singapore - acted as the data intermediary. Both SingHealth and IHiS were found to have breached the protection obligations to ensure reasonable security arrangements under s 24 of PDPA.[107] Given the "highly sensitive and confidential personal data",[108] SingHealth and IHiS were ordered by PDPC to pay a financial penalty of S$250,000 and $750,000, respectively.

Box 7.1 - HIV patients and confidentiality of information

It was discovered in January 2019 that information of 14,200 people with HIV including their names, contact details and medical information had been stolen and leaked online. The leakage was due to the acts of a Singaporean doctor who had access to the HIV Registry by virtue of his position as head of MOH's National Public Health Unit (NPHU) and his boyfriend from the United States who was HIV positive and had been convicted previously for fraud and drug-related offence (The Straits Times, 28 January 2019 at https://www.straitstimes.com/singapore/data-of-14200-singapore-patients-with-hiv-leaked-online-by-american-fraudster-who-was). HIV patients in Singapore face challenges in the workplace. A recent study based on one acute hospital setting in Singapore indicated challenges relating to the: (1) ability to ensure secrecy of diagnosis from employers; (2) ability to secure financial resources for treatment and sustenance; (3) ability to ensure stable health to meet job requirements; (4) ability to cognitively sit with the concerns of uncertainty and limitations in career; and (5) ability to work through discriminatory workplace practices (Tan et al. 2013). What appropriate measures (both pre and post-breach) could be undertaken to mitigate such risks?

---

104 See *My Digital Lock Pte Ltd* [2018] SGPDPC 3 at [33], *per* Yeong Zee Kin (Personal Data Protection Commission).
105 (Cap 256A, 2015 Rev Ed).
106 Section 50(3), PDPA. See *My Digital Lock Pte Ltd* [2018] SGPDPC 3 at [55] and [59]-[62] (where the claim extends beyond protection of complainant's personal data to other areas such as the laws on the protection of privacy and harassment under the Protection from Harassment Act).
107 *Singapore Health Services Pte Ltd and others* [2019] SGPDPC 3 (14 January 2019).
108 This included clinical episode information, clinical documentation, patient diagnosis and health issues and Dispensed Medication Records.

7.5 Access to and ownership of patient information

Under the PDPA, the individual is entitled to request for access to personal data in the possession or control of an organisation such as a medical clinic or hospital.[109] Such access is, however, subject to certain caveats stated in the statute. For example, an organisation is not required to provide individuals with personal data or other information where the personal data in question is "opinion data" kept solely for an evaluative purpose.[110] Further, organisations must not provide access to personal data or other information if providing access could reasonably be expected to cause immediate or grave harm to the safety or to the physical or mental health of the individual who made the request, or reveal the identity of the individual who provided the personal data and that individual does not consent to the disclosure of his identity.[111] The Advisory Guidelines by PDPC indicate that the PPDA does not confer property or ownership rights *per se* with respect to personal data.[112]

Case authorities suggest that patients do not have an unfettered right of access at common law, though they may be granted access to their personal medical information in the possession of their doctors for a medical purpose[113] or for the purpose of litigation.[114] Such right of access has been denied even for such limited purposes.[115] Furthermore, access to medical information may be refused to the patient if it would be detrimental to his health or condition and this is determined by the doctor acting in the best interests of the patient.[116]

The patient does not have any proprietary right or interest in the information contained in the medical records created by the doctor at common law.[117] In the UK, it was held that the patient does not own the prescription forms and his or her personal information contained therein. In *R v Department of Health, ex p Source Informatics Ltd*,[118] the company, Source Informatics, obtained information from general practitioners and pharmacists about drugs prescribed for their patients in the prescription forms and sold the information to pharmaceutical companies for the latter's marketing purposes. This was part of a scheme in which general practitioners and pharmacists who participated were paid modest sums by Source

---

109 Personal Data Protection Act (Act 26 of 2012), section 21.
110 Paragraph 1(a) in the Fifth Schedule, PDPA.
111 Section 21(3), PDPA.
112 Advisory Guidelines on Key Concepts in the PDPA (updated 9 Oct 2019), para 5.30.
113 See *McInerney v. MacDonald* [1992] 2 SCR 138 (a patient should be entitled to examine and obtain copies of his or her medical records from the patient's physician as well as medical reports from previous physicians that the physician may have received and which the physician considered in administering advice or treatment; however, the medical records remained the property of the physician).
114 *R v Mid Glamorgan Family Health Services Authority and Another ex p Martin* [1995] 1 WLR 110 (applicant's purpose was to know more about his "childhood, development and history").
115 See eg, *Breen v Williams* [1996] 138 ALR 359 (Australian High Court) (access sought for purpose of litigation in US; no common law right of access to medical records).
116 *R v Mid Glamorgan Family Health Services Authority and Another ex p Martin* [1995] 1 WLR 110 (medical records were made by health authority prior to and therefore not subject to the UK Access to Health Records Act 1990 or Data Protection Act 1984).
117 *Breen v Williams* [1996] 138 ALR 359.
118 [2000] 1 All ER 786.

Informatics. The information entered into by the pharmacists contained the doctor's name, the patient's name, the date of prescription, the product and the quantity prescribed. The information eventually passed to the company were, however, anonymised in that it did not contain information of the individual patient's identity. The UK Department of Health issued a policy document stating that the duty of confidence owed to patients remained notwithstanding the anonymisation of information and that general practitioners and pharmacists would incur legal risks if they participated in the scheme. The applicants challenged the policy guidance decision by means of judicial review proceedings against the Department of Health.

The English Court of Appeal held that a patient, lacking any proprietary claim to the prescription form or to the information it contained, did not possess the "right to control the way the information was used provided only and always that his privacy was not put at risk". It would therefore not be a breach of confidence for general practitioners and pharmacists to disclose to a third party, without the patient's consent, the anonymised information contained in the prescription forms. The conscience of a reasonable pharmacist would not be troubled by the use of the patients' prescriptions as it did not invade the individual patient's privacy.

In this regard, the Singapore PDPC Advisory Guidelines for the Healthcare Sector (revised 28 March 2017) appears to be consistent with the stance in *Source Informatics* on the issue of anonymised data[119]:

> As good practice, Health Organisation ABC should consider if it is able to achieve the same purposes without using personal data. For example, using anonymised datasets that do not relate to any identifiable individual. Health Organisation ABC will not need to obtain consent from individuals if the personal data in its possession is anonymised before use. Consent is also not required if Health Organisation ABC uses and discloses the anonymised data.

7.6 Disclosure of patient's genetic information

In Chapter 3, we discussed the various scenarios in which the doctor or hospital may owe a duty of care to the patient including providing relevant information concerning the patient's health condition as part of medical advice. Does this extend to genetic information to be obtained by the doctor or hospital that may infringe the confidentiality of another patient such as a family member? One's genetic make-up carries with it uniquely identifying characteristics concerning his origin and other persons he is related to. Genetic information can also predict diseases in individuals and family members. A positive result in genetic testing indicates a predisposition to the disease.

In *ABC v St Georges' Health NHS*,[120] the claimant's father contracted Huntington's disease which is a genetic disease. He was convicted of manslaughter on the grounds of diminished responsibility. The defendants NHS Trust responsible for treating the father kept it confi-

---

119 Page 10.
120 [2017] PIQR P15.

dential from the claimant who was pregnant. The father did not wish his daughters to know "as he felt they might get upset, kill themselves, or have an abortion".[121] The claimant gave birth to a healthy baby but she, as a single mother of the child, was diagnosed with Huntington's disease. When she discovered her father's disease, she initiated a claim against the defendants. She claimed that if she had been informed of her father's diagnosis, she would have sought to be tested for Huntington's disease and would have terminated the pregnancy rather than run the risk that her child might be dependent on a seriously ill single parent or become an orphan, and the risk that her child might inherit the disease.

On the defendants' application to strike out the claim in negligence on the ground that there was no duty of care to begin with, the Court of Appeal refused to do so, holding that there was an arguable case that the defendants NHS might owe the claimant a duty of care to inform her of her father's diagnosis in the light of her pregnancy. Though doctors generally owe a duty of confidentiality to patients, it is not absolute and may be counter-balanced by a public interest in disclosure. It was already recognised under existing law that, in certain circumstances, a professional duty to disclose information can arise. The court cited the UK General Medical Council (GMC) report on confidentiality[122] which referred to justifications for disclosure and the need to "still seek the patient's consent to disclosure if practicable and consider any reasons given for refusal".

In the subsequent trial of the action,[123] Yip J held that the second defendants owed a duty, but the claim failed on breach and causation. The decision not to disclose was supported by a responsible body of medical opinion which had not been proved to be illogical. Furthermore, the judge was not certain on the evidence adduced about what the claimant would have done if she were faced with information about her father's condition.

We should briefly mention three relevant US court decisions. In *Safer v Pack*,[124] the New Jersey appellate court held that the defendant owed a duty to the claimant to warn her when she was a young child that she would contract a genetic disease (a form of colon cancer) which she was diagnosed with subsequently. Significantly, it added that the duty was owed to all members of the immediate family of the patient who may be adversely affected. The cases of *Tarasoff v Regents of the University of California*[125] (cited in *ABC v St Georges' Health NHS*) and *Palmer v Tees Health Authority*[126] involved the disclosure of information pertaining to psychiatric patients (see Chapter 6). The Supreme Court of California in *Tarasoff* held that a therapist had a duty of care to warn an identifiable third party that she was at risk of being murdered.[127] On the other hand, there was no proximity in *Palmer* between the defendant (psychiatrist) and the victim.

---

121 Para 11.
122 See updated guidance published by the GMC in 2009.
123 *ABC v St George's Healthcare NHS Trust & Ors* [2020] EWHC 455 (QB) (28 February 2020).
124 (1996) 677 A 2d 1188 (Sup Ct App Div).
125 (1976) 551 P.2d 334.
126 [2000] PIQR 1.
127 See also *Resiner v Regents of the University of California* (1995) 37 Cal Rptr 2d 518 (that doctors owe duty to future and current sexual partners as foreseeable victims of HIV patient and doctor did not inform patient of HIV positive status).

In Singapore, the BAC (2005) Report had already recommended disclosure of genetic information in limited circumstances where the "nondisclosure of the test result may endanger the life of a third party" and expressed agreement with the National Medical Ethics Committee's position that a physician's duty of confidentiality may be overridden if the following conditions are met[128]:

"(a) separate efforts by two physicians to elicit voluntary consent to disclosure have failed, despite the patient or client fully understanding the implications of such refusal;
(b) there is a high probability both that harm will occur to identifiable individuals or society at large if the information is withheld and that the disclosed information can actually be used to avert harm;
(c) the harm that identifiable individuals (if any) would suffer would be serious; and
(d) appropriate precautions are taken to ensure that only the genetic information needed for diagnosis and/or treatment of the disease in question is disclosed".

Adopting a different approach from the *ABC* case and BAC (2005) Report discussed above, Denbo (2006) argued that doctors should not be required to disclose genetic information to third parties without having first obtained the express consent of the patient suffering from a genetic disease, especially if the information reveals a health condition for which there is no cure. This is because the disclosure of genetic information may cause adverse psychological and emotional impact on individuals. However, she granted that an exception to confidentiality would apply if the patient is a minor child. Kovalesky (2008)[129] applied a more moderate approach by balancing the concerns of the doctor for legal certainty and the patient's or relatives' need to be fully informed, but would grant doctors the discretion rather than impose a duty on them to disclose the genetic information.

A related question is the right to know one's genetic origin by tracing the biological parents. In the UK decision of *Rose and another v Secretary of State for Health and another*,[130] it was held that the claimants, who were conceived by artificial insemination with sperm from donors, had a right to obtain information relating to their biological parents even if the information regarding the donors were confidential information.

7.7 Medical ethics and disciplinary cases

This section discusses disciplinary cases on confidentiality that involve both applicable laws as well as ethical guidelines on confidentiality.

---

128 Para 4.2.2.
129 More specifically, that doctors should inform patients that their conditions are genetically transmissible and allow them their own independent choice of whether to disclose such information to their kin; and if patient decides against disclosure, to allow doctors to exercise their discretion and professional judgement on whether to make such a disclosure to the patient's kin in view of the latter's health concerns.
130 (2003) 69 BMLR 83.

158 *Confidentiality*

The most notable decision is *SMC v Soo Shuenn Chiang*.[131] Dr Soo, a psychiatrist, was charged with (i) failing to verify the identity of a caller claiming to be the husband of one of his patients before issuing, in reliance on information provided by the caller, a memorandum containing confidential medical information about that patient; and (ii) failing to take appropriate steps to ensure that the confidential medical information in the memorandum was not accessible to unauthorised persons. The patient had a history of psychiatric problems, including depression, alcohol misuse, and a risk of self-harm. The caller informed Dr Soo that the patient was suicidal and had to be brought to the Institute of Mental Health ("IMH") for an urgent assessment of her suicide risk.

Dr Soo pleaded guilty to the charge of professional misconduct under s 53(1)(d) of the Medical Registration Act.[132] He was fined $50,000 for breach of confidentiality by the Disciplinary Tribunal (DT).[133] Subsequently, the SMC applied to the High Court for a review of the DT's decision on the ground that the penalty imposed on Dr Soo was manifestly excessive and/or seriously or unduly disproportionate. Shortly thereafter, the SMC decided, based on new findings of facts, to amend its application to the High Court for Dr Soo's conviction and sentence to be set aside.

Dr Soo was under the impression that the caller was the patient's husband. Dr Soo left the memorandum with his clinic staff, with instructions that it should be handed to the husband. However, unknown to Dr Soo, it was the brother who collected the memorandum from the clinic staff later that day. The brother subsequently used the memorandum to get a Personal Protection Order (PPO) issued by the Family Court against the patient.

Dr Soo was eventually acquitted by the High Court of the charges. Upon considering the various ethical guidelines, the High Court opined that[134]:

> a doctor may disclose a patient's confidential medical information without her consent when: (a) he reasonably regards it as necessary to protect the patient from potentially serious self-harm; (b) disclosure is in the patient's best interests; and (c) the patient's consent cannot reasonably be obtained. In such circumstances, we consider that the disclosure should be made to those closest to the patient, such as her next of kin.

The doctor was justified in assessing there was a real risk of suicide on the part of the patient and the memorandum was provided with the objective to obtain assistance from the police or ambulance staff to quickly send her to IMH. To expect the doctor to call the patient directly to verify the identity of the caller was, according to the court, tantamount to "defensive medicine" (*ie*, avoiding perceived legal risks rather than acting in the patient's best interests).[135] The High Court took note of the the absence of specific information on the complainant's next of kin in her electronic records and that the details about the complainant, her medical history and reported medical emergency from the caller corresponded with the information in the electronic records and the doctor's understanding of the complainant's medical

---

131 [2020] 3 SLR 1129.
132 (Cap 174, 2014 Rev Ed).
133 Singapore *Medical Council v Dr Soo Shuenn Chiang* [2018] SMCDT 11.
134 [2020] 3 SLR 1129 at [55].
135 [2020] 3 SLR 1129 at [61].

condition.[136] Moreover, the doctor had given specific instructions to his clinic staff to release the memorandum to the patient's husband.[137] Dr Soo had therefore discharged his duty to maintain the complainant's confidentiality whilst the responsibility of verifying the identity of the person collecting the memorandum would fall on the clinic staff who released it. In the aftermath of this episode, the Ministry of Health issued guidelines on communicating medical information over the phone by healthcare providers and institutions.[138]

The ethical guidelines referred to by the High Court included the ECEG 2002 on "Responsibility to maintain medical confidentiality",[139] and the Guidelines on the Practice of Psychiatry 1997 which provide that a psychiatrist may make such disclosure "to avert inevitable danger to others".[140] In a similar vein, the SMC Ethical Code and Ethical Guidelines (2016 Edition) ("ECEG 2016") provide that disclosure of patients' confidential medical information without their consent is generally defensible when, among other situations, "it is necessary in order to protect patients or others from harm" or "where such disclosure is in patients' best interests".[141]

The *SMC Handbook on Medical Ethics* (2016 Edition) ("HME 2016"), which is a secondary source expounding on the ECEG 2016, notes that a doctor may decide to disclose a patient's confidential medical information to prevent potentially serious harm to the patient herself.[142] Furthermore, "[i]n such cases, if an attempt to secure voluntary disclosure is unsuccessful, impossible, or contrary to the very purpose of disclosure", the doctor may disclose the information without the patient's consent. An example of such circumstances is where there is a "risk of serious harm, such as ... self-harm". The HME 2016 reminds doctors that "except for statutory requirements and urgent situations", they "should be slow to decide to breach medical confidentiality".

The SMC Disciplinary Tribunal has sanctioned doctors for unauthorised access to medical databases and records including the information relating to persons who may not be existing patients under their care.[143] Disciplinary sanctions have been meted out based on offences committed by the doctor under the Computer Misuse Act[144] implying a defect in character

---

136 [2020] 3 SLR 1129 at [74].
137 [2020] 3 SLR 1129 at [82].
138 https://www.todayonline.com/singapore/moh-issues-guidelines-medical-practitioners-information-disclosure.
139 Guideline 4.2.3.1 reads: A doctor shall respect the principle of medical confidentiality and not disclose without a patient's consent, information obtained in confidence or in the course of attending to the patient. However, confidentiality is not absolute. It may be overridden by legislation, court orders or when the public interest demands disclosure of such information. ... There may be other circumstances in which a doctor decides to disclose confidential information without a patient's consent. When he does this, he must be prepared to explain and justify his decision if asked to do so. ...
140 Guideline 2b.
141 Guideline C7(5).
142 (HME 2016, section C7.2).
143 SMC ECEG 2016 states that the doctor must not access confidential patient information if he is not involved in any aspect of the patients' care: section C7.
144 (Cap 50A, 2007 Rev Ed).

160   Confidentiality

which makes the doctor unfit for the medical profession,[145] and for accessing and reading the electronic medical records of two patients without authorisation and consent.[146]

With respect to a conviction on a charge of failing to obtain informed consent, factors to consider for sentencing include the materiality of the information that was not furnished to the patient, the extent to which the patient's autonomy to make an informed decision on his treatment was undermined by the doctor's failure, and the possibility and materiality of harm ensuing from the failure.[147] On the last factor, where the harm is not an element of the charge, the causation of harm would be an "aggravating" factor whilst the absence of harm would have "neutral consideration" without "mitigating value".[148]

The SMC ECEG Guidelines 2016 has laid down other principles on medical confidentiality[149] including that medical doctors ensure the security of the system used for storing medical records, not use patients' information in a court proceeding, disciplinary or formal inquiry as a means to embarrass or otherwise pressurise any party involved, not refer to patients' information beyond what is reasonable and relevant when they need to defend their reputation in the public domain, and in the context of teaching, to ensure that students or trainees only access patients' information for legitimate educational purposes.

Box 7.2 – The ethics of health surveillance

The Nuffield Council of Bioethics recommended the following guidelines on surveillance during the COVID pandemic:

(a) To assess and predict trends in infectious disease it is acceptable for anonymised data to be collected and used without consent, as long as any invasion of privacy is reduced as far as possible. It may be ethically justified to collect non-anonymised data about individuals without consent if this means that significant harm to others will be avoided

…

(b) The avoidance of significant harm to others who are at risk from a serious communicable disease may outweigh the consideration of personal privacy or confidentiality, and on this basis it can be ethically justified to collect non-anonymised

---

145   *Singapore Medical Council v Dr Leo Kah Woon* [2018] SMCDT 12 (suspension from practice for three months for unauthorised access to patient database of a hospital to obtain the information relating to suspected extra-marital affair of doctor's wife).
146   *In the Matter of Dr Singh Tregon Randhawa* [2011] SMCDC 2017 (penalty of $10,000 imposed on doctor who accessed medical data of former patient of his with whom he had a relationship to find out if she had a sexually transmitted disease and accessed a second patient's data to find out when she would have appointments at the hospital so he could avoid confronting her).
147   *Lam Kwok Tai Leslie v SMC* [2017] 5 SLR 1168 at [90].
148   *Yong Thiam Look Peter v SMC* [2017] 4 SLR 66 at [12].
149   Section C7.

> data about individuals for the purpose of implementing control measures. However, any overriding of privacy or confidentiality must be to the minimum extent possible to achieve the desired aim
>
> ...
>
> (c) Liberty-infringing measures to control disease, such as quarantine and isolation, can be justified if the risk of harm to others can be significantly reduced
>
> ...
>
> (see "Guide to the ethics of surveillance and quarantine for novel coronavirus" https://www.nuffieldbioethics.org/assets/pdfs/Guide-to-the-ethics-of-surveillance-and-quarantine-for-novel-coronavirus.pdf).
>
> Do you agree with the principles? Why or why not?

7.8 Procedural matters

In general, a litigant has the right to obtain confidential information relevant to the alleged wrongdoing for a potential lawsuit subject to the specific rules for pre-action discovery and interrogatories in the Rules of Court.[150] The rules are underpinned by principles of justness and necessity in balancing the parties' interests including any confidentiality obligations.[151] Applications for pre-action disclosures can only be granted in relation to intended proceedings in a Singapore court.[152]

Disclosure of the identity of a *source* of information (namely medical records of a patient) may at times be required of a party who has "participated" or been "involved" in the alleged wrongdoing. The litigant is entitled to apply to the court for a *Norwich Pharmacal* order.[153] In the House of Lords' decision of *Ashworth Security Hospital v MGN Ltd*,[154] the defendants newspapers, which had published an article containing verbatim extracts from the patient's medical records, obtained the information from an intermediary. The patient in question was a convicted murderer who was on a hunger strike and had engaged in a media campaign concerning his treatment at the hospital. The source of the information was likely an employee at the hospital who was suspected of having supplied the information to the intermediary for payment in breach of his duty of confidentiality under his contract of employment. The order to disclose the source was found to be necessary and proportionate and therefore justifiable on the ground of deterrence against the same or similar wrongdoings in the future.[155]

---

150 O 24 r 6(5) and O 26A r 1(5) of the Rules.
151 *Intas Pharmaceuticals Ltd v DealStreetAsia Pte Ltd* [2017] 4 SLR 684, per George Wei J.
152 *Intas Pharmaceuticals Ltd v DealStreetAsia Pte Ltd* [2017] 4 SLR 684, per George Wei J (discovery and interrogatories); *Dorsey James Michael v World Sport Group Pte Ltd* [2014] 2 SLR 208 (interrogatories).
153 *Norwich Pharmacal v Customs and Excise Commissioners* [1974] AC 133.
154 [2002] 1 WLR 2033, applying *Norwich Pharmacal Co v Customs and Excise Comrs* [1974] AC 133.
155 [2002] 1 WLR 2033 at 2052-2053.

7.9 Conclusion

Confidentiality is one of the hallmarks of the medical profession that applies to both clinical practice and medical research. In general, patient information should be kept confidential unless there is consent/agreement by the patient, public interest in disclosure, and legal requirement for disclosure. Medical doctors may be liable for breach of confidence in accessing, acquiring, or disclosing confidential information about their patients or for the misuse of private information in circumstances where there is a reasonable expectation of privacy concerning the information. A healthcare organisation has to discharge statutory obligations to protect personal data based on the principles of consent and circumscribed purpose(s), take steps to ensure accuracy of data, correct and remove data where necessary, failing which the aggrieved party may take legal action for breach of statutory duty. The law is complemented by ethical guidelines in SMC ECEG (2016) and others stressing the importance of medical confidentiality and, at the same time, carving out exceptions allowing disclosure in limited circumstances. The significance of such ethical guidelines and the law can be gleaned from disciplinary proceedings against doctors charged for violating confidentiality. On more specific matters, it would appear from common law and PDPC guidelines that the patient, though he may have access to medical data concerning his condition in the doctor's possession, does not own the medical data. It is possible that a doctor's omission to reveal genetic information that can cause serious risks to a patient will subject him to a negligence lawsuit even if it means the doctor has to divulge the confidential genetic information of another patient. This controversial issue has yet to be decided by the Singapore courts. Finally, healthcare institutions and doctors should be aware that parties who participated or were involved in wrongdoing may be compelled by litigants to reveal the sources of confidential information in their custody including a patient's health information.

References

Aplin, T., Bently, L., Johnson, P., et al. (2012). *Gurry on Breach of Confidence*, Second Edition (Oxford University Press: Oxford).

BAC (2005). Bioethics Advisory Committee Report on "Genetic Testing and Genetic Research" (Nov).

Benn, S.I. (1975). "Privacy, Freedom, and Respect for Persons" in Wasserstrom, R. (ed) *Today's Moral Problems* (MacMillan Publishing Company: New York).

Denbo, S. (2006). "What Your Genes Know Affects Them: Should Patient Confidentiality Prevent Disclosure of Genetic Test Results to a Patient's Biological Relatives?" 43(3) *American Business LJ* 561.

Giliker, P. (2015). "A Common Law Tort of Privacy: The Challenges of Developing a Human Rights Tort" 27 *SAcLJ* 761.

Herring, J. (2018). "Confidentiality", Chapter 5 in Herring, J. *Medical Law and Ethics*, 7th edition (Oxford University Press: Oxford), pp. 228-277.

Kovalesky, M. (2008). "To Disclose or Not to Disclose: Determining the Scope and Exercise of a Physician's Duty to Warn Third Parties of Genetically Transmittable Conditions" 76 *U of Cincinnati L Rev* 1019.

Saw, C.L. & Chan, G. (2005). "The House of Lords at the Crossroads of Privacy and Confidence" 35 *Hong Kong Law Journal* 91-102.

Stauch, M. & Wheat, K. (2015). "Confidentiality, Privacy and Access to Medical Records", chapter 5 in Stauch, M. & Wheat, K. *Text, Cases and Materials on Medical Law and Ethics*, Fifth Edition (Routledge: New York), pp. 213-255.

Tan, S.Y., Ow Yong, L.M., Yuet, E.F.J., et al. (2013). "Securing and Sustaining Employment: Concerns of HIV Patients in Singapore" 52(10) *Social Work in Health Care* 881-898, DOI: 10.1080/00981389.2013.827148.

Taylor, M. (2017). "Confidentiality and Data Protection", chapter 12 in Laing, J. & McHale, J. (eds) *Principles of Medical Law,* 4th Edition (Oxford University Press: Oxford), pp. 643-711.

Wei, G. (2002). "Confidential Information, Trade Secrets, Privacy, Genetic Discrimination, Genetic Engineering and the Life Sciences", ch 2 in Wei, G. *An Introduction to Genetic Engineering: Life Sciences and the Law* (NUS Press: Singapore), pp. 55-95.

Westin, A.F. (1967). *Privacy and Freedom* (Atheneum: New York).

8 Complementary and alternative medicine[†]

8.1 Introduction

In the SMC Handbook on Medical Ethics, the term "complementary and alternative medicine (CAM) refers to a broad domain of purported healing resources that encompasses all health systems, modalities and practices with their accompanying theories and beliefs which fall outside conventional health systems and medical practice".[1] Complementary medicine may be used along with conventional medicine, such as to alleviate stress, reduce pain and anxiety, and manage symptoms.[2] Alternative medicine is used in place of conventional medicine and is typically built upon systems of theory and practice, such as homeopathic and naturopathic medicine.[3]

Integrative medicine, which combines complementary therapies with mainstream patient care, has been gaining popularity among patients with cancer and other chronic illness.[4] Complementary therapies including acupuncture, massage therapy, mind-body techniques

---

[†] The author thanks Rennie Whang, graduate from SMU's JD programme, for her thorough research work and assistance.

1 Singapore Medical Council, *Handbook on Medical Ethics* (2016 Edition), <https://www.healthprofessionals.gov.sg/smc/guidelines/smc-ethical-code-and-ethical-guidelines-(2002-and-2016-editions)-and-handbook-on-medical-ethics-(2016-edition)> (accessed 28 April 2020) ("*SMC Handbook on Medical Ethics*"), p. 64. See also the National Centre for Complementary and Integrative Health "The Use of Complementary and Alternative Medicine in the United States" which described CAM as "a group of diverse medical and health care systems, practices, and products that are not generally considered part of conventional medicine". For the World Health Organization, the terms "complementary medicine" or "alternative medicine" refer to a "broad set of health care practices that are not part of that country's own tradition and are not integrated into the dominant health care system" (cited in Kaan (2015, at p. 422)).

2 Lim Kae Shin, "Complementary and Alternative Medicine: Myths and Truths" <https://www.pss.org.sg/know-your-medicines/safe-use-medicines/complementary-and-alternative-medicine-myths-and-truths#.XZxJ-0YzblU> (accessed 8 October 2019).

3 National Cancer Centre Singapore, *Complementary and Alternative Medicine: A Guide For People With Cancer* (October 2018 Rev Ed) <https://www.nccs.com.sg/patient-care/cancer-types/Documents/NCCS_CAM%20%28Eng%29_1018.pdf> (accessed 8 October 2019).

4 Cassileth et al. (2007, at p. 265).

and herbal supplements are used to reduce symptoms and side effects that may arise independently or as a result of standard treatments such as surgery or radiation.[5]

CAM also covers "long-held historical or traditional practices".[6] In Singapore, traditional Chinese medicine ("TCM") is the most widely used,[7] followed by traditional Malay (Jamu) medicine, and traditional Indian (Ayurvedic) medicine.[8] The level of regulation varies for each of these practices. TCM practitioners are the only category governed by statute and professional rules in Singapore.[9] Outside traditional practices, though the Parliament had discussed about the status of chiropractic practitioners in Singapore, there is as yet no licensing or regulatory framework on chiropractic practice.[10]

According to the SMC Handbook on Medical Ethics, CAM is a "justifiable alternative to conventional medical therapy" where the latter has been tried and failed, or if there is no better alternative in conventional medicine.[11] For example, it may be reasonable to try acupuncture for chronic headaches or backaches, where there is no diagnosable disease and conventional medicine can only alleviate and not cure.[12] CAM may be used as an "added modality to conventional medicine" including helping cigarette smokers stop smoking (as part of managing chronic lung disease) and to relieve the side effects of cancer chemotherapy.[13] The SMC has also noted that practices previously regarded as CAM may sometimes be incorporated into mainstream conventional medicine via "quality scientific evidence or general acceptance by the medical community" and may be offered by doctors as an "integral part of conventional medicine".[14]

Certain hospitals in Singapore integrate acupuncture services into their provision of medical services.[15] Registered doctors who also practice CAM must do so in an ethical manner.[16] Among other things, a doctor practicing or availing his patients of CAM must restrict this to modalities specifically approved by the SMC, be duly trained to so practice, cannot mislead patients as to the appropriateness of use and expected benefits of CAM nor claim superiority

---

5 Cassileth et al. (2007, at p. 265).
6 SMC Handbook on Medical Ethics, at p. 64.
7 Lim et al. (2005, at p. 19).
8 Lim et al. (2005, at p. 19).
9 Cf the Malaysia approach which enacted a statute governing traditional and complementary medicine generally in its Traditional and Complementary Medicine Act 2016 at http://tcm.moh.gov.my/en/upload/aktaBI2016.pdf.
10 Singapore Parliament Reports, "Licensing of Chiropractic Practice" (11 January 2010), Vol 86. It was mentioned in Parliament that the Ministry for Health was studying the matter: Singapore Parliament Reports, "Allied Health Professions Bill" (10 January 2011), Vol 87.
11 *SMC Handbook on Medical Ethics*, at p. 66.
12 *SMC Handbook on Medical Ethics*, at p. 66.
13 *SMC Handbook on Medical Ethics*, at p. 66.
14 *SMC Handbook on Medical Ethics*, at p. 64.
15 Singapore Parliament Report (26 April 2010), Vol 87.
16 Singapore Medical Council, *Ethical Code and Ethical Guidelines* (2016 Edition), <https://www.healthprofessionals.gov.sg/smc/guidelines/smc-ethical-code-and-ethical-guidelines-(2002-and-2016-editions)-and-handbook-on-medical-ethics-(2016-edition)> (accessed 10 November 2019) ("SMC Ethical Code and Guidelines") at p. 30.

of service merely on the basis of offering CAM alongside conventional medicine. The doctor must ensure he is acting in the patients' best interests and have medical reasons for offering SMC-approved CAM services, and must not use CAM in disregard of medical needs that are better met through conventional medicine.[17] Medical practitioners practising CAM must also provide sufficient information about the approved CAM treatment so that patients can give informed consent.[18]

A registered doctor who avails his patients of SMC-approved CAM practiced by non-doctors would be regarded as having only delegated care, and retains responsibility for the patient's overall care.[19]

8.2 Traditional Chinese medicine

TCM practices form the most significant part of all forms of CAM practices in Singapore.[20] A survey by the Ministry of Health ("MOH") in 1994 found that 45% of Singaporeans had consulted TCM practitioners at some point, and about 12% of outpatients were seen by TCM practitioners.[21] In 2019, there were 2,284 TCM practitioners in active practice, with another 761 not in active practice.[22]

TCM has been said to play a complementary role in Singapore's healthcare system.[23] It is neither meant to replace Western medicine in Singapore, nor act as an alternative form of medical treatment.[24] That said, it is used for a wide variety of ailments, including cancer, chronic pain, dermatological conditions, and other chronic diseases.[25] Public healthcare institutions have incorporated some of these therapies into patient care, where evidence has shown that they are efficacious and safe, such as acupuncture for pain management and post-stroke rehabilitation.[26]

---

17 SMC Ethical Code and Guidelines, at pp. 30–31.
18 *SMC Handbook on Medical Ethics*, at p. 67.
19 SMC Ethical Code and Guidelines, at p. 31.
20 Ministry of Heath, *Traditional Chinese Medicine: A Report by the Committee on Traditional Chinese Medicine* (October 1995) at 1.1.
21 *Ministry of Health, Traditional Chinese Medicine: A Report by the Committee on Traditional Chinese Medicine* (October 1995), at 2.4 and 2.8.
22 MOH Singapore, "Number of Traditional Chinese Medicine Practitioners" <https://data.gov.sg/dataset/number-of-traditional-chinese-medicine-practitioners> (accessed 28 April 2020).
23 See for *eg*, Singapore Parliamentary Debates, *Official Report* (15 March 1996), vol 65 at col 1384 (Budget, MOH) (Dr Aline K. Wong, Senior Minister of State for Health); Singapore Parliamentary Debates, *Official Report* (11 September 2017), vol 94 no 50, at p. 36 (Pioneer Generation Package Coverage for Traditional Chinese Services) (Mr Gan Kim Yong, Minister for Health); Singapore Parliamentary Debates, *Official Report* (6 August 2018), vol 94 no 81, at p. 78 (Treatments that Blend Western and Traditional Chinese Medicine) (Mr Gan Kim Yong, Minister for Health).
24 Singapore Parliamentary Debates, *Official Report* (15 March 1996), vol 65 at col 1384 (Budget, MOH) (Dr Aline Wong, Senior Minister of State for Health).
25 Foon and Yeh (2017, at p. 115).
26 Singapore Parliamentary Debates, *Official Report* (6 August 2018), vol 94 no 81, at p. 78 (Treatments that Blend Western and Traditional Chinese Medicine) (Mr Gan Kim Yong, Minister for Health).

Complementary and alternative medicine 167

The MOH provides funding to support the professional development of registered TCM professionals, course providers and service providers.[27] TCM has been increasingly popular as a career with the number of practitioners rising by 16% between 2012 and 2017.[28] In 2017, about 21% of registered practitioners were degree holders.[29]

TCM practitioners, unlike conventional medical practitioners, cannot issue medical leave certificates. The Government's position in 2000 when the Bill was debated was that it was premature to consider this issue and that it would ultimately depend on the recognition by employers regarding the professional standards of TCM practitioners.[30] In 2016, the Minister for Manpower stated that the Employment Act mandates that employers grant medical leave to employees who have obtained medical certificates from a Government medical officer or private medical practitioners who are registered under the Medical Registration Act (MRA). Hence, TCM practitioners would have to be formally registered under the MRA in order for them to issue medical certificates recognised by employers.[31] TCM expenses are not covered under the MediSave scheme though private insurance policies may include coverage for TCM treatment expenses.

8.2.1 Laws and regulations governing the practice of TCM

The Traditional Chinese Medicine Practitioners Act[32] ("TCMPA") was passed by Parliament in 2000 to regulate the practice of TCM in Singapore.[33] Under the TCMPA, a person who wishes to carry out any "prescribed practice" of TCM must be registered and have in force a practising certificate.[34] The TCMPA allows the Minister for Health to declare any type of

---

27 MOH Singapore, "Traditional Chinese Medicine Development Grant" <https://www.moh.gov.sg/research-grants/traditional-chinese-medicine-development-grant> (accessed 8 November 2019).
28 Singapore Parliamentary Debates, *Official Report* (11 February 2019), vol 94 no 89 (Second Reading of the Traditional Chinese Medicine Practitioners (Amendment) Bill) (Mr Louis Ng Kok Kwang, Member of Parliament for Nee Soon GRC).
29 Singapore Parliamentary Debates, *Official Report* (11 February 2019).
30 Singapore Parliamentary Debates, *Official Report* (14 November 2000), vol 72 at col 1139 (Second Reading of the Traditional Chinese Medicine Practitioners Bill) (Mr Chan Soo Sen, Parliamentary Secretary to the Minister for Health).
31 See MOM website at <https://www.mom.gov.sg/newsroom/parliament-questions-and-replies/2016/0913-written-answer-by-mr-lim-swee-say-pq-on-recognition-of-medical-certificates-issued-by-traditional-chinese-medicine-practitioners> (accessed 28 April 2020).
32 (Cap 333A, 2001 Rev Ed) ("TCMPA").
33 Singapore Parliamentary Debates, *Official Report* (14 November 2000), vol 72 at cols 1126–1128 (Second Reading of the Traditional Chinese Medicine Practitioners Bill) (Mr Chan Soo Sen, Parliamentary Secretary to the Minister for Health).
34 TCMPA, section 24(1) and (6). The procedure for registration of TCM physicians is governed by the Traditional Chinese Medicine Practitioners Act (Cap 333A, Sections 14(4) and 38), Traditional Chinese Medicine Practitioners (Registration of Traditional Chinese Medicine Physicians) Regulations; while the registration of acupuncturists is governed by the Traditional Chinese Medicine Practitioners Act (Cap 333A, Section 14(4)), Traditional Chinese Medicine Practitioners (Registration of Acupuncturists) Regulations.

168 *Complementary and alternative medicine*

TCM practice a "prescribed practice" if he is of the opinion that regulation of the practice is in the public interest.[35] At present, these "prescribed practice(s)" consist of acupuncture, the diagnosis, treatment, prevention or alleviation of any disease or its symptom(s), or the prescription of any herbal medicine, and the regulation of the functional states of the human body based on TCM.[36] The regulated TCM practices are those of the acupuncturists[37] and TCM general practitioners and do not currently cover Chinese herbalists and herbal dispensers. The registered TCM practitioner may, however, prescribe, dispense or supply herbal medicine on medical grounds upon consultation and diagnosis.[38]

The statutory model is primarily based on self-regulation by the TCM practitioners, largely similar to the MRA model for medical practitioners. The Traditional Chinese Medicine Practitioners Board ("TCMPB" or "Board") which was established under the TCMPA[39] registers TCM practitioners, accredits TCM institutions and courses, and regulates the professional conduct and ethics of registered TCM practitioners.[40]

Currently, approved local TCM schools include the Singapore College of TCM, Institute of Chinese Medical Studies, and Nanyang Technological University.[41] TCMPB also recognises Bachelor's degrees from eight TCM institutions in China.[42] From 2 January 2013, TCMPB introduced the Continuing Professional TCM Education programme on a voluntary basis.[43] This has since been changed to a compulsory requirement from 1 April 2020.[44]

Under the TCMPA, the Board may cancel the registration of a registered practitioner if it is satisfied that he obtained his registration by a fraudulent or incorrect statement, or has had any of his relevant qualifications or foreign registration withdrawn or cancelled, or has ceased to carry on the prescribed practice of TCM for which he is registered.[45]

---

35 TCMPA, section 14(1).
36 Traditional Chinese Medicine Practitioners Act (Cap 333A, Section 14(1)), Traditional Chinese Medicine Practitioners (Prescribed Practices of Chinese Medicine) (Consolidated Order), O 1.
37 The reason given in Parliament was that "acupuncture is an invasive procedure that carries risks of injury and infection": Singapore Parliamentary Debates, *Official Report* (14 November 2000), vol 72 at col 1128 (Second Reading of the Traditional Chinese Medicine Practitioners Bill) (Mr Chan Soo Sen, Parliamentary Secretary to the Minister for Health).
38 TCM Ethical Code and Ethical Guideline s (ECEG) 2006, at para 4.1.3.
39 TCMPA, section 3. It includes five to nine members to be appointed by the Minister for Health, including one registered medical practitioner, one Registrar (ex-officio), and two registered persons with at least ten years' experience in any prescribed practice of TCM.
40 TCMPA, section 4. TCMPB <https://www.healthprofessionals.gov.sg/tcmpb/en> (accessed 9 November 2019).
41 TCMPB, "Registration Requirements" <https://www.healthprofessionals.gov.sg/tcmpb/en/registration-requirements> (accessed 9 November 2019).
42 TCMPB, "Registration Requirements". Applicants with foreign TCM qualifications must also fulfil practice experience requirements.
43 TCMPB, "Continuing Professional TCM Education" <https://www.healthprofessionals.gov.sg/tcmpb/en/continuing-professional-tcm-education> (accessed 28 April 2020).
44 TCMPB, "Continuing Professional TCM Education". TCMPA, section 17(5A)(a); Traditional Chinese Medicine Practitioners (Amendment) Act 2019 (Commencement) Notification 2020.
45 Section 19(1).

Other grounds for cancellation include a finding that the practitioner has failed to comply with any condition his registration is subject to, has contravened any relevant regulations under the TCMPA on the practice and conduct of registered practitioners, or has been convicted of an offence involving fraud or dishonesty, or which implies a defect in character rendering him unsuitable to remain registered.[46] A finding that the practitioner was guilty of any professional misconduct or negligence, or "any improper act or conduct" rendering him unfit to remain registered; or that he was unable to carry out the prescribed practice safely due to a mental or physical disability are grounds for cancellation as well.[47] It is noted that in relation to the grounds mentioned in this paragraph, the Board may instead caution or censure the practitioner, issue a letter of advice or order an undertaking to abstain from the conduct complained of, impose a penalty of up to $50,000, alter the practitioner's class of registration, impose certain conditions for his registration for up to three years, order that the complaint be referred for mediation; or suspend his registration for up to three years.[48] However, for the last ground of cancellation – namely inability to practice safely due to a disability – the Board may, instead of cancelling his registration, suspend it for up to 12 months, alter his class of registration, or modify its conditions for up to three years.[49]

Save for the ground of ceasing to practice, any complaint against a registered practitioner in relation to any of the abovementioned grounds must be in writing.[50] Under Part IVA of TCMPA, the Board must start reviewing a complaint within two weeks of receipt and complete such a review within three months.[51] The Board may make an interim order, where it appears that a practitioner must stop practising as soon as possible, as it would likely endanger the public for him to continue.[52]

Under the usual review process, if the Board does not dismiss any complaint for being frivolous, vexatious, misconceived or lacking in substance, it must then refer the complaint to an Inquiry Committee.[53] For the purposes of an Inquiry, which must in turn be completed within six months from referral (subject to time extensions), the Committee must direct one or more investigators to look into the matter and afford the practitioner an opportunity to be heard on the complaint.[54] The Committee has to report its findings and recommendation to the Board for its consideration and action.[55]

Before exercising its power to cancel the practitioner's registration or impose the other possible measures, the Board will notify the practitioner of its intention and give him an

---

46 Section 19(1).
47 Section 19(1).
48 Section 19(2).
49 Section 19(2A).
50 Section 26B(2).
51 Section 26C(1).
52 Section 26H.
53 Section 26C(3) and (4).
54 Section 26E.
55 Sections 19(3)(b), 26E and 26G.

170 Complementary and alternative medicine

opportunity to be heard personally or by counsel.[56] Where the Board imposes such measures against a practitioner, it may also order him to pay costs.[57]

The TCM practitioner is entitled to appeal to the Singapore High Court against a decision of the Board to impose these measures.[58] However, no further appeals are allowed once the High Court has rendered its judgement.[59]

The TCMPA further provides that a registered practitioner may request the Board to, among others, cancel or suspend his registration[60] if he believes that his fitness to practice has been impaired due to a mental or physical disability, or that the quality of his professional services is not of a standard reasonably expected of a practitioner.[61] However, this avenue of voluntary cancellation or suspension is not available if the Board believes there is evidence of certain grounds for cancellation,[62] or an inquiry has already started based on a complaint.[63]

A practitioner whose registration has been cancelled under these provisions may apply to the Board to be re-registered from three years after the date of the cancellation.[64]

As part of the Traditional Chinese Medicine Practitioners (Practice, Conduct and Ethics) Regulations, a registered practitioner is required to keep proper records, including with the particulars required by guidelines set by the Board; and must conspicuously display his certificate of registration and practising certificate at his principal place of practice.[65] Any advertising must also be done in accordance with the Board's guidelines.[66] Overall, he must comply with "all standards of professional conduct and ethics" and "pronouncements on professional matters" as determined and issued by the Board,[67] to which we now turn.

8.2.2 Ethical Code and Guidelines for TCM practitioners

The Ethical Code and Ethical Guidelines for TCM Practitioners (*"TCMPB Ethical Code and Ethical Guidelines"*) published by the Board apply to both TCM physicians and acupuncturists

---

56 Section 19(3)(a).
57 Section 20(1).
58 Section 21(1).
59 Section 21(2).
60 Section 26A.
61 Section 26A(1).
62 Namely, being convicted of an offence involving fraud or dishonesty, or which implies a defect in character rendering him unsuitable to remain registered, or that the practitioner was guilty of any professional misconduct or negligence, or "any improper act or conduct" rendering him unfit to remain registered: section 26A(3)(a).
63 Section 26A(3)(b).
64 Section 23(1) and (3)(a). The practitioner cannot make such an application for re-registration more than once in the space of a year (section 23(3)(b)).
65 Traditional Chinese Medicine Practitioners Act (Cap 333A, Section 14(4)), Traditional Chinese Medicine Practitioners (Practice, Conduct and Ethics) Regulations, regulations 3 and 4.
66 *Id*, regulation 5.
67 *Id*, regulation 2(2).

registered under the TCMPA.[68] They are intended to guide TCM practitioners as to the "minimum standards required of all TCM practitioners".[69] Serious disregard or persistent failure to meet these standards can harm patients and the profession, and may therefore lead to disciplinary proceedings.[70] These proceedings will be discussed in greater detail below.

Upon being admitted as a registered TCM Practitioner, every practitioner must pledge to, among others, "dedicate (his) life to the service of humanity, practice my profession with conscience and dignity, make the health of my patient my first consideration", similar to the pledge for registered medical practitioners (see Chapter 2) and comply with the *TCMPB Ethical Code and Ethical Guidelines*.[71]

We should highlight certain important ethical guidelines including:

1   Good Clinical Care

    A TCM practitioner must provide medical care only after adequately assessing a patient's condition.[72] It is only in "exceptional or emergency circumstances" that diagnosis or treatment may be offered without personal contact.[73] Remote consultations – where a previously unknown patient might initiate consultation over the Internet – is inappropriate, and no consultation fee may be received in relation to such consultations.[74] However, remote consultations may be permitted if it is a matter of continuing care, although if it appears the patient has developed a new problem or complication, the practitioner must "endeavor to see the patient personally…before offering further treatment".[75] While a TCM practitioner may delegate another TCM practitioner or student to provide treatment or care on his behalf, he retains responsibility for the overall management of the patient in question.[76]

    Furthermore, a TCM practitioner must provide his patient with "competent, compassionate and appropriate care", including necessary and timely visits, appropriate investigations, and conveying the results of investigations to the patient.[77] If he avails his patient of any supporting medical service, he must be "reasonably confident" as to the standard and reliability of this service, and is responsible for adequately providing it.[78] Additionally, a TCM practitioner must only use "appropriate and generally accepted

---

68   TCMPB, "Ethical Code and Ethical Guidelines for TCM Practitioners" (January 2006) <https://www.healthprofessionals.gov.sg/tcmpb/en/ethical-code-and-ethical-guidelines> (accessed 10 November 2019) at p. 2.
69   TCMPB, "Ethical Code and Ethical Guidelines for TCM Practitioners", at p. 5.
70   TCMPB, "Ethical Code and Ethical Guidelines for TCM Practitioners", at p. 5.
71   TCM Practitioner's Pledge, at p. 6.
72   TCM Practitioner's Pledge, at p. 8.
73   TCM Practitioner's Pledge, at p. 8.
74   TCM Practitioner's Pledge, at p. 8.
75   TCM Practitioner's Pledge, at pp. 8–9.
76   TCM Practitioner's Pledge, at p. 9.
77   TCM Practitioner's Pledge, at p. 9.
78   TCM Practitioner's Pledge, at p. 9.

methods of TCM treatment".[79] If he is in doubt regarding whether a treatment is unorthodox, he must clarify in writing with the Board before proceeding with the treatment.[80]

A TCM practitioner is not allowed to offer treatment packages in the form of guaranteeing a cure.[81] Finally, he must practice within his competence. Where he believes it is exceeded, he must offer to refer the patient to another TCM practitioner or a registered medical practitioner with the required expertise.[82]

2   Informed Consent and Patient's Right to Information

A TCM practitioner must ensure a patient under his care is "adequately informed" about his medical condition and treatment options, so he can participate in making decisions about treatment.[83] If a procedure needs to be performed, the patient must be made aware of its benefits, risks, and possible complications of the procedure, and any available alternatives.[84] If the patient is a minor or of diminished ability to give consent, this information must be provided to his parent, guardian or person responsible for him to consent on his behalf.[85]

In relation to the patient's medical management, the TCM practitioner must provide "adequate information" to a patient for him to make informed choices.[86] This must be communicated to the best of the practitioner's ability, clearly, and in a language understood by the patient.[87] Furthermore, the practitioner is to respect a patient's choice in accepting or rejecting advice or treatment offered, after ensuring that the patient understands the consequences of his choice.[88] The practitioner must also facilitate the obtaining of a second opinion, if the patient so desires.[89]

If a patient's relatives request that the patient not be informed that he has a fatal or socially embarrassing disease, a TCM practitioner must not withhold such information from the patient unless he determines that it would be in the patient's best interests to do so.[90] Thus, TCM practitioners are to "recognise the role of the family" in this decision about whether to disclose a diagnosis to a patient, and must address the family's concerns adequately.[91]

3   Medical Confidentiality

A TCM practitioner has a responsibility to maintain medical confidentiality, and must obtain a patient's consent before disclosing any information obtained in confidence or

---

79   TCM Practitioner's Pledge, at p. 9.
80   TCM Practitioner's Pledge, at p. 9.
81   TCM Practitioner's Pledge, at p. 9.
82   TCM Practitioner's Pledge, at p. 9.
83   TCM Practitioner's Pledge, at p. 12.
84   TCM Practitioner's Pledge, at p. 12.
85   TCM Practitioner's Pledge, at p. 12.
86   TCM Practitioner's Pledge, at p. 13.
87   TCM Practitioner's Pledge, at p. 13.
88   TCM Practitioner's Pledge, at p. 13.
89   TCM Practitioner's Pledge, at p. 13.
90   TCM Practitioner's Pledge, at p. 13.
91   TCM Practitioner's Pledge, at p. 13.

Complementary and alternative medicine

in the course of attending to him. However, confidentiality is "not absolute", and may be over-ridden by legislation, court orders or when the public interest demands disclosure.[92] While there may be other circumstances where a TCM practitioner might decide to disclose confidential information without a patient's consent, should he do so, he "must be prepared to explain and justify his decision" if questioned.[93]

8.2.3 Criminal liabilities

Under the TCMPA, unqualified persons who carry out any prescribed practice of TCM – that is, persons who are not registered and/or do not have a valid practicing certificate authorising them to practice – or who have held themselves out as so qualified are liable on conviction to a fine of up to $25,000 or imprisonment of up to six months, or both.[94] The extent of harm caused is a relevant consideration in sentencing.[95] This punishment extends to a person who employs another to carry out a prescribed practice for which he is not qualified, although he may prove in defence that he did not know the employee was unqualified and that he had exercised due diligence to ascertain whether the employee was qualified.[96]

The TCMPA also provides for possible imprisonment and fines in instances of fraudulent registration,[97] false answers to or the knowing obstruction of an officer authorised by the Board to investigate, or the intentional alteration, suppression or destruction of information which he has been required by an investigator to provide, among others.[98] Similarly, a person who fails to provide information as required by an investigator without a reasonable excuse may be liable.[99]

The Act also provides for possible fines for offences relating to a failure to inform the Registrar of changes in particulars,[100] and failure to surrender a certificate of registration or practising certificate if a practitioner has had his registration cancelled or suspended.[101]

Furthermore, a TCM practitioner may be found to be criminally liable under the Penal Code.[102] In *Lim Poh Eng v Public Prosecutor*,[103] the offender, a TCM practitioner, was convicted under section 338 of the Penal Code for having caused grievous hurt to a patient. He had negligently failed to attend to her complaints adequately after prescribing colonic washouts

---

92 TCM Practitioner's Pledge, at p. 12.
93 TCM Practitioner's Pledge, at p. 12.
94 Section 24(1), (4) and (6). The punishment stated above is for a first-time offender; in the case of a second or subsequent conviction, the offender would be liable to a fine of up to $50,000 or imprisonment of up to 12 months, or both.
95 *Public Prosecutor v Kong Tong Hong* [2017] SGDC 218 at [32] and [40].
96 Sections 24(2), (4) and (5).
97 Section 26. See *PP v Zhong Zhi Li* [2007] SGDC 126.
98 Sections 30(1)–(4).
99 The possibility of self-incrimination is such a reasonable excuse: sections 30(5) and (6).
100 Sections 12(3) and (4).
101 Sections 16(2) and (3); 17(6), (6A) and (7).
102 Singapore Penal Code (Cap 224, 2008 Rev Ed).
103 [1999] 1 SLR(R) 428 ("*Lim Poh Eng*").

174 Complementary and alternative medicine

and failed to refer her to a hospital for treatment.[104] It was later found that the colonic washouts had caused a perforation in the patient's anal canal, which later led to gangrene. The patient was left with permanent loss of her rectum and would have to wear a colostomy bag indefinitely.[105] Lim's sentence of ten months' imprisonment and compensation order was upheld by the High Court. Significantly, the High Court decided that the standard of negligence in criminal and civil cases is the same.[106] However, there are two essential differences between a tort in negligence and criminal liability involving negligence: (i) breach of the standard of negligence must be proved beyond reasonable doubt in a criminal case; and (ii) in a crime involving negligence, negligence is not the sole criterion of liability.[107] For example, in a case involving section 338 of the Penal Code, the Prosecution would, in addition to proving negligence, have to prove the other elements of grievous hurt to a person and that the act endangered human life or personal safety.[108] It is noted that, in line with the objective nature of negligence, the accused's conduct is measured against that of a reasonable person with the knowledge, experience and skill expected of such a person.[109] Thus, a trainee would be held to the same standard as a qualified professional.[110]

Similarly, there have been cases in Australia where CAM practitioners[111] were found criminally liable for deaths that resulted where their advice meant that the patient did not receive conventional treatment, or where conventional treatment was sought far too late. For example, a naturopath in New South Wales was sentenced to five years' jail for the manslaughter of an 18-day-old baby with a heart defect which could be treated only by surgery. He had treated the baby with herbal drops and a "Mora machine", declared him cured, and advised the baby's parents against surgery.[112] In *R v Thomas Sam*,[113] a homeopath who demonstrated "clear reluctance" to obtain and follow through specialist medical advice and treatment for his infant daughter who had severe, protracted eczema and weight loss – and instead opted to apply homeopathic treatment and remedies – was found guilty of manslaughter by criminal negligence.[114]

---

104 *Lim Poh Eng* at [1].
105 *Lim Poh Eng* at [10].
106 *Lim Poh Eng* at [20].
107 *Lim Poh Eng* at [27].
108 *Lim Poh Eng* at [27].
109 As stated by the High Court in *Ng Keng Yong v Public Prosecutor* [2004] 4 SLR(R) 89 ("*Ng Keng Yong*") at [79], citing Mustill LJ in *Wilsher v Essex Area Health Authority* [1987] QB 730, the duty of care is tailored not to the actor, but "the act which he or she elects to perform"; Yeo et al. (2018, at [4.41]).
110 *Ng Keng Yong* at [79].
111 See Freckelton (2012).
112 *The Age*, "Naturopath guilty of manslaughter" (13 February 2004) <https://www.theage.com.au/national/naturopath-guilty-of-manslaughter-20040213-gdicpd.html> (accessed 11 December 2019).
113 [2009] NSWSC 1003 (unreported).
114 [2009] NSWSC 1003 at [30] and [132]. The court found the first accused person, Thomas Sam, culpable according to both the "reasonable parent" and the "reasonable homeopath" tests: [142]. His conviction and sentence (as well as those of his wife) were affirmed on appeal by the New South Wales Court of Criminal Appeal in *Thomas Sam v R* [2011] NSWCCA 36.

8.2.4 Civil liabilities

The TCM practitioner should ensure that the patient has consented to the treatment or procedure. Proper explanation of at least the broad nature and purpose of the treatment or procedure should be given by the TCM practitioner in order to avoid allegations under the tort of battery.

The Singapore courts have not directly ruled on the issue of whether a TCM practitioner is to be held to the same standard of care and skill as a qualified medical practitioner in the tort of negligence. In *Ang Tiong Seng v Goh Huan Chir*,[115] the Court of Appeal found it unnecessary to decide on the question. Even if it were assumed that the standard of care and skill expected was not as high as that to be expected from a qualified medical practitioner, the third defendant in the case, a Chinese physician, was found guilty of a "high degree of negligence" when he applied a very tight bandage to the plaintiff's arm and did not remove it to inspect the arm even when the plaintiff complained of severe pain.[116] The plaintiff's arm later had to be amputated due to gangrene.[117]

In the context of the tort of negligence, should a TCM practitioner be judged by the standards of a reasonable TCM practitioner or that of a reasonable registered medical practitioner or somewhere in between? Given limited case law on the negligence of TCM practitioners in Singapore, court decisions on the negligence of medical doctors may be applicable by analogy.[118] In this regard, we should explore whether the *Bolam*[119] test with the *Bolitho*[120] addendum in relation to diagnosis and treatment, and the three-stage test in *Hii Chii Kok*[121] for advice, as discussed in Chapter 3, may apply to TCM practitioners.

With respect to the *Bolam* test, one preliminary question is whether the TCM practitioners who may be called to testify in court to determine the standard of care of a defendant would represent the respectable opinion of a "profession". Given their education and training, specialisation or expertise and adherence to a code of ethics, TCM practitioners should be regarded as a profession in itself. Additionally, given the regulatory framework of the TCMPA today, and the relevance of industry guidelines in determining the standard of care,[122] the courts would likely hold a TCM practitioner to these guidelines.

Under the *Bolitho* test, the expert opinion would have to be based on logic to reach a defensible conclusion. In order to reach a defensible conclusion, the expert opinion would

---

115 [1968–1970] SLR(R) 778 ("*Ang Tiong Seng*") at [4].
116 *Ang Tiong Seng* at [4].
117 *Ang Tiong Seng* at [6]–[7].
118 This was the same approach taken by Weir (2017, at p. 112).
119 *Bolam v Friern Hospital Management Committee* [1957] 1 WLR 582. It is noted that the *Bolam* test was applied by the High Court of Johor Bahru in *Abdul Rahman bin Abdul Karim v Abdul Wahab bin Abdul Hamid* [1996] 4 MLJ 623 in relation to a traditional eye healer who was registered under the Medical Act 1971.
120 *Bolitho v City and Hackney Health Authority* [1998] AC 232.
121 *Hii Chii Kok v Ooi Peng Jin London Lucien and another* [2017] 2 SLR 492.
122 The High Court in *D'Conceicao Jeanie Doris (administratrix of the estate of Milakov Steven, deceased) v Tong Ming Chuan* [2011] SGHC 193 referred to the SMC ECEG as evidence of the position of "a reasonable body of medical opinion" (at [130]–[131]).

have to be internally consistent and ensure coherence with the existing state of medical knowledge. An interesting question is how these criteria are to be dealt with in respect of TCM practitioners. It may be argued for instance that the nature of TCM practice – being more intuitive and individualised to the patient – may not easily lend itself to such objective tests of internal and external consistency and coherence as applied in conventional medicine.

Reference may be made to the English case of *Shakoor (administratrix of the estate of Shakoor (deceased) v Situ (t/a Eternal Health Co)* on the standard of an alternative medical practitioner insofar as treatment is concerned.[123] The English High Court found that in adjudicating on the standard of care of an alternative medical practitioner, it would not be enough to judge him by the ordinary practitioner "skilled in that particular art", but to also consider whether the alternative medical practitioner had taken account of the fact that he was practicing his art alongside orthodox medicine.[124]

In the case, it was found that the defendant – a qualified TCM practitioner but not qualified as a doctor of orthodox medicine – who had prescribed a traditional recipe of Chinese herbal medicine[125] to a patient who later died from acute liver failure was not negligent. This was because, judging him by the appropriate equivalent orthodox specialty of an ordinary careful general practitioner, although he had failed to notice letters and warnings in orthodox medical publications, these would not in any case have put him on notice that the preparation was too hazardous to prescribe.[126] The orthodox medical publications were "overall equivocal and did not paint a consistent picture of serious risk".[127] Moreover, there was disagreement between the expert witnesses in the case as to whether a reasonable general practitioner in the UK would have noticed those letters and warnings in the orthodox medical journals.

It should be noted that the defendant was not holding himself out as an orthodox medical practitioner but only as a TCM practitioner. It would therefore not be fair to adjudge him based purely on the standard of an orthodox medical practitioner. As mentioned, the standard expected of such a practitioner would require him to take account of the alternative medicine that is practised alongside orthodox medicine. Under this standard, there is no requirement for the practitioner to have read orthodox medical journals but only to have obtained access to the relevant information through the association which was responsible to search the relevant literature and promptly report to the alternative practitioner.[128] Fordham (2011, at p. 11) argued that such a standard strikes a fair balance between alternative practitioners and patients and also allows patients access to alternative medicine and safeguards their welfare.

---

123 [2001] 1 WLR 410 ("*Shakoor*").
124 *Shakoor* at 417.
125 In Singapore, as mentioned above, there is no specific regulation for traditional Chinese herbalists or herb dispensers.
126 *Shakoor* at 420. In *Bawden v Marin* [1990] SASC (2 July 1990) (unreported), the South Australian Supreme Court held that a chiropractor who allegedly caused broken ribs by negligent spinal manipulation to the standard of a competent chiropractor, not a medical practitioner. However, as the evidence of a medical practitioner was admitted into testimony, the case also suggests that such evidence may be appropriate in deciding the liability of a chiropractor, although the evidence of another chiropractor was ultimately preferred: Weir (2017, at p. 127).
127 *Shakoor* at 420.
128 *Shakoor* at 417.

> **Box 8.1 - *Shakoor* on standard of care for TCM practitioners**
>
> Based on *Shakoor*, a TCM practitioner may be liable in negligence for prescribing medication or administering a treatment that injures his patient even if the medication or treatment is accepted by TCM practitioners generally. This can happen if the TCM practitioner did not take account of knowledge in conventional medicine of potential harmful effects to the extent it is available to TCM practitioners generally. Is this fair to the TCM practitioner? What do you think is the justification for this additional requirement with respect to TCM practitioners?

With respect to giving advice, the TCMPB Ethical Code and Ethical Guidelines contain similar guidelines as for medical practitioners, namely that the TCM practitioner has to keep his patient "adequately informed" about his medical condition and treatment options to allow for the patient's participation in decision-making on treatment as well as the content of the information to be disclosed (namely concerning the benefits, risks, and possible complications of the procedure, and any available alternatives).[129] This approach is similar to that stated in *Hii Chii Kok* with respect to the standard of care of medical practitioners in giving medical advice.

The patient must, in addition to proving breach of duty, show that the TCM practitioner's negligence caused the damage he suffered. For example, but for the TCM practitioner's negligence in misdiagnosing the symptoms and failing to refer the matter to a medical practitioner, the patient would have sought the opinion of a medical practitioner who would have administered the proper treatment to prevent the damage. Alternatively, the patient could prove that the TCM practitioner's negligence had materially contributed to his damage. The general principles of remoteness of damage based on foreseeability of the type of harm suffered and the egg-shell skull rule should also apply to TCM practitioners under the tort of negligence.

The usual rules on contributory negligence will apply (for example, where the patient fails to comply with instructions to take prescribed medication when he could reasonably foresee the adverse effects of such non-compliance, or the patient failed to communicate his symptoms for the doctor to make the correct diagnosis or give proper treatment), though a successful defence on this ground is not common in medical negligence to begin with.[130] It is an open question whether the defence of *volenti non fit injuria*, as applied in several cases in the United States, will be available to a CAM or TCM practitioner here. That is, the practitioner could argue that the client had voluntarily assumed the risk of "go[ing] outside currently approved medical methods in search of an unconventional treatment".[131] The client

---

129 TCMPB Ethical Code and Ethical Guidelines, at p. 12.
130 Weir notes that the defence of contributory negligence may not be often available in the medical context due to discrepancies in power between doctor and patient: Weir (2017, at pp. 136-137); Stone and Matthew (1996, at pp. 169-172); Laing and McHale (2017, at para [6.71]).
131 *Schneider v Revici*, 817 F 2d 987 at 995 (2nd Cir. 1987) ("*Schneider v Revici*").

178 *Complementary and alternative medicine*

cannot then argue that he had received treatment without reference to orthodox medicine. However, it would appear that this defence is subject to a knowledge requirement: the patient must have been aware of the risks of refusing conventional treatment, and the basic tenets of his selected unconventional alternative.[132] Furthermore, the defence would rarely succeed in this context, as few people would expressly or impliedly consent to the risks of negligent medical treatment.[133]

Apart from the above, practitioners could also be made liable for misrepresentation, or under the Consumer Protection (Fair Trading) Act[134] for unfair practices in relation to representations made regarding the efficacy of treatment. This has been the case, for example, in Australia, where the Supreme Court of Victoria found that statements by a clinic to the effect that its complementary therapies could cure cancer or stop its progress, among others, were misleading or deceptive within the meaning of section 9 of the Fair Trading Act 1999 (Vic).[135] The Singapore courts have, in interpreting the CPFTA, considered the Australian courts' approaches on similar statutory prohibitions against misleading or deceptive conduct and unconscionable conduct.[136]

8.2.5 *Disciplinary cases*

The "rules and standards of the TCM profession" determine whether any conduct complained of amounts to professional misconduct.[137] The TCMPB Ethical Code and Ethical Guidelines is meant as a guide to the conduct that could amount to professional misconduct.[138]

It is noted that a registered TCM practitioner who commits professional misconduct overseas may be prosecuted under the TCMPA. The High Court in *Huang Danmin v TCMPB*[139]

---

132 *Kirschner v Keller*, 70 Ohio App 111 at 112; Feasby (1997, at p. 63); *Schneider v Revici*, at 995-996.
133 Feasby (1997, at p. 63). Bearing in mind the three requirements to establish the defence, *viz*, that the plaintiff (i) acted freely and voluntarily; (ii) acted with full knowledge of the nature and extent of the risk of harm created by the defendant's negligence; and (iii) expressly or impliedly consented to the abovementioned risks: Chan and Lee (2016, at para 8.024). There are no reported medical negligence cases in Australia or the UK which confirm the applicability of the *volenti* defence: Weir (2017, at p. 135).
134 (Cap 52A, 2009 Rev Ed) ("*CPFTA*").
135 *Noone (Director of Consumer Affairs Victoria) v Operation Smile (Aust) Inc* [2012] VSCA 91. Section 9 of the Act, which has since been repealed, prohibited conduct that was misleading or deceptive or was likely to mislead or deceive. Similarly, the Federal Court of Australia found that unconscionable conduct under section 51AB of the Trade Practices Act 1974 (Cth) was made out in *Australian Competition and Consumer Commission v Nuera Health Pty Ltd* [2007] FCA 695, as the respondents claimed that their products ranging from fruit and vegetable juice diets to colonic irrigation, as part of "The Rana System", could cure cancer. These cases were noted by Freckelton (2011, at p. 654).
136 *Freely Pte Ltd v Ong Kaili* [2010] 2 SLR 1065 at [19]-[20]. CPFTA has been applied in relation to the sale of health supplements: https://www.case.org.sg/consumer_guides_casestudies_archive.aspx?month=June&year=2017.
137 *TCMPB Ethical Code and Guidelines*, at p. 21.
138 *TCMPB Ethical Code and Guidelines*, at p. 21.
139 [2010] 3 SLR 1108 ("*Huang Danmin*").

held such an extraterritorial ambit served the underlying purpose of the TCMPA, did not create any enforcement problems as the cancellation of a practitioner's registration could be enforced easily, and did not create any comity problems as such cancellation would not prevent a practitioner from practising TCM elsewhere.[140] In *Huang Danmin*, the appellant, a Singapore-registered TCM practitioner, was found guilty of professional misconduct in respect of treatment administered in his Johor clinic, on a patient with terminal rectal cancer whom he had met in Singapore. Thus, the High Court found that the respondent, TCMPB, was correct in taking into account such treatment in considering the appellant's guilt under the TCMPA, as he was treating the patient at the Johor clinic in the capacity of a registered TCM practitioner.[141]

In *Huang Danmin*, the High Court considered the provision in the *TCMPB Ethical Code and Guidelines* which state that a TCM practitioner must only use "appropriate and generally accepted methods of TMC treatment".[142] It noted that a practitioner's failure to do so would be a breach of the *TCMPB Ethical Code and Guidelines* and could amount to professional misconduct. Whether a particular TCM practice is established depends on whether it is "generally accepted as an appropriate treatment for a particular ailment…a purely factual question", relying substantially on its general acceptance among TCM practitioners in Singapore and elsewhere.[143] It added that while the court of three judges had previously formulated factors to determine whether a particular medical practice was generally accepted,[144] it was of the view that this "should not be transplanted wholesale to TCM practice" due to, among others, differences in the development and documentation of the two types of practice.[145]

When the TCMPB has discharged its burden of proving that the treatment was not generally accepted by the TCM profession,[146] the practitioner may defend himself by showing

---

140 *Huang Danmin* at [33]-[39].
141 *Huang Danmin* at [40].
142 *Huang Danmin* at [44].
143 *Huang Danmin* at [45] and [47]. An example of an inappropriate or not generally accepted method of TCM treatment is the insertion of surgical thread under the skin: TCMPB, "Suspension of Registration as TCM Practitioners – Yap Kwok Ann and Xia Rongrong" (31 January 2020). <https://www.healthprofessionals.gov.sg/docs/librariesprovider12/default-document-library/press-release---tcmp-joseph-yap-xia-rongrong_31-jan-20.pdf> (accessed 29 April 2020).
144 *Gobinathan Devathasan v Singapore Medical Council* [2010] 2 SLR 926 ("*Gobinathan Devathasan*") (the essential factors for a particular medical practice to be generally accepted were that (a) there had to be at least "one good study"; (b) the results of the study can be replicated and reproduced under the same sort of like treatment parameters and conditions; (c) the study had been written up in publications and presented at meetings; (d) the study had received peer review; (e) the study had clear cut results and the sample had to be statistically significant; and (f) the study had to have some form of controls such as randomised double-blind trials).
145 *Huang Danmin* at [47].
146 In this case, the need to call TCM experts to show the appellant's treatment was contrary to TCM practice was dispensed with as the TCMPB possessed the requisite experience and knowledge about TCM practice: *Huang Danmin* at [53]-[54].

"some evidence that the treatment may do some good but will do no harm to the patient".[147] However, the appellant in *Huang Danmin* was unable to show this, as it appeared that he did not know what exactly an aspect of the treatment in question – namely the use of an "electrothermal needle" machine to insert a needle into the patient's tumour area – could do for the patient.[148]

Other notable instances of professional misconduct have included the prescription or dispensation of western medicine[149] as well as failing to act within the limits of one's own competence by trying to interpret and provide a diagnosis based on Western medical reports, and recommending that surgery to treat breast and lung cancer (as recommended by the patient's Western doctors) should be delayed.[150]

> **Box 8.2 – Comparing TCM practice and conventional medical practice**
>
> Overall, how does the regulation of TCM practice whether via legislation, subsidiary legislation or ethical code and guidelines compare with that for medical practice? Is there more convergence than divergence? What are the reasons for convergence and/or divergence in your view?

8.2.6 Regulation of Chinese proprietary medicines

Chinese herbal medicines may be categorised as raw herbal medicines and Chinese Propriety Medicines ("CPM").[151] The government imposes minimal control on the import, export, sale

---

147 *Huang Danmin* at [48]. *Gobinathan Devathasan v Singapore Medical Council* [2010] 2 SLR 926 ("*Gobinathan Devathasan*").
148 *Huang Danmin* at [55]. The appellant had also administered injections to the patient which was contrary to established TCM practice (*Huang Danmin* at [51]).
149 TCMPB, "Suspension of Registration of TCM Physician – Lim Kim Hock" (9 July 2012) <https://www.healthprofessionals.gov.sg/docs/librariesprovider12/press-releases/2012-07-09-lim-kim-hock---press-release-(jul-2012).pdf>; Suspension of Registration of TCM Physician – Tang Yeow Leong @ Tan Yeow Leong" (8 October 2012) < https://www.healthprofessionals.gov.sg/docs/librariesprovider12/press-releases/2012-10-08-tang-yeow-leong---press-release-(oct-2012).pdf> (both accessed 10 November 2019).
150 TCMPB, "Suspension of Registration as TCM Practitioner – Chua Beng Chye" (24 September 2018). <https://www.healthprofessionals.gov.sg/docs/librariesprovider12/press-releases/press-release--suspension-of-registration-as-tcm-practitioner-chua-beng-chye-(final).pdf> (accessed 10 November 2019). It was found that a third option Mr Chua had put to the patient – to postpone the surgery for three months to undergo TCM treatment administered by him, with a CT scan after two months to determine the effectiveness of treatment – could "result in higher risk of mortality", and was neither "an appropriate and generally accepted method of TCM treatment" nor "an option at all".
151 Yee et al. (2005, at p. 134).

and distribution of the former as most have low toxicity or, if they do, would be controlled under the Poisons Act.[152]

A CPM refers to a medicinal product which is in the form of a finished product, such as a capsule or tablet, and contains one or more active ingredients from any plant, animal or mineral, or any combination of sources.[153] All the active ingredients must be documented for use in TCM.[154] All CPM are regulated by the Health Sciences Authority ("HSA") and must comply with safety and quality criteria before they can be sold in Singapore.[155] For example, labelling of the medicine must comply with the Medicines (Labelling of Chinese Proprietary Medicines) Regulations.[156] Furthermore, CPM dealers must be licensed by the HSA.[157] As with traditional Malay and Indian Medicines, the advertisement or promotion of CPM for sale requires a permit from the HSA.[158]

8.3 Traditional Malay medicine

8.3.1 Introduction to Malay jamu medicine

Malay healing practices are said to emphasise harmony between mental, physical and spiritual spheres.[159] Traditional Malay healers are the main providers of Malay medicine. They include *pawang*, a shaman of magic who may conduct rituals and divination ceremonies, *dukun/bomoh*, a general practitioner who treats fevers, headaches and other ailments, and *bidan* or midwives.[160] Apart from this, women at home traditionally often brewed their own

---

152 (Cap 234, 1999 Rev Ed); Yee et al. (2005, at p. 134).
153 Medicines (Traditional Medicines, Homeopathic Medicines and other Substances) (Exemption) Order (Cap 176, O 6, 2005 Rev Ed), paras 2(a) and (b); Health Sciences Authority, "Regulatory Overview of Chinese Proprietary Medicines" <https://www.hsa.gov.sg/chinese-proprietary-medicines/overview> (accessed 11 November 2019).
154 Medicines (Traditional Medicines, Homeopathic Medicines and other Substances) (Exemption) Order (Cap 176, O 6, 2005 Rev Ed), para 2(c); Health Sciences Authority, "Regulatory Overview of Chinese Proprietary Medicines".
155 MOH Singapore, "TCM Practitioners" <https://www.moh.gov.sg/hpp/tcm-practitioners> (accessed 11 November 2019).
156 Medicines (Labelling of Chinese Proprietary Medicines) Regulations (Cap 176, Rg 13, 2005 Rev Ed).
157 HSA, "Regulatory Overview of Chinese Proprietary Medicines". See also Medicines (Licensing, Standard Provisions and Fees) Regulations (Cap 176, Rg 6, 2000 Rev Ed), Regulations 3(2), 3(3), 3(4); Second, Third and Fourth Schedules.
158 Medicines (Medical Advertisements) Regulations (Cap 176, Rg 2, 2000 Rev Ed), Regulation 3; HSA, "Advertisements and Promotions of Medical Products" <https://www.hsa.gov.sg/traditional-medicines/advertisements-and-promotions-of-medicinal-products> (accessed 11 November 2019). Note also Part VI of the Medicines Act (Cap 176, 1985 Rev Ed) regarding the advertising of medicinal products.
159 Zakaria and Zainal (2017, at p. 129).
160 Nadirah Norruddin, "Magic or Medicine? Malay Healing Practices" (October 16, 2018) 14(3) *BiblioAsia* <http://www.nlb.gov.sg/biblioasia/2018/10/16/magic-or-medicine-malay-healing-practices/> (accessed 11 November 2019).

herbal remedies known as *jamu*.[161] Today, *jamu* is also commercially produced and sold in various forms including ointments, oils, tonics or compresses for external use as well as powders, tablets, pills, tonics and capsules.[162] Traditional Malay healers may recommend unprocessed herbal medications, spiritual treatments, or traditional Malay massage, among others.[163]

8.3.2 Regulation

Traditional Malay medicine is not subject to approvals and licensing by HSA for their importation, manufacture and sale.[164] However, HSA prohibits the addition of medicinal ingredients such as steroids into these products.[165] Furthermore, dealers must ensure that their products are safe and conform to guidelines on toxic heavy metal limits, microbial limits, labelling, certain prohibited ingredients, and ingredients derived from animals and endangered species.[166] They must also adhere to guidelines on advertisements and promotions.[167]

8.4 Traditional Indian medicine

8.4.1 Introduction to Ayurvedic medicine

Ayurveda, or the "science of life" is said to be not only a system of medicine, but also a way of life.[168] It has developed into eight specialised branches and two major schools, the School of Physicians and the School of Surgeons.[169] Under Ayurvedic theory, all matters in the universe – including the human body – are composed of *Panchamahabhuta* and Ayurvedic treatment principles are based on correcting the imbalances of *Panchamahabhutas* in the body.[170] Several studies have suggested that Ayurvedic treatment may be beneficial in managing osteoarthritis.[171]

---

161 Zakaria and Zainal (2017, at p. 130).
162 Tuschinsky (1995, at p. 1588).
163 Ikram and Ghani (2015, at p. 726).
164 HSA, "Regulatory Overview of Traditional Medicines" <https://www.hsa.gov.sg/traditional-medicines/regulatory-overview-of-traditional-medicines> (accessed 11 November 2019).
165 HSA, "Regulatory Overview of Traditional Medicines".
166 HSA, "Regulatory Overview of Traditional Medicines". For example, in respect of labelling, product labels must include the ingredients and their strengths in English: Medicines (Labelling) Regulations (Cap 176, Rg 5, 2000 Rev Ed), Regulation 4. The labels also cannot suggest that the product will prevent, alleviate or cure a number of ailments, including blindness, cancer, cataracts, diabetes and kidney diseases: Medicines Act (Cap 176, 1985 Rev Ed), section 51(1).
167 HSA, "Regulatory Overview of Traditional Medicines". Including the Medicines (Medical Advertisements) Regulations (Cap 176, Rg 2, 2000 Rev Ed) and Part VI of the Medicines Act (Cap 176, 1985 Rev Ed).
168 Ayurveda Association of Singapore ("AAOS") "About Ayurveda" <https://aaos.org.sg/about-us/about-ayurveda/> (accessed 29 April 2020); Shroff (2017, at p. 19).
169 Kurup (1983, at pp. 50–51).
170 Vikas et al. (2016, at p. 154).
171 National Centre for Complementary and Integrative Health, "Ayurvedic Medicine: In Depth" <https://nccih.nih.gov/health/ayurveda/introduction.htm> (accessed 11 November 2019); Sharma et al. (2013); Kessler et al. (2018).

8.4.2 Regulation

In Singapore, the regulatory framework for Ayurvedic medicine is the same as that for traditional Malay medicine.[172]

8.5 Conclusion

The scope of CAM, which covers a wide range of traditional and more modern practices that are complementary and/or alternative to conventional medicine, is not set in stone. Registered medical practitioners are allowed to practice CAM (currently acupuncture) alongside conventional medicine subject to SMC's ethical guidelines. TCM practice – the most prevalent CAM practice in Singapore – has been regulated by statute and subsidiary legislation since 2000 but not traditional Malay and Indian medicine. TCM practitioners are bound by a professional code of practice with guidelines on good clinical care, informed consent, confidentiality that are broadly similar to those applicable to registered medical practitioners. Errant TCM practitioners are subject to criminal sanctions, discipline by the Board and civil liabilities under tort law. Questions about the appropriate standard of care expected of TCM practitioners in the tort of negligence and the relevance of legal tests applicable to medical practitioners remain to be determined by the courts. The HSA continues to exercise control over the ingredients used, the safety aspects and the advertising and promotion of Chinese proprietary medicines and products derived from traditional Malay and Indian medicine.

References

Cassileth, B., et al. (2007). "Complementary Therapies for Cancer Pain" 11 *Current Pain and Headache Reports* 265-269.
Chan, G. & Lee, P.W. (2016). *The Law of Torts in Singapore,* 2nd Ed (Academy Publishing: Singapore).
Feasby, C. (1997). "Determining Standard of Care in Alternative Contexts" 5 *Health LJ* 45.
Foon, Y.F. & Yeh, C.L. (2017). "Steroids in Traditional Chinese Medicine: What is the Evidence?" 58(3) *Singapore Medical Journal* 115-120.
Fordham, M. (2001). "The Standard of Care Applicable to Practitioners of Alternative Medicine" *Singapore Journal of Legal Studies* 1-11.
Freckelton, I. (2011). "Unscientific Health Practice and Disciplinary and Consumer Protection Litigation" 18 *Journal of Law and Medicine* 645-668.
Freckelton, I. (2012). "Death by Homeopathy: Issues for Civil, Criminal and Coronial Law and for Health Service Policy" 19(3) *Journal of Law and Medicine* 454-78.
Ikram, R.R.R. & Ghani, M.K.A. (2015). "An Overview of Traditional Malay Medicine in the Malaysian Healthcare System" 15 *Journal of Applied Sciences* 723-727.
Kaan, T.S.H. (2015). "Traditional, Complementary and Alternative Medicine" in Joly, Y. & Knoppers, B.M. (eds) *Routledge Handbook of Medical Law and Ethics* (Routledge: London), pp. 419-442.
Kessler, C.S. et al. (2018). "Effectiveness of an Ayurveda Treatment Approach in Knee Osteoarthritis – A Randomized Controlled Trial" 26 *Osteoarthritis and Cartilage* 620-630.
Kurup, P.N.V. (1983). "Ayurveda," in Bannerman, R.H., Burton, J., & Ch'en, W.-C. (eds) *Traditional Medicine and Health Care Coverage: A Reader for Health Administrators and Practitioners* (World Health Organisation: Geneva).
Laing, J. & McHale, J. (2017). (eds) *Principles of Medical Law* (Oxford University Press: Oxford).

---

172 HSA, "Regulatory Overview of Traditional Medicines" <https://www.hsa.gov.sg/traditional-medicines/regulatory-overview-of-traditional-medicines> (accessed 11 November 2019).

Lim, M.K., et al. (2005). "Complementary and Alternative Medicine Use in Multiracial Singapore" 13 *Complementary Therapies in Medicine* 16-24.

Sharma, M.R., et al. (2013). "Multimodal Ayurvedic Management for *Sandhigatavata* (Osteoarthritis of Knee Joints)" 34(1) *Ayu* 49-55.

Shroff, F.M. (2017). "What is Ayurvedic Health Care and How is it Applicable to the Modern Day?" 1(2) *Journal of Nutrition and Human Health* 17-29.

Stone, J. & Matthew, J. (1996). *Complementary Medicine and the Law* (Oxford University Press: Oxford).

Tuschinsky, C. (1995). "Balancing Hot and Cold - Balancing Power and Weakness: Social and Cultural Aspects of Malay *jamu* in Singapore" 41(11) *Social Science & Medicine* 1587-1595.

Vikas, B., Pankaj, S., & Sahana, C. (2016). "Panchamahabhuta Siddhanta and Chikitsa - A Bird's Eye View" 11(3) *European Journal of Biomedical and Pharmaceutical Sciences* 154-159.

Weir, M. (2017). *Law and Ethics in Complementary Medicine: A Handbook for Practitioners in Australia and New Zealand*, 5th Edition (Allen & Unwin: Sydney).

Yee, S.-K., Chu, S.-S., Xu, Y.-M., et al. (2005). "Regulatory Control of Chinese Proprietary Medicines in Singapore" 71 *Health Policy* 133-149.

Yeo, S., Morgan, N., & Chan, W.C. (2018). *Criminal Law in Malaysia and Singapore*, 3rd Ed (LexisNexis: Singapore).

Zakaria, F. & Zainal, H. (2017). "Traditional Malay Medicine in Singapore" 45(131) *Indonesia and the Malay World* 127-144.

9 Reproduction

9.1 Introduction

Discussions concerning reproduction often trigger reflective views as well as feelings of gratitude and awe about the beginning of human existence and life. Modern technologies have enabled us to better control birth and its timing, allowed infertile couples to have babies with their DNA and even to exercise greater control over the characteristics of the offspring we desire based on predictive genetic information. Reproduction is not solely a medical issue in Singapore, where the total fertility rate is below replacement levels, but is also affected by and impinge on socio-economic inequalities, raising questions about the work-life balance of parents, educational demands and opportunities for the young and future generations and invite deeply religious and cultural views about human life.

Reproduction and its technologies have also given rise to a tussle of rights amongst family members, claims by parents and children against doctors and geneticists for negligence and generated significant impact on social and family policies. Controversial issues concerning the balancing of the mother's right to her body and the unborn child's rights, the determination of parentage of a child born via *in vitro* fertilisation (IVF), the attendant responsibilities of parenthood and the child's welfare will be discussed.

This chapter covers a wide range of legal and ethical issues relating to reproduction starting with contraception and sterilisation, followed by abortion,[1] assisted reproduction,[2] surrogacy, and finally, reproductive genetics.[3]

9.2 Contraceptives and sterilisation

The common contraceptives include the condom, the female contraceptive pill, the intrauterine device (IUD), injections and sterilisation. Condoms and contraceptive pills prevent fertilisation from taking place. The IUD and "morning after" pill, on the other hand, prevent the fertilised egg from being implanted in the uterus. These forms of contraception also vary in terms of the extent of availability (*eg*, whether it can be bought over the counter or

---

1 See Jackson (2017).
2 See Freeman (2017a).
3 See Freeman (2017b).

only under prescription by pharmacists), costs, the reliability or success rates, the potential side effects, and the degree of permanence or irreversibility of the procedures such as sterilisation.

With respect to the issue of capacity to consent to receiving contraceptives, the doctor is permitted at common law to give contraceptive advice to minors below the age of 16 years without parental consent provided the child is sufficiently mature to understand the medical, social and family issues involved in the decision-making.[4] Where the person lacks the mental capacity to give consent to contraceptives, the decision may be made on her behalf based on the best interests approach.[5]

Contraceptives may fail to perform as they should and claims may be made based on breach of contract or negligence. With regard to the latter, a legal duty of care may be owed by the manufacturer or retailer to the purchaser or ultimate consumer[6] as the case may be. The purchaser or consumer would have to further prove that the manufacturer or retailer was negligent, the negligence caused the plaintiff's injury and the type of damage was reasonably foreseeable. Where the plaintiff was aware that the contraception (eg, condom) failed to work, but omitted to take reasonable steps (such as by taking the "morning-after" pill) to avoid the unwanted pregnancy, she may not be able to recover damages.[7]

Sterilisation methods include vasectomies for males and tubal occlusions for females. Treatment for sexual sterilisation in a health institution and by an authorised registered medical practitioner with the requisite obstetric and surgical qualifications is legal in Singapore.[8] The medical practitioner has to give the person a "full and reasonable explanation as to the meaning and consequences of that treatment" prior to the treatment for sterilisation.[9] The following persons are entitled to give consent to treatment for sterilisation under the Voluntary Sterilization Act[10]:

(i)   a married or an unmarried person who is 21 years of age or older[11]; and
(ii) a married person who is below 21 years of age.[12]

Where the person is an unmarried person who is below 21 years of age, the person and at least one parent or guardian of the person must give consent to the treatment.[13]

---

4   *Gillick v West Norfolk and Wisbech Area Health Authority* [1986] AC 112.
5   *A Local Authority v Mrs A and Mr A* [2011] 2 WLR 878 (Mrs A lacked capacity to decide due to Mr A's influence; courts considered whether it was in her best interest to receive contraception but did not compel Mrs A to use contraception).
6   See *Donoghue v Stevenson* [1932] AC 562; *TV Media Pte Ltd v De Cruz Andrea Heidi* [2004] 3 SLR(R) 543.
7   *Richardson v LRC Products* [2000] L1 Med Rep 280 (claim against condom manufacturer for fracture of condom during sexual intercourse which led to claimant's pregnancy based on the UK Consumer Protection Act).
8   Voluntary Sterilization Act (Cap 347), sections 3 and 4.
9   Section 3(3).
10 (Cap 347, 2013 Rev Ed).
11 Section 3(2)(a).
12 Section 3(2)(b).
13 Section 3(2)(c).

For a person who lacks mental capacity, decisions made on his or her behalf should be made in the person's best interests. The decision to proceed with sterilisation may be based on therapeutic[14] as well as non-therapeutic reasons.[15] The nature of the contraception (such as the degree of intrusiveness) may be relevant.[16] The interests of carers or parents[17] is not a relevant consideration. The approval of the courts would be required as to whether the treatment is necessary in the person's best interests. For a married person, the spouse is entitled to make the application to the court[18]; for an unmarried person, the application may be made by the person's parent or guardian.[19]

The medical practitioner is immune from criminal and civil liability if he carries out the sterilisation treatment with the proper and valid consent from the person under the statute, and the sterilisation treatment was not carried out negligently.[20] The determination as to whether the treatment was negligent or not would be made by reference to the *Bolam*[21] and *Bolitho*[22] tests as affirmed in the Singapore Court of Appeal decision of *Hii Chii Kok*[23] (Chapter 3). If the issue is whether the medical practitioner has given adequate disclosure of information (including the risks of pregnancy) prior to the sterilisation treatment, such a determination will be assessed based on what a reasonable patient would regard as material information according to the test in *Hii Chii Kok*.[24]

Where it is proved that but for the medical practitioner's negligence in failing to give adequate medical advice prior to the sterilisation treatment, the woman would not have proceeded to give birth to the child, she would normally be able to recover damages for pain and suffering and medical expenses associated with the pregnancy and delivery. In *Thake v Maurice*,[25] the defendant (doctor) explained to the plaintiffs (husband and wife) the nature of the vasectomy operation which involved the cutting of the husband's vas deferens. The defendant negligently omitted to warn the plaintiffs that there was a small risk that after the operation there could be a "recanalisation" of the vas such that the wife would become fertile again. It was reasonably foreseeable that the defendant's breach would cause damage to the plaintiffs and damages for ante-natal pain and suffering was allowed.

---

14 *A Trust v H (An Adult)* [2006] 2 FLR 958 (patient suffered from schizophrenia and delusional beliefs; total abdominal hysterectomy to remove cancerous cyst in ovaries in her best interests).
15 *Re B (A Minor)* [1987] 2 FLR 314 (mentally incapable minor would be mentally disturbed by pregnancy and would not be able to understand pregnancy and care for child and no practical alternative to sterilisation).
16 *Re S (Adult Patient)* [2001] Fam 15 (hysterectomy invasive compared to less intrusive contraceptive coil according to medical experts).
17 *Re B (A Minor)* [1987] 2 FLR 314.
18 Section 3(2)(d).
19 Section 3(2)(e).
20 Section 8.
21 *Bolam v Friern Hospital Management Committee* [1957] 1 WLR 582.
22 *Bolitho v City and Hackney Health Authority* [1998] AC 232.
23 *Hii Chii Kok v Ooi Peng Jin London Lucien* [2017] 2 SLR 492.
24 Note that a bill has been introduced in the Singapore Parliament on 3 September 2020 seeking to change the legal approach relating to medical advice.
25 [1986] 2 WLR 337.

188 *Reproduction*

It is less clear whether the mother would be able to recover for losses in bringing up the child. In *McFarlane v Tayside Health Board*,[26] after a vasectomy performed on the husband, he was informed by the doctor that he could resume sexual intercourse without the use of contraceptives. His wife, however, became pregnant and delivered a healthy daughter. The claim for the costs of bringing up the daughter was dismissed. As a matter of policy, looking after the child should be regarded overall as a joy that outweighs the expenses (see *McFarlane* and other related cases in the section on "Wrongful conception and birth claims" below). The child's claim for wrongful life would likely fail based on public policy considerations (see "Wrongful life claims by child" below).

9.3 Abortion

The reasons for legalising abortion in Singapore raised by the Minister for Health in Parliament in 1969 included medical considerations (to safeguard the physical and mental health of the pregnant woman), eugenic considerations (to avoid or reduce the risks of giving birth to mentally handicapped or deformed children), humanitarian considerations (where the pregnancy was due to sexual crimes such as rape and incest), social and environmental considerations (faced by the mother and family in having to bring up the child), legalisation as a means to deal with the practical problem of illegal abortions, a secondary consideration to control population growth, and the failures of contraceptives.[27] Opponents have argued, amongst others, that abortion destroys the foetus which constitutes human life or the beginning of human life, questioned the effectiveness of the bill to reduce illegal abortions and noted the relative success of family planning programmes in Singapore at that time. That was one of the rare parliamentary bills in which the Whip was lifted for the members. After much controversy and debate, the bill was passed upon the Second Reading,[28] sent to the Select Committee and eventually passed after the Third Reading in 1969.[29] The statute with some modifications was reviewed five years later by Parliament, debated and passed in 1974.[30]

9.3.1 The law on abortion

Abortion is allowed in Singapore under conditions specified in the Termination of Pregnancy Act (TPA).[31] It is not an offence if the pregnancy is terminated by an authorised medical practitioner in an approved institution[32] acting on the request of a pregnant woman and with her written consent.[33] There is no legal minimum age for a person seeking an abortion. Further,

---

26 [2000] 2 AC 59.
27 Singapore Parliament Reports, Abortion Bill, Vol. 28, cols 860-875 (8 April 1969), Minister for Health.
28 Passed with 32 ayes, 10 noes, 2 abstentions and 14 absent: Singapore Parliament Reports, Abortion Bill, Vol. 28 (10 April 1969).
29 Singapore Parliament Reports, Abortion Bill, Vol. 29, cols 339-349 (29 December 1969).
30 Singapore Parliament Reports, Abortion Bill, Vol. 33, cols 1099-1137 (6 November 1974).
31 (Cap 324) (1985 Rev Ed).
32 Section 3(2).
33 Section 3(1).

parental consent is not strictly required for minors who wish to undergo abortion.[34] This is provided the minor possesses sufficient maturity and understanding to give valid consent. Moreover, unmarried pregnant women below 16 years of age shall be referred by the authorised medical practitioner to a counselling centre or facilities directed by the Director of Medical Services.[35]

The authorised medical practitioner is entitled to carry out the treatment to terminate pregnancy on a pregnant woman who is a citizen of Singapore or is the wife of a citizen of Singapore, holder, or is the wife of a holder, of a work pass issued under the Employment of Foreign Manpower Act[36] or who has been resident in Singapore for a period of at least four months immediately preceding the date on which such treatment is to be carried out.[37] The medical practitioner may also carry out such treatment if it is "immediately necessary to save the life of the pregnant woman".[38]

Abortion is prohibited[39] where the pregnancy is of more than 24 weeks duration unless the treatment is "immediately necessary to save the life or to prevent grave permanent injury to the physical or mental health of the pregnant woman". If the pregnancy is more than 16 weeks but less than 24 weeks' duration, it has to be carried out by an authorised medical practitioner with surgical and obstetric qualifications or special skill in such treatment based on his practice or appointment in an approved institution. The period from which the foetus becomes viable varies depending on the state of medical technology.[40] When the issue was raised in Parliament, the Minister for Health decided in 2008 to retain the 24-week period based on expert opinion on the viability of the foetus.[41]

---

34 See *Singapore Parliament Reports*, 9 October 2000, Vol 72 (Minister for Health), col 963
… it has been observed that the pregnant girls are often in a very desperate situation and likely to resort to extreme measures. If parental consent is made compulsory, some may even resort to suicide. There is also the possibility of going to unlicensed practitioners for abortion locally or in neighbouring countries with its inherent dangers of botched up operations, severe infection and death. Besides surgical procedures there is also a possibility of them taking 'medicines' purported to cause abortions which may be harmful to health or be dangerous.
35 Termination of Pregnancy Regulations (Cap 324, Rg 1), Reg 5(2).
36 (Cap 91A, 2009 Rev Ed).
37 TPA, section 3(3).
38 TPA, section 3(3).
39 Section 4.
40 See *Roe v Wade* 410 US 113 (1973) (if the foetus is viable, the state has a legitimate interest to protect its potential life and statutes prohibiting abortion after viability except when necessary to preserve the life or the health of the mother would not be unconstitutional).
41 Singapore Parliament Report, 27 August 2008, Vol 84, col 3300 (Minister for Health). The expert opinion quoted by the Minister stated that
… babies born after 24 completed weeks of gestation should have a very good chance of surviving intact and the most optimal care should be offered to them. Between 22 to 24 weeks gestation, survival rates dip sharply, even in the presence of the latest technologies, and the disability rates will also climb sharply, especially disabilities in the moderate and severe range.

190 *Reproduction*

The statute allows for conscientious objections by any person (including a medical practitioner) to participation in any treatment to terminate a pregnancy.[42] The conscientious objection may be due to religious considerations, personal values or other reasons.

A person who is concerned with the keeping of medical records in connection with treatment to terminate a pregnancy or participates in any treatment to terminate a pregnancy shall not disclose any facts or information relating to the treatment unless the pregnant woman gives express consent to disclosure[43] or disclosure is made to specified bodies or parties (*eg*, officer in Ministry of Health and Attorney-General) for specified purposes (*eg*, criminal proceedings and *bona fide* research).[44] It is an offence to compel or induce a pregnant woman against her will, by means of coercion or intimidation, to undergo treatment to terminate pregnancy.[45]

The Penal Code contains provisions that protect the unborn child. The act of voluntarily causing a woman with child to miscarry is an offence.[46] Where the act was committed without the consent of the woman, the punishment for the offence is a longer maximum term of imprisonment.[47] The same applies to (i) a person who, with intent to cause the miscarriage of a woman with child, commits an act which causes the death of such woman[48]; or (ii) one who, with intent to destroy the life of a child capable of being born alive, by any intentional act causes a child to die before it has an existence independent of its mother or by such act causes the child to die after its birth (unless such act is immediately necessary to save the life of the mother).[49] A person who is guilty of causing the death of a quick unborn child by an act amounting to culpable homicide is liable to a maximum of ten years' imprisonment.[50]

9.3.2 The ethics of abortion

The ethical arguments for and against abortion have generally revolved around questions concerning the foetus' moral status and right to life, the mother's right to her body, the condition of the foetus and child to be born, and the social impact of allowing or prohibiting abortion.

On the status of the foetus, various views have been proffered: a human being at conception,[51] potential to develop into a human being, a human being only after a certain period of time from conception, and that it is not a human being until birth. If the foetus

---

42 Section 6. See *Janaway v Salford Area Health Authority* [1989] AC 537 (receptionist typing a letter referring patient to consultant with a view to possible termination of pregnancy did not amount to participation in treatment).
43 TPA, section 7.
44 Termination of Pregnancy Regulations (Cap 324, Rg 1), Reg 12.
45 TPA, section 5.
46 Section 312.
47 Section 313.
48 Section 314.
49 Section 315.
50 Section 316.
51 Declaration of Geneva (1948) (physician's oath: "I will maintain the utmost respect for human life from the time of conception"), adopted by the General Assembly of the World Medical Association, Geneva, Switzerland, September 1948 and amended by the 22nd World Medical Assembly, Sydney, Australia, August 1968.

possesses human life, then intentionally killing a foetus without justification would constitute murder. At common law, the foetus was not regarded as a distinct legal person; neither was it an "adjunct of the mother".[52] Instead, it was regarded as a "unique organism".[53]

It has also been stated that the foetus does not have separate interest from the mother.[54] Further, the foetus' need for medical assistance does not prevail over the mother's rights not to proceed with induced delivery. Doing so against the mother's autonomy would constitute a trespass to person.[55]

Thomson (1971)[56] argued from the ethical perspective that a woman is entitled to "defend her life against the threat to it posed by the unborn child, even if doing so involves its death". Furthermore, the mother's rights with respect to her body must be respected. Thomson gave the following vivid analogy[57]:

> You wake up in the morning and find yourself back to back in bed with an unconscious violinist. A famous unconscious violinist. He has been found to have a fatal kidney ailment, and the Society of Music Lovers has canvassed all the available medical records and found that you alone have the right blood type to help. They have therefore kidnapped you, and last night the violinist's circulatory system was plugged into yours, so that your kidneys can be used to extract poisons from his blood as well as your own. The director of the hospital now tells you, "Look, we're sorry the Society of Music Lovers did this to you - we would never have permitted it if we had known. But still, they did it, and the violinist now is plugged into you. To unplug you would be to kill him. But never mind, it's only for nine months. By then he will have recovered from his ailment, and can safely be unplugged from you".

The violinist himself may have a right to life. Nonetheless, it does not give him the right to demand that he use your kidneys for nine months[58] even if it means that without the kidney, the violinist would perish. After all, "the body that houses the child is the mother's body".[59] On this basis,

> unborn persons whose existence is due to rape have no right to the use of their mothers' bodies, and thus that aborting them is not depriving them of anything they have a right to and hence is not unjust killing.[60]

---

52 *Attorney-General's Reference (No 3 of 1994)* [1998] AC 245 at 256, per Lord Mustill.
53 [1998] AC 245 at 256, per Lord Mustill; and 267, per Lord Hope ('separate organism from the mother from the moment of its conception").
54 *Re MB (An Adult: Medical Treatment)* [1997] 2 FCR 54 at [60], per Butler-Sloss LJ. See also McLachlin J in *Winnipeg Child and Family Services (Northwest Area) v G* 3 BHRC 611 ("foetus's complete physical existence is dependent on the body of the woman").
55 *St George's Healthcare NHS Trust v S* [1999] Fam 26.
56 Thomson (1971, at p. 53).
57 Thomson (1971, at pp. 48-49).
58 Thomson (1971, at p. 55).
59 Thomson (1971, at p. 54).
60 Thomson (1971, at p. 58).

192 Reproduction

With regard to the rights of the mother versus the foetus, Singer (2000, at pp. 156-157) opined that the rights of a mother as an actual human being with capacity for reasoning should prevail over that of a foetus which is unconscious albeit with the potential to become a person in the future.

It is arguably acceptable to allow the mother the choice to undergo an abortion in order to avoid giving birth to a child with serious deformities or disabilities such as haemophilia and Down's syndrome. It may, however, have the effect (albeit unintended) that children with such disabilities are perceived as less worthy than those who are not disabled. We will see such an argument surface again below in the context of claims by the mother and/or the child for damages arising from the negligence of doctors or geneticists in diagnoses or medical advice.

In a multi-racial and religious society such as Singapore, the issue of abortion can give rise to different religious and cultural viewpoints. Catholics, for example, may oppose abortion taking the view that the foetus is a human person at conception. The liberal attitude of Mill is that unless there is harm to others, the moral actors including those with different religious persuasions should be permitted to make up their own minds on a matter of private morality:

> That the only purpose for which power can be rightfully exercised over any member of a civilised community, against his will, is to prevent harm to others... ... He cannot rightfully be compelled to do or forbear because it will be better for him to do so, because it will make him happier, because in the opinions of others, to do so would be wise or even right.

The statute allows for abortions but does not compel anyone to undergo or to participate in any abortion.

Box 9.1 – Reflecting on the ethics and law on abortion

How do you think the ethical considerations and perspectives can inform the law on abortions? Should abortions be permitted? If so, what are the permissible circumstances?

9.4 Assisted reproduction

Technology has enabled reproduction through various artificial methods notwithstanding infertility. In 1983, the late Emeritus Professor Ratnam delivered the first test-tube baby in Asia through IVF in KK Women's and Children's Hospital (KKH). In 1989, National University Hospital (NUH) was instrumental in enabling the conception of a baby via MIST (Micro-Insemination Sperm Transfer).[61]

According to the Ministry for Health's Licensing Terms and Conditions on Assisted Reproduction Services 2020 (LTC-ARS 2020), Assisted Reproduction ("AR") refers to clinical treatments and laboratory procedures involving:

(a) the removal or attempted removal of oocytes from a woman for any purpose; or

---

61 Sim (2016, at p. 251).

(b) the handling of human oocytes or embryos for the purpose of procreation, including In-vitro Fertilisation (IVF), Gamete Intrafallopian Transfer (GIFT), Zygote Intrafallopian Transfer (ZIFT), Intra-cytoplasmic Sperm Injection (ICSI), gamete/embryo/ovarian tissue cryopreservation, gamete/embryo donation (for any purpose) and embryo biopsy for preimplantation genetic diagnosis (PGD).[62]

AR Centres shall carry out AR procedures for the purpose of procreation only on a married woman and only with the consent of her husband whether or not her husband's semen is used and ensure that informed consent for the AR procedure is obtained from both the patient and her husband.[63] The patients and their respective husbands must be adequately advised, counselled and provided with all relevant and material information including the risks of the procedures depending on the ages of the patients, the success rates for the procedures and the impact of older patients on the welfare of the child.[64] The AR Centres have to keep all information obtained during counselling strictly confidential.[65] Express written consent (which shall be witnessed) from all patients and their respective husbands for AR services must be obtained.[66] The storage and disposal of gametes/embryos shall be carried out strictly in accordance with the written instructions of the couple.[67] There are detailed guidelines on the storage, disposal and transfer of gametes and embryos in the LTC-ARS 2020.[68]

Screening tests for donors and patients undergoing AR must be carried out with respect to certain conditions including hepatitis B, hepatitis C, syphilis and Human Immunodeficiency Virus (HIV),[69] as well as rubella for patients[70] and Cytomegalovirus for donors.[71]

Age limits with respect to the donors of sperm and oocytes for AR procedures are specified.[72] AR centres have to ensure that a genetic link to one of the intended parents

---

62 https://www.moh.gov.sg/licensing-and-regulation/regulations-guidelines-and-circulars/details/revised-licensing-terms-and-conditions-on-assisted-reproduction-services-imposed-under-section-6(5)-of-the-private-hospitals-and-medical-clinics-act-cap-248, para 2.2.
63 LTC-ARS 2020, para 5.3.
64 Para 5.7.
65 Para 5.9.
66 Such consent shall include consent for carrying out all key procedures and processes, including but not limited to: (a) the examination and treatment procedures; (b) the number of embryos to be transferred; (c) the storage (including the location of storage)/disposal/transfer of gametes/embryos; and (d) any intended donation of gametes/embryos: LTC-ARS 2020, para 5.10.
67 Para 5.38. On the partner's right to withdraw consent to continuing storage of embryo and IVF treatment, see *Evans v Amicus Healthcare Ltd* (2004) 2 FLR 766 (English Court of Appeal).
68 Paras 5.38–5.52.
69 Paras 5.15 and 5.16.
70 Para 5.17.
71 Para 5.19.
72 They are: (a) oocytes donated by women between the ages of 21 and 35 at the point of oocyte removal; (b) sperm donated by men between the ages of 21 and 40 at the point of sperm removal; and (c) embryos created from oocytes removed from women between the ages of 21 and 35 at the point of oocyte removal: see LTC-ARS 2020, para 5.29.

of the child is maintained as far as possible; otherwise, the express written consent of the persons donating the embryo must be obtained.[73] Moreover, the man whose sperm is used to fertilise the oocyte must not be biologically related[74] to the woman whose oocyte is used.[75] Inter-generational gamete (*eg*, mother-to-daughter oocyte donation or father-to-son sperm donation) or embryo donation is permitted only with approval from a Hospital Ethics Committee and with express written consent from the donor(s).[76] There is also a limit of three live-birth events as a result of donations from a donor of gametes or embryos.[77]

In Singapore, egg-freezing (or oocyte cryopreservation) is currently allowed only on medical grounds for women with genetic conditions associated with high risk of ovarian cancer and women who might lose their fertility through medical treatments such as chemotherapy. There have been proposals to allow egg freezing on non-medical grounds (*ie*, social egg-freezing). The reasons include: the process of donating eggs is tedious; it may be difficult to reach out to egg donors; couples undergoing IVF would prefer using their own eggs; and the quality and quantity of the eggs will decrease as the woman ages.[78] Social egg-freezing, if permitted, it would enable more women to exercise reproductive autonomy rather than as an option only for the financially well-off who can pay for such procedures overseas. That being said, other factors impacting on any proposal for social egg-freezing such as the low success rates in terms of achieving live births and the unintended consequences of delayed motherhood[79] should be carefully considered.

The issue of parentage is dealt with under the Status of Children (Assisted Reproduction Technology) Act.[80] The presumed position is that the gestational mother who carried the child as a result of a fertilisation procedure will be regarded in law as the mother of the child under section 6. Section 7 states that where the child was brought about with the sperm

---

73 Para 5.25.
74 The term "biologically related" only refers to first and second degree biological relatives, meaning that an oocyte shall not be fertilised with sperm from the woman's biological brother (including half-brother), father, son, grandfather, grandson, uncle or nephew: LTC-ARS 2020, para 5.26.
75 Para 5.26.
76 Para 5.28.
77 Para 5.30.
78 Afifah Darke, "'Doing it for myself': The women freezing their eggs to raise their chances of conceiving" CNA, 25 March 2019 at https://www.channelnewsasia.com/news/singapore/social-egg-freezing-singapore-women-ivf-11314552.
79 Lee Geok Ling and Eric Blyth, "Commentary: Should Singapore allow healthy women to freeze their eggs?" CAN, 3 Dec 2017 at https://www.channelnewsasia.com/news/singapore/commentary-should-singapore-allow-healthy-women-to-freeze-their-9380582.
80 (Cap 317A, 2015 Rev Ed). The Minister for Law stated in Parliament that the Ministry had considered the Singapore Academy of Law's Law Reform Committee Report (26 September 1997) at https://www.sal.org.sg/Resources-Tools/Law-Reform/Status-of-Children-Born-through-Artificial-Conception: see Singapore Parliament Reports, Status of Children (Assisted Reproduction Technology) Bill, Vol 90 (12 August 2013).

of the gestational mother's husband/*de facto* partner,[81] the husband to whom she was married at the time or after the fertilisation procedure, or the *de facto* partner to whom she was married after the fertilisation procedure, shall be treated as the father of the child.[82] Where the child was not brought about with the sperm of her husband/*de facto* partner, the husband/*de facto* partner will nonetheless be treated as the father of the child unless he did not consent to the gestational mother undergoing the fertilisation procedure at the time the procedure was carried out.[83] Further, even if the husband/de facto partner did not consent to the fertilisation procedure, he will be considered the father of the child if he nevertheless through a course of conduct accepted the child as a child of the marriage or relationship, as the case may be, knowing that the child was not brought about with his sperm.[84] Where no man was regarded as the legal father based on the above provisions, the "*de facto* partner" will only be considered as the legal father of the child if an application is made to the court and the court, in its discretion, declares so.[85] Sub-section 7(7) deals with the situation where two or more men are to be treated as the father of a child by virtue of one or more provisions in section 7. In such an instance, only the man who is to be treated as the father of the child earlier in time by virtue of a provision in section 7 shall be treated as the father of the child.

In a case where the child was born as a result of any mistake, negligence, recklessness or fraud, in which the egg, sperm or embryo used in the fertilisation procedure undergone by the gestational mother was not the egg, sperm or embryo intended to be used, the legal parents of the child shall be determined in accordance with section 6 or 7 above as if –

(a) the mistake, negligence, recklessness or fraud had not occurred; and
(b) the child was brought about with the egg, sperm or embryo intended to be used by the gestational mother or, where applicable, her husband or her de facto partner, as the case may be, and not the egg, sperm or embryo actually used.[86]

Finally, where the woman who is to be treated as the mother of a child under the statute is married to the man who is to be treated as the father of the child under the statute, the child shall be treated as legitimate and a child of the marriage.[87]

---

81 The term "*de facto* partner", in relation to a gestational mother (whether married or not) at a given point in time, means the man, if any, with whom the gestational mother is living in a relationship as if he were her spouse at that point in time: section 2.
82 Section 7(1) and (4).
83 Section 7(2) and (5).
84 Section 7(3) and (6).
85 Section 8.
86 Section 9. See also *L Teaching Hospital NHS Trust v A* [2003] EWHC 259 (QB) involving a mix-up of sperm sample (a husband whose wife had given birth following the mistaken use of another man's sperm during *in vitro* fertilisation treatment could not be considered the child's legal father under section 28 of the Human Fertilisation and Embryology Act 1990 as he had not consented to the placing in his wife of the actual embryo used).
87 Section 11.

9.5 Surrogacy

There are generally two forms of surrogacy:

(a) Traditional surrogacy: where the surrogate is the biological mother and the surrogate's own egg is artificially inseminated with the intended father's (or a donor's) sperm.
(b) Gestational surrogacy: where the surrogate carries a baby that is conceived through fertilising the egg of the intended mother or a donor with the sperm of the intended father or a donor.

Surrogacy is "commercial" in nature where the surrogate mother is paid a fee for her reproductive services over and above the reimbursement of pregnancy-related expenses. The "altruistic" form of surrogacy refers to an arrangement where the surrogate mother is not paid or paid only the amount of pregnancy-related expenses.

Surrogacy arrangements can lead to the exploitation of financially poor people who are attracted to serve as surrogate mothers for payment of money. In an unregulated market environment, the consequence might be a race to the bottom as commissioning parents seek out the best prices and terms for surrogate mothers especially those from poorer developing countries.[88] These financially needy women may be under significant economic duress or pressure to consent to renting their wombs in exchange for payments, family sustenance and livelihood.

The LTC-ARS 2020 states that AR Centres shall not carry out surrogacy "where a woman is artificially impregnated, whether for monetary consideration or not, with the intention that the child is to be given and adopted by some other person or couple".[89]

In Singapore, the High Court (Family Division) in *UKM v AG*[90] opined that there is no settled government policy against surrogacy in Singapore even though surrogacy is not available under the LTC-ARS 2020 issued by the Ministry of Health. The use of surrogacy arrangements is not criminalised in Singapore. It also stated that Government ministers have approached surrogacy as a "very sensitive delicate issue" and appeared to be deliberating upon it instead of arguing against it. In fact, the judgement noted that the Ministry of Social Development and Family had overseen adoption cases which involved the use of surrogacy. Nonetheless, though there is no firm government policy against surrogacy, the Chief Justice noted that surrogacy is an "ethically complex and morally fraught issue".[91]

The status of children born through surrogacy can be a source of contention. We have heard of the Baby M case[92] where the surrogate mother refused to give up custody. One of the commissioning parents (the husband) eventually obtained custody of the child with visitation rights granted to the surrogate. Another more recent example is the Baby Gammy case where the surrogate mother gave birth to twins in Thailand one of which was born with Downs' syndrome. In the circumstances, the commissioning couple decided to abandon the

---

88 Ryznar (2010, at p. 1011).
89 Para 5.54.
90 [2018] SGHCF 18 at [167]-[186].
91 [2018] SGHCF 18 at [179].
92 *In re Baby M*, 537 Am 2d 1227, 109 NJ 396 (NJ 1988).

baby with Downs' syndrome and only brought back the other twin.[93] Such disputes may have a significant impact on the child's welfare and well-being. In commercial surrogacy arrangements where the identity of the surrogate mother and donors are kept confidential, this may hinder the child from knowing his or her origin and parentage.[94]

As stated in the Status of Children (Assisted Reproduction Technology) Act, the gestational mother is presumed to be the legal mother of the child. This includes the surrogate mother. Furthermore, the husband or partner of the surrogate may be treated presumptively as the legal father under the statute. It is common, however, for the surrogate mother and her husband or partner to relinquish their rights to the child to the commissioning parents via an agreement signed by all the parties.

9.5.1 Surrogacy arrangements and adoption of child

In *UKM v AG* as mentioned above, the appellant, a gay man, applied to the court to adopt his biological child under the Adoption of Children Act.[95] The child was conceived through IVF and was birthed in the US by a surrogate mother. She was paid by the appellant and his same-sex partner (who were both Singapore citizens) for the reproductive services she provided. An egg from an anonymous donor was fertilised by the appellant's sperm and then implanted in the womb of the surrogate mother, a US citizen (*ie*, gestational surrogacy). Under the surrogacy agreement signed by the parties, the surrogate mother was to carry the baby to term, deliver him, and relinquish her rights over him. The appellant then brought the child to Singapore.

At this juncture, the statutory regime should be briefly mentioned. Section 377A of the Singapore Penal Code criminalises sexual conduct between males; and a marriage solemnised between two males would be regarded as void under the Women's Charter.[96] Attempts have been made to repeal section 377A without avail as at the time of the proceedings, but it should be noted that the statutory provision is not proactively enforced in Singapore.

The District Judge dismissed the appellant's adoption application.[97] Though the surrogate mother had consented to the appellant's application for an adoption order, the learned District Judge opined that the requirement that the adoption would be for the welfare of the child[98] was not satisfied. The appellant sought adoption of the child through the "back door" (*ie*, foreign surrogacy arrangements) which was not obtainable through the "front door" in Singapore. Further, the child would continue to have food, shelter, a good education and an adequate support system regardless of whether he would be adopted by the appellant.

The High Court overruled the decision of the District Court. Sundaresh Menon CJ held that allowing the adoption would increase the child's prospects of remaining in Singapore as

---

93 Pascoe (2018, at p. 466).
94 This would contravene Art 7.1 of the United Nations Convention on Rights of the Child ("…as far as possible, the right to know and be cared for by his or her parents"): see Pascoe (2018, at p. 469).
95 (Cap 4, 2012 Rev Ed).
96 Section 12(1).
97 *Re UKM* [2018] SGFC 20.
98 Adoption of Children Act, s 5(1)(b).

it would entitle him to apply for citizenship. The related care arrangements would promote the child's welfare (which includes his sense of security and emotional well-being). In addition, there were no strong countervailing policies (legal and socio-economic policies) that would override this consideration based on the child's welfare. Menon CJ noted that although the adoption would violate the policy against the formation of same-sex family units (ie, with two homosexual parents and a child or a single homosexual parent and a child) contrary to traditional parenting norms in Singapore,[99] such a policy did not arise from the Adoption of Children Act. Further, it was unclear whether the appellant was deliberately seeking to violate any public policy since the public policy could not be articulated precisely at the relevant time. Hence, on the whole, the policy reasons were not strong enough to override the consideration based on the child's welfare. It may be argued, however, that the issue of the formation of same-sex family unit should be relevant to the assessment of the child's welfare given that welfare has a broad scope; and that the issue of adoption is connected to foundational social institutions of parenthood and family.[100]

9.5.2 Claim for surrogacy expenses

Given the controversy surrounding surrogacy and its legal status, an interesting question has arisen in England relating to the recoverability of the costs of surrogacy arrangements due to medical negligence. In *Whittington Hospital NHS Trust* v XX,[101] the hospital had negligently failed to detect the plaintiff's cervical cancer from smear tests and biopsies. But for the negligence, the plaintiff would not have developed cancer. As a result of the delayed diagnosis, she could not undergo fertility-saving surgery due to her condition, and was advised to undergo chemotherapy. Prior to that, she underwent ovarian stimulation and egg harvest to generate eggs which were cryopreserved. The subsequent chemotherapy caused irreparable damage to her uterus and ovaries, premature menopause, vaginal stenosis and atrophy of vaginal tissues rendering intercourse impossible. Nonetheless, she and her partner wanted to have their own biological children through surrogacy and intended to have four children. In addition to damages for pain and suffering and loss of amenities, she claimed for the expenses of four commercial surrogacy arrangements in California arising from the negligently inflicted infertility either using her own eggs, or where necessary, using donor eggs and her partner's sperm. The plaintiff's "preferred solution" was a Californian surrogacy which is lawful there and the second-best solution would be lawful surrogacy arrangements in the UK.

The UK Supreme Court held that the costs of surrogacy arrangements whether with the patient's eggs or donor eggs and lawfully conducted in the UK would be recoverable by the patient provided the prospects of surrogacy success are reasonable, and that it was clear that the claimant intended to pursue surrogacy. As for the costs of commercial surrogacy arrangements in California (which are prohibited in the UK), the majority of the Supreme Court held that they would also be recoverable provided the treatment programme and the costs involved are reasonable. The items in the Californian bill would be claimable if the

---

99 [2018] SGHFC 18 at [207].
100 See Tan (2019, at pp. 269–270).
101 [2020] UKSC 14.

surrogacy had taken place in the UK. The UK statute does not criminalise the surrogate or commissioning parents. Furthermore, the government's position on surrogacy has shifted recognising it as a valid way of creating family relationships including same sex relationships, and the use of assisted reproduction techniques has become more widespread and socially acceptable in the UK. Hence, awards of damages for foreign commercial surrogacy would no longer be contrary to public policy.

Lord Carnwarth dissented (with whom Lord Reed agreed) on the issue of foreign commercial surrogacy. His Lordship opined that damages to fund the cost of foreign commercial surrogacy arrangements should not be allowed as it would be "contrary to that principle for the civil courts to award damages on the basis of conduct which, if undertaken in this country, would offend its criminal law".[102] His Lordship also stated that "[a]lthough this case is not concerned with illegality as such, the underlying principle of coherence or consistency in the law is of broader application".[103] Further, despite the majority's observations about the shift in government policy in surrogacy, Lord Carnwarth stated that "[t]here has ... ... been no change to the critical laws affecting commercial surrogacy".[104]

Though *Whittington* is not legally binding on Singapore courts, it may be persuasive. In Singapore, there is no strong government policy against surrogacy as noted in *UKM v AG*. Following *Whittington*, this may allow some leeway for a patient to make an argument for the recovery of foreign surrogacy expenses. Singapore, however, does not recognise to the same extent as the UK the legal and attitudinal changes regarding same-sex family relationships though the use of assisted reproduction techniques is fairly common here. The Singapore case of *Man Mohan Singh*[105] suggested that there is no right to replace deceased children via IVF treatment following a car accident in which the plaintiffs' children died due to the defendant's negligence (Chapter 3). In that case, the Court of Appeal also took into account the subjective nature of the plaintiffs' post-accident choices to seek fertility treatment and the low success rates for IVF, and refused the claim for the costs of fertility treatment. As such, the damages (the costs of fertility treatment) were too remote. It is argued that *Man Mohan Singh* should not in itself bar a claim for surrogacy expenses. After all, the factual matrix in *Whittington* is quite different involving a hospital's negligence which had directly caused the plaintiff (patient) – who had desired to bear four children with her husband – to be infertile.

9.6 Reproductive genetics

Broadly speaking, there are two objectives in reproductive genetics namely therapy and enhancement through selection of certain genetic traits. With respect to PGD, BAC (2005) Report recommended that preimplantation genetic testing should be allowed to "prevent the transmission of a serious disease in genetically at-risk couples to the next generation".[106] BAC

---

102 [2020] UKSC 14 at [66].
103 [2020] UKSC 14 at [64].
104 [2020] UKSC at [67].
105 *Man Mohan Singh s/o Jothirambal Singh v Zurich Insurance (Singapore) Pte Ltd* [2008] 3 SLR(R) 735.
106 Para 28.

200 Reproduction

(2005) Report also recommended allowing Preimplantation Tissue Typing (PTT) in combination with PGD to allow couples to have a healthy child who is also immunogenetically compatible, as a potential stem cell donor, to a sick sibling.[107]

The issue of mitochondrial donation has been explored in Singapore with a view to preventing the transmission of mitochondrial diseases from a woman to her offspring. The UK Parliament has passed the Department of Health's draft Human Fertilisation and Embryology (Mitochondrial Donation) Regulations in 2015 to allow mitochondrial donation for the prevention of serious mitochondrial diseases. Singapore's BAC (2018) Consultation Paper on mitochondrial genome replacement therapy (MGRT) sought the views of the public as to whether to allow women suffering from various mitochondrial diseases[108] the chance to bear genetically related children free from those diseases through egg or embryo manipulation using one or more of the MGRT techniques.[109] If successful, the application of the techniques can prevent or mitigate foreseeable injuries to the unborn children. One main concern, however, relates to health risks to the child due to potential incompatibility between the nuclear and mitochondrial DNA. The other is the notion of the "three-parent child" who will inherit genetic material from two prospective parents as well as the donor though the Consultation Paper noted that the nuclear DNA from the prospective parents would likely outweigh the amount of mitochondrial DNA from the donor.[110]

9.6.1 Selection of sex and genetic traits

Sex selection for non-medical reasons is generally unacceptable, according to BAC (2005), as it may "promote or reinforce gender stereotyping and discrimination" and "promote gender imbalance in the population structure, which in turn may have undesirable social implications".[111] In this regard, we note that the LTC-ARS 2020 specifically prohibits sperm sorting techniques in sex selection.[112]

With respect to the issue of parental selection of genetic traits in unborn children, BAC (2005) Report raised the concern that PGD

---

107 Para 31. On the power of HFEA in UK to authorise tissue typing and PGD, see *R (Quintavalle) v Human Fertilisation and Embryology Authority* [2005] 2 AC 561.
108 The disorders and affected organs and tissues include encepthalopathy (brain), myopathy (muscle), cardiomyopathy (heart muscle), deafness (inner ear) and diabetes (endocrine system): see para 9.
109 The three techniques discussed in the BAC (2018) Consultation Paper were (a) Maternal Spindle Transfer (maternal chromosomes are held in a structure called the spindle-chromosome complex); (b) Pronuclear Transfer (pronuclei are structures visible in the egg within 10 hours after penetration by the sperm at fertilisation); and (c) Polar Body Transfer (polar bodies are small cells produced during oogenesis or egg formation).
110 Para 71.
111 Para 4.46.
112 Para 5.54.

may be used to select certain desired traits (for example, intelligence, colour of hair, sports ability or musical talent) for the "enhancement" of children, which thereby devalue and alter the way in which society views those who do not possess the desirable traits.[113]

It was also concerned about the potential costs of PGD which can only be afforded to the rich thereby resulting in social stratification.[114] In addition, the child may "experience increased pressure to fulfil the expectation of this genetic potential" and the parent-child relationship may be adversely affected with "parental love" being "dependent on a child having characteristics that the parents hoped for, but rather as individuals in their own right" and allowing parents to exercise "control over the result of conception".[115]

Sandel (2004) had similarly warned against the "hubris of the designing parents, in their drive to master the mystery of birth" which "threatens to banish our appreciation of life as a gift". On the other hand, Savulescu (2007) has gone beyond the parental right to choose to advocating that parents *ought* morally to choose desirable genetic traits of their unborn children. He referred to Procreative Beneficence as the "principle of selecting the best child of the possible children one could have". In response to objections, he argued that "[f]ar from playing God, attempting to control our genetic fate is 'playing human' - trying to improve the odds of doing well in an uncertain world of difficulty, threat and misfortune". He also took the view that allowing selection would reduce inequality if the procedures are "cheap and affordable". Procreative beneficence is connected to the wider debate on genetic enhancements. In that regard, Savulescu (2012) opined that genetic enhancements will not only improve the functioning of the human system but also "increase the chances of leading a good life" (the welfarist argument).

Box 9.2 - Designer babies and parental rights

Do parents have the right to select desirable genetic traits such as intelligence and athleticism for their children if the medical technology is available? If so, should doctors facilitate or enable the exercise of such a right?

9.6.2 Human cloning and human stem cell research

Cloning is the reproduction of genetic material of an ancestor-organism without sex.[116] The process is known as somatic cell nuclear transfer where the nucleus of an adult cell is taken from an existing organism and implanted or fused into the egg. The egg still contributes the mitochondrial DNA albeit not a significant amount of genetic material. Nonetheless, the clone would still be genetically different from the ancestor.

---

113 Para 4.37.
114 Para 4.38.
115 Para 4.44.
116 Pence (2012, at p. 194).

202 *Reproduction*

Human cloning is prohibited in Singapore under the Human Cloning and Other Prohibited Practices Act (HCOPPA).[117] No person shall place any human embryo clone in the body of a human or the body of an animal[118] regardless of the survivability of the human embryo clone.[119] The following acts are prohibited under the statute:

(a) developing any human embryo, that is created by a process other than the fertilisation of a human egg by human sperm for a period of more than 14 days[120];
(b) developing any human embryo outside the body of a woman for a period of more than 14 days[121];
(c) removing any human embryo from the body of a woman for the purpose of collecting a viable human embryo[122];
(d) placing any human embryo in an animal[123];
(e) placing any human embryo in the body of a human, other than in a woman's reproductive tract[124];
(f) placing any animal embryo in the body of a human for any period of gestation[125];
(g) placing any embryo in the body of a woman knowing that, or reckless as to whether, the embryo is a prohibited embryo[126];
(h) knowingly import any prohibited embryo into Singapore[127]; or knowingly export any prohibited embryo out of Singapore[128];
(i) giving or offering valuable consideration to another person, *or* receiving, or offering to receive, valuable consideration[129] from another person for the supply of any human egg, human sperm or human embryo.[130] Any contract or arrangement entered into by any person in contravention of this prohibition will be void unless it is only for the

---

117 (Cap 131B, Rev Ed 2005). The provisions are based on Tasmania law.
118 Section 5.
119 Section 6.
120 Section 7.
121 Section 8.
122 Section 9.
123 Section 10(a).
124 Section 10(b).
125 Section 10(c).
126 Section 11.
127 Section 12(a).
128 Section 12(b).
129 Valuable consideration includes any inducement, discount or priority in the provision of a service to the person, but does not include the payment of reasonable expenses incurred by the person in connection with the supply: section 13(5).
130 Section 13(1). The "supply" does not refer to the provision of any service for facilitating the donation and receipt of any human egg, human sperm or human embryo by receiving, storing, processing and subsequently implanting the donated human egg, human sperm or human embryo in the body of another human: section 13(4).

reimbursement of any reasonable expenses[131] incurred by a person in relation to the supply of any human egg, human sperm or human embryo.[132]

The statutory enactment was influenced by the BAC (2002) Report. In particular, the BAC (2002) Report recommended that research involving human embryos should be permitted subject to the 14-day period of the embryo's development. The position of the Catholics and Protestants groups which responded to the BAC (2002) Report was that the embryo from conception is already a human person. Hence, they rejected the destruction of embryos arising from human stem cell research and advocated instead that human embryonic research should be carried out using adult stem cells derived from competent consenting adults or from umbilical cord blood (Kaan 2010).[133] On the other hand, the Muslim and Jewish groups responded that human life does not begin at conception (Kaan 2010).[134] The BAC (2002) Report eventually adopted a "moderate approach" on the form of respect to be accorded to a human embryo[135] based on the following ethical values[136]:

> the results must be both just and sustainable. 'Just' refers to the obligation to respect the common good, that there must be fair sharing of the costs and benefits. 'Sustainable' refers to an obligation to respect the needs of generations yet unborn. The principles include the concepts of beneficence and nonmaleficence, that of encouraging the pursuit of social benefits while avoiding or ameliorating potential harm.

9.6.3 Genetic defects, mix-ups and inadequate advice

The availability of genetic technology has brought about significant benefits to couples who desire to have children of their own. Genetic counselling plays an important complementary role. The BAC (2005) Report recommended that genetic counselling provide sufficient and unbiased information to enable full and informed choices to be exercised and appropriate support to the patient and family members.[137] Notwithstanding, errors at the microscopic level can still happen and may amplify the adverse consequences for humans and the yet-to-be-born. We will consider the potential claims of parents and the child respectively against geneticists, embryologists and medical doctors amongst others in the tort of negligence primarily.

---

131 This includes, but is not limited to, expenses relating to the collection, storage or transport of the egg or sperm and expenses relating to the storage or transport of the embryo: section 13(5).
132 Section 13(2) and (3).
133 Paras 63–66.
134 Paras 71–74.
135 At p. 7.
136 At p. 21.
137 Para 40.

9.6.3.1 Wrongful conception and birth claims by parents

The mother's claims for pain and suffering and medical costs associated with pregnancy and delivery are generally allowed. But the parents' claims for the expenses in bringing up the child are more controversial. The Singapore Court of Appeal has recently allowed recovery for loss of genetic affinity which we will discuss below.

The English cases on wrongful birth claims have not been entirely consistent with regard to recovery of damages. In *McFarlane v Tayside Health Board*,[138] the parents sued the doctor for a failed vasectomy operation performed on the father as a result of which the mother gave birth to a healthy child. It was held that the parents could recover damages for pain and suffering related to the pregnancy and birth of the child[139] and special damages for the extra expenses and loss of earnings associated with pregnancy and birth.[140] However, they could not recover for the financial costs of raising the child. Important reasons included the reluctance to treat a normal healthy child as a financial liability as opposed to a "mixed blessing" bringing "joy and sorrow, blessing and responsibility"[141] and that the rewards of parenthood could not be quantified.

In a subsequent case where the child was born disabled, the parents successfully claimed for the *additional* costs of raising the child *with a disability*.[142] The decision seemed to contradict the rationale in *McFarlane* that the child should not be treated as a financial liability and that the rewards of parenthood could not be quantified. Moreover, by allowing the additional costs for a disabled child, it may imply that a disabled child is worth less than a healthy child. Shortly thereafter, the majority judges[143] in *Rees v Darlington Memorial Hospital NHS Trust*,[144] applying *McFarlane*, denied a claim for the additional costs of raising a normal child due to the mother's poor eyesight. Instead, the parents were entitled to recover a conventional sum for the denial of personal autonomy to limit the size of her family.[145]

Taking a different stance, the majority judges of the High Court of Australia[146] in *Cattanach v Melchior*[147] allowed the costs of raising a normal child until the age of 18 arising from the doctor's negligent failure to advise the mother of the conception. McHugh and Gummow JJ referred to the loss as "financial damage that the parents will suffer as the result of their legal responsibility to raise the child".[148] Kirby J noted that the loss claimed for was reasonably foreseeable and not too remote.[149] He also regarded the claim as based on a loss

---

138 [2000] 2 AC 59; Lord Millett dissenting.
139 The majority of the House of Lords except Lord Millet.
140 Lord Hope, Lord Steyn and Lord Slynn.
141 *McFarlane v Tayside Health Board* [2000] 2 AC 59 at 113-114.
142 *Parkinson v St James and Seacroft University Hospital NHS Trust* [2002] QB 266.
143 Lord Bingham, Lord Nicholls, Lord Millett and Lord Scott.
144 [2004] 1 AC 309.
145 *Rees v Darlington Memorial Hospital NHS Trust* [2004] 1 AC 309 at [8], *per* Lord Bingham.
146 McHugh, Gummow, Kirby and Callinan JJ (Gleeson CJ Hayne and Heydon JJ dissenting).
147 [2003] 215 CLR 1.
148 *Cattanach v Melchior* [2003] 215 CLR 1 at [90].
149 *Cattanach v Melchior* [2003] 215 CLR 1 at [179].

consequential upon physical injury to the mother rather than pure economic loss.[150] However, the common law position has been overruled by legislation in some states in Australia.[151]

Unlike Australia, Singapore has denied the recovery of costs of bringing up the child but allowed the claim for loss of genetic affinity based on a unique set of facts. In the landmark case of *ACB v Thomson Medical Centre Pte Ltd*,[152] a Singapore Chinese woman married to a German man of Caucasian descent wanted to have a child via IVF. There was a serious mix-up in the laboratories of the medical centre which performed the IVF. Instead of the appellant's husband's sperm, the appellant's egg was fertilised by the sperm of an unknown Indian donor. As a result, the baby's skin tone and colour were different from the appellant and her husband. The appellant claimed in negligence for pain and suffering relating to the pregnancy and mental distress as well as upkeep costs to raise the baby. The Singapore Court of Appeal rejected the claim for upkeep costs based on the following reasons:

(a) The obligation to maintain one's child is an obligation at the heart of parenthood and cannot be a cognisable head of loss[153]; and
(b) The upkeep claim was fundamentally inconsistent with the nature of the parent-child relationship and would place the appellant in a position where her personal interests as a litigant would conflict with her duties as a parent.[154]

Instead, a new head of damage was recognised. Damage to the appellant's interest in "genetic affinity" is a cognisable injury.[155] The Court of Appeal acknowledged the appellant's "interest in maintaining the integrity of her reproductive plans" as she had made a conscious decision to have a child with her husband to "maintain an intergenerational genetic link and to preserve "affinity".[156] The interest in affinity exists at the bilateral level between parent and child, multilaterally between the parents and their extended relations, child's relationship with his siblings as well as the family's relationship with the wider community of which they are part.[157]

Though the claim for damages was treated as one for non-pecuniary losses, the Court of Appeal decided to benchmark the award for loss of genetic affinity to a percentage (30%) of the financial costs of raising the baby. The court felt that the award should allow for substantial damages that "properly reflects sufficiently the seriousness of the Appellant's loss and is *just, equitable, and proportionate* in the circumstances of the case".[158] It considered the alternative of awarding a conventional sum as in *Rees* for loss of personal (reproductive) autonomy – a vindicatory rather than a compensatory approach – but eventually rejected it.

---

150 *Cattanach v Melchior* [2003] 215 CLR 1 at [149].
151 Civil Liability Act 2002 (NSW) Pt 11; Civil Liability Act 2003 (Qld) Ch 2 Pt 5.
152 [2017] 1 SLR 918.
153 [2017] 1 SLR 918 at [86].
154 [2017] 1 SLR 918 at [86].
155 It cited Norton (1999).
156 [2017] 1 SLR 918 at [135].
157 [2017] 1 SLR 918 at [128].
158 [2017] 1 SLR 918 at [150] (emphasis in original).

Commentators have noted other possible claims, for example, for mental distress arising from the invasion of the mother's bodily autonomy (which is akin to trespass to the person)[159] since the sperm from a third party donor was implanted in her womb without informed consent. Alternatively, based on the vindicatory approach, it has been proposed that a new tort that is actionable *per se* and strict, in contrast to negligence, be created to "address mistakes in the course of assisted reproduction which lead to the birth of a child that is different in some significant way to that contemplated by the clinic and the intending parents" (Mulligan 2020, at p. 72). In the assessment of damages, insofar as loss of genetic affinity is concerned, Norton (1999) had argued that the strength of the parents' preferences for such affinity should provide a coherent basis for the damages recoverable.

9.6.3.2 Wrongful life claims by child

The disabled child's claim based on "wrongful life" for the damages he or she allegedly suffered are generally not recoverable. In contrast to wrongful birth claims where courts are called to assess the mother's claim for the costs of bringing up the child, the central issue in a wrongful life claim for damages concerns the worth of the child's existence. In *JU v See Tho Kai Yin*,[160] it was alleged that the defendant (an obstetrician and gynaecologist) had negligently failed to advise a pregnant woman of the increased risks of having a baby with chromosomal abnormalities due to the woman's age. The woman claimed that, as a consequence, she was prevented from exercising her option to abort the baby. With respect to the claim by the disabled child (who was born with Downs' syndrome) for pain and financial hardship as a result of being born, the High Court ruled that such an action would be contrary to public policy as it violated the sanctity of human life. The Singapore court had followed the position in *McKay v Essex Area Health Authority*[161] denying wrongful life claims. Stephenson LJ in *McKay*[162] stated that to impose a duty "would mean regarding the life of a handicapped child as not only less valuable than the life of a normal child, but so much less valuable that it was not worth preserving". Both Stephenson LJ and Ackner LJ highlighted the impossibility of valuing "non-existence" over existence, however handicapped the child may be.

The sanctity of life argument does not imply that "the right to life must be protected at all costs".[163] In end-of-life decision-making, courts have for example sanctioned withholding life-sustaining treatment to a patient in a persistent vegetative state based on the "best interests" test[164] (Chapter 10). Hence, it may be argued that sanctity of life should not be treated as an absolute value that will negate all claims in wrongful life.

---

159 Fordham (2015, at p. 6).
160 [2005] 4 SLR(R) 96.
161 [1982] QB 1166.
162 [1982] QB 1166 at 1180.
163 Fordham (2005, at p. 403).
164 *Airedale NHS Trust v Bland* [1993] AC 789.

The majority of the High Court of Australia has endorsed this common law position against the recovery of claims based on wrongful life in *Waller v James*[165] and *Harriton v Stephens*[166] albeit with a powerful dissent. In *Harriton v Stephens*, it was held that a doctor who negligently failed to diagnose rubella in a pregnant patient did not owe a duty of care to the patient's child born with congenital disabilities. The majority decided, consistent with *McKay*, that to allow the child's claim for damages was tantamount to making a comparison between the child's life with disabilities and the state of non-existence if the doctor were not negligent. As Callinan J put it, "[i]t is not logically possible for any person to be heard to say 'I should not be here at all' because a non-being can say nothing at all".[167] Kirby J, however, voiced a strong dissent, stating that the term "wrongful life" is a misnomer as the child exists, and the non-existence is purely "hypothetical".[168] Thus, the real question should be whether the doctor should pay for the child's suffering and loss,[169] and healthcare providers should not be immune from the consequences of their negligent conduct that results in the lifelong and substantial suffering of the child.[170]

9.7 Conclusion

Reproduction is both a biological as well as a social fact. It has been an intrinsic part of humankind and human nature since time immemorial. Yet, new medical technologies are continually prompting developments and changes in the laws and ethics applicable to age-old issues such as birth control, surrogacy and what it means for parents to bring up their children. Insofar as birth control methods such as contraceptives and sterilisation are concerned, there are legal safeguards on obtaining consent from minors, ensuring the best interests of mentally incapable patients and duties owed by doctors to patients in implementing or advising on birth control. Abortion is legalised in Singapore. Notwithstanding the controversy surrounding the abortion issue globally, the practice may be defensible in a limited number of situations from the ethical and social perspectives. Assisted reproduction techniques, which are conducted by licensed assisted reproduction centres according to ministerial guidelines, are not administered in Singapore for the purpose of giving birth to a baby through surrogacy. Yet there is no firm government policy against surrogacy; nor are such arrangements criminalised in Singapore. This gives rise to interesting issues on adoptions of children born via foreign surrogacy arrangements and claims for foreign surrogacy expenses. However, human cloning is clearly prohibited in Singapore and the ethics of "designer babies" has been questioned by the Bioethics Advisory Committee. The approaches to wrongful conception and birth claims by parents vary depending on the jurisdictions concerned with no consistent

---

165 (2006) 226 CLR 136.
166 (2006) 226 CLR 52.
167 *Harriton v Stephens* (2006) 226 CLR 52 at [206].
168 *Harriton v Stephens* (2006) 226 CLR 52 at [101].
169 *Harriton v Stephens* (2006) 226 CLR 52 at [10], [96], [118] and [155].
170 *Harriton v Stephens* (2006) 226 CLR 52 at [153]. See *Turpin v Sortini* 182 Cal Rptr 337 (1982) (refusing the child's claim for general damages for wrongful life).

overarching principle as yet[171] whilst the general denial of wrongful life claims by the child has encountered strong dissent and critique by courts and academic commentators.

References

BAC (2002). *Ethical, Legal and Social Issues in Human Stem Cell Research, Reproductive and Therapeutic Cloning*: A Report from the Bioethics Advisory Committee, Singapore (21 June).

BAC (2005). *Genetic Testing and Genetic Research*: A Report from the Bioethics Advisory Committee, Singapore (November).

BAC (2018). *Ethical, Legal and Social Issues Arising from Mitochondrial Genome Replacement Technology* – A Consultation Paper (19 April).

Fordham, M. (2005). "A Life Without Value: *JU and Another v See Tho Kai Yin*" *Sing JLS* 395-406.

Fordham, M. (2015). "An IVF Baby and a Catastrophic Error – Actions for Wrongful Conception and Wrongful Birth Revisited in Singapore" *Sing JLS* 1-9.

Fox, D. (2017). "Reproductive Negligence" 117 *Columbia Law Review* 149.

Freeman, M. (2017a). "Medically Assisted Reproduction" in Laing, J.M. & McHale, J.V. (eds) *Principles of Medical Law*, Fourth Edition (Oxford University Press: Oxford), pp. 755-834.

Freeman, M. (2017b). "Reproductive Genetics" in Laing, J.M. & McHale, J.V. (eds) *Principles of Medical Law*, Fourth Edition (Oxford University Press: Oxford), pp. 835-849.

Jackson, E. (2017). "Abortion" in Laing, J.M. & McHale, J.V. (eds) *Principles of Medical Law*, Fourth Edition (Oxford University Press: Oxford), pp. 850-885.

Kaan, S.H.T (2010). "At the Beginning of Life" 22 *SAcLJ* 883-918.

Mulligan, A. (2020). "A Vindicatory Approach to Tortious Liability for Mistakes in Assisted Human Reproduction" 40 *Legal Studies* 55-76.

Norton, F. (1999). "Assisted Reproduction and the Frustration of Genetic Affinity: Interest, Injury, and Damages" 74 *NYU Law Review* 793.

Pascoe, J. (2018). "Sleepwalking Through the Minefield: Legal and Ethical Issues in Surrogacy" 30 *SAcLJ* 455.

Pence, G. (2012). "Cloning" in Kuhse, H. & Singer, P. (eds) *A Companion to Bioethics* (Wiley-Blackwell: Hoboken, NJ), pp. 193-203.

Ryznar, M. (2010). "International Commercial Surrogacy and its Parties" 43 *John Marshall Law Review* 1009.

Sandel, M. (2004). "The Case Against Perfection". The Atlantic (April) at www.theatlantic.com/doc/200404/sandel

Savulescu, J. (2007). "In Defence of Procreative Beneficence" 33 *Journal of Medical Ethics* 284-288.

Savulescu, J. (2012). "Genetic Enhancement" in Kuhse, H. & Singer, P. (eds), *A Companion to Bioethics* (Wiley-Blackwell: Hoboken, NJ), pp. 216-234.

Sim, J. (2016). "National University Hospital" in Lee, C.E. & Satku, K. (eds) *Singapore's Health Care System: What 50 years have achieved* (World Scientific: Singapore), pp. 247-256.

Singer P. (2000). *Writings on an Ethical Life* (The Ecco Press: New York).

Tan, S.H. (2019). "Surrogacy, Child's Welfare, and Public Policy in Adoption Applications" *Sing JLS* 263.

Thomson, J.J. (1971). "A Defense of Abortion" 1 *Philosophy and Public Affairs* 47-66.

---

171 *Eg*, see Fox (2017) on reproductive negligence to deal with misconduct that (1) imposes unwanted pregnancy or parenthood, (2) deprives wanted pregnancy or parenthood, and (3) confounds efforts to have or avoid a child born with particular traits.

10 End of life

10.1 Introduction

Singapore is experiencing an ageing population with increased average life expectancy. On average, the last 8-10 years of a person's life in Singapore are likely to be spent in poor health (IPS Report 2019, at p. 17). Many of the elderly persons may be suffering from long-drawn chronic illnesses. Due to Singapore's self-reliance model, a significant burden of health financing for the elderly would fall on themselves, their family members and caregivers (see Chapter 1).

The provision of long-term and palliative care in Singapore is mainly drawn from the voluntary welfare organisations (VWOs) and charity sector on an ad-hoc basis and supported by grants from the Ministry for Social and Family Development (IPS Report 2019, at p. 21). Palliative care is available in government acute care hospitals and community hospitals. Home hospice care is provided free of charge from grants by the Ministry for Health, National Council for Social Services (NCSS) and sponsors whilst fees are charged for inpatient hospice care though subsidies are available subject to means-testing (IPS Report 2019, at p. 75).

The Report on the National Strategy for Palliative Care (2011) made some recommendations concerning the national delivery of palliative care, its affordability, the need for adequately trained staff on palliative care and for establishing evidence-based standards of care. The National Guidelines for Palliative Care by the National Strategy for Palliative Care Implementation Taskforce in 2015 emphasised the assessment of patients with terminal illnesses and support for the caregivers of such patients.

Advanced care planning (ACP) in Singapore – which is coordinated by the Agency for Integrated Care – aims to promote increased understanding of individuals about their present and future health plans in conversations with their family members and healthcare professionals. Improving the "quality of death"[1] in Singapore involves not merely medical but also social aspects (for example, building community and networks for the elderly through

---

1 Quality of Death Index by the Economist Intelligence Unit ranked Singapore 12th out of 80 countries based on the scores in 20 quantitative and qualitative indicators across five categories (Palliative and healthcare environment, Human resources, Affordability of care, Quality of care and Community engagement): see http://www.lienfoundation.org/sites/default/files/2015%20Quality%20of%20Death%20Report.pdf at pp. 9 and 15.

a network of VWOs, grassroots and community groups and government agencies) as well as cultural and spiritual dimensions (by providing emotional and psychological support for the patient). Public education about legal matters (eg, the drafting of wills, creation of lasting powers of attorney and advance medical directives) and ethical issues (eg, the preservation of autonomy of patients and family support in decision-making) pertaining to end-of-life issues for the community at large would also be important.

With this brief introduction of the socioeconomic and policy aspects, we can now focus on the doctors' role in end-of-life matters as well as the legal and ethical aspects relating to the determination of death, the creation and regulation of advance medical directives, the withdrawal or refusal of life-sustaining treatment and physician-assisted euthanasia.

10.2 Definition of death

Death in a sense defies definition. From the philosophical perspective, it is a state of non-existence which falls outside our human-describable experience. Those reflecting on death (or the process of dying) may find that they need to also unravel the mystery of its metaphysical counterparts (that is, life and living, respectively). Certain religious beliefs may speak of death in spiritual terms (eg, of the soul leaving the body) which may not be entirely amenable to scientific proof.

For specific purposes relating to health law and medical ethics, we need a legal definition of death that can be empirically determined in order to delineate the circumstances when medical practitioners are entitled to issue death certificates under the Registry of Births and Deaths Act,[2] to apply the concept to criminal law cases on murder and culpable homicide and to deal with legal procedures pertaining to the removal of human tissues and organs from deceased persons in the Human Organ Transplant Act ("HOTA")[3] and Coroners' inquiries into the causes of death.[4]

In the past, the common law approach has been to leave the determination of death to the medical experts (Kaan 1992). In 1998, the Interpretation Act, by way of a statutory amendment, stipulated two definitions of death.[5] Under existing law, a person is regarded to have died when there has occurred either –

(a) irreversible cessation of circulation of blood and respiration in the body of the person; or
(b) total and irreversible cessation of all functions of the brain of the person.

---

2 (Cap 267, 1985 Rev Ed), section 19.
3 (Cap 131A, 2012 Rev Ed).
4 The focus of the Coroner's inquiry is the "cause of and circumstances connected with the death" to ascertain where possible (a) the identity of the deceased; and (b) how, when and where the deceased came by his death: section 27(1) of the Coroner's Act (Cap 63A, 2012 Rev Ed). "Any death in Singapore that occurred, directly or indirectly, as a result of any medical treatment or care" is subject to such an inquiry: see Third Schedule of the statute. See also Lee et al. (2008).
5 Section 2A via Act 22 of 1998 – Interpretation (Amendment) Act 1998.

Both the concepts of cardiac and brain death have been referred to in criminal[6] and tort cases.[7] The enquiry as to whether there has been irreversible cessation of circulation of blood and respiration is to be determined according to the standards of medical practice.[8] On the other hand, total and irreversible cessation of all functions of the brain is determined according to statutorily prescribed criteria.[9] The determination of brain death can only be carried out if certain statutory conditions are satisfied.[10] The Interpretation (Determination and Certification of Death) Regulations[11] further stipulate the main criteria for determining brain death,[12] and these criteria may be supplemented by other tests.[13] Death is required under statute to be certified by two medical practitioners who possess relevant postgraduate medical qualifications and who have not been excluded by the relevant statutes.

Previously, cardiac death was the only yardstick for death. The advancements made by medical technology allowed for a patient's heart to be removed whilst being kept alive by

---

6 Eg, *Wang Wenfeng v Public Prosecutor* [2012] 4 SLR 590 at [43] (dismissing the possibility of sudden cardiac death of victim based on evidence); *Public Prosecutor v Chan Lie Sian* [2017] SGHC 205 at [54] (deceased's brain death due to brain injuries in a murder case); *Murgan s/o Ramasamy v Public Prosecutor* [1994] SGCA 30 at [11] and [12] (medical evidence concerning the brain death of victim in a murder case).

7 *Goh Guan Sin (by her litigation representative Chiam Yu Zhu) v Yeo Tseng Tsai and another* [2019] SGHC 274 at [13] (reference to brain death in one of the tests used to assess patient's state in respect of a medical negligence claim by patient who was in a persistent vegetative state after undergoing surgery to remove a brain tumour).

8 Section 2A(2).

9 Section 2A(3).

10 The three conditions are:
    (a) the person's condition is undoubtedly due to irremediable structural brain damage and the diagnosis of any disorder which can lead to the irreversible cessation of all functions of the person's brain must have been fully established;
    (b) that there is no suspicion that the person's condition is due to depressant drugs, hypothermia or metabolic and endocrine factors; and
    (c) that the person's cessation of spontaneous respiration is not caused by neuromuscular blocking agents or other drugs.

11 Rg 1, G.N. No. S 505/1998.

12 The criteria are as follows:
    (a) the pupils are fixed and non-reactive to strong light;
    (b) there is no corneal reflex;
    (c) there is no spontaneous motor response to painful stimulus, excluding spinal reflexes;
    (d) there is no oculocephalic reflex;
    (e) there is no gag reflex or reflex response to tracheobronchial stimulation;
    (f) there is no vestibulo-ocular response on instillation of 50 cubic centimetres of ice-cold water into each ear; and
    (g) there is no spontaneous respiration even with carbon dioxide tension at 50 millimetres or more of mercury.

13 The supplementary tests (in the First Schedule to the Regulations) are:
    1. Cerebral angiography to confirm that there is no intracranial blood flow.
    2. Radionuclide scan to confirm that there is no intracranial perfusion.

212 *End of life*

machines to enable blood circulation before a new heart is transplanted. It was also possible to restart a person's heart through cardiopulmonary resuscitation (CPR). To allow for heart transplants from living donors, cardiac death as the sole criterion of death would no longer be tenable given the medical technology. A report by the Ad Hoc Committee of the Harvard Medical School (1968) had argued instead for brain death. This concept of brain death was subsequently accepted in a US court decision.[14] Both concepts of cardiac death and brain death are now incorporated in the US' Uniform Determination of Death Act which is a model state law that was approved in 1981[15] and applied in most US states.

The Singapore Academy of Medicine published guidelines for the determination of brain death "in the deeply comatosed patient" in 1985 (Kaan 1992, at p. 318).[16] Statutorily, death was defined in the HOTA in 1987 according to the brain death criteria. Under the statute, the time of the donor's death has to be accurately determined so as to allow the removal of the deceased person's organs. The HOTA provision meant that in 1987, there was one statutory definition of death and possibly another outside of the statute or at common law (Kaan 2011). Prior to the Interpretation Act amendment in 1998 and Regulations, the High Court referred to brain death in a criminal case without citing the HOTA or common law.[17] With the addition of the aforementioned definitions of death in the Interpretation Act, the provision defining death in the HOTA was no longer necessary and was thereby deleted. The definitions in the Interpretation Act would now apply generally not only with respect to the HOTA but also the Medical (Therapy, Education and Research) Act[18] which allows people to pledge their organs or any body parts for the purposes of transplant, education or research upon their death. A study has indicated, however, a resistance to the notion of brain death amongst a majority of respondents in Singapore and this may have had an impact on their willingness to donate their organs or those of family members upon death (Liu et al. 2019).

In England, death, at common law, was defined as brain stem death in *Airedale NHS Trust v Bland*[19] and other cases.[20] A person in persistent vegetative state such as Bland would not be regarded as brain stem dead and was still alive. Bland's cerebral cortex lost all its functions and activity but his brain stem was functioning. He could not see, hear or taste or communicate with others and was fed by a nasogastric tube. We will examine this case in greater detail below.

The hospital or medical clinic in which the deceased person is receiving medical treatment or care must preserve all medical records, healthcare records and any other document in its

---

14 *Tucker's Administrator* v. *Lower* (Ct Law & Eq., Richmond, Virginia, 25 May 1972, No. 2831 (cited in Kaan 1992, at p. 312).
15 It was approved by the National Conference of Commissioners on Uniform State Laws, in cooperation with the American Medical Association, the American Bar Association, and the President's Commission for the Study of Ethical Problems in Medicine and Biomedical and Behavioral Research.
16 Citing Devathasan (1985).
17 *PP v Othman bin Hussain & Anor* [1991] SGHC 168 (reference to brain death involving offence of culpable homicide not amounting to murder).
18 (Cap 175, 2014 Rev Ed).
19 [1993] AC 789 at 863, *per* Lord Goff and 878, *per* Lord Browne-Wilkinson. See also *Auckland Area Health Board v Attorney General* [1993] 1 NZLR 235.
20 *Auckland Area Health Board v Attorney General* [1993] 1 NZLR 235; and *Re A (A Child)* [2015] EWHC 443.

possession pertaining to the medical treatment or care of the deceased.[21] The Coroner has the power to order a forensic pathologist to investigate the cause of and circumstances connected with the death,[22] and upon consulting the pathologist, order a post-mortem examination to be conducted on the deceased person to establish the manner and cause of death.[23] The pathologist who conducted the post-mortem will be required to certify the medical cause of death and submit a report to the Coroner[24] for the purpose of the inquiry into the cause and circumstances of death.

10.3 Advanced medical directives

Doctors, family members and the loved ones of patients who are suffering from terminal illnesses may have to confront thorny issues. From the clinical perspective, if the dying patient is suffering from pneumonia, should the doctor prescribe antibiotics which may tackle the infection but is otherwise ineffective in improving the patient's condition?[25] Should the doctor continue to place a dying patient on a life support system even it would merely prolong the latter's life without any prospect of recovery? What are the views of family members and loved ones?

These decisions are not only vexing but also profoundly personal. In Singapore, a person who is 21 years old[26] is entitled to make a medical directive under the Advance Medical Directive (AMD) Act expressing his wish not to be subjected to the "extraordinary life-sustaining treatment in the event of his suffering from a terminal illness".[27] The words "terminal illness" refer to an incurable condition caused by injury or disease from which there is no reasonable prospect of a temporary or permanent recovery where –

(a) death would, within reasonable medical judgement, be imminent regardless of the application of extraordinary life-sustaining treatment; and
(b) the application of extraordinary life-sustaining treatment would only serve to postpone the moment of death of the patient.

There is no specific definition for "imminent death" in AMD Act. The term "extraordinary life-sustaining treatment" means any "medical procedure or measure which, when administered to a terminally ill patient, will only prolong the process of dying when death is imminent, but excludes palliative care".[28] This means that palliative care will continue even when the directive has been carried out. "Palliative care" includes the provision of reasonable medical

---

21 Coroner's Act (Cap 63A, 2012 Rev Ed), section 8.
22 Section 16.
23 Section 18.
24 Section 20.
25 Singapore Parliament Reports, Advance Medical Directive Bill (5 December 1995) Vol 65, col. 352 (Minister for Health).
26 AMD Act, section 3(1).
27 Section 3.
28 Section 2.

procedures for the relief of pain, suffering or discomfort; and the reasonable provision of food and water.[29]

The statute also stipulates that extraordinary life-sustaining treatment shall not be withheld or withdrawn from a patient known to the medical practitioner to be pregnant so long as it is probable that the foetus will develop to the point of live birth with continued application of extraordinary life-sustaining treatment.[30]

Procedurally, the directive must be witnessed by two persons (including one medical practitioner)[31] present at the same time. The medical practitioner has to ensure that the person making the directive is at least 21 years old, not mentally disordered, has made the directive voluntarily and without inducement or compulsion, and has been informed of the nature and consequences of making the directive.[32] The directive must also be registered with the Registrar of AMD.[33] Revocation of the AMD is allowed and the requirements are more relaxed than those for making the AMD. The person may revoke the AMD orally or in writing in the presence of at least one witness, and the revocation shall, as far as practicable, be registered.[34]

Where a medical practitioner responsible for the treatment of a person reasonably believes that the person is suffering from a terminal illness, requires extraordinary life-sustaining treatment and is unconscious or incapable of exercising rational judgement, the medical practitioner may issue a certificate sent to the Registrar of AMD.[35] If the Registrar confirms the person has made an AMD, the medical practitioner should seek the unanimous opinion of two other medical practitioners[36] or a committee of three specialists[37] that the patient is terminally ill. These requirements must be satisfied before the medical practitioner may act in accordance with the directive.

If the patient is conscious or capable of exercising rational judgement at the relevant time, he or she is entitled at common law to make a decision as to the treatment (including the use of extraordinary life-sustaining treatment) as long as he is able to do so.[38]

A medical practitioner is immune from criminal or civil liability or professional discipline for professional misconduct if he made a decision in good faith and without negligence concerning the following matters: (a) whether the patient was or was not suffering from a

---

29 Section 2. In *Re (on the Application of Burke) v General Medical Council* [2005] 3 FCR 169 (common law duty to provide artificial nutrition and hydration (ANH) for a capacitated patient as long as it prolongs his life and where it is in accordance with patient's expressed wishes, but common duty to provide ANH to patient is subject to the patient's wishes to reject ANH).
30 Section 10(6).
31 Section 3(2). Further, the witness cannot be a beneficiary under the patient's will or any policy of insurance or be entitled to any interest in the patient's estate or CPF moneys: section 3(3).
32 Section 4.
33 Section 5.
34 Section 7.
35 Section 9(1).
36 Section 9(3).
37 Section 9(5) and (6).
38 Section 12.

terminal illness; (b) whether he has revoked or intended to revoke a directive; (c) whether the patient was capable of understanding the nature and consequences of the directive; and (d) whether the directive was valid.[39] The non-application of extraordinary life-sustaining treatment to, or the withdrawal of extraordinary life-sustaining treatment from, a person suffering from a terminal illness is not a cause of death if it resulted from compliance with the directive.[40] Medical doctors may register their conscientious objections to the AMD[41] and are thereby excluded from participating as witnesses to the making of AMDs and from the certification of terminal illnesses.

Hospitals and their staff responsible for the care of patients cannot ask them whether they have made an AMD or intend to make one.[42] The requirement or prohibition of an AMD cannot be a condition for the receipt of medical or healthcare services.[43]

The AMD Act is based on the principle of personal autonomy. During the parliamentary debates in 1995, it was suggested that though individual autonomy is important, family consultation should be encouraged.[44] Nevertheless, the making of an AMD is ultimately a personal decision. The individual's decision to make the AMD may relieve his or her family members from the sometimes difficult decision whether to withdraw the extraordinary life-sustaining treatment when the individual is suffering from a terminal illness not to mention the potential conflicts amongst family members.[45] It should be highlighted that under the Mental Capacity Act ("MCA"),[46] family members do not make decisions with respect to life-sustaining treatment for the incapacitated patient.

The acceptance of AMDs implicitly suggests that that there may come a time when life is not worth living for a person who is suffering from a terminal illness. This raises the question of whether the law, by providing for an individual person to make an AMD, is indirectly endorsing such a perspective of human life. In this regard, the sanctioning of AMDs has been used by proponents as an argument for allowing some form of physician-assisted euthanasia (see Section 10.5). On the religious front, it should be noted that the National Medical Ethics Committee (NMEC) had conducted consultations with the major religious groups prior to the AMD Bill. The Fatwa Committee of the Muslim Religious Council of Singapore, for example, had expressed agreement with AMDs.[47]

---

39 Section 19.
40 Section 20.
41 Section 19(1).
42 Section 15.
43 Section 16.
44 Singapore Parliament Reports, Advance Medical Directive Bill (5 December 1995) Vol 65, col 374-375.
45 There may be attendant healthcare costs issues: see Chan (2010).
46 (Cap 177A, 2010 Rev Ed), section 13(8).
47 Singapore Parliament Report, Advance Medical Directive Bill (5 December 1995) Vol 65, col 368 (Member of Parliament Encik Harun bin A Ghani)

> Islam allows anyone with sound mind to make a will or advance medical directive stating that he does not want or refuse to accept any treatment to prolong his life when his illness is incurable and terminal and that there is no hope of him to continue living. This is allowed because a patient who is terminally ill cannot live longer and is prepared to endure the suffering and wants to die

Assuming that an AMD is registered in Singapore, is there any recourse for the patient if his wishes under the AMD are not respected by the medical doctor? There is no court decision in Singapore on this issue. Reference may be made to the situation where patients may express their end-of-life wishes by means of a "Do Not Resuscitate" (DNR) Order. This was in response to medical technology that allows physicians to administer CPR in order to save the patient suffering from cardiac arrest. The DNR order – which states that the physician should not attempt CPR or/and any resuscitation measures – is not the same as an order not to treat the patient; notwithstanding a DNR order, the patient may still receive medical care, medication and surgery (Hodge 2019, at pp. 175-176). In some cases, administering resuscitation measures can cause injuries to the patient. Even if no injuries were caused, physicians who did not comply with the DNR orders would have administered the medical procedures without the patient's consent.

Should the doctor disregard a DNR order, can the patient claim for damages? In the US, such claims have generally been disallowed.[48] There have, however, been more recent cases where the courts refused to strike out the claim upon the defendant's application for summary judgement or where the dispute was settled and enforced by the court.[49] One notable exception which allowed the claim was *Koerner v Bhatt*,[50] where an 89-year-old woman who gave a DNR order had subsequently suffered from cardiac arrest. Notwithstanding the DNR order, the hospital resuscitated her. Though she continued to live for another six months, the resuscitation measures had caused her pain and suffering. She claimed for "wrongful prolongation of life". The New Jersey court noted the "fundamental right of individuals to make health care decisions to have life prolonging medical or surgical means or procedures provided, withheld or withdrawn". The New Jersey Advance Directive for Health Care Act only immunises from liability medical providers who did not take action to save a person's life and does not apply in the present case where the doctor took resuscitation measures. With respect to the claim for wrongful prolongation of life, the court held that as the doctor failed to comply with the patient's DNR order, the plaintiff was entitled to recover damages arising from the defendants' negligent failure to follow her advance directive. In doing so, the court relied on wrongful birth cases which "compensate victims who have increased expenses resulting from a medical professional's negligent failure to identify remedial diseases before they become permanent".

---

peacefully and calmly. This is because he believes that his destiny is in the hands of God and the time has come for him to go and that he will die.

48 *Egs, Anderson v St Francis-St George Hospital* 671 NE 2d 225 (Ohio 1996); *Wright v. Johns Hopkins Health Systems Corp.* 728 A.2d 166 (Md. 1999); *Taylor v Muncie Medical Investors* 727 NE 2d 466 (Ind Ct App 2000).
49 *Eg, Doctors Hospital of Augusta, LLC v Alicea* 788 SE 2d 392 (Ga. 2016); *Weisman v Maryland General Hospital* (see Docket Proceedings at 3, Entry No. 73/0, Weisman, No. 24-C-16-004199 indicating that a motion was filed to enforce a settlement agreement reached between the parties during a 14 September 2017 mediation).
50 No. L-002983-13 (NJ Super Ct Law Div, Morris Cty 2017).

Box 10.1 – Personal reflections on AMDs

Have you made an AMD? What are your reasons for making an AMD or deciding not to do so? Do the reasons relate to the existing legal framework and/or its implementation?

10.4 Withholding, refusal of life-sustaining treatment and death

This section discusses end-of-life issues arising from decisions to withhold or to refuse treatment in circumstances where the decision would likely lead to the patient's death. In addition to consent issues, we will examine cases where the patients could not or would not have been capable of giving consent such as PVS patients and conjoined twins. The application of best interests and the defence of necessity inevitably involve difficult questions on the quality and sanctity of life itself.

10.4.1 Patient autonomy

Under the common law, mentally competent patients have the right to refuse treatment. Cardozo J, in *Schloendorff v Society of New York Hospital*[51] recognised that "[e]very human being of adult years and sound mind has a right to determine what shall be done with his own body…". This extends to cases where the patient was likely to die unless treatment was administered. In *Re B (Consent to Treatment: Capacity)*,[52] the patient, a tetraplegic, was adjudged mentally competent to make the decision not to be kept artificially alive by the use of a ventilator. Two consultant psychiatrists attested to her mental capacity. The fact that she had not experienced rehabilitation or lacked experience in ICU did not mean that she lacked mental capacity. In the patient's assessment, the weaning programme offered by hospital would have meant a slow and painful death. Her mental capacity was commensurate with the decision made.[53] Hence, the NHS trust was held liable for ignoring her wishes and was required to pay nominal damages for trespass to person.

In practice, one issue that has arisen in Singapore is the tendency of some family members to request doctors and nurses to withhold information from elderly patients about their adverse health conditions (Krishna and Menon 2014). Further, instead of the patient who is mentally capable of making a decision, the family members may sometimes decide on behalf of the elderly patient so as not to burden or cause anguish to him or her. This alleged practice of "collusion" amongst the family members, doctors and nurses, which may be based on good

---

51 (1914) 105 NE 92 at 93.
52 [2002] EWHC 429 (Fam). See also *Brightwater Care Group (Inc) v Rossiter* (2009) 40 WAR 84 (where the Western Australian Supreme Court recognised the right of self-determination of quadriplegic who expressed wish not to continue receiving artificial nutrition and hydration through a tube into his stomach).
53 The court cited *Re T (adult: refusal of treatment)* [1993] Fam 95 at 113 which stated that "the more serious the decision, the greater the capacity required".

intentions, can be contrary to the concept of patient autonomy and what is envisaged in the MCA and ethical guidelines for the medical profession.

With respect to end-of-life care, the SMC's ECEG (2016)[54] highlight the doctor's role to help "patients, their families and the community to deal with the consequences of irreversible or fatal illnesses and the reality of impending death". In order to preserve "patient autonomy" where possible, doctors are enjoined to "engage patients through good communications to elicit their preferences and goals of treatment, while helping them to understand the limits of medical treatment". In particular, the doctor has to "respect patients' wishes not to receive specific treatments" though the doctor is "not obliged to provide or continue treatments that [the doctor may] deem inappropriate, non-beneficial or even harmful in view of the natural course of the underlying disease".

10.4.2 Patient's best interests

Where the patient is mentally incapacitated, treatment may be administered based on the best interests of the patient. Difficult decisions arise when the patient is in a coma and tied to a life support system. The withholding of treatment via the life support system will likely result in the death of the patient (though some patients have been known to live several years after the withdrawal of the life support system). How would the "best interests" test be applied in cases where death is likely? Do doctors or family members have the right to decide whether the treatment should be withheld in such circumstances? What happens when they disagree?[55]

Determining the best interests of the patient entails the consideration of not merely the patient's life and its value but also the patient's pain and suffering and diminished quality of life (should the life be prolonged) as well as the pain and suffering involved in the proposed treatment.[56] The SMC's ECEG (2016) recognise that doctors may consult family members or those close to them to help them determine what would be the patients' best interests. Where the patient is a baby or young child, an alternative approach based on "the standpoint of the reasonable and responsible parent who has his or her child's best interests at heart" has been suggested.[57]

---

54 Section A7.
55 In the long-drawn *Terri Schiavo* case in the United States, there was a tussle between the patient's husband who wanted her feeding tube removed and the patient's parents who filed court applications to block the husband's decision. The parties argued over what they believed were the patient's wishes concerning life support. After several years of litigation, the court system eventually upheld the original decision to remove the feeding tube (*Schiavo ex rel. Schindler v. Schiavo*, 403 F 3d 1223 (11th Cir. 2005)). Terri died in 2005.
56 See the English Court of Appeal decision in *Re J (a minor) (wardship: medical treatment)* [1991] Fam 33 at 46, *per* Lord Donaldson of Lymington MR and 55, *per* Taylor LJ (that J, a very premature baby with perinatal brain damage, should not be resuscitated by mechanical ventilator, an invasive procedure, in the event of convulsions requiring resuscitation).
57 *Re J (a minor) (wardship: medical treatment)* [1991] Fam 33 at 52, *per* Balcombe LJ.

It is also relevant to mention the MCA[58] which requires the decision-maker to ensure on behalf of a person who is mentally incapacitated that the act is done or the decision is made in the person's best interests. Where the decision relates to whether life-sustaining treatment is in the best interests of the patient, the decision-maker must not be motivated by a desire to bring about the patient's death.[59] We will examine two major English cases relating to a patient in a persistent vegetative state and conjoined twins.

10.4.2.1 PVS patients

In the English case of *Airedale NHS Trust v Bland*,[60] as mentioned above, the patient was in a persistent vegetative state and in coma for three years. He was kept alive by means of artificial hydration and nutrition that was administered through a nasogastric tube. According to his doctors, he would maintain his state for several years if the treatment he was receiving were to be continued. The NHS Trust sought a declaration from the courts on future medical care. The House of Lords held that the doctors were authorised to withdraw the tube.

First, it regarded the principle of sanctity of life as not absolute. Further, existence in a persistent vegetative state with no prospect of recovery is not a benefit. In fact, Lord Goff stated that the doctor was not under a duty to prolong the life of a patient under his care regardless of circumstances.[61] In the present case, as the treatment would be futile, the termination of artificial feeding through the tubes and antibiotics would be justified.[62] Here, the question was not whether it was in the best interests of the patient that he should die but rather "whether it is in the best interests of the patient that his life should be prolonged by the continuance of this form of medical treatment or care".[63] To this question, the House of Lords responded with a negative answer where the doctors' decision to withdraw the tube was supported by a responsible body of medical opinion. Lord Goff also noted that Bland, who was not capable of any feeling, would not suffer any pain or distress from the discontinuance of the artificial feeding.[64]

A distinction was drawn between acts and omissions. The withdrawal of artificial hydration and nutrition[65] was regarded as an omission to provide care even though the withdrawal would in practice require someone to remove the nasogastric tube; it was stated that "discontinuation of life support is, for present purposes, no different from not initiating life

---

58 (Cap 177A, 2010 Rev Ed).
59 Section 6(5).
60 [1993] AC 789. See also Finnis (1993).
61 [1993] AC 789 at 865.
62 [1993] AC 789 at 869.
63 [1993] AC 789 at 868.
64 [1993] AC 789 at 870; applied in *Frenchay Healthcare National Health Service Trust v S* [1994] 1 WLR 601 (not in patient's best interests to permit the gastronomy tube that became dislodged to be reinserted as there was no hope of recovery and patient did not have "conscious being" at all).
65 See Kennedy & Grubb (1993).

220 End of life

support in the first place".[66] Lord Goff opined that doing an act actively to bring a patient's life to an end is

> to cross the Rubicon which runs between on the one hand the care of the living patient and on the other hand euthanasia – actively causing his death to avoid or to end his suffering. Euthanasia is not lawful at common law.[67]

Lord Browne-Wilkinson in *Bland* expressed, however, some difficulties with the act-omission distinction[68]:

> Finally, the conclusion I have reached will appear to some to be almost irrational. How can it be lawful to allow a patient to die slowly, though painlessly, over a period of weeks from lack of food but unlawful to produce his immediate death by a lethal injection, thereby saving his family from yet another ordeal to add to the tragedy that has already.

Keown (1997, at p. 501) disagrees with the act-omission distinction and gave an example to show that *Bland* would result in a "radical inconsistency":

> Imagine the following scenario. X is a patient in PVS who is free of any suffering and who has made no request to be killed. X's doctor decides that, because X's life is worthless, he would be better off dead, and stops his tube-feeding with intent to kill. In the next bed is Y, a patient dying in agony who, after serious reflection, begs the doctor to kill him by lethal injection. The doctor, fearful of prosecution, refuses. A third patient, A, moved by Y's predicament, draws a pistol, holds it to the doctor's head and threatens "If you don't inject Y, I will shoot you dead". The doctor, to save his own life, administers a lethal drug to Y. The doctor's killing of X is lawful; his killing of Y is murder.[69]

On the question of benefit to a PVS patient and his interests, it was not clear from the case why Bland's lack of awareness or feeling would necessarily prevent him from continuing to receive benefit via the feeding tube. Following the approach under the existing MCA framework, it is arguable that the determination of best interests should not be made by sole reference to medical opinion under the *Bolam* test but should be assessed in a more holistic manner by the judges themselves.[70] Further, with regard to determining the patient's best interests, Lord Goff referred to[71]:

---

66 [1993] AC 789 at 866. Switching off or disconnection of a ventilator has also been regarded as a withdrawal of treatment and the original disease suffered by the patient was the cause of death not the withdrawal: *Auckland Area Health Board v Attorney General* [1993] 1 NZLR 235 at 254, *per* Thomas J.
67 [1993] AC 789 at 865.
68 1993] AC 789 at 885.
69 Note that duress is not a defence to murder at common law: see *Abbott v R* [1976] 3 All ER 140 (PC), at 145, *per* Lord Salmon ("From time immemorial it has been accepted by the common law of England that duress is no defence to murder, certainly not to murder in the first degree").
70 See *Goh Guan Sin (by her litigation representative Chiam Yu Zhu) v Yeo Tseng Tsai and another* [2019] SGHC 274 (where the judge did not apply the "best interests" test in MCA to the doctor's decision to proceed with a medical procedure for a mentally incapacitated patient that resulted in her persistent vegetative state).
71 [1993] AC 789 at 867.

the established rule that a doctor may, when caring for a patient who is, for example, dying of cancer, lawfully administer painkilling drugs despite the fact that he knows that an incidental effect of that application will be to abbreviate the patient's life. Such a decision may properly be made as part of the care of the living patient, in his best interests; and, on this basis, the treatment will be lawful.

This appears to relate to the doctrine of double effect (Chapter 2). Under the doctrine, doctors may administer treatment to alleviate patient's suffering even if there is an obvious risk of a side effect that renders death likely or even certain.[72] In this regard, the ECEG (2016) remind the doctor that he "must not commit or participate in any act where [the doctor's] primary intention is to hasten or bring about death". At the same time, the doctor has to "offer good palliative care where necessary to minimise suffering in the course of life-limiting illnesses".

10.4.2.2 Conjoined twins

Moving on to the case of conjoined twins, it is noted from the outset that the majority of conjoined twins are stillborn. Even where such twins are born alive, their prospects are usually dim (Sheldon and Wilkinson 1997, at p. 149). The decision - whether to separate the twins[73] to enhance their life-prospects or enable independent living when it is likely to result in the death of one or both of them - can be extremely difficult and heartbreaking at times. Should one twin sacrifice his or her life so that the other might enjoy better life-prospects? Who is to decide who lives or dies? The parents, family members and/or doctors? When such matters are brought to the courts for a decision, judges are compelled to find a legal answer to what is essentially a moral dilemma involving philosophical and religious/spiritual dimensions (Choo 2001).

In *re A (Children) (Conjoined Twins: Surgical Separation)*,[74] the conjoined twins J and M were joined at the pelvis. J sustained M's life by circulating oxygenated blood to a common artery. The doctors wanted to undertake an operation to separate the twins. If there were no operation, both J and M would die within a few months. However, if the operation were carried out, M will die within minutes but J would enjoy a reasonable prospect of survival. The parents were devout Catholics and did not wish to give consent to the operation. The matter was brought before the English Court of Appeal which decided to allow the operation to proceed[75] based on three main reasons.

---

72 *R v Cox* (1992) 12 BMLR 38 at 41.
73 It has been reported that Singapore hospitals have carried out operations to separate conjoined twins in a few cases. It included two successful operations for Nepalese ten-month-old twins Ganga and Jumana in 2001 (Singapore General Hospital) and South Korean four-month-old twins Min Ji Hye and Min Sa Rang in 2009 (Raffles Hospital). Unfortunately, the separation procedure for Iranian adult twins Laleh and Ladan Bijani conducted in 2003 was not successful.
74 [2001] Fam 147.
75 Applied in *State of Queensland v Nolan* [2001] QSC 174 (operation to separate the twins Alyssa and Bethany - who have separate brains but are joined at the head and shared the cranial draining veins

First, whilst the operation would amount to a positive act of surgery and was not merely an omission, there was no intention to kill M though the doctors had foresight of M's accelerated death if the operation were carried out. The primary purpose of the operation was to preserve J's life.

Second, the decision was justified by balancing the interests of the twins. It was acknowledged that there was a conflict of duties to J and M respectively. Whilst the operation would be in J's best interests, it would clearly not be in M's best interest as it would deny her inherent right to life. The Court of Appeal sought to balance the interests of both J and M by considering whether the operation was worthwhile, each twin's condition and the relative advantages and disadvantages for each twin from the treatment, rather than to compare the quality of life for each twin as the latter approach would violate the principle based on sanctity of life (and also the equality in the value of life).[76] Yet, it is noted that the question of the worth of the life to be saved or prolonged is inextricably bound up with the issue of the worthwhileness of the treatment in a life-death situation (Phang 2001, at pp. 91-92).

In such a scenario, the "least detrimental alternative" according to the English Court of Appeal was to allow J the advantage of enjoying a normal life even at the cost of sacrificing M's life. In comparison, though the operation would grant M independent bodily integrity upon separation of the twins, that would last only for brief moments. If the operation were not carried out, M's continued life would be one of pain and discomfort and that would be to M's disadvantage.

On the comparison between the twin's exercise of their right to live, Ward LJ stated[77]:

> Mary may have a right to life, but she has little right to be alive. She is alive because and only because, to put it bluntly, but none the less accurately, she sucks the lifeblood of Jodie and she sucks the lifeblood out of Jodie. She will survive only so long as Jodie survives. Jodie will not survive long because constitutionally she will not be able to cope. Mary's parasitic living will be the cause of Jodie's ceasing to live. If Jodie E could speak, she would surely protest, "Stop it, Mary, you're killing me." Mary would have no answer to that. Into my scales of fairness and justice between the children goes the fact that nobody but the doctors can help Jodie. Mary is beyond help.

Third, the operation was an act of necessity to avoid inevitable and irreparable evil. Brooke LJ referred[78] to the three requirements in the doctrine of necessity: (i) the act is needed to avoid inevitable and irreparable evil; (ii) no more should be done than is reasonably necessary for the purpose to be achieved; (iii) the evil inflicted must not be disproportionate to the evil avoided. As the interests of J must be preferred to the conflicting interests of M, the three requirements were satisfied in this case. Robert-Walker LJ also agreed with the applica-

---

and blood flow whilst Alyssa's kidney removed waste from bloodstream of both girls – in order to save Alyssa's life though immediate prospect would be Bethany's death).

76 That "every life has an equal inherent value" at 187-188, per Ward LJ; and at 214, per Brookes LJ that in the eyes of the law "Mary's right to life must be accorded equal status with her sister Jodie's right to life".
77 [2001] Fam 147 at 197.
78 [2001] Fam 147 at 240.

tion of defence of necessity. In addition, according to Ward LJ, the doctors should go to J's defence and remove the threat of fatal harm to her from M.[79]

The English court's first argument that the primary objective of the operation was to save J and not to kill M appears related to the doctrine of double effect. Here there are two effects: the good effect from saving J's life and the bad effect of killing M. The doctrine states that the good effects cannot proceed from the bad effects. In this case, it may be argued that it was the killing of M via the operation that would allow J to live. If this argument is accepted, the doctrine cannot be used to justify the decision to proceed with the operation. It might be countered, however, that the killing of M is *not* the *means* to save J; rather, it is the operation that caused M to die and J to live (Sheldon and Wilkinson 1997, at p. 160). Interpreted in this narrow sense, this requirement concerning the relationship between the bad and good effects may be satisfied.

Annas (1987, at p. 28) argued for the application of the double effect doctrine in a limited scenario where

> twin A threatens twin B merely because its body requires more support than their shared hearts can provide. Then one is relieving the pressure on twin B's heart by tying off the carotid artery, and twin A's death becomes an inevitable but unintended result of a good act.

Analogising to the present case, and noting Ward LJ's dictum that M was "sucking the lifeblood" of and "parasitic" on J, it may be argued that the operation would constitute a "good act" in relieving pressure on J's part in sustaining M's life even if it is inevitable that M would die.

The conjoined twins case gives rise to the knotty jurisprudential and ethical issue as to whether killing a person to save another life or lives may be justified. In the oft-discussed case of *R v Dudley and* Stephens,[80] the accused persons who killed and ate a cabin boy whilst stranded out at sea could not avail themselves of the defence of necessity even though eating the boy saved their lives. The present case might be distinguished from *Dudley* in that it is the doctors who are deciding whether to proceed with an operation which would likely kill M and to save J's life as opposed to one making a decision borne out of self-preservation. Further, there is no good reason to choose to kill the boy in *Dudley* as opposed to the other adults, unlike the circumstances in the present case where it is more obvious which twin should die or live. From the ethical perspective, using the analogy of an organ donation, though Utilitarianism *per se* would seem to favour killing a person (for his organs) in order to save other people (who need the organs) if it maximises overall welfare (a net saving of lives), Utilitarians would likely be cautious against extending this principle lest it imply support for organ harvesting (Sheldon and Wilkinson 1997, at p. 155). Yet, an egalitarian rights-based approach would inevitably lead to a clash of rights between M and J without any resolution unless a clear distinction is made between the rights of each twin with reference to the circumstances (*eg*, Ward LJ's judgement).

---

79 [2001] Fam 147 at 204.
80 (1884) 14 QBD 273.

> **Box 10.2 – The conjoined conundrum**
>
> Does the conjoined twins case give rise to a true ethical dilemma where there are no justifiable or satisfactory answers?

10.5 Physician-assisted euthanasia

The issue of euthanasia tends to provoke or evoke strong emotions even disgust at times from both sides of the divide. Media reports of high-profile cases – for example, of Dr Jack Kevorkian who had used a machine loaded with lethal medication that was administered to Janet Adkin, a schoolteacher suffering from Alzheimer's disease – attract significant attention. Though acquitted of charges several times, he was finally convicted of second-degree murder in 1999.

It is useful from the outset to differentiate the forms of euthanasia. The most controversial is voluntary euthanasia which takes place upon the patient's request and the physician executes the final act. Where the final act is executed by the patient with the assistance of a physician, it is known as physician-assisted suicide. In some cases, the patient may not be physically capable of executing the final act due to disability. Non-voluntary euthanasia occurs when the patient does not have the capacity to request or consent to euthanasia or did not express his wish when he had capacity. Involuntary euthanasia is performed on a person who has expressed that he does not want to die or he is not asked for his decision. Most people would frown on involuntary euthanasia. There is also a distinction between euthanasia that is described as active (based on a positive act) or passive (an omission such as withdrawing life support).

10.5.1 The Singapore position

Euthanasia including physician-assisted suicide is not allowed in Singapore. The object of the AMD Act was distinguished from euthanasia. Section 17 of the AMD Act explicitly states that nothing in the statute authorises any act that causes or accelerates death as distinct from that which permits the dying process to take its natural course. The Act also states that nothing in the statute condones, authorises or approves the abetment of suicide, mercy killing or euthanasia.

The offence of attempted suicide – formerly under section 309 of the Penal Code[81] – has been repealed in Singapore.[82] The Penal Code Review Committee (2018) stated "there is a growing recognition that treatment, not prosecution" is the appropriate response for such cases, and that repealing section 309 would allow these individuals to be "more appropriately managed by the healthcare and social assistance systems".[83] Abetting someone to

---

81 Section 309: Whoever attempts to commit suicide, and does any act towards the commission of such offence, shall be punished with imprisonment for a term which may extend to one year, or with fine, or with both [repealed].
82 Act 15 of 2019.
83 Para 13.

commit suicide remains an offence.[84] A doctor is not absolved from criminal liability for physician-assisted suicide under the General Exceptions (namely section 81[85] and 88[86] Penal Code based on "good faith") if he had assisted in the suicide of the patient intending the death of the latter. In such cases, the doctor may have intended to do so in order to relieve the patient's suffering but that would still amount to an intention to terminate the patient's life as a *means* to the end (of relieving suffering) (Keown 2012, at p. 29).

Notwithstanding the current legal position against euthanasia, various arguments based on ethics and public policy have been made for and against the legalisation of euthanasia.[87] Toh and Yeo (2010) have taken the position that if palliative care cannot meet the patient's physical, mental or emotional needs, physician-assisted suicide should be legalised for terminally ill patients facing imminent death and suffering unbearably. This position was argued for on the grounds of autonomy, quality of life and consistency with AMD Act amongst others. On the other hand, Tan (2017) has argued for the criminalisation of euthanasia based on the sanctity of life as well as the impact on the role of the medical profession. These considerations will be further discussed below.

10.5.2 Other jurisdictions

Physician-assisted suicide is legal in the Netherlands, Luxembourg, Belgium, Switzerland, Colombia, Canada, parts of Australia[88] and several states in the United States including the states of Oregon, Washington and Montana. In Oregon, the Death with Dignity Act[89] allows physicians to prescribe lethal drugs to a patient who requests for them under stringent conditions (but prohibits lethal injection, mercy killing or active euthanasia).

In *re Quinlan*,[90] the Supreme Court of New Jersey granted a comatose patient in persistent vegetative state the right to discontinue life support if there was no prospect of her recovering from her condition based on the substituted judgement approach. In *Nancy Beth*

---

84 Section 306: If any person attempts or commits suicide, whoever abets the commission of such attempted suicide or suicide shall be punished with imprisonment for a term which may extend to ten years, and shall also be liable to fine.
85 Section 81: Nothing is an offence merely by reason of its being done with the knowledge that it is likely to cause harm, if it be done in good faith for the purpose of preventing or avoiding other harm to person or property.
86 Section 88: Nothing, which is not intended to cause death, is an offence by reason of any harm which it may cause, or be intended by the doer to cause, or be known by the doer to be likely to cause, to any person for whose benefit it is done in good faith, and who has given a consent, whether express or implied, to suffer that harm, or to take the risk of that harm.
87 See Menon (2013).
88 States of Victoria and Western Australia.
89 The statute has recently been amended by Senate Bill 579 passed by the 2019 Oregon legislative assembly: https://www.oregon.gov/oha/PH/PROVIDERPARTNERRESOURCES/EVALUATIONRESEARCH/DEATHWITHDIGNITYACT/Documents/statute.pdf.
90 70 NJ 10, 355, A. 2d 647 at 663 (1976) (that patient would choose to withdraw life support if she were miraculously lucid for an interval and perceptive of her irreversible condition).

226   End of life

Cruzan,[91] Cruzan was in a persistent vegetative state due to a car accident and was not competent to refuse life-sustaining treatment. The guardian sought to discontinue artificial nutrition and hydration. The United States Supreme Court held that the state of Missouri has the right to require clear and convincing evidence as to the patient's prior expressed wishes to be allowed to die. The evidence that Cruzan had told her housemate a year before the accident that she did not want to live should she face life as a "vegetable" was not sufficiently clear and convincing; and there was no reference to any withdrawal of medical treatment or artificial nutrition and hydration.[92] Finally, the US Supreme Court opined that the state of Missouri was not required to accept the substituted judgement of close family members where there was no proof that their views would reflect that of the patient.

Arguably, both *Quinlan* and *Cruzan* impliedly recognised a right to die. Yet it may be within constitutional parameters for a state to prohibit physician-assisted euthanasia. In *Washington v Glucksberg*,[93] the US Supreme Court held that the statute applicable in the state of Washington that prohibited physician-assisted suicide was not unconstitutional. The prohibition was rationally related to the State's legitimate governmental interests (which included the preservation of human life, preventing suicide and identifying, studying and treating its causes, maintaining the integrity and ethics of the medical profession, protecting vulnerable groups from the risks of coercion and undue influence in respect of physician-assisted suicide, and the concern with the slippery slope to voluntary euthanasia).[94] The Supreme Court also distinguished assisted suicide from the withdrawal of life-sustaining treatment in *Cruzan*.[95] In *Vacco v Quill*,[96] the US Supreme Court did not consider New York State's prohibition of assisted suicide to be contrary to the Equal Protection clause in the US Constitution. The state's prohibition against assisted suicide and permitting withdrawal of life-sustaining treatment respectively do not differentiate between persons. The Supreme Court also stated that assisted suicide and withdrawal of life-sustaining treatment are rationally distinct and consistent with principles of causation and intent.[97]

In *Carter v Canada*,[98] the Supreme Court of Canada decided in 2015 that the prohibition of assisted suicide in the Criminal Code[99] unjustifiably infringed upon section 7 of the Canadian Charter of Rights and Freedoms (on the right to life, liberty and security of the person). The *Carter* decision in effect allowed physician-assisted death for a competent adult person who (i) clearly consents to the termination of life and (ii) has a grievous and irremediable medical condition (including an illness, disease or disability) that causes enduring suffering that is

---

91   *Cruzan v Director, Missouri Department of Health* 110 S Ct 2841 (1990).
92   110 S Ct. 2841 (1990) at [7].
93   521 US 702; 117 S Ct 2258 (1997).
94   117 S Ct 2258 at 2272-2274 (1997).
95   117 S Ct 2258 at 2270 (1997).
96   521 US 793 (1997); 117 S Ct 2293 (1997).
97   117 S Ct 2293 at 2298 (1997).
98   2015 SCC 5.
99   Section 241(b) of the Criminal Code R.S.C. 1985, c. C-46 states that everyone who aids or abets a person in committing suicide commits an indictable offence. Section 14 states that no person may consent to death being inflicted on them.

intolerable to the individual in the circumstances of his or her condition. The Supreme Court was of the view that the erstwhile prohibition had the effect of forcing some individuals to take their own lives prematurely, for fear that they would be incapable of doing so when they reached the point where suffering was intolerable, and denied an individual faced with a grievous and irremediable medical condition the right to make decisions concerning their bodily integrity and medical care and may therefore leave them to endure intolerable suffering. The Parliament of Canada later passed federal legislation in June 2016 that allowed eligible Canadian adults to request medical assistance in dying.[100] Amendments are being proposed to the federal legislation at the time of writing.[101]

In the Netherlands, the Dutch Supreme Court held in a 1984 case[102] that the physician who assisted in the suicide could raise the defence of necessity. The Termination of Life on Request and Assisted Suicide (Review Procedures) Act[103] which took effect in 2002 stipulates due care criteria for the physician who assists in the patient's suicide. Article 2 states that in order to establish "due care", the physician must:

(a) be satisfied that the patient has made a voluntary and carefully considered request;
(b) be satisfied that the patient's suffering was unbearable, and that there was no prospect of improvement;
(c) have informed the patient about his situation and his prospects;
(d) have come to the conclusion, together with the patient, that there is no reasonable alternative in the light of the patient's situation;
(e) have consulted at least one other, independent physician, who must have seen the patient and given a written opinion on the due care criteria referred to in a. to d. above; and
(f) have terminated the patient's life or provided assistance with suicide with due medical care and attention.

In the UK, challenges have been made against section 2 of the UK Suicide Act which prohibits assisted dying. The House of Lords decision in *R (Pretty) v Director of Public Prosecutions*[104] denied a "right to die" based on the European Convention of Human Rights (ECHR). However, the European Court in Strasbourg in *Pretty v United Kingdom*[105] later recognised the right to die under article 8 of the European Convention of Human Rights. It opined however, that, due

---

100 See "An Act to amend the Criminal Code and to make related amendments to other Acts (medical assistance in dying)" SC 2016 c 3, at https://laws-lois.justice.gc.ca/eng/AnnualStatutes/2016_3/FullText.html (accessed on 1 May 2020).
101 The bill was proposed on 24 February 2020 by the Minister of Justice and Attorney-General of Canada: see https://www.justice.gc.ca/eng/csj-sjc/pl/ad-am/index.html. The website states that the bill seeks to amend the *Criminal Code* to allow medical assistance in dying for eligible persons who wish to "pursue a medically assisted death, whether their natural death is reasonably foreseeable or not" to "support greater autonomy and freedom of choice for eligible persons, and provide safeguards to protect those who may be vulnerable".
102 *Schoonheim*, Netherlands Jurisprudentie 1985, no 106.
103 See https://www.ieb-eib.org/ancien-site/pdf/loi-euthanasie-pays-bas-en-eng.pdf.
104 [2002] 1 AC 800.
105 [2002] 35 EHRR 1; see also subsequent cases of *Haas v Switzerland* (2011) 53 EHRR 33, para 51, *Koch v Germany* (2013) 56 EHRR 6, paras 46 and 51, and *Gross v Switzerland* (2014) 58 EHRR 7, para 60

228   End of life

to the diversity of views, the European states enjoy a wide margin of appreciation concerning this issue. It also ruled that the interference with the right under the prohibition on assisted suicide in the UK Suicide Act was justified in order to protect the rights of vulnerable people.

Another legal challenge arose in *R (Purdy) v DPP*.[106] Purdy, who was suffering from multiple sclerosis, wanted to commit suicide in Switzerland and her husband to assist her. She argued that the law was not sufficiently clear as to the circumstances in which a prosecution for assisted suicide under the Assisted Suicide Act 1961 would be brought. The House of Lords accepted the European court's ruling in *Pretty* concerning the right to die under Article 8 of ECHR, and held that the DPP should provide clear guidance on whether the husband would be prosecuted for assisted suicide. The DPP must also provide guidelines as to the facts and circumstances to be taken into account in such cases whether it would be appropriate to prosecute for assisted suicide, which the DPP did, following the House of Lords' decision.

In the subsequent Supreme Court decision in *R (Nicklinson) v Ministry of Justice*,[107] it was recognised that, based on the wide margin of appreciation given to member states in *Pretty*, the UK courts are entitled to make their own decisions on the UK statute's compatibility with ECHR. In this regard, the majority decided that Parliament would be better placed to decide on whether section 2 of the UK Suicide Act was incompatible with the European Convention of Human Rights though the courts would have the constitutional authority to declare incompatibility if Parliament does not act on it.[108] Overall, the judgement was "sympathetic towards the legalisation of assisted dying" (Wicks 2015, at p. 145) without explicitly stating so. The applicants complained to the European Court of Human Rights[109] about the *Nicklinson* decision to no avail. At that time, proposals were made by the Commission for Assisted Dying for legislative reforms and a private members' bill ("Assisted Dying" bill) was tabled in the UK Parliament though it eventually failed at the second reading debate in 2015.

10.5.3 Specific Issues on euthanasia

The debate on euthanasia has generated a whole gamut of difficult ethical, legal and public policy issues. The following sets out some salient arguments on both sides of the divide and their limits as well as safeguards should the legalisation route be pursued.

10.5.3.1 Killing

One core issue is whether the objections against killing of a person will apply equally to voluntary euthanasia. Singer (1993, at pp. 194-196) examined four arguments against killing a person: (a) classical utilitarianism (that the potential victim would fear his own death); (b)

(which allowed for "a right to decide how and when to die, and in particular the right to avoid a distressing and undignified end to life" cited in *Pretty v UK* (2002) 35 EHRR 1.
106 [2010] 1 AC 345.
107 [2014] 3 WLR 200.
108 Two judges (Lady Hale and Lord Kerr) took the view that the statutory provision prohibiting assisted dying is a disproportionate interference with Article 8 of ECHR (on the right to respect for private life) since it goes beyond what is necessary to achieve its stated aim of protecting the vulnerable and was therefore incompatible with Article 8.
109 Applications nos 2478/15 and 1787/15.

preference utilitarianism (that killing thwarts a victim's desire to continue living); (c) theory of rights (that one's desire to continue living corresponds with his right to life); and (d) respect for the autonomous choice of a rational agent. He contended that the four objections to killing are not applicable to voluntary euthanasia where the person in question who is mentally capable wants to die. It may be countered that there are limits to respect for autonomy and that what amounts to preferences and rational judgement is a matter for debate.

10.5.3.2 The act-omission distinction

Opponents of physician-assisted suicide argue that there is a distinction between AMD in which the doctors, in withdrawing extra-ordinary life sustaining treatment, allow death to take its natural course and physician-assisted suicide when the physician assists in causing death. In *Airedale NHS Trust v Bland*,[110] the House of Lords held that it was lawful for the doctors to discontinue life-sustaining treatment to a PVS patient based on the ground that the cessation of treatment amounted to an omission[111] instead of an active act. As mentioned above, Lord Goff draws a distinction between a case of a doctor withholding treatment which might prolong a patient's life and that of administering a lethal drug to bring the patient's life to an end even if it is prompted by the humanitarian desire to end the latter's suffering.[112] Lord Browne-Wilkinson analysed the conduct of the doctors as an omission to feed and the removal of the nasogastric tube is merely an incident of that omission.[113] However, such a distinction has also been described as illogical[114] or artificial in ethical terms.[115]

10.5.3.3 Sanctity and quality of life and patient autonomy

Keown (1997) noted that the traditional doctrine of the sanctity of life holds that human life is created in the image of God and therefore, possessed an intrinsic dignity. The notion of sanctity of life is that "one ought never intentionally to kill an innocent human being" and that the "right to life" is essentially a right not to be intentionally killed.[116] On the other hand, the argument based on "Quality of life" (with a capital "Q") takes the view that where the life of certain patients falls below a certain threshold (a measure of the *worthwhileness of life*), it is right to terminate the life.[117] Alternatively, assessments of "quality of life" (with a small "q") can be used to determine the *worthwhileness of a treatment* for a patient based on the risks and benefits of the treatment which is less morally objectionable than to assess the worth of a patient's life.

Proponents of physician-assisted euthanasia argue that terminally ill patients should have the right to choose death when the quality of life has deteriorated below a minimum threshold (in physical, mental, emotional and spiritual terms). This is often associated with the

---

110 [1993] AC 789.
111 [1993] AC 789 at 866, *per* Lord Goff.
112 [1993] AC 789 at 865.
113 [1993] AC 789 at 882.
114 [1993] AC 789 at 875, *per* Lord Lowry.
115 [1993] AC 789 at 887, *per* Lord Mustill.
116 At 482–483.
117 Keown (1997, at p. 486).

notion of a dignified death. van Zyl (2000, at p. 183) argued that allowing a person to die in such circumstances can be an act of "responsible benevolence" (provided it is based on scientific knowledge, expertise and practical wisdom in understanding the patient's experiences) underpinned by the "virtue of respectfulness" (in order to advance the patient's interests by taking into account his life's plan, values and beliefs).

Euthanasia allows for the alleviation of unbearable suffering for certain vulnerable people. The value of the life to the person subject to unbearable suffering cannot be assessed without taking account of the intense physical and mental suffering to be borne by the person. The instrumental value of life holds that life is a means to things that make life worth living. Where a person is deprived of the enjoyment or appreciation of those things due to severe disability, life to that person may not be worth living.

10.5.3.4 Plurality of religious views

Toh and Yeo (2010) argued that as there is no consensus amongst the main religions in Singapore (Christianity, Islam, Buddhism and Hinduism) on whether euthanasia is wrong, and given the pluralistic nature of Singapore society, the people should have the right to decide about end-of-life matters including euthanasia.

10.5.3.5 Uncertainties or miracles of life

Patients in a coma or suffering from terminal illnesses have been known to recover though the doctors regarded treatment as futile. Even if euthanasia is legalised, caution should be exercised before proceeding with euthanasia in a particular case as the process is irreversible. It is argued that stringent medical checks and certification by the doctors that the illness is terminal, the suffering is unbearable, there are no alternatives to relieve the patient's suffering and that the patient's decision is voluntary and informed would be necessary.

10.5.3.6 Slippery slope arguments and unintended effects of legalising euthanasia

If euthanasia were to be allowed for certain categories of persons such as the terminally ill, will it inevitably be extended to other categories such as those with disabilities or who suffer psychic pain? Will it also lead to a "weakening of respect for the sanctity of life" and affect the worthwhileness of certain treatments for such categories of persons (Tan 2017)?

When the State allows euthanasia for certain vulnerable people, it may send a signal that the lives of such vulnerable people are not worth living. Moreover, allowing euthanasia could have the effect albeit unintended that the elderly and vulnerable may choose euthanasia in order that they do not burden their family members and loved ones. Even if euthanasia were allowed, it is important to ensure that the patient in question has clearly made a voluntary and informed decision to die as opposed to acting under depression, undue pressure or influence.

10.5.3.7 Impact on medical profession and its role

Another argument is that the doctors' relationship with patients would change considerably if doctors are allowed, instead of treatment, to offer death as an option to the patients. Such an option would run counter to the Hippocratic Oath to use treatment to help the sick according to my ability and judgment, but never with a view to injury and wrongdoing. Neither will I administer a poison to anybody when asked to do so, nor will I suggest such a course.

Should euthanasia be legalised, the doctor's judgement in such end-of-life decisions would be crucial. Will medical doctors be able to discern that the patient had freely and voluntarily made the request to terminate his life (Keown 2012, at p. 73) or that the suffering was unbearable? To what extent would doctors make their own assessments of the merits of a patient's request? Would this lead to medical assessments to terminate the patient's life even when patient is not capable of making a request (Keown 2012, at p. 77)? There is a related concern that allowing euthanasia would also lead to changes in attitudes towards palliative care. Instead of exploring the benefits of palliative care, is there a danger that doctors would incline towards proposing euthanasia for their patients?

10.6 Conclusion

End-of-life matters are indeed complex, multi-faceted and interdisciplinary. They are not only intimately connected with the work of medical and legal experts but also intersect with the socioeconomic, cultural, psychological and religious/spiritual dimensions. Insofar as the law is concerned, death is determined based on either cardiac death according to the practice of the medical profession or brain death based on certain statutory criteria for purposes such as death certification and organ transplants upon death. At law, medical doctors and family members have to respect the patient's autonomous choice on treatment to the extent he is mentally capable of making the decision even if the decision may lead to the patient's death. Where the patient is mentally incapable (*eg*, the cases of PVS patients and conjoined twins), the decision whether to administer or withdraw treatment must be made in his best interests taking into account the worthwhileness of treatment, his personal preferences and values, the sanctity of life and quality of life assessments. Singaporeans are entitled to make an advance directive on the withdrawal of extra-ordinary life-sustaining treatment should they encounter a terminal illness. This autonomy to make such a directive has been contrasted with the purported right to choose physician-assisted euthanasia which is currently denied in Singapore. Globally, we have also seen pro-euthanasia developments in jurisdictions such as Canada and Netherlands in the new millennium. In contemplating the direction of the society and the law on this vexed issue, recourse may be made to the ethical debates on, amongst others, autonomy and its limits, the potential effects on the medical profession, the emphasis on palliative care and the slippery slope arguments should euthanasia be legalised.

References

Ad Hoc Committee of the Harvard Law Medical School to Examine the Definition of Death (1968). "A Definition of Irreversible Coma" 205 *Journal of the American Medical Association* 337-340.
Annas, G.J. (1987). "Siamese Twins: Killing One to Save the Other" 17 *Hastings Center Report* 27.
Chan, J.W.T. (2010). "Significant Bioethical Issues at the End of Life" 22 *SAcLJ* 948.
Choo, H.T. (2001). "The 14th Singapore Law Review Lecture: Termination of Non-Viable Life" 13 *SAcLJ* 267.
Lee et al. (2008). *Coroner's Practice in Medical Cases* (Academy Publishing: Singapore).

Devathasan, G. (1985). "Brain Death: Concept, Controversies and Guidelines" 14(1) *Annals of the Academy of Medicine Singapore* 1-3.

Finnis, J.M. (1993) "Bland, Crossing the Rubicon?" 109 *LQR* 329.

Hodge, S.D. (2019). "Wrongful Prolongation of Life – A Cause of Action That May Have Finally Moved Into the Mainstream" 37 *Quinnipiac Law Review* 167.

Institute of Policy Studies (IPS) (2019) (Yvonne Arivalagan and Christopher Gee). *Leaving Well: End-of-Life Policies in Singapore*, July at https://lkyspp.nus.edu.sg/docs/default-source/ips/ips-exchange-series_no-13_leaving-well-end-of-life-polices-in-singapore_web.pdf.

Kaan, T. (1992). "The End of Life: Defining Death in Singapore" 4 *SAcLJ* 310.

Kaan, T. (2011). "Shifting Landscapes: Law and the end of life in Singapore" in Chan, W.C. (ed) *Singapore's Ageing Population: Managing Healthcare and End-of-life Decisions* (Routledge Contemporary Southeast Asia Series: Abingdon), pp. 137-161.

Kennedy, I. & Grubb, A. (1993). "Withdrawal of Artificial Hydration and Nutrition: Incompetent Adult" 1 *Medical Law Review* 359.

Keown, J. (1997). "Restoring Moral and Intellectual Shape to the Law after Bland" 113 *LQR* 481.

Keown, J. (2012). *Euthanasia, Ethics and Public Policy: An Argument Against Legalisation* (Cambridge University Press: Cambridge)

Krishna, L.K.R. & Menon, S. (2014). "Understanding the Practice of Collusion of End of Life Care in Singapore" 2014 *JMED Research* 1-8.

Liu, C.W., Yeo, C., Lu, B.Z. et al. (2019). "Brain Death in Asia: Do Public Views Still Influence Organ Donation in the 21st Century?" 103(4) *Transplantation* 755-763.

Menon, S., Chief Justice of Singapore (2013). "Euthanasia: A Matter of Life or Death?", speech delivered at the *Singapore Medical Association Lecture 2012* (9 March) and published in *SMA News* (March).

National Strategy for Palliative Care (2011). Report coordinated by Lien Centre for Palliative Care, Duke-NUS Graduate Medical School.

Penal Code Review Committee (2018). Report submitted to Ministry of Home Affairs and Minister for Law (August) at https://www.mha.gov.sg/docs/default-source/default-document-library/penal-code-review-committee-report3d9709ea6f13421b92d3ef8af69a4ad0.pdf.

Phang, A. (2001). "Conjoined Twins: The Limits of Reason and the Transcendent Hope – Part Two", 147 *Law & Just – Christian Law Review* 89.

Sheldon, S. & Wilkinson, S.C. (1997). "Conjoined Twins: The Legality and Ethics of Sacrifice" 5 *Medical Law Review* 149.

Singer, P. (1993). *Practical Ethics* (Cambridge University Press: Cambridge).

Tan, S.H. (2017). "The Case against Physician-Assisted Suicide and Voluntary Active Euthanasia" 29 *SAcLJ* 375.

Toh, P.S. & Yeo, S. (2010). "Decriminalising Physician-Assisted Suicide in Singapore" 22 *SAcLJ* 379.

van Zyl, L. (2000). *Death and Compassion: A Virtue-based Approach to Euthanasia* (Ashgate: London).

Wicks, E. (2015). "The Supreme Court Decision in Nicklinson: One Step Forward on Assisted Dying: Two Steps Back on Human Rights" 23(1) *Medical Law Review* 144-156.

11 Human organs, tissues and biological materials

11.1 Introduction

This chapter discusses the legal and ethical issues dealing with human organs, tissues and biological materials. One major concern is the availability of human organs and tissues that may be used to save the lives of people suffering from major ailments. Apart from therapeutic purposes, such organs and tissues may be useful for biomedical research.

Due perhaps to the naturally intimate and intrinsic connections with our own body parts and materials, this topic tends to generate strong visceral responses and raise a whole gamut of difficult questions pertaining to autonomy, justice and rights. As efforts are made to ensure an adequate supply, to what extent should we require explicit consent from donors to remove and use their tissues? In the case of organ transplants, is it appropriate to presume consent on the part of potential donors but allow them to opt out if they so wish? Should we allow commercial trading of organs on an arms-length basis? How should we allocate human tissues and organs to those who need them in a fair and just manner? Do we "own" our organs, tissues and body parts, and if so, what are the implications of such property interests?

In 2002, the Bioethics Advisory Committee had issued a Consultation Paper on "Human Tissue Research" emphasising the rights of donors in requiring, amongst others, consent to the use of their tissues and the confidentiality of tissue information. This paper has contributed to the preparation of the BAC's *Ethical Guidelines for Human Biomedical Research* in 2015 and subsequent legal reforms. We will focus on the specific legal and regulatory frameworks pertaining to the removal, use, storage and donations of human tissues (Human Biomedical Research Act (HBRA)), organ transplants (Human Organ Transplant Act (HOTA)) and donations of human body parts for medical research, education and other purposes (Medical (Therapy, Education and Research) Act (MTERA)). This will be followed by a discussion of the controversial issue of whether we have property interests in human bodies and parts and a brief examination of the ethical and legal considerations relating to bioprinting of human organs and tissues.

11.2 The human tissues regulatory framework

The human tissues regulatory framework is set up under the HBRA[1] and subsidiary legislation. The scope of "human tissue" under this regulatory framework is broad, encompassing

---

1 (No 29 of 2015).

any human biological material[2] but excludes the following: (i) hair shafts, nail plates, naturally excreted bodily fluids and waste products such as saliva, sweat, urine and faeces,[3] and (ii) any other human biological material that is not individually identifiable and has been processed in such a manner that its functional, structural and biological characteristics are substantially manipulated as compared to the time of collection.[4] Human tissues would include cord tissues, cord blood, bone marrow, human skin grafts and human bone chips.

Research institutions are allowed to operate tissue banks that carry out tissue banking activity.[5] The tissue banks would have to submit reports, implement standards, policies and procedures, take appropriate remedial measures, ensure compliance with requirements for the export or removal of human tissues with respect to tissue banking activity under their supervision and control,[6] and abide by specific regulations.[7]

We will examine below the laws and regulations relating to the requirements of consent from living donors, the restrictions on the use and removal of human tissues, donations of human tissues from deceased persons, and the prohibitions against commercial transactions involving human tissues.

11.2.1 Consent requirements

The consent of donors and related parties is vital for the removal and use of human tissues. According to the HBRA, consent from the tissue donor must be given in writing in the presence of a witness after the requisite information[8] has been provided and explained to the tissue donor (or to persons authorised to give consent on the donor's behalf).[9] The information to be provided include the nature of the research or other specific purposes, the reasonably foreseeable risks, renunciation of the donor's rights to the tissue and any intellectual property rights that may be derived from the use of the tissue, whether individually identifiable information obtained from the tissue donor will be used and so on.[10]

---

2 This means any biological material obtained from the human body that consists of, or includes, human cells: section 2.
3 The reason given for the exclusion is that there would be "very little risk to the human donor in the collection of such material": see Parliament Reports, *Human Biomedical Research Bill* (18 August 2015), Vol. 93 (The Minister of State for Health).
4 Section 2 read with Schedule 1.
5 Tissue banking activity is defined as "a structured and an organised activity involving human tissue for the purposes of facilitating current or future research or for public health or epidemiological purposes or any combination of such purposes including any of the following activities: (a) the collection, storage, procurement or importation of human tissue; (b) the supply, provision or export of human tissue.": section 2.
6 Section 35.
7 The Human Biomedical Research (Tissue Banking) Regulations 2019 took effect from 1 November 2019: https://sso.agc.gov.sg/SL/HBRA2015-S702-2019?DocDate=20191021.
8 Section 12.
9 Section 6.
10 The full list of information is contained in section 12(2).

Where the prospective tissue donor is an adult who lacks mental capacity to consent to the removal or use of any human tissue and the removal of human tissue from that adult is primarily for a therapeutic or diagnostic purpose, the appropriate consent must be obtained from the donee or deputy who is authorised to give consent to such removal or use on behalf of the adult.[11] Where there is no authorised donee or deputy, consent is to be obtained from any of the following persons in the following order of priority: the spouse; an adult son or daughter; either parent or a guardian; an adult brother or sister; any other person named by the adult as someone to be consulted on the matter in question or on matters of that kind.[12]

Where the prospective tissue donor is a minor who possesses sufficient understanding and intelligence to enable the minor to understand what is proposed in the procedure, consent must be obtained from both the minor and at least one adult parent or guardian of the minor.[13] If the minor lacks sufficient understanding and intelligence to understand what is proposed in the procedure and the removal of the tissue is primarily for a therapeutic or diagnostic purpose, consent must be obtained from at least one adult parent or guardian of the minor.[14] Where the minor lacks mental capacity and the removal of the tissue is primarily for a therapeutic or diagnostic purpose, consent has to be obtained from a deputy who is authorised to give consent for the removal or use of the tissue on behalf of the minor; or at least one adult parent or guardian of the minor.[15]

A donor of human tissue or any person who is authorised to give consent on the donor's behalf may withdraw the consent to the use of the donor's tissue for research if (i) the tissue is individually identifiable and has not been used for the research; or (ii) the tissue is individually identifiable and has been used for the research but it is practicable to discontinue further use of the tissue for the research.[16] Certain exemptions from the consent requirements are allowed in the regulations.[17]

11.2.2 Restrictions relating to human tissues

There are specific restrictions against the removal of human tissues for research purposes. Removal of human tissue is prohibited unless – [18]

(a) where the tissue is to be removed for a therapeutic or diagnostic purpose but will also be or is likely to be used for research purposes, appropriate consent has been obtained for these research purposes in addition to the consent obtained for the therapeutic or diagnostic purpose; or

---

11 Section 9(1)(a).
12 Section 9(1)(b).
13 Section 10(1)(a).
14 Section 10(1)(b).
15 Section 10(1)(c).
16 Section 14(2).
17 Human Biomedical Research (Requirements for Appropriate Consent – Exemption) Regulations 2019 at https://sso.agc.gov.sg/SL/HBRA2015-S703-2019?DocDate=20191021.
18 Section 37(1).

(b) where the tissue is to be removed for a research purpose, appropriate consent has been obtained for the tissue to be removed from the donor.

Special protection is afforded to more vulnerable groups. Human tissue from any of the following persons cannot be removed unless the removal of the tissue was primarily for a therapeutic or diagnostic purpose:[19]

(a) an adult who lacks mental capacity;
(b) a minor who lacks mental capacity;
(c) a minor who lacks sufficient understanding and intelligence to give consent.

The above requirements may be waived by an institutional review board if the removal of the tissue involves no more than minimal risk to that person, and there are reasonable grounds for believing that the proposed areas of research cannot be carried out without the use of the tissue from the class of persons to which that person belongs.[20] There are also other consent requirements for the storage, use, supply, import of human tissue for the purpose of research.[21]

Compelling a person to donate human tissue by means of coercion or intimidation, or through deception or misrepresentation, is a criminal offence.[22] The confidentiality relating to individually identifiable information of any donor of human tissue is protected though such information may be disclosed in specified circumstances (such as consent given by the donor or his legal representative, a court order, public availability of the information, public interest for disclosure, and other right under the statute or other written law).[23]

11.2.3 Tissue donation from deceased persons

Where the prospective research subject or tissue donor is a deceased person, the appropriate consent (a) for the use of the deceased person's individually identifiable biological material, body or any part of the body or health information; or (b) for the removal or use of human tissue for research from the deceased person, must be obtained from any of the following persons in the order of priority stated: the spouse; an adult son or daughter; either parent or a guardian of the deceased person at the time of the person's death; an adult brother or sister; the administrator or executor of the estate of the deceased person; any other person authorised or under obligation to dispose of the body of the deceased person.[24]

11.2.4 Prohibition of commercial trading of human tissues

Any purported contract or an arrangement under which a person agrees, for valuable consideration to the sale or supply of any human tissue from his or her body or from the body

---

19 Section 37(2).
20 Section 37(3).
21 Section 37(4) to (8).
22 Section 38.
23 Section 39.
24 Section 11(1).

Human organs, tissues, biological materials 237

of another person, whether before or after his or her death or the death of the other person, would be rendered void under the HBRA.[25] Moreover, such a person would be criminally liable.[26] The same would apply to any person who – [27]

(a) gives or offers to give valuable consideration for the sale or supply of, or for an offer to sell or supply, any human tissue from the body of another person other than for the purpose of transplantation to his or her body;
(b) receives valuable consideration for the sale or supply of, or for an offer to sell or supply, any human tissue from the body of another person;
(c) offers to sell or supply any human tissue from the body of another person for valuable consideration;
(d) initiates or negotiates any contract or arrangement for the sale or supply of, or for an offer to sell or supply, any human tissue from the body of another person for valuable consideration other than for the purpose of transplantation to his or her body; or
(e) takes part in the management or control of a body corporate or body unincorporate whose activities consist of or include the initiation or negotiation of any contract or arrangement referred to in paragraph (*d*).

Hence, criminal liability extends to direct contracting parties, initiating or negotiating parties, intermediaries and participants as specified above. However, the following contracts, arrangements and schemes are exempted:[28]

(a) a contract or an arrangement providing only for the reimbursement of any expenses necessarily incurred by a person in relation to the removal of human tissue in accordance with the provisions of any other written law;
(b) any scheme introduced or approved by the Government granting medical benefits or privileges to any human tissue donor and any member of the donor's family or any person nominated by the donor; and
(c) any contract, arrangement or valuable consideration providing only for the defraying or reimbursing, in money or money's worth, of such costs or expenses that may be reasonably incurred by a living person in relation to –
   (i) the removal, transportation, preparation, preservation, quality control or storage of any human tissue;
   (ii) the costs or expenses (including the costs of travel, accommodation, domestic help or child care) or loss of earnings so far as are reasonably or directly attributable to that person supplying any human tissue from his or her body; and
   (iii) any short-term or long-term medical care or insurance protection of that person which is or may reasonably be necessary as a consequence of his or her supplying any human tissue from his or her body.

---

25 Section 32(1).
26 Section 32(2).
27 Section 32(3).
28 Section 32(4).

238 *Human organs, tissues, biological materials*

Advertisements relating to the buying or selling in Singapore of any human tissue or of the right to take any human tissue from the body of a person are prohibited.[29]

11.3 Human Organ Transplant Act

The HOTA[30] was first enacted in 1987 and implemented based on the presumed consent of donors to donate their kidneys when they have died in accidents. Those who do not wish to donate their kidneys may opt out. Such an approach was justified by virtue of the need to save the lives of those who require the donated kidneys. Subsequently, in 2004, an amendment Bill was debated in Parliament.[31] The parliamentary Whip was lifted to allow the members to debate and vote on the Bill based on their religious and ethical beliefs. The scope of the statute was subsequently expanded to cover non-accidental deaths (such as deaths from medical conditions) and other organs (liver, heart, corneas). Separate registers are kept for each organ. Regulations were also put in place with respect to living donor organ transplantation. The previous age limit of 60 years for cadaveric donors has been removed since 2009.

Muslims were initially excluded from the HOTA. This was because, for Muslims, consent must be obtained by *waris* (or next-of-kin) of the intended donor according to a fatwa. However, any Muslim was entitled to opt in if he or she so desired. The MKAC (Muslim Kidney Action Committee) encouraged Muslims to opt in. Those Muslims who decided to opt in would qualify for the benefits under the HOTA (such as the right to receive organ donation and subsidised treatment). In 2008, the Fatwa Committee of MUIS (which is the acronym for the Islamic Religious Council of Singapore) accepted the position that Muslims may be included under the HOTA. Based on the 2008 fatwa, there is presumed consent on the part of the *waris*.[32]

To enhance public education on the HOTA especially the opt-out and opt-in system, a notification letter would be sent to all citizens and permanent residents who are about to turn 21 years old, explaining the requirements and implications of the HOTA. Publicity campaigns have begun since 2008 to raise public awareness and understanding about organ donation. Teams comprising senior clinicians, medical social workers, nurses and transplant coordinators sought to engage family members of donors during the organ donation process.[33]

We will first discuss the HOTA covering the regulations concerning the donations of human organs from cadavers, living donor transplants, and the prohibitions against organ trading, followed by the voluntary pledge of donations for medical education and research under the MTERA.

---

29 Section 33.
30 (Cap 131A, Rev Ed 2012).
31 Singapore Parliament Reports, Human Organ Transplant (Amendment) Bill (5 Jan 2004), Vol 77.
32 Singapore Parliament Reports, Human Organ Transplant (Amendment) Bill, (21 January 2008), Vol 84 (Minister for Health).
33 Singapore Parliament Reports, "Public Education on Organ Donation under Human Organ Transplant Act" (14 April 2014), Vol. 91.

11.3.1 Organ removal from donors upon death for transplant

The removal of organs from the body of a person who has died in the hospital for the purpose of organ transplantation must be authorised by a designated officer of the hospital.[34] The unauthorised removal of organs from the body of a deceased person is a punishable offence. A citizen or a permanent resident of Singapore of 21 years and above may register his objection[35] with the Director of Medical Services to the removal of the organ from his body after his death.[36]

For persons whom the designated officer has reason to believe was mentally disordered, the removal of organ cannot be authorised unless the consent of the parent or guardian to such removal is obtained.[37] The authority of the designated officer for the removal of organs is also subject to the Coroner's consent to the removal.[38] Further, only a medical practitioner in a hospital has the authority to remove and to transplant an organ.[39]

Questions have been raised as to when a donor is considered dead so that his organ may be removed for the purpose of transplant to another person; and whether there are sufficient safeguards to ensure that doctors do not prematurely diagnose brain death. First, the patient's death must be certified by two doctors based on statutory clinical criteria. After brain death has been certified, the patient's status as an organ donor would have to be verified by the Organ Donor Registry. The donation and transplant can only be carried out upon death if the patient had not objected to organ donation previously. The transplant coordinator from the National Organ Transplant Unit and doctor in-charge would communicate with the family members about the patient's decision to be an organ donor. It has been noted that the process of removal of the organ is "extremely time-sensitive"; beyond a certain time frame (within 24 hours after the certification of brain death), the organs may no longer be suitable for transplantation.[40]

With respect to the selection of proposed recipients of any organ removed, a person who has not registered any objection with the Director to the removal of the organ shall have priority over a person who has registered such objection.[41] A person may withdraw his objection.[42] The person who has withdrawn such objection for at least two years[43] shall have the same priority as a person who has not registered any such objection. The criteria for the selection and prioritisation of recipients have been reported in parliamentary reports as follows: (i) the extent of tissue matching; (ii) those who opted out enjoyed lower priority than those who did not opt out; and (iii) the length of time the patients had been on the waiting list.

---

34 Section 5.
35 See section 9.
36 Section 5(2).
37 Section 5(2)(e).
38 Section 6(1).
39 Section 7.
40 Singapore Parliament Reports, "Number of Successful Organ Transplants Resulting from Human Organ Transplant Act" (13 May 2013), Vol. 90 (Minister for Health).
41 Section 12(a).
42 Section 11.
43 Section 12(b) refers to the period of two years from the date of receipt of the withdrawal by the Director provided he has not registered again any such objection since that date.

> **Box 11.1 – The HOTA and fairness**
>
> Do you agree with the opt-out system under the HOTA? And do you find the priority scheme for organ recipients to be fair and reasonable?

11.3.2 Donation of organs by living persons

With respect to a living donor organ transplant,[44] the organ can be removed in a hospital only with the written authorisation of the Transplant Ethics Committee (TEC) of the hospital, and the donor's consent to the removal.[45] The consent must not be given pursuant to a prohibited contract or arrangement for the sale and supply of organs or blood under the HOTA[46] or obtained by virtue of any fraud, duress or undue influence.[47] The donor must not be mentally disordered and must be able to understand the nature and consequence of the medical procedures he has to undergo.[48]

Hence, for living donor organ transplants, the hospital would be obligated to set up a TEC.[49] It must consist of a minimum of three members with at least one medical practitioner not employed by or otherwise connected with the hospital and at least one lay person.[50] Requests for organ transplants are evaluated by the TEC which may authorise the carrying out of a specific organ transplant.[51] The composition and functions of the TEC is regulated by the Director of Medical Services,[52] and the TEC is immune from liability for anything done in good faith in the exercise of its functions.

Furthermore, under the HOTA, any information or document relating to the identity of the organ donor and recipient must be kept confidential.[53]

11.3.3 Prohibition of sale and supply of organs and blood

There is a concern that human organs and body parts may be treated as commodities to be bought and sold resulting in the devaluation of human life. A market for organs would also privilege the wealthy who have greater financial capacity to purchase the organs at

---

44 This means the removal of a specified organ from the body of any living person for the purpose of its transplantation into the body of another living person: section 2.
45 Section 15A(1).
46 Section 15A(2)(c)(i).
47 Section 15A(2)(c)(ii).
48 Section 15A(2)(b).
49 Section 15B.
50 Section 15B(2).
51 Section 15B(3).
52 Section 15C.
53 Section 18(1). This is subject to exceptions in 18(2) such as disclosures for the purpose of administering and enforcing the HOTA, and disclosures pursuant to a court order and for the purpose of hospital administration and *bona fide* medical research.

the expense of the poor who may need them (Herring 2018, at pp. 474-476). Although allowing organ trading may alleviate the shortage of supply and enable access to human organs that are indeed essential to save lives, such supply cannot be totally unregulated and left to the wishes of willing sellers and buyers. To that end, HOTA prohibits commercial transactions for the sale and supply of organs and blood subject to certain exceptions.

Similar to the case for human tissues, a contract or an arrangement under which a person agrees for "valuable consideration" to the "sale or supply of any organ or blood from his body or from the body of another person" shall be void.[54] A person who enters into such a contract or an arrangement is guilty of a criminal offence which is punishable with a fine or imprisonment.[55] In criminal sentencing, the court may take into account the extreme ill-health of the accused person suffering from end-stage renal failure and who may be seeking an organ transplant without any intention to exploit the potential donor, and exercise "judicial mercy" in sentencing.[56] In another case, the poor socio-economic circumstances of the potential donor of organs and his exploitation by a syndicate such that he committed the offence of entering into an arrangement to supply his organ was relevant to sentencing.[57] On the other hand, a deterrent sentence would be imposed where the accused person had abetted the illegal organ supply and made profits by acting as a "runner" to facilitate the commercial trading of organs,[58] where the accused person was convicted of abetment by aiding,[59] or worse, if the accused person had, in abetting the illegal organ supply, taken advantage of the donors and donees, acted with deceit and schemed to mislead the hospital's TEC.[60]

In addition, similar to the prohibition against tissue trading, criminal sanctions extend to not only the directing contracting parties but also those initiating or negotiating such prohibited arrangements, the intermediaries and participants having management and control of entities undertaking such activities.[61]

The statute exempts certain acts from criminal liability. For example, a contract or an arrangement providing only for the reimbursement of any expenses necessarily incurred by person in relation to the removal of blood is not prohibited.[62] The Code of Ethics for

---

54 Section 14(1).
55 Section 14(2).
56 *Public Prosecutor v Tang Wee Sung* [2008] SGDC 26 (fine of $7,000 for first charge of entering into prohibited arrangement for valuable consideration; one day's imprisonment and fine of $10,000 for the second charge of making false declaration that he did not pay money for the kidney).
57 *Public Prosecutor v Sulaiman Damanik and Another* [2008] SGDC 175 at [36]-[39].
58 *Public Prosecutor v Sulaiman Damanik and Another* [2008] SGDC 175 at [55] and [58]. The abettor Toni was sentenced to three months' imprisonment.
59 *Whang Sung Lin v Public Prosecutor* [2010] 2 SLR 958 (four months' imprisonment).
60 *Wang Chin Sing v Public Prosecutor* [2009] 1 SLR(R) 870.
61 Section 14(2A).
62 Section 14(3)(a). See also section 14(3)(b):
   (b) any scheme introduced or approved by the Government granting medical benefits or privileges to any organ or blood donor and any member of the donor's family or any person nominated by the donor.

Blood Donation and Transfusion (2000 and amended in 2006) issued by the International Society of Blood Transfusion (ISBT) – which has also been adopted by the World Health Organisation – also refers to the concept of "non-remunerated" blood donation.[63] The concept of "defraying and reimbursing" the costs and expenses of the donor also applies to organ donation.[64]

The Minister may exempt from prohibition the sale or supply of a specified class or classes of product derived from any organ or blood that has been subjected to processing or treatment.[65] Where the product in question has not been specifically exempted by the Minister, the vendor or supplier for the sale or supply of such a product remains criminally liable if the organ or blood from which the product was derived was obtained under a void contract or an arrangement for the sale and supply of organs or blood as mentioned above.[66] Furthermore, advertisements relating to the "buying or selling in Singapore of any organ or blood or of the right to take any organ or blood from the body of a person" are prohibited under the statute.[67]

The Health Sciences Authority (HSA) administers blood donation at various locations in Singapore. A person who knows that he has HIV is prohibited from donating blood to a blood bank in Singapore; and he is deemed to know that he has HIV Infection if a serological test or other test for the purpose of ascertaining the presence of HIV Infection carried out on him has given a positive result and the result has been communicated to him.[68] Non-compliance

---

63 A donation is considered "non-remunerated" if the person gives blood, plasma or cellular components without payment for it", either in the form of cash, or in kind which could be considered a substitute for money. This would include time off work other than that reasonably needed for the donation and travel. Small tokens, refreshments and reimbursements of direct travel costs are compatible with voluntary, non-remunerated donation": see https://www.isbtweb.org/fileadmin/user_upload/ISBT_Code_of_Ethics/Code_of_ethics_new_logo_-_feb_2011.pdf.
64 Section 14(3)(c) states –
   (c) any contract, arrangement or valuable consideration providing only for the defraying or reimbursing, in money or money's worth, of such costs or expenses that may be reasonably incurred by a person in relation to –
       (i) the removal, transportation, preparation, preservation, quality control or storage of any organ;
       (ii) the costs or expenses (including the costs of travel, accommodation, domestic help or child care) or loss of earnings so far as are reasonably or directly attributable to that person supplying any organ from his body; and
       (iii) any short-term or long-term medical care or insurance protection of that person which is or may reasonably be necessary as a consequence of his supplying any organ from his body.
   See The Declaration of Istanbul on Organ Trafficking and Transplant Tourism made on 2 May 2008 (that: "Comprehensive reimbursement of the actual, documented costs of donating an organ does not constitute a payment for an organ but is rather part of the legitimate costs of treating the recipient" and clause 7 on reimbursable expenses).
65 Section 14(4).
66 Section 14(5).
67 Section 15.
68 Infectious Diseases Act (Cap 137, 2003 Rev Ed), section 24.

will attract criminal penalties. At common law, a person who has contracted HIV from donated blood may pursue a negligence action against the blood banks if the recipient is able to prove that the inadequacies of the bank's donor screening procedures had materially contributed to the contraction of HIV.[69]

11.4 Medical (Therapy, Education and Research) Act

The MTERA[70] which was enacted in 1972 sets out rules concerning the donation of human bodies and body parts of deceased persons to approved hospitals and medical schools for medical education and research. A person who is not mentally disordered and 18 years of age or above may pledge to donate any of his other organs and tissues (*eg*, lungs, bones and skin) upon his death, for the purpose of transplantation to a specified individual, *or* to an approved hospital or medical or dental school for medical or dental education, research, advancement of medical or dental science, therapy or transplantation under MTERA.[71] In section 2, "part", in relation to a human body, includes organs, tissues, eyes, bones, arteries, blood, other fluids and other portions of a human body. Hence, the purposes and subject matter of donation provided in MTERA are broader than those in the HOTA. Another material difference is that the MTERA allows for Singaporeans to pledge their organs by opting-in.

Unlike organ transplants under the HOTA in which the donated organs are intended for a common pool of recipients on the waiting list, a donor is entitled to specify the organ recipient under the MTERA. The gift may be made by a donor either in writing or orally in the presence of two or more witnesses during a last illness.[72] The gift may be revoked by the donor.[73] Muslims who wish to donate their organs can make a pledge to that effect under the MTERA.

Aside from the donor, certain persons in the following order of priority (spouse, adult son or daughter, either parent, an adult brother or sister, a guardian of the deceased at the time of his death, and any person authorised or obliged to dispose of the deceased's body) are authorised[74] to give all or any part of the body of the deceased person after death or immediately before death for the abovementioned purposes.[75]

The donee shall not accept the body or part of body if he has actual notice of contrary indications by the deceased person or that a gift by a member of a class is opposed by

---

69 *Walker Estate v York Finch General Hospital* [2001] 1 SCR 647.
70 (Cap 175, Rev Ed 2014) at https://sso.agc.gov.sg/Act/MTERA1972. Cf the US Revised Uniform Anatomical Gift Act (amended in 2008) drafted by the National Conference of Commissioners on Uniform State Laws which regulates the donations of organs to increase the supply. It revised the earlier 1968 and 1987 Uniform Acts relating to organ donation throughout the United States.
71 Section 3 read with section 7.
72 Section 8.
73 Section 9.
74 There must not be any actual notice of contrary indications by the deceased person, or actual notice of opposition of a member of the same class or a prior class: section 4(1).
75 Section 4 read with the Schedule.

a member of the same class or a prior class.[76] A donee may accept or reject a gift of a body or part of a body.[77] Where a part of the body has been removed, the surviving spouse, next-of-kin or other person under obligation to dispose of the body will have custody of the remainder of the body.[78]

Where the body of a deceased person has not been claimed from an approved hospital or from an institution maintained on public funds for more than 24 hours after death, the Director of Medical Services may authorise in writing the use of the body or any specified part for the purposes of medical or dental education, research, advancement of medical or dental science, therapy or transplantation.[79]

The removal of any part of a body shall be carried out by a registered medical practitioner who is satisfied that the death of the deceased person has been determined and certified in accordance with section 2A of the Interpretation Act (*ie*, cardiac death or brain death).[80]

11.5 Whither property rights in human body or parts

At common law, the cadaver is "nullius in bonis" (or in the goods of no one).[81] That is, there is no property in a corpse.[82] A person's directions by will that his body be cremated did not impose a legal obligation on the executors as the person had no property right in his body.[83] The executors nonetheless had a right to the custody of the body for the purpose of burial.

It is generally accepted that, as a starting point, we have *personal* rights in our own bodies and its parts before they are removed (Dworkin and Kennedy 1993, at p. 298). Cardozo J stated in *Schoendorff v Society of New York Hospital*[84] that "[e]very human being of adult years and sound mind have a right to determine what shall be done with his body".

The general common law position since time immemorial is that a living human body is incapable of being owned. Relatedly, it was stated that a person does not even "possess" his body or any part of it.[85] Strictly speaking, if there were no property rights at all over human body or the body parts, those who take or use them should not be regarded as having committed any legal wrong. This is subject, however, to subsequent common law developments and legal claims discussed below.

---

76 Section 5.
77 Section 11(1).
78 Section 11(3).
79 Section 12.
80 Section 16(2).
81 Sir Edward Coke, *Institutes of the Laws of England* Part III (1797 ed), p. 203 cited in *Yearworth v North Bristol NHS Trust* [2009] 3 WLR 118 at 128.
82 *Re Sharpe* (1856-1857) Dears and B 160.
83 *Williams v Williams* (1882) 20 Ch D 659 at 663.
84 (1914) 105 NE 92.
85 *R v Bentham* [2005] 1 WLR 1057 at [8] (unsevered hand or finger as part of a person, not a thing to be possessed by person).

It may be appropriate to first consider if existing statutory provisions are consistent with or indicate any property rights or interests over body parts. In Singapore, a post-mortem examination ordered by the Coroner may only be performed by a pathologist or a medical practitioner under the supervision of a pathologist. The pathologist who conducts or supervises a post-mortem examination may perform an operation on the body and retain any part or contents of the body or any other substance in order to determine the manner or cause of death.[86] Under the law, in respect of a reportable death, the Coroner possesses "control" over the deceased body and its parts in Singapore until such time that the Coroner orders the release of the body for burial or cremation.[87]

The opt-out system based on presumed consent under the HOTA for donations of organs upon death may suggest that, as a general default position, the organs do not belong to the person though they may specifically opt out from donating the organs by registering an objection. However, the MTERA allows individual persons to opt in by pledging donations of body parts which may indicate the opposite (ie, that the donor has rights over its body parts in order to be in a position to give consent to the donation). The relationship between consent and (property) rights raises the proverbial "chicken and egg" syndrome: does the reference to consent under the statute mean that the person has property rights over the removed body part or should the existence of property rights be the basis for the consent to be given in the first place? A middle (possibly safer) approach might be that the statutory provisions should have no bearing on property rights; if Parliament had intended to make a determination on property rights over human body parts, it would have stated so more clearly.

11.5.1 Common law developments

The general common law position that there is no property in a corpse was modified somewhat in the bizarre Australian case of *Doodeward v Spence*[88] involving the corpse of a two-headed baby. The doctor who had been attending its mother preserved the corpse in spirits. After the doctor died, the corpse was sold. Subsequently, the claimant came into possession of the corpse and exhibited it for profit. A police officer confiscated the corpse in order to bury it. The claimant successfully sued for detinue. Griffith CJ stated[89]:

> when a person has by the lawful exercise of work or skill so dealt with a human body or part of a human body in his lawful possession that it has acquired some attributes differentiating it from a mere corpse awaiting burial, he acquires a right to retain possession of it, at least against any person not entitled to have it delivered to him for the purpose of burial, but subject, of course, to any positive law which forbids its retention under the particular circumstances.

---

86 Coroner's Act (Cap 63A, 2012 Rev Ed), section 19. See also Lee et al. (2008).
87 Coroners' Act (Cap 63A, 2012 Rev Ed), section 22 read with section 2 on the meaning of "body" which includes any part of the deceased person.
88 (1908) 6 CLR 406.
89 (1908) 6 CLR 406 at 414.

Though Barton J agreed, Higgins J dissented on the basis that there could be no ownership of a human corpse.

The subsequent case of *Dobson v North Tyneside Health Authority*[90] agreed with the *Doodeward* principle that a body part could be owned if subjected to the exercise of work and skill. A woman had died of brain tumours. The doctor at the hospital removed her brain and preserved (or fixed) it in paraffin. The deceased's body was returned to her family and buried. Subsequently, the plaintiffs (the mother and infant son of the deceased) sued the hospital in negligence for failing to detect the tumours. The issue of whether the tumours were benign or malignant was important to the lawsuit. In this regard, the plaintiffs alleged that the doctor failed to preserve either the deceased's brain or sections of the brain tumours making it impossible to determine whether the tumours were benign or malignant.

On the facts, no skill was exercised by the doctor on the deceased's brain by fixing it in paraffin. The court stated that the plaintiffs did not have any property right over the deceased's brain. Furthermore, the removal of the brain was lawfully performed by the doctor in the course of the post-mortem at the coroner's request. The plaintiffs' claim in conversion failed as they could not show that they had actual possession or the immediate right to possession at the time the brain was disposed of or that the doctor had committed any wrong.

The dissection of human material into tissues in a post-mortem has been held to constitute the exercise of work and skill by the pathologists sufficient to confer property rights under the *Doodeward* exception.[91] This does not mean that the accrual of property rights depended exclusively on the exercise of work and skill on the human body or a part of the body. In *Yearworth v North Bristol NHS Trust*,[92] the English Court of Appeal was of the view that the

> distinction between the capacity to own body parts or products which have, and which have not, been subject to the exercise of work or skill is not entirely logical. Why, for example, should the surgeon presented with a part of the body, for example, a finger which has been amputated in a factory accident, with a view to re-attaching it to the injured hand, but who carelessly damages it before starting the necessary medical procedures, be able to escape liability on the footing that the body part had not been subject to the exercise of work or skill which had changed its attributes?

It preferred the approach in *R v Kelly*[93] in which Rose LJ stated:

> It may be that if, on some future occasion, the question arises, the courts will hold that human body parts are capable of being property ... ... even without the acquisition of different attributes, if they have a use or significance beyond their mere existence. This may be so if, for example, they are intended for use in an organ transplant operation, for the extraction of DNA or, for that matter, as an exhibit in a trial.

---

90 [1997] 1 WLR 598 at 601.
91 *Re Organ Retention Litigation* [2005] QB 506 at [160].
92 [2009] 3 WLR 118 at 135.
93 [1999] QB 621 at 631 (Court of Appeal (Criminal Division)).

Hence, instead of placing emphasis solely on skill and work done on the human body parts, the focus has shifted to the use or value of the parts.

11.5.2 Legal claims and rights

The term "property" would typically denote a bundle of rights including the right to use, transfer and dispose of the property as well as to exclude others from using the property. We will examine below the scope of legal rights and the different legal causes of action that may be or have been brought with respect to the removal, use, disposal or destruction of human body parts, organs or tissues, the underlying arguments and likelihood of success. Certain causes of action are based on some indicia of proprietary interests in the human tissue or body part whilst others are more personal in nature (such as human dignitary interests and mental well-being). As we examine these cases, it would be useful to bear in mind the arguments raised above against commercial trading of human organs, tissues and blood such as the commoditisation of human bodies and parts and market inequality. None of the cases below, it seems, would support a free market for the buying and selling of body parts.

11.5.2.1 Property damage

In *Yearworth v North Bristol NHS Trust*,[94] the claimants were diagnosed with cancer and had to undergo chemotherapy treatment. The defendant hospital's fertility storage unit, licensed under the UK Human Fertilisation and Embryology Act 1990, offered to freeze and store their sperm samples as the chemotherapy treatment might affect the fertility of the sperm sample. The claimants consented. However, in the process of freezing the sperm samples, the liquid nitrogen fell below the requisite level and the semen was destroyed.

The claimants successfully sued for property damage in the tort of negligence. The English court took the view that the claimants had ownership of the sperm which they had ejaculated for the sole purpose of using it for their benefit. There was a sufficient nexus between the incident of ownership (the right of the men to use the sperm) and the nature of the damage consequent upon the breach of the duty of care (their inability to use it for the specific purpose). Such a narrow concept of property right vis-à-vis the sperm was, according to the court, permitted within the framework of the Human Fertilisation and Embryology Act 1990.

11.5.2.2 Psychiatric harm and/or mental distress

Apart from the claim in property damage, an alternative claim succeeded in *Yearworth v North Bristol NHS Trust*[95] for the recovery of damages for psychiatric injury and/or mental distress under the law of bailment. The defendant hospital was liable as a gratuitous bailee with respect to the sperm samples to which the claimants possessed sufficient rights

---

94 [2009] 3 WLR 118.
95 [2009] 3 WLR 118.

248 Human organs, tissues, biological materials

as bailors. Here there was a breach of bailment due to a specific promise extended by the defendant to the claimants.[96]

The doctrine of bailment was also relevant in the Canadian case of *Mason v Westside Cemeteries Ltd*[97] which concerned the cremated remains of the plaintiff's parents that were placed in urns and kept by a funeral home. The plaintiff instructed the funeral home to transfer the urns to Westminster cemetery (the defendant) to keep the urns temporarily. When the plaintiff asked for the urns, however, the defendant could not locate them. The court stated that next of kin have the right to direct the disposition of the remains of their loved ones subject to statutory restrictions. The Westminster cemetery was the bailee of the remains in the urn. The defendant did not know what had happened to the urns and could not thereby show that the loss of the remains in the urns was not due to its negligence. The defendant would have reasonably contemplated that the plaintiff would have suffered mental distress from the loss of his parents' ashes and the urns. The judge treated the bailment as more akin to contract than tort of negligence and awarded damages for mental distress on that basis.

The plaintiff also recovered the amount of moneys he paid to the funeral home for the internment of the ashes at the defendant's cemetery. In assessing special damage, the learned judge noted there was no market value for the ashes and, despite the plaintiff's argument based on the sentimental value attached to the ashes and urns, decided not to assign a monetary value to the ashes and instead awarded a nominal sum for the loss of the ashes and urns.

In the UK, a claim for psychiatric harm suffered by mourners at a funeral procession – which arose from the displacement of the coffin bearing the body of their close relative due to the defendant's negligence in driving the car that collided with the hearse – was successful.[98]

In a separate case, inquiries were conducted in the UK in response to allegations concerning the retention of organs in the British Royal Infirmary and the Alder Hey Children's Hospital in Liverpool. The organs of children were removed and retained without the knowledge of the parents. Herring (2018, at p. 447) noted that the doctors might have placed emphasis on the greatest good to remove tissues based on utilitarian reasoning at the expense of individual rights to one's bodily materials. This episode also reminds us that the remains of human bodies may hold "emotional social importance for the surviving relatives" and this might call for legal protection (Kaan 2000, at p. 496). In the case of *Re Organ Retention Litigation*,[99] deceased children's organs were removed post-mortem by medical professionals without the consent of parents though they had consented to the post-mortem itself. It was held that the hospital owed a duty of care to the parents to inform them of the purpose of

---

96 The English court cited *Graham v Voigt* (1989) 95 Fed LR 146; (1989) ACTR 11 (Supreme Court of the Australian Capital Territory); *Mason v Westside Cemeteries Ltd* (1996) 135 DLR (4th) 361 (Ontario Court, General Division).
97 (1996) 135 DLR (4th) 361 (Ontario Court, General Division).
98 *Owens v Liverpool Corp* [1939] 1 KB 394.
99 Also known as *A and B v Leeds Teaching Hospitals NHS Trust; Cardiff and Vale NHS Trust* [2005] QB 506 (surgeons had right to possession of organs having invested work and skill on the organs; but owed a duty to parents and had to compensate damages for psychiatric harm).

the post-mortem and what it entailed including the retention of organs.[100] The practice of not warning parents that the organs of their deceased children might be removed and retained was not a justifiable practice. The facts also suggested that some parents thought that tissues would be removed from the deceased children's bodies but did not know that could include the removal of whole organs.[101] The hospital was obliged to compensate for psychiatric harm in the tort of negligence.

11.5.2.3 Commercial profits from research

Would patients have an economic interest in their removed body parts or tissues so as to claim for commercial benefits that may be generated from research derived from the use of their body parts or tissues? Will this depend on whether they have any proprietary interests in their body parts and tissues? This issue of potential medical research and commercial profits through patents is important not least because living matter is patentable under the law.[102] Patents allow inventors a monopoly over the invention for a certain number of years to exploit the commercial benefits of the invention.

In *Moore v Regents of the University of California*,[103] the claimant (Moore) was suffering from leukaemia. One of the defendants, a physician, obtained his consent to the removal of his spleen and other body parts without revealing that they were to be used in research. The physician and other parties[104] produced a cell-line of great economic potential from the use of Moore's spleen in the treatment of leukaemia, which they subsequently patented. The claimant sued the physician for a share of the profits alleging (i) breach of the physician's fiduciary duty to disclose facts relevant to the claimant and/or for operating upon him without having obtained his informed consent; and (ii) conversion described as a "tort that protects against interference with possessory and ownership interests in personal property".

The majority judges[105] of the Supreme Court of California allowed the claim based on non-disclosure and lack of informed consent. The information concerning the use of the spleen for research was material to the patient's decision. Moreover, the doctor failed to disclose to the patient his personal (economic) interests that might affect his professional judgement. The majority held, however, that the claim for conversion of the body parts failed. First, case precedents and statute law did not indicate that the claimant would be the owner of the

---

100 Gage J at [199] regarded the parents as primary victims. Note that Singapore has abandoned the distinction between primary and secondary victims for psychiatric harm: see *Ngiam Kong Seng v Lim Chiew Hock* [2008] 3 SLR(R) 674.
101 Gage J held at [125] that consent to the post-mortem includes consent to procedures such as the removal and retention of organs necessarily involved in a post-mortem. As such, the claim for wrongful interference with the body of the child failed (at [161]).
102 *Diamond v Chakrabarty* (1980) 447 U.S. 303 (genetically engineered bacteria is patentable subject matter).
103 (1990) 793 P 2d 479.
104 University researcher, university regents and licensees of rights to patented cell-line and its products.
105 Panelli J (Lucas CJ, Eagleson and Kennard JJ concurring); and Arabian J concurring in a separate judgement.

body parts following removal or even the patented cell-line and its products.[106] Second, the majority judges thought that allowing the action in conversion would have hindered valuable research[107]:

> In effect, what Moore is asking us to do is to impose a tort duty on scientists to investigate the consensual pedigree of each human cell sample used in research. To impose such a duty, which would affect medical research of importance to all of society, implicates policy concerns far removed from the traditional, two-party ownership disputes in which the law of conversion arose. Invoking a tort theory originally used to determine whether the loser or the finder of a horse had the better title, Moore claims ownership of the results of socially important medical research, including the genetic code for chemicals that regulate the functions of every human being's immune system.

Panelli J also noted that if the cause of action in conversion were allowed, parties who were involved in the research without knowledge of the patient's lack of informed consent would nevertheless remain liable since conversion is by its nature a strict liability tort.[108] A subsequent and analogous US decision has endorsed a similar position that there is no property interest in the donated human tissues[109] in order to avoid hindering medical research. Another decision[110] has denied any ownership interest of certain donors who had given informed consent to donate their biological materials for medical research to a particular institution such that they were unable to issue instructions as to the transfer of those biological materials to another party.

Broussard and Mosk J in *Moore* dissented on this issue of conversion. Broussard J opined that as the patient possessed the "right to control the use" of the body part upon removal, the doctor by withholding the material information from the patient before the removal had wrongfully interfered with the patient's right to control.[111] Mosk J argued that we must not allow the human body to be subject to "indirect abuse" by "economic exploitation" for the benefit of another.[112] In particular, where parties are not on equal bargaining positions, a party may be "unjustly enriched" from commercial profits generated at the expense of the other who had contributed the human tissues; and this would run contrary to "fundamental fairness".[113] The learned judge also observed that the non-disclosure cause of action would not apply to a significant group of potential defendants outside the physician-patient relationship.[114] This would mean that the other parties (*ie*, non-doctors) would not be liable to the

---

106 (1990) 793 P 2d 479 at 489, *per* Panelli J.
107 (1990) 793 P 2d 479 at 487-488.
108 (1990) 793 P 2d 479 at 494.
109 *Greenberg v. Miami Children's Hosp. Research Inst., Inc.*, 264 F. Supp. 2d 1064 at 1076 (S.D. Fla. 2003) (plaintiffs, donors and non-profit organisation who had provided funding and information to defendants, succeeded on unjust enrichment claim but failed in claims for conversion, breach of informed consent or fiduciary duties, fraudulent concealment).
110 *Wash. Univ. v. Catalona*, 490 F.3d 667 at 673 and 677 (8th Cir. 2007).
111 (1990) 793 P 2d 479 at 499.
112 (1990) 793 P 2d 479 at 515.
113 (1990) 793 P 2d 479 at 516.
114 (1990) 793 P 2d 479 at 521.

claimant for non-disclosure and this is where the alternative cause of action based on the tort of conversion would have been important to protect potential claimants.[115]

Are there alternative legal approaches to or explanations of *Moore*? One preliminary question is whether the patient might have impliedly abandoned his rights to the discarded body part (Dworkin and Kennedy 1993, at p. 311).[116] If the patient was given to understand by the doctor that the body part would be used for a specific purpose (therapy) but was instead applied to a different purpose (research), this implied abandonment approach would not be very persuasive. Alternatively, it may be argued that under English common law, the patient's consent to the removal of the spleen was invalidated by the doctor's failure to disclose the real purpose for the removal – arguably a form of deception on the doctor's part – which was fundamental to the patient's decision. If so, it would constitute a trespass to the person as a separate cause of action (Dworkin and Kennedy 1993, at p. 312).

It should be noted that under the HBRA, the act of the physician in removing the human tissue without obtaining consent for the research purpose in addition to the consent obtained for the therapeutic or diagnostic purpose would attract criminal penalties.[117] Further, as part of the process of obtaining informed consent, the donor would likely be taken to have renounced his or her rights to the tissue and any intellectual property rights that may be derived from the use of the tissue.[118] These provisions should, to a large extent, preempt or reduce the likelihood of a *Moore*-like dispute surfacing.

11.5.2.4 Disposition by will

The US decision in *Hecht v Superior Court for Los Angeles County*[119] considered the issue of whether the deceased's sperm was something capable of disposition by his will. The court held that, at the time of his death, he had sufficient decision-making authority in relation to the use of his sperm for it to amount to "property" for the purpose of the state's Probate Code. In Australia, the court in *Bazley v Wesley Monash IVF*[120] held that semen constitutes "property, the ownership of which vested in the deceased while alive and in his personal representatives after his death".

11.5.2.5 Demand for return

In *Bazley*,[121] on the basis of a bailment for reward between the person who had provided his semen (bailor) and the IVF centre (bailee), where the bailee agreed to store the semen, the bailor or the personal representative of the bailor was entitled to demand for the return of

---

115 See Tan (2003).
116 Broussard J in *Moore* would appear to agree with the abandonment approach if the doctor had no prior knowledge of any commercial value of the patient's organ: (1990) 793 P 2d 479 at 500.
117 Section 37(1) read with (11).
118 Section 12(2).
119 (1993) 20 Cal Rptr 2d 275.
120 [2011] 2 Qd R 207 at [33].
121 [2011] 2 Qd R 207 at [33].

the semen in a condition that preserved the essential characteristics of the frozen semen capable of being used. The bailor had passed away without leaving any written directive with regard to the semen.

> **Box 11.2 – Does ownership really matter?**
>
> Given the discussion above, does it matter whether we legally own our human bodies or parts? Is the existing position at common law defensible even if it does not give us a definitive answer on proprietary interests in human bodies and parts?

11.6 Bioprinting of human tissues and organs

In bioprinting, the stem cells are put into a bio cartridge together with proteins and other biological materials to generate living tissues.[122] 3D bioprinting of bioinks involve living cells (stem cell lines) and biomaterial scaffolds for growing these cells into tissues. Bioink refers to "biomaterial ink engineered to convey living cells through a printing process for the purpose of fabricating biological constructs" (Gilbert et al. 2018, at p. 74).

There are potential benefits to be derived from customising treatments for patients and in producing human tissues and organs that may be used in transplants in order to save lives. This is particularly useful where there is a shortage of supply or donations of organs. On the other hand, there could be risks to the patient's health from transplants using foreign biomaterials and patients may object to the cells (eg, from animals) used for bioprinting. Further, the effects of the transplant process and the use of certain implants from bioprinting may be irreversible. In some cases, the removal of the transplants or implants might have adverse effects on the patient. As a result, clinical trials involving such irreversible treatments or implants would likely be administered only when the patient is in a life-threatening or desperate situation.

In addition to therapeutic purposes, bioprinting can also be utilised for human enhancements. This may be resisted on the ground that the process is non-natural and contrary to humanity especially when the effects are irreversible (Patuzzo et al. 2018, at p. 340). There is also the need for human biomedical research on bioprinting to obtain consent from the donors of the tissues and organs, as well as to ensure the patients are properly informed of the origin of the tissues and organs and the risks of the treatment or enhancement.

11.7 Conclusion

Strict statutory requirements relating to consents and authorisations apply to the removal and use of human tissues for the purposes of therapy and research. Specific procedures attend to organ transplants (including the opt-out system, authorisations for cadaveric donations and ethics approvals for living donor transplants) and the voluntary pledging of body

---

122 https://www.asiaone.com/health/3d-printers-real-human-tissue-become-reality-singapore.

parts for education, therapy and research. The prohibition against commercial dealings with human tissues, organs and blood are enforced by criminal sanctions with exceptions for arrangements that provide for reimbursement of expenses. There is thus far no statutory or common law endorsement of a general property right or interest in one's human body and parts though some limited form of property interests is recognised at common law. Moreover, claimants can rely on alternative non-proprietary analyses (such as breach of informed consent or fiduciary duties). As for bioprinting, despite its potential benefits to alleviate the problem of shortage of human organs and tissues, the jury is still out on its ethical acceptability in view of the risks of physical harm, irreversible effects and the implicit endorsement of human enhancement.

References

Bioethics Advisory Committee (2002). Consultation Paper on "Human Tissue Research" (27 February) at https://www.bioethics-singapore.gov.sg/files/publications/consultation-papers/human-tissue-research.pdf.
Lee et al. (2008). *Coroner's Practice in Medical Cases* (Academy Publishing: Singapore).
Dworkin, G. & Kennedy, I. (1993). "Human Tissue: Right in the Body and its Parts" 1 *Medical Law Review* 291.
Gilbert, F., O'Connell, C.D., Mladenovska, T. et al. (2018). "Print Me an Organ? Ethical and Regulatory Issues: Emerging from 3D Bioprinting in Medicine" 24 *Sci Eng Ethics* 73-91.
Herring, J. (2018). "Organ Donation and Ownership of Body Parts" in Herring, J. *Medical Law and Ethics*, 7th edition (Oxford University Press: Oxford), pp. 432-492.
Kaan, S.-H.T. (2000). "Rights, Ethics and the Commercialisation of the Human Body" *Singapore Journal of Legal Studies* 483.
Patuzzo, S., Goracci, G., Gasperini, L. et al. (2018). "3D Bioprinting Technology: Scientific Aspects and Ethical Issues" 24 *Sci Eng Ethics* 335-348.
Tan, B.H. (2003). "Property Rights in Human Tissue – Calling a Spade, A Spade" 15 *SAcLJ* 61.

12 Human biomedical research, medical innovations and information technologies in healthcare[†]

12.1 Introduction

Research seeks to contribute to and grow generalisable knowledge for public good, and human biomedical research is the specific area of research relating to the improvement of health and well-being that involves human subjects.[1] The goal of human biomedical research for public good and its reputation are highly prized. Yet there have been a number of improprieties and misconduct relating to biomedical research involving the administration of unnecessary experiments on humans and the lack of informed consent from subject participants,[2] the unauthorised retention of human biological materials by hospitals[3] as well as serious injuries[4] and death[5] suffered by research participants in clinical trials. Singapore's human biomedical research is similarly not immune from misconduct[6] and errors, and in this regard, she has set up a regulatory, legal and ethical infrastructure to maintain and enhance accountability and to mitigate potential risks.

[†] The author would like to thank Wan Ding Yao a law student at Singapore Management University for his research assistance.

1 See NMEC (1997) Guidelines, paragraph 2.2.1 which defines human research as "studies which generate data about human subjects which go beyond what is needed for the individual's well-being. The primary purpose of research activity is the generation of new information or the testing of a hypothesis".

2 *Eg*, Tuskegee experiment in 1972 on black US males with respect to treatment of syphilis though there were generally available treatments.

3 Royal Liverpool Children's Hospital (Alder Hey) and Bristol Infirmary.

4 *Eg*, multiple organ failure suffered by six men in drug trials conducted by Northwick Park Hospital in London in 2006: see McHale (2017, at p. 715).

5 Ellen Roche died in a study on asthma conducted by John Hopkins University in 2001: see McHale 2017 at 713.

6 See *eg, Shorvon Simon v Singapore Medical Council* [2006] 1 SLR(R) 182 at [9] and [11] (former director of National Neuroscience Institute and lead Principal Investigator of a research project found guilty by the Disciplinary Committee of charges of professional misconduct relating to breach of confidentiality, failure to give informed consent to patients, failure to obtain ethics approvals and failure to act in patients' best interests).

The major actors in Singapore's human biomedical research are the research institutions, government agencies, researchers under the supervision of research institutions, funders, ethics review committees (in particular the Institutional Review Boards or IRBs), and research subjects. The Ministry of Health (MOH) including the statutory agencies such as the Health Sciences Authority (HSA) regulate the use of medical devices and clinical trials for medicinal products. The Ministry of Health issued a directive in 1998 for hospitals to set up ethics committees to govern research relating to new medical devices and procedures that involve the participation of human subjects or the use of human tissues and organs. The National Medical Ethics Committee's (NMEC) *Ethical Guidelines on Research Involving Human Subjects* in 1997 provide "a broad framework of ethical principles which local ethics committees should take into consideration in their deliberations and to suggest procedures which these committees should follow in the decision making process". Another body – the Bioethics Advisory Committee (BAC) – was set up in 2000 to address the ethical, legal and social issues arising from biomedical sciences research in Singapore. Furthermore, the MOH also established the *Governance Framework for Human Biomedical Research* as well as issued *Operational Guidelines for Institutional Review Boards* in 2007. The BAC's recommendations in *Research Involving Human Subject Guidelines for IRBs* (2004)[7] were implemented in 2006 by means of a directive by the MOH to all registered medical practitioners.

On the legislative front, the Human Cloning and Other Prohibited Practices Act had already been enacted in 2005. At that time, the Medicines (Clinical Trials) Regulations[8] promulgated under the Medicines Act[9] was the only set of regulations concerning clinical trials for human biomedical research. There was no overarching regulatory framework for human biomedical research until the enactment of the HBRA in 2015. Its objective was to "build strong legislative foundations to facilitate research while ensuring high ethical standards and protection for human subjects" and to maintain its "reputation as a biomedical hub of international standing".[10] This statute has two main parts: (i) the human biomedical research regulatory framework which will be a focal area in this chapter, and (ii) the human tissue regulatory framework which we have already examined in Chapter 11.

Just as human biomedical research seeks to enhance human well-being through improving our scientific knowledge and applying it to clinical practice, the use of medical and information technologies have significantly influenced both clinical practice as well as biomedical research. The development of new medical devices for diagnostic and therapeutic purposes, the digitisation of patient health records for easy access and use for diagnoses and treatments, and the use of robotic surgery in hospitals are merely examples of the potential reach and impact of technology in the healthcare sector. These technological developments have in turn generated a slew of legal, professional and ethical issues pertaining to the requirement of informed consent obtained from patients, confidentiality of data, accuracy of the

---

7   See https://www.bioethics-singapore.org/files/publications/reports/research-involving-human-subjects-guideline-for-irbs-full-report.pdf.
8   Cap. 176, 2000 Rev Ed, RG 3.
9   (Cap. 176) (1985 Ed).
10 Parliamentary Report on "Human Biomedical Research Bill" (17 August 2015), Vol 93 (The Minister of State for Health), p. 71.

outputs from the technologies, bias against certain groups of patients, and the challenges in ascertaining the responsibility of technology developers and the users (including doctors and healthcare professionals).

12.2 Laws and regulations on human biomedical research

We will begin with the basic legal rules under the Human Biomedical Research Act (HBRA) 2015[11] followed by the regulations on clinical trials for medicinal and therapeutic products.

12.2.1 Definition of human biomedical research

It is important to first ascertain the scope of the HBRA. There are two meanings for the term "human biomedical research". The first meaning in section 3(2) involves two limbs based on the purpose and the content of the research respectively:

Any research that is intended to study –

(a) the prevention, prognostication, diagnosis or alleviation of any disease, disorder or injury affecting the human body;
(b) the restoration, maintenance or promotion of the aesthetic appearance of human individuals through clinical procedures or techniques; or
(c) the performance or endurance of human individuals,
where the research involves –
   (i) subjecting an individual to any intervention (including any wilful act or omission) that has a physical, mental or physiological effect (whether temporary or permanent) on the body of the individual;
   (ii) the use of any individually identifiable human biological material; or
   (iii) the use of any individually identifiable health information.

Section 3(3) of HBRA refers to the second definition of "human biomedical research" based on the involvement of specified biological materials and entities:

Any research that involves –

(a) human gametes or human embryos;
(b) cytoplasmic hybrid embryos;
(c) the introduction of any human-animal combination embryo into an animal or a human;
(d) the introduction of human stem cells (including induced pluripotent stem cells) or human neural cells into an animal at any stage of development (including a prenatal animal foetus or animal embryo); or
(e) any entity created as a result of any process referred to in paragraph (c) or (d).

Furthermore, the Second Schedule excludes the following list of research, studies and matters from the definition of "human biomedical research":

1   Research and studies on normal human psychological responses and behaviours –
    (a) which are not designed or intended to study psychiatric or psychological disorders; and

---

[11] (No. 29 of 2015). See Labude (2016).

(b) which involve no more than minimal risk to the research subject.
2. Research, studies and tests to measure human intelligence –
   (a) which are not designed or intended to study mental or intellectual disability; and
   (b) which involve no more than minimal risk to the research subject.
3. Public health research on infectious diseases conducted for the purposes of and in accordance with section 59A of the Infectious Diseases Act (Cap. 137).[12]
4. Collection and compilation by the National Registry of Diseases of health information for epidemiological or statistical purposes in accordance with the National Registry of Diseases Act (Cap. 201B).[13]
5. Collection and compilation of health information for statistical purposes in accordance with the Statistics Act (Cap. 317).
6. Clinical trials of health products conducted in accordance with the Health Products Act (Cap. 122D).
7. Clinical trials of medicinal products conducted in accordance with the Medicines Act (Cap. 176).

The BAC (2010) report on *Human-Animal Combinations in Stem Cell Research – A Report* recommended that cytoplasmic hybrids (in which the nuclei of cells from the human body are injected into enucleated animal eggs) and animal chimeras (in which human stem cells are injected into animals) should be allowed on grounds of scientific merit subject to putting in place a regulatory framework and compliance with ethical requirements. Animal eggs have been used due to the shortage of human eggs. Scientific advantages include nuclear reprogramming,[14] improved understanding of genetic diseases and stem cells for clinical applications. However, the BAC (2010) report noted the concern over the "creation of entities in which human sentience or consciousness might be expected to occur" so as to justify specific prohibitions or restrictions relating to hybrids and chimeras.

The BAC (2010) report has been influential in legal reforms. In the HBRA, certain categories of human biomedical research stated below have been *prohibited* under the HBRA[15]:

1. Human biomedical research involving the development of human-animal combination embryos beyond 14 days or the appearance of the primitive streak, whichever is the earlier.
2. Human biomedical research involving the implantation –
   (a) of a human-animal combination embryo into the uterus of an animal; or
   (b) of a human-animal combination embryo into the uterus of a human.

---

12 See McHale (2010) (proposing justifications for exceptions to privacy and decision-making autonomy based on public interest in the UK with respect to epidemiological research, anonymised data and public health emergencies).
13 See McHale (2010).
14 That is, a process whereby the nucleus of a somatic cell is transformed to acquire the characteristics and potential of an embryonic cell nucleus: BAC Report 2010, footnote 10.
15 Section 30 and Third Schedule.

3   Human biomedical research involving the introduction of human stem cells (including induced pluripotent stem cells) or human neural cells into the brain of living great apes whether prenatal or postnatal.
4   Human biomedical research involving the breeding of animals which have had any kind of human pluripotent stem cells (including induced pluripotent stem cells) introduced into them.

Other types of human biomedical research[16] are *subject to restrictions* (such as the requirement to give notifications and obtain approvals, reviews by IRBs, and the conduct of research by specific persons in specific premises).[17] The restricted category is as follows:

1   Human biomedical research involving human eggs or human embryos.
2   Human biomedical research involving –
   (a) the following types of human-animal combination embryos:
      (i) cytoplasmic hybrid embryos;
      (ii) human-animal combination embryos created by the incorporation of human stem cells (including induced pluripotent stem cells);
      (iii) human-animal combination embryos created in-vitro by using –
         (A) human gametes and animal gametes; or
         (B) one human pronucleus and one animal pronucleus;
   (b) the introduction of human stem cells (including induced pluripotent stem cells) into a prenatal animal foetus or animal embryo;
   (c) the introduction of human pluripotent stem cells (including induced pluripotent stem cells) into a living postnatal animal but excludes the introduction of such human pluripotent stem cells into immunodeficient mice solely for the analysis of teratoma induction;
   (d) the introduction of human stem cells (including induced pluripotent stem cells) or human neural cells into the brain of a living postnatal animal; or
   (e) any entity created as a result of any process referred to in sub-paragraphs (*b*), (*c*) and (*d*).

The Minister for Health has the power to exempt human biomedical research from the scope of the HBRA.[18] The statute does not specifically cover nanotechnology and synthetic technologies in human biomedical research but where the research involves subjecting an individual to any intervention, or where there is use of individually identifiable biological material or health information,[19] it would be regulated under HBRA.

12.2.2 Consent requirements

Unlike the case of a typical doctor-patient relationship where there is a duty owed by a treating physician to act in the best interests of a patient, biomedical research does not usually

---

16 See the Fourth Schedule.
17 Section 31.
18 Section 57.
19 Section 3(2).

confer direct benefit on the human research subject (Kaan 2004, at para 9.4). A treatment may be regarded as an activity where its "sole purpose is to serve the interests of the patient for whom it is administered" whilst research would normally refer to activities that "serves to either generate additional data that is not necessary for the treatment of a patient or 'new information'" (Chan 2013, at p. 101). There are also systemic design features and methodologies associated with biomedical research (such as the use of placebo controls and randomised investigations conducted on research subjects) that differentiate it from therapy or treatments for individual patients.

Consent to be obtained from the research subject, as it is for patients, remains crucial. First, the consent from the research subject must be in writing in the presence of a witness after the requisite information[20] has been provided and explained to the research subject (or to persons authorised to give consent on the subject's behalf).[21] Where an adult research subject lacks mental capacity, the consent may be obtained instead from the donee or deputy who is authorised to give consent to the biomedical research on behalf of the adult, or where there is no authorised donee or deputy, the following persons in the order of priority: the spouse; an adult son or daughter; either parent or a guardian; an adult brother or sister; any other person named by the adult as someone to be consulted on the matter in question or on matters of that kind.[22]

If the prospective research subject is a minor who has sufficient understanding and intelligence to enable the minor to understand what is proposed in the biomedical research, consent must be obtained from both the minor and at least one adult parent or guardian of the minor.[23] The IRB may waive the requirement to obtain the consent of at least one adult parent or guardian of the minor.[24] One of the grounds for IRB waiver is that the proposed research "involves no more than minimal risk to the research subjects".[25]

Where the minor does not have sufficient understanding and intelligence to enable the minor to understand what is proposed in the biomedical research and there are reasonable grounds for believing that biomedical research of comparable effectiveness cannot be carried out without the participation of the class of minors to which the minor belongs, consent must then be obtained from at least one adult parent or guardian of the minor.[26] On the other hand, if the minor lacks mental capacity and there are reasonable grounds for believing that biomedical research of comparable effectiveness cannot be carried out without the participation of the class of minors to which the minor belongs, consent must be obtained from a deputy who is authorised to give consent to the biomedical research on behalf of the minor; or at least one adult parent or guardian of the minor.[27]

---

20 Section 12.
21 Section 6.
22 Section 7.
23 Section 8(1)(a).
24 Sections 8(1)(b) and 13.
25 Section 13(2)(a).
26 Section 8(1)(c).
27 Section 8(1)(d).

The concept of informed consent is one core aspect of human biomedical research. The appropriate consent must be obtained after the research subject or, where applicable, the person authorised to give consent, has been informed of a list of specified information such as the nature and purpose of the biomedical research, reasonably foreseeable risks and benefits from the biomedical research, compensation and treatment available to the research subject in the event of injury and so on.[28] To ensure that autonomy is given due respect, a research subject or any person who is authorised to give consent on the subject's behalf may, at any time, withdraw the consent to the subject's participation in the human biomedical research.[29]

At common law, the principle of informed consent in the context of medical research was applied in *Halushka v University of Saskatchewan*.[30] The research participant in that case was not informed of the risks associated with the procedure and likely effects. The researchers informed the subject that a new drug was to be tested but did not inform the subject that it was an anaesthetic of which they had no previous knowledge and the risks involved in the use of the anaesthetic. Moreover, the subject was only told that the catheter would be inserted in the vein in his arm but the catheter was in fact advanced through his heart. The Canadian court held that the subject of medical experimentation is "entitled to a full and frank disclosure of all the facts, probabilities and opinions which a reasonable man might be expected to consider before giving his consent".[31] Moreover, the researchers were to be placed in a "fiduciary" position towards the subjects.[32]

12.2.3 Regulation of human biomedical research

The HBRA covers the supervision and control exercised by the research institution over human biomedical research,[33] and the duties of the researchers in the conduct of such research.[34] A research institution must appoint one or more IRBs to review human biomedical research conducted under the supervision and control of that research institution.[35] That the IRB is part of and is accountable to the research institution has raised questions about the IRB's independence and impartiality (Chan 2010). This problem is mitigated in part by mandating a minimum number of external parties in the IRB. According to the regulations, an IRB must comprise not less than five individuals including the chairman who must be a medical practitioner, at least one external scientific person and at least one external lay person.[36] It is obligatory for a member of an IRB to declare any conflicts of interest or potential conflicts of interest at the IRB meeting in relation to a matter under consideration by the IRB.[37] A

---

28 Section 12(1).
29 Section 14(1).
30 (1965) 53 DLR (2d) 436.
31 (1965) 53 DLR (2d) 436 at [29].
32 (1965) 53 DLR (2d) 436 at [29].
33 Sections 21, 23 and 24.
34 Section 22.
35 Section 15.
36 Human Biomedical Research Regulations 2017 (No S 621), reg 11.
37 Section 19.

researcher who is aggrieved by the decision of the IRB not to grant approval for the research is entitled to appeal to the research institution which appointed the IRB, and the research institution may direct the IRB to reconsider or refer the matter to another IRB.[38]

Human biomedical research cannot be conducted if the appropriate consent of a person for participation as a research subject, including the use of his or her biological material or individually identifiable health information, has not been obtained.[39] Waiver may, however, be given by IRB in accordance with the specified statutory criteria.[40] A person who compels another to participate as a subject in human biomedical research by means of coercion or intimidation, or by means of deception or misrepresentation, is guilty of an offence.[41]

Reasonable steps and safeguards must be taken to protect individually identifiable information or human biological material against accidental or unlawful loss, modification or destruction, or unauthorised access, disclosure, copying, use or modification.[42] With respect to any information or human biological material which was individually identifiable but which has been rendered non-identifiable, the researcher cannot identify the person from whom such information or material was obtained unless the consent of the subject is obtained or reidentification is allowed.[43] As a general rule, the researcher cannot disclose any individually identifiable information of any research subject which has come to his or her knowledge in the course of discharging his or her functions or duties.[44]

A researcher conducting research must immediately report to his or her research institution any "serious adverse event" which has occurred to a research participant.[45] The research institution would have to report the matter to the Director of Medical Services.[46] It has to also establish a system to prevent or control the spread of any communicable disease from any human biological material used in transplantational human biomedical research[47] as well as to ensure the safety and welfare of the research subjects.[48]

12.2.4 Clinical trials of medicinal and therapeutic products

The clinical trials with respect to medicinal and therapeutic products are governed by separate regulations. The term "medicinal product" is defined in the Medicines Act[49] as a substance or article which is manufactured, sold, supplied, imported or exported for use by being administered to human beings or animals for a medicinal purpose and/or used as an ingredient in the preparation of a substance or article which is to be administered to human beings

---

38 Section 21.
39 Section 25.
40 Section 13 read with the Fifth Schedule.
41 Section 26.
42 Section 27.
43 This is subject to certain statutory exceptions: see section 28.
44 Section 29.
45 Human Biomedical Research Regulations 2017, reg 9.
46 Human Biomedical Research Regulations 2017, reg 10.
47 Human Biomedical Research Regulations 2017, reg 10B.
48 Human Biomedical Research Regulations 2017, reg 10C.
49 Section 3(1).

or animals for a medicinal purpose.[50] Medicinal products include cell, tissue and gene therapy products, as well as complementary health products (eg, Chinese proprietary medicines).[51] The Medicines (Clinical Trials) Regulations 2016[52] made under the Medicines Act[53] apply to all clinical trials of medicinal products which are aimed at investigating, under the direction of medical doctors or dentists, whether and to what extent the product in question has beneficial or harmful effects on patients.[54] On the other hand, the Health Products (Clinical Trials) Regulations 2016 regulate clinical trials of a health product categorised as a therapeutic product in the Health Products Act.[55] Therapeutic products include chemical drugs and biologics.

Clinical trials of therapeutic products will require a Clinical Trial Authorisation (CTA) for high-risk therapeutic products or a Clinical Trial Notification (CTN) for low-risk therapeutic products which have already been reviewed by HSA for product registration (Ho and Chang 2019, at p. 351). For medicinal products, a clinical trial certificate must be obtained from the HSA before the commencement of a trial.[56] To obtain the certificate, the principal investigator who is conducting the trial and two specialists who are not conducting the trial must certify in writing, amongst others, that the trial is required on "potential subjects who are facing a life-threatening situation to determine the safety or efficacy of a medicinal product", the available treatments or procedures are "unproven or unsatisfactory" and that there is "a reasonable prospect that participation in the trial will directly benefit the potential subjects" even if their consent or that of their legal representatives cannot be obtained.

The sponsor of the clinical trial has to "evaluate during the trial on an ongoing basis the safety of the investigational medicinal product"[57] and promptly notify all principal investigators of the trial concerning the safety of the subjects of the trial could be adversely affected and findings that could impact on the conduct of the trial. More specifically, the sponsor is required

---

50 In the Medicines Act, "a medicinal purpose" means any one or more of the following purposes:
   (a) treating or preventing disease;
   (b) diagnosing disease or ascertaining the existence, degree or extent of a physiological condition;
   (c) contraception;
   (d) inducing anaesthesia;
   (e) otherwise preventing or interfering with the normal operation of a physiological function, whether permanently or temporarily, and whether by way of terminating, reducing or postponing, or increasing or accelerating, the operation of that function or in any other way.
51 HSA's Clinical Trials Guidance 2017 at https://www.hsa.gov.sg/docs/default-source/clinical-trials/hsa_ctb_guidance_determining_cta_ctn_ctc_2may2017.pdf.
52 No. S 335.
53 (Cap. 176) (1985 Ed.), section 18.
54 Section 2 of the Medicines Act.
55 (Cap. 122D), First Schedule
56 Para 8.
57 Para 4(4).

to notify the HSA in writing of any "serious breach"[58] during the clinical trial.[59] The clinical trial certificate may include a condition requiring the sponsor to obtain and maintain insurance to provide compensation in the event of injury or loss arising from the clinical trial.[60]

The clinical trial must be supervised by a principal investigator who is a qualified practitioner (ie, a registered medical practitioner or dentist). Only the investigator or a person who is assisting and acting under the instructions of such investigator may treat or administer any investigational medicinal product of the trial to a subject of the trial.[61]

In addition to the stringent requirements for the authorisation and conduct of the clinical trials, there are specific regulations relating to the obtaining of consent from the subject in clinical trials,[62] and consent requirements in emergency situations.[63] The consent required for a person to be a subject must be obtained by an investigator who is a qualified practitioner.[64] It is also stipulated that section 6 of the Mental Capacity Act applies for the purpose of determining what is in the "best interests" of a subject in a clinical trial.[65] Full and reasonable explanation[66] of various matters including but not limited to the purpose of the trial, procedures, risks, benefits, expenses, the access to the health records and confidentiality, withdrawal of participation, and expected duration of the trial, must be given to a a subject, a legal representative, or a family member in relation to a clinical trial. Complementary with the regulations, the HSA has issued the Clinical Trials Guidance 2017[67] which state that clinical trials for therapeutic and medicinal products would also have to abide by international guidelines[68] and standard operating procedures. During the COVID-19 pandemic, a special set of guidelines[69] were issued on the contingency measures to be undertaken to ensure the safety of trial participants who may have been subject to restrictions (eg, due to quarantines and stay home notices), and to deal with interruptions of the investigational product supply chain or challenges in conducting on-site monitoring visits by sponsors.

---

58 This means a breach during a clinical trial which is likely to affect to a significant degree -
   (a) the safety, or physical or mental integrity, of any subject of the trial; or
   (b) the scientific value of the trial.
59 Para 11.
60 Para 9(2).
61 Para 5.
62 Para 16.
63 Para 17.
64 Para 18.
65 Para 18(7).
66 Para 19(1) lists the full information.
67 https://www.hsa.gov.sg/docs/default-source/clinical trials/hsa_ctb_guidance_determining_cta_ctn_ctc_2may2017.pdf.
68 The ICH E6(R2) Good Clinical Practice (GCP) Guidelines. ICH refers to the International Council for Harmonisation of Technical Requirements for Pharmaceuticals for Human Use, an international non-profit association. The guidelines were developed through a process of scientific consensus in tandem with regulatory and industry experts: https://www.ich.org/page/mission.
69 Guidance on the Conduct of Clinical Trials In Relation to the COVID-19 Situation (March 2020) https://www.research.nhg.com.sg/wps/wcm/connect/dd08a7804dcf1012acc0ae8b7731585b/HSA+COVID19+Guidance+Clinical+Trials+27Mar2020.pdf?MOD=AJPERES.

264   *Research, innovations and technologies*

Labelling requirements for medicinal and health products used in clinical trials are also put in place to protect subjects by identifying the product, the proper use and storage of the product and to enable product traceability from manufacture, import, supply to its return and destruction.[70] The onus for product labelling falls on the manufacturers, importers, suppliers including sponsors and investigators who supply investigational products and auxiliary products for the purpose of a clinical research to ensure compliance with specific regulations.[71]

> **Box 12.1 – Efficiency versus efficacy in clinical trials?**
>
> To what extent is it justifiable to allow researchers to skip steps in or to expedite clinical trials in order to develop vaccines as quickly as possible during the COVID-19 pandemic?

12.3 Ethical guidelines for human biomedical research

Unlike the statutory rules, the ethical principles on human biomedical research are not legally authoritative. These ethical principles generally complement the statutory rules. As noted above, several BAC report recommendations have led to legal reforms culminating in the HRBA. We will examine the BAC (2015) *Ethics Guidelines for Human Biomedical Research* which incorporated guidelines from seven previous BAC reports namely:

- The Stem Cell Report. *Ethical, Legal and Social Issues in Human Stem Cell Research, Reproductive and Therapeutic Cloning* (2002)
- The Tissue Report. *Human Tissue Research* (2002)
- The IRB Report. *Research Involving Human Subjects: Guidelines for IRBs* (2004)
- The Genetics Report. *Genetic Testing and Genetic Research* (2005)
- The Personal Information Report. *Personal Information in Biomedical Research* (2007)
- The Egg Donation Report. *Donation of Human Eggs for Research* (2008)
- The Human-Animal Combinations Report. *Human-Animal Combinations in Stem Cell Research* (2010).

The BAC's *Ethics Guidelines for Human Biomedical Research* have also drawn from the following external and/or international documents and declarations:

- *The Nuremberg Code* (1949)[72]

---

70 Clinical Trials Guidance (January 2018), Health Sciences Authority at https://www.hsa.gov.sg/docs/default-source/clinical-trials/hsa_ctb_guidance_labelling_mp_tp_31jan2018.pdf, para 1.2.
71 *Egs*, Health Products (Therapeutic Products as Clinical Research Materials) Regulations and the Medicines (Medicinal Products as Clinical Research Materials) Regulations.
72 The Code consists of ten ethical principles for research on humans as stated in the 1947 Judgement of the international criminal court in the Nuremberg Doctor Trials (Trials of War Criminals before the Nuremberg Military Tribunals under Control Council Law No 10 1949). The principles are as follows:
  1 the voluntary consent of the human subject is absolutely essential.

- The World Medical Association Declaration of Helsinki: *Ethical Principles for Medical Research Involving Human Subjects* (1964, revised 2013)[73]
- The Belmont Report: *Ethical Principles and Guidelines for the Protection of Human Subjects of Research* (1979)[74]

---

2. the experiment should be such as to yield fruitful results for the good of society, unprocurable by other methods or means of study, and not random and unnecessary in nature.
3. the experiment should be so designed and based on the results of animal experimentation and a knowledge of the natural history of the disease or other problem under study, that the anticipated results will justify the performance of the experiment.
4. the experiment should be so conducted as to avoid all unnecessary physical and mental suffering and injury.
5. no experiment should be conducted, where there is an *a priori* reason to believe that death or disabling injury will occur; except, perhaps, in those experiments where the experimental physicians also serve as subjects.
6. the degree of risk to be taken should never exceed that determined by the humanitarian importance of the problem to be solved by the experiment.
7. proper preparations should be made and adequate facilities provided to protect the experimental subject against even remote possibilities of injury, disability, or death.
8. the experiment should be conducted only by scientifically qualified persons. The highest degree of skill and care should be required through all stages of the experiment of those who conduct or engage in the experiment.
9. during the course of the experiment, the human subject should be at liberty to bring the experiment to an end, if he has reached the physical or mental state, where continuation of the experiment seemed to him to be impossible.
10. during the course of the experiment, the scientist in charge must be prepared to terminate the experiment at any stage, if he has probable cause to believe, in the exercise of the good faith, superior skill and careful judgement required of him, that a continuation of the experiment is likely to result in injury, disability, or death to the experiment subject.

73 This is a statement of ethical principles for medical research involving human subjects, including research on identifiable human material and data. The Declaration is addressed primarily to physicians, but the WMA encourages others involved in medical research to also adopt these principles. It contains General Principles and more specific operational principles, including Risks, Burdens and Benefits; Vulnerable Groups and Individuals; Scientific Requirements and Research Protocols; Research Ethics Committees; Privacy and Confidentiality; Informed Consent; Use of Placebo; Post-trial Provisions; Research Registration and Publication and Dissemination of Results; and Unproven Interventions in Clinical Practice.

74 The report was issued by the National Commission for the Protection of Human Subjects (US) established under the National Research Act (Pub. L. 93-348) in 1974. It focuses on three cardinal ethical principles:
  (a) respect for persons (including "autonomous individuals" and "individuals with diminished autonomy") as applied to the practice of obtaining informed consent for research (based on criteria of information, comprehension and voluntariness);
  (b) beneficence (such as to maximise the possible benefits and minimise the possible harms) as applied to the assessment of risks and benefits in research; and
  (c) justice (to each person, an equal share, according to individual need, according to individual effort, according to societal contribution, and according to merit) as applied to the selection of human subjects for research.

266 Research, innovations and technologies

- The International Ethical Guidelines for Biomedical Research Involving Human Subjects (2002)[75]
- The United Nations Educational Scientific and Cultural Organisation (UNESCO): *Universal Declaration on Bioethics and Human Rights* (2005).[76]

The five main ethical principles[77] for human biomedical research in BAC's *Ethics Guidelines for Human Biomedical Research* are:

1   *respect for persons* (respecting their right to make their own decisions without being coerced, misled, or kept in ignorance and protecting their welfare and interests)
2   *solidarity* (the subordination of individual interest to that of a group based on common interests)
3   *justice* (principle of fairness and equality under the law, equitable access to the benefits of research, and the burden of supporting it within society)
4   *proportionality* (regulation of research should be in proportion to the possible threats to autonomy, individual welfare, or the public good)
5   *sustainability* (that research should not jeopardise or prejudice the welfare of later generations).

More specific guidelines are found in the BAC *Ethics Guidelines for Human Biomedical Research* (Executive Summary).[78] These ethical guidelines overlap with as well as supplement the legal rules. The following sub-sections outlines aspects of the guidelines that are supplementary to the legal rules:

---

75 These guidelines were published by the Council for International Organizations of Medical Sciences (CIOMS), an international non-governmental organisation in official relations with the World Health Organization. Similar to the Belmont Report, the basic ethical principles are respect for persons, beneficence and justice. In addition, the guidelines cover the following specific topics: ethical justification and scientific validity of research; ethical review; informed consent; vulnerability – of individuals, groups, communities and populations; women as research subjects; equity regarding burdens and benefits; choice of control in clinical trials; confidentiality; compensation for injury; strengthening of national or local capacity for ethical review; and obligations of sponsors to provide healthcare services.
76 The Declaration provides for 15 principles relating to: human dignity and human rights; benefit and harm; autonomy and individual responsibility; consent; persons without the capacity to consent; respect to human vulnerability and personal integrity; privacy and confidentiality; equality; justice and equity; non-discrimination and non-stigmatisation; respect for cultural diversity and pluralism; solidarity and cooperation; social responsibility and health; sharing of benefits; protecting future generations; and protection from the environment, the biosphere and biodiversity. In particular, it enjoins states to take legislative and administrative measures, among others, to give effect to the Declaration's principles in accordance with international human rights law.
77 Paras 2.3–2.12.
78 The cited paragraphs in sections 12.3.1–12.3.6 refer to the specific paragraphs in the Executive Summary.

12.3.1 Ethics governance

This covers the review of human biomedical research by IRBs.[79] The submitted research should take into account the extent of the identifiable risk or sensitivity of the research.[80] An expedited review is allowed for research that involves "no more than minimal risk" to research participants, and exemptions from review must involve "no likelihood of harm" to research participants.[81] Minimal risk refers to "an anticipated level of harm and discomfort that is no greater than that ordinarily encountered in daily life, or during the performance of routine educational, physical, or psychological tasks".[82]

12.3.2 Consent to participation

Consent for participation in research must be given voluntarily and in the absence of coercion, deception or undue influence. Research participants may be reimbursed for legitimate expenses. Any other payment, whether monetary or in kind, should not amount to an inducement, and should be approved by an IRB. Keeping research participants in ignorance of a research hypothesis, or of which intervention group they have been assigned to, does not amount to deception. However, the need to keep participants ignorant of a research hypothesis should be disclosed and justified to the satisfaction of the IRB.

For research involving vulnerable persons not lacking mental capacity,[83] consent should be taken by independent third parties, whenever possible. With regard to research involving patients, consent for participating in research should be clearly separated from consent for treatment. When a researcher is also the attending physician, the consent for research should ideally be taken by an independent third person.

12.3.3 Personal information

All biomedical research involving personal information, whether identified or de-identified, will be subject to IRB review.[84] Personal information used for research should be de-identified as early as possible, and stored and managed as de-identified information.[85]

Information should remain in the care of and for the use of the researcher and not as the continued property of the research participant or 'donor'. An organisation that collects and de-identifies personal data for processing and storage is still considered to hold personal data if it retains the ability to re-identify the data.

---

79 The IRB should "combine appropriate expertise with some lay representation to reinforce the objectivity and impartiality of the process": see para 3.
80 Para 4.
81 Para 4.
82 Para 5.
83 For example, prisoners, uniformed personnel, and employees.
84 Para 21.
85 Para 23.

Research participants are entitled to expect that their data will not be used for purposes other than those for which they have given consent, and the information should not be disclosed to any third party, including employers or insurance companies.

12.3.4 Biobanking and research involving human biological materials

For research using foetal tissues, consent for the termination of pregnancy should be separate from the consent for obtaining foetal tissue or any tissue related to the pregnancy for research.[86] For women undergoing fertility treatment, consent for the donation of surplus oocytes or embryos for research should be separate from the consent for treatment. The treating physician should not also be the researcher seeking consent for the donation of oocytes or embryos for research.[87] Women wishing to donate eggs specifically for research must be of sound mind, clearly understand the nature and consequences of the donation, and have freely given explicit consent, without any inducement, coercion or undue influence.[88]

12.3.5 Human genetic research

Participation in genetic research should be voluntary, whether directly or by contribution of biological materials or personal information.[89] When clinically significant findings are discovered in the course of any genetic research, researchers should ensure that affected participants are informed, if they have indicated their desire to know.[90]

12.4 Medical innovations and information technologies in healthcare

Medical technology is evolving rapidly to improve delivery of medical services. Two applications at the cutting-edge are nanobiotechnology and neurotechnology. Nano-particles due their size can pass through cell membranes. In nanobiotechnology, nano-artefacts deliver lethal drugs to targeted cells to destroy them. It is also employed in *in vitro* diagnostics, biomaterials and implants. The risks involve the toxicity levels of the nano-particles which are small enough to be inhaled or ingested by humans. The nano-particles could invade the bloodstream and attack human organs causing serious harm. In the area of neurotechnology, brain implants in paralysed patients enable them to control robotic arms and brain imaging is utilised to diagnose and treat neurological diseases. Functional magnetic resonance imaging (fMRI) measures the brain's electrical activity whilst transcranial direct current stimulation (tDCS) devices stimulate brain activity electrically. Research is already ongoing to develop brain-computer interfaces (BCIs) to "read" a person's mind or neurons and "translate" them into words on a computer.[91] This technology raises novel issues concerning individual privacy to the brain and the security

---

86 Para 32.
87 Para 34.
88 Para 35.
89 Para 44.
90 Para 45.
91 Sigal Samuel, "Brain-Reading tech is coming. The law is not ready to protect us", 20 Dec 2019 at https://www.vox.com/2019/8/30/20835137/facebook-zuckerberg-elon-musk-brain-mind-reading-neuroethics.

of brain data. On neurotechnologies more generally, Ienca and Andorno (2017) highlighted four novel human rights that might be relevant in future: right to cognitive liberty (to use or refuse coercive uses of emerging neurotechnologies), the right to mental privacy (to protect against illegitimate access to a person's brain information and to prevent the indiscriminate leakage of brain data), the right to mental integrity (to protect against forced intrusion into and alteration of a person's neural processes), and the right to psychological continuity (personal identity consisting in experiencing oneself as persisting through time as the same person). The OECD Council has issued the *OECD Recommendation on Responsible Innovation in Neurotechnology* (11 December 2019) to "address the ethical, legal and social challenges raised by novel neurotechnologies while promoting innovation in the field".[92]

This section discusses how the courts, SMC and the legal and disciplinary processes regulate the use of innovative treatments and untested practices by medical practitioners, the use of information technology (such as electronic health records, telemedicine, robotics and artificial intelligence) to enhance the provision of medical services and the potential pitfalls and legal and ethical issues that might arise.

12.4.1 Innovative treatments and untested practices

The general position adopted in Singapore is that a balance should be struck between allowing innovative treatments with its underlying commercial considerations and ensuring the safety of the patient. This position and how the balancing exercise is carried out can be gleaned from a scrutiny of both court decisions and ethical guidelines.

The ECEG 2002 (clause 4.1.4) and 2016 (section B6) respectively refer to treatments that are "not generally accepted" by the profession and "outside the context of a formal and approved clinical trial" and to what extent such treatments can be administered. More specifically, the ECEG 2016 state that doctors must treat patients only according to "generally accepted methods, based on a balance of available evidence and accepted best practices" and that treatments that are not generally accepted must be offered to patients only in the context of formal and approved clinical trials. Innovative therapy may however be offered when conventional therapy is "unhelpful and it is a desperate or dire situation".[93] The ECEG 2016 also added that there must be "professional consensus on the use of innovative therapy in the particular clinical situation". It is not clear as to the extent of "professional consensus" required and how such "consensus" may be proved since innovative therapy is not likely to

---

92 https://www.oecd.org/science/recommendation-on-responsible-innovation-in-neurotechnology.htm. The Recommendations consisted of nine principles: 1. Promoting responsible innovation 2. Prioritising safety assessment 3. Promoting inclusivity 4. Fostering scientific collaboration 5. Enabling societal deliberation 6. Enabling capacity of oversight and advisory bodies 7. Safeguarding personal brain data and other information 8. Promoting cultures of stewardship and trust across the public and private sector 9. Anticipating and monitoring potential unintended use and/or misuse.

93 See Article 35 of the Declaration of Helsinki (2008) which states that,
In the treatment of a patient, where proven interventions do not exist or have been ineffective, the physician, after seeking expert advice, with informed consent from the patient or a legally authorized representative, may use an unproven intervention if in the physician's judgement it offers hope of saving life, re-establishing health or alleviating suffering.

be widely practised. Moreover, ECEG 2016 also remind us that consent must be obtained from patients if they are able to give it.

We examine below two disciplinary cases that deal with clause 4.1.4 of the ECEG 2002 followed by a medical negligence case. First, the novel use of therapeutic ultrasound on a patient with a chronic and complicated neurological syndrome did not give rise to professional misconduct in *Gobinathan Devathasan v SMC*.[94] On the clause in ECEG 2002, the court stated that patients should be treated with "time tested methods where the benefits and risks have been well researched and documented", and that doctors should ensure that to conform to generally accepted practices is to ensure that "patients suffer no harm".[95] The factors for determining whether a particular medical treatment is generally accepted were as follows:

(a) there had to be at least "one good study";
(b) the results of the study can be replicated and reproduced under the same sort of like treatment parameters and conditions;
(c) the study had been written up in publications and presented at meetings;
(d) the study had received peer review;
(e) the study had clear-cut results and the sample had to be statistically significant; and
(f) the study had to have some form of controls such as randomised double-blind trials.

The court in *Gobinathan* opined that the proper legal approach towards treatment that is not generally accepted is to shift the burden onto the doctor to show the patient will not come to harm as this would strike "a correct balance between two important considerations in medicine, *viz*, promoting innovation and progress, provided that the patient's well-being is not compromised".[96]

This legal approach was elaborated upon in *Pang Ah San v Singapore Medical Council*.[97] The patient suffered a stroke and required permanent tube feeding. The doctor recommended the use of and performed the loop Percutaneous Endoscopic Gastrostomy ("loop-PEG") tube, which he had developed, to feed the patient. However, the patient's health condition deteriorated and she died shortly thereafter. The doctor was charged for providing treatment to the patient that was not generally accepted by the profession and outside the context of a formal and approved clinical trial, in breach of clause 4.1.4 of ECEG 2002.

Rajah JA, delivering judgement on behalf of the High Court, noted that the doctor could have applied to the IRBs and ethics committees for review and approvals to conduct clinical trials.[98] His Honour also cited *Low Chai Lin v SMC*[99] for the proposition that the assessment of whether a particular medical treatment is generally accepted is scientific and not empirical (which is based solely on the numbers of doctors engaged in it). The treatment accepted by a number of doctors may after all be unethical or illegitimate. The learned judge, however,

---

94 [2010] 2 SLR 926.
95 [2010] 2 SLR 926 at [45].
96 [2010] 2 SLR 926 at [62].
97 [2014] 1 SLR 1094.
98 [2014] 1 SLR 1094 at [30].
99 [2013] 1 SLR 83.

stated that where an overwhelming majority of doctors endorses a certain treatment, it is *prima facie* evidence that it is generally accepted.[100]

The expression "not generally accepted by the profession" should mean "not generally known or used". A particular treatment is generally accepted (*ie*, a standard treatment) where "the potential benefits and risks of that treatment and the ability to control these are approaching a level of predictability that is acceptable to the medical community in general".[101] The High Court added that[102]:

> ... standard treatments may lose their status of being "generally accepted" if there is a rejection of the standard treatment by the profession, or if the underlying assumptions about the safety and efficacy of the standard treatment ought to be seriously questioned in the light of advances in medical knowledge, provided that there are viable alternatives to that treatment... ...
>
> A particular treatment will only be caught by the prohibition against offering innovative treatments in Clause 4.1.4 if that particular treatment is significantly different from the standard treatment that is generally accepted by the profession... ...
>
> Important factors in assessing whether a particular treatment is significantly different from the standard treatment are the increase in the amount of risks, the addition of new types of risks, and a significant increase in the degree of ignorance of the risks.

In the present case, as the "use of the loop-PEG tube significantly increased the risks of leakage of gastric contents into the peritoneal cavity, hence rendering the loop-PEG procedure significantly different from the standard PEG procedure/tube", the loop-PEG procedure was "not generally accepted by the profession".[103] In addition, the High Court stated that "experimental and innovative treatment which is *therapy* administered in the best interests of the patient is permissible"[104] though this principle did not apply to the case at hand.[105]

The Disciplinary Committee (or Tribunal) have in a number of cases ruled against medical practitioners who have offered or given treatments that were not medically proven at the relevant time *and* outside the context of a formal and approved clinical trial: offering via advertisements the use of stem cell skin therapy or stem cell therapy for facial and body rejuvenation,[106] offering to use cell therapy for anti-ageing and rejuvenation,[107] the use of Bioresonance Machine to treat the patient's smoking habits, allergies and behavioural issues as a result of autism,[108] performing the Aqualift Dermal Filler (ADF) procedure and injecting

---

100 [2014] 1 SLR 1094 at [50].
101 [2014] 1 SLR 1094 at [55]-[56] citing (Cowan 1985, at p. 621).
102 [2014] 1 SLR 1094 at [56]-[57].
103 [2014] 1 SLR 1094 at [59].
104 [2014] 1 SLR 1094 at [61] citing Chan (2013) and BAC (2004) Guidelines, paras 3.21 to 3.23.
105 [2014] 1 SLR 1094 at [108].
106 *In the matter of Dr ADP* [2010] SMCDC 13 (fine and censure).
107 *In the Matter of Dr AAT* [2009] SMCDC 8 (fine and censure).
108 *In the Matter of Dr ABO* [2010] SMCDC 12 (the doctor pleaded guilty to the charge and was fined and censured).

the patient with Aqualift Hydrophilic Gel (AHG) filler material for breast augmentation,[109] advertising certain procedures as "detox medicine", and offering face treatment using oxygen.[110]

We will now turn to the medical negligence case of *Rathanamalah d/o Shunmugam v Chia Kok Hoong*[111] in which the use of a novel surgical technique, or novel combination of surgical procedures on a patient suffering from eczema was held to be not negligent. The defendant doctor had combined endovenous laser therapy with foam sclerotherapy in an unorthodox fashion in treating the plaintiff. Expert evidence indicated that the novel technique posed minimal risk and had the potential to reduce the risk of injury. The court reasoned that there was no evidence that no responsible body of medical opinion, logically held, would support such innovation.[112] This is arguably an innovation-friendly inversion of the *Bolam/Bolitho* standard that was first articulated in the Scottish case of *Hunter v Hanley*[113] in which Lord President Clyde had stated that "[i]n the realm of diagnosis and treatment, there is ample scope for genuine difference of opinion".

In addition to the *post hoc* regulation of innovative treatments and untested practices in terms of SMC disciplinary actions and medical negligence, it has been proposed that there should also be *ex ante* regulation through peer oversight processes such as requiring clinical registries to collate information of innovative therapies and the institutional supervision of the development processes prior to the use of such innovative treatments in order to protect patients and public health (Chan 2013, at pp. 127-129; Cowan 1985, at p. 630).

12.4.2 Telemedicine and telehealth products

Telemedicine facilitates the delivery of healthcare resources in a timely manner to those who need it, helps to bridge the distance, and saves travel time and money. This has become even more important during the COVID-19 pandemic. In the *National Telemedicine Guidelines* (January 2015)[114] ("NTG"), telemedicine refers to "the systematic provision of healthcare services over physically separate environments via Information and Communications Technology (ICT)", and is applicable in four main domains as follows:

- Tele-collaboration: interactions between onsite and remote healthcare professionals for clinical referral, co-diagnosis, supervision or case review

---

109 *In the matter of Dr Chan Heang Kng Calvin* [2017] SMCDT 6 (the applications to the Health Sciences Authority to register the AHG were not approved. The doctor pleaded guilty to the charge as well as other charges including the failure to inform patient of the lack of published clinical studies and data on the safety of ADF procedure or AHG. The DT suspended the doctor for six months).
110 *In the Matter of Dr ABU* [2011] SMCDC 2.
111 [2018] 4 SLR 159.
112 [2018] 4 SLR 159 at [127].
113 1955 SLT 213; [1955] SC 200.
114 https://www.moh.gov.sg/docs/librariesprovider5/licensing-terms-and-conditions/national-telemedicine-guidelines-for-singapore-(dated-30-jan-2015).pdf.

- Tele-treatment: interactions between remote healthcare professionals and patients/caregivers for direct clinical care such as triage, history, examination, diagnosis and treatment, and remote robotic surgery
- Tele-monitoring: biomedical and other forms of data collection directly from patients (or through caregivers) via remote systems, which are used by healthcare professions for vital signs monitoring and home nursing
- Tele-support: using online services to support the patient and caregiver, such as health education, care administration, and treatment prompts in chronic disease management

Beyond these domains, exchanging information for clinical purposes between providers and patients/caregivers over electronic media also falls within Telemedicine's definition.

The NTG are broad and generic, and individual specialities are encouraged to customise the NTG to meet the specific requirements of their respective fields. The NTG state that duty of care must be established in all telemedicine encounters and the responsibilities of patient/caregivers and roles of health professionals should be clarified. Healthcare professionals are enjoined to collaborate with each other to clearly define their roles and responsibilities. Further, the patient and caregiver should be given clear and explicit directions during the telemedicine encounters as to who has ongoing responsibility for any required follow-up and ongoing healthcare. With respect to standard of care in Telemedicine delivery, the overall standard must not be any less compared to a service not involving telemedicine. Where a face-to-face consultation is not reasonably practical, it is permitted to deliver care exclusively via Telemedicine as this is better than not having any access to care at all. On the other hand, where face-to-face consultations are reasonably practical, the delivery of Telemedicine must not compromise the overall quality of care provided as compared with non-Telemedicine care delivery.

In this regard, the SMC ECEG 2016 contains a specific section on Telemedicine[115] as to its "responsible" provision. Medical practitioners are enjoined to "provide the same quality and standard of care as in-person medical care" and ensure they have "sufficient training and information to manage patients through telemedicine". With respect to the provision of healthcare by a medical practitioner via robotic procedures performed by other doctors remotely, the medical practitioner "retains responsibility for the overall management of the patients". Sufficient information including information on the limitations of telemedicine that may affect the quality of care must be provided to patients in order that proper consent may be given.

Healthcare organisations must ensure that patient information and records are protected by having a confidentiality policy in place, and comply with applicable existing legislation and regulations such as the Personal Data Protection Act (PDPA) and the SMC Ethical Code and Ethical Guidelines (ECEG). On informed consent, healthcare providers should share relevant information, such as the objective of the Telemedicine interaction, care documentation requirements, risks and benefits, costs, and alternative choices before commencing any Telemedicine interaction.

---

115 Section A6.

The Ministry for Health has sought to encourage selected telemedicine providers to participate in a regulatory sandbox – the Licensing Experimentation and Adaptation Programme (LEAP)[116] – to develop innovative methods and tools in order to better understand the evolving nature of telemedicine and to jointly partake in the creation of appropriate regulatory frameworks. During the COVID-19 pandemic, pre-approvals were granted for a number of new teleconsultation (video) solutions.[117]

Before we discuss telehealth products, let us briefly examine the regulations pertaining to medical devices generally. The HSA regulates medical devices by requiring formal registration except for the class A medical devices (low risk) and conducts evaluations on the devices based on their risk classifications. The registrants of the medical devices have to notify the HSA of changes that affect the safety, quality and efficacy of the registered device pursuant to the Health Products (Medical Devices) Regulations. Apart from risk-based regulation, HSA also makes reference to approvals already given by certain regulatory agencies for the medical devices and/or their prior safe marketing history.

Telehealth products are instruments, apparatus, machines or software (including mobile applications) that are involved in the provision of healthcare services over physically separate environments via info-communication technologies. Similar to Telemedicine, it is classified into four domains in the HSA's *Regulatory Guidelines for Telehealth Products* (2019)[118]:

- Tele-collaboration (*eg*, an online platform that facilitates sharing of information between physicians for peer consultation purpose)
- Tele-treatment (*eg*, a robotic surgery system that allows a surgeon to perform surgery on a patient even though they are not physically in the same location)
- Tele-monitoring (*eg*, a portable SpO2 patient monitoring system that is intended for spot-checking or continuous monitoring of oxygen saturation of arterial haemoglobin where the readings can be transmitted to the physician for monitoring)
- Tele-support (*eg*, a mobile application that provides educational information to patients on diseases and medications)

A Telehealth product intended for medical purposes by the Product Owner (PO), will be classified as a medical device and would be regulated by HSA as Telehealth Medical Device and is subject to the following medical device regulatory controls: product registration, dealer's license requirements and post-market obligations. It should be noted that not all Telehealth products are medical devices. Some Wellness Devices merely encourage users to improve or maintain a healthy lifestyle and are not considered medical devices. The PO should ensure that the product is labelled with a clarification statement or equivalent that is sufficiently clear so as to avoid it being mistakenly used for medical purposes.

---

116 https://www.moh.gov.sg/home/our-healthcare-system/licensing-experimentation-and-adaptation-programme-(leap)---a-moh-regulatory-sandbox.

117 https://www.imda.gov.sg/-/media/Imda/Files/About/Media-Releases/2020/Annex-A_New-Teleconsultation-Video-Solutions-Supported-by-PSG.pdf?la=en.

118 https://www.hsa.gov.sg/docs/default-source/hprg-mdb/regulatory-guidelines-for-telehealth-products-rev-2-1.pdf.

Standalone Medical Mobile Applications (*ie*, software for which PO intends to perform a medical function *per se* without controlling or affecting other hardware medical devices such as medical sensors) are regulated by the HSA if the application is distributed in Singapore via local online platforms.[119] Like all other medical devices, the Standalone Medical Mobile Applications are subject to similar regulatory controls relating to product registration, dealer's license requirements and post-market obligations.

As a final note, telepharmacy and tele-pharmaceutical care services in Singapore allow access to medicines, remote medication review, patient counselling and education, pharmacist consults, and medication adherence monitoring.[120]

12.4.3 Electronic health records and big data

The National Electronic Health Record (NEHR) is a patient data exchange system for the purpose of enabling clinicians and healthcare professionals to view patient health records across the health establishments in Singapore including community hospitals, GP clinics, clinical laboratories, and nursing homes. Medical information shared on NEHR include the discharge summaries (which summarise the patient's recent hospitalisation record and treatment received), laboratory test results, medical operation reports, X-ray and other radiological test results, patient diagnoses, allergies, medicines prescribed and emergency department reports. This allows doctors and healthcare professionals taking care of the patient to obtain a more holistic view of and more expeditious access to the patient's medical history and condition. This is particularly important in emergency situations when speed in obtaining relevant medical information concerning the patient is of the essence. Moreover, certain patients who are elderly or mentally infirm may not be able to recall or communicate relevant medical information to the doctors. To allow for such holistic use of medical data, interoperability of computer systems is required to link data kept by various medical hospitals and institutions, research institutions and government agencies.

Electronic data may be aggregated for the purpose of detecting trends and making predictions. Big data allows for predictive analysis of trends relating to diseases and symptoms globally or in certain regions or countries. During the COVID-19 pandemic, big data was used to predict and to reduce the spread of the coronavirus. For example, a heat map was developed to detect the users who were experiencing symptoms of COVID-19 and ascertain if they were staying home in order to contain the spread.[121] An app known as TraceTogether was developed in Singapore to trace infected persons by allowing users who have downloaded the app on their smart phones to detect other users who may be within close proximity during a specified period. Big data can generate information for clinical practice for the benefit of patients as well as in medical research to enhance the store of generalisable knowledge on health and well-being. However, obtaining consent from patients to use their personal data

---

119 *Eg*, the Apple Store and Google Play Store.
120 See also Pharmaceutical Society of Singapore's Guidelines for Telepharmacy and Tele-Pharmaceutical Care Services.
121 https://www.mobihealthnews.com/news/europe/evergreen-life-build-covid-19-heat-map-new-mental-health-app-launched-uk-and-many-more.

276 Research, innovations and technologies

for specific purposes would be impractical where the aggregated data may be used in a wide range of contexts and in ways that are quite removed from the original source of information.

12.4.4 Robotics and artificial intelligence

In 1993, the Singapore General Hospital (SGH) used virtual reality surgery to remove brain tumours and arteriovenous malformations (Ang 2016, at pp. 225-226). About 20 years later, in 2012, SGH began using the *daVinci* robot-assisted surgical system for minimally invasive procedures to remove cancers in the throat, tongue and tonsils. Changi General Hospital's online pharmacy enables the purchase of homecare and medical supplies via Internet and online healthcare assessment tools. Since 2014, the Tan Tock Seng Hospital's (TTSH) outpatient pharmacy automation system has been providing automated, radio-frequency identification (RFID) technology, and robotic technology to ensure accurate medication packing and dispensing to patients. The robotic endoscopy system (Master and Slave Transluminal Endoscopic Robot or MASTER) has been employed by the National University Hospital (NUH) to perform endoscopic submucosal dissection in patients (Sim 2016, at p. 254).

The Centre for Healthcare Assistive & Robotics Technology (CHART)[122] in Singapore – which involves healthcare professionals, academia and research institutions in co-developing and test-bedding healthcare solutions with assistive robots – builds prototypes of smart systems and technologies.[123] It has developed the Tutti bathing system (that includes a wheelchair docked directly onto a bathtub to allow patients to take private baths), Rimo the robot that facilitates communications between bed-bound patients and friends who live far away, autonomous robotic floor scrubbers and cleaners and a leg rehabilitation robot for physiotherapy.[124] The Soutenir Gait Assessment robot has the capacity to capture gait parameters to customise rehabilitation interventions and exercises in order to cater to the patient's needs.[125] The design of care robots that interact with patients should, as far as possible, be based on ethical principles (such as respecting autonomy and being responsive to needs) in ways that are sensitive to the caring values, practices and contexts in which they are placed (van Wynsberghe 2013).

The uses of artificial intelligence in clinical practice and healthcare sector generally are myriad. Clinical Decision Support Systems (CDSS) platforms utilise machine learning to make diagnostic decisions and predictions of treatment outcomes based on EHR data as described above. The diagnostic recommendations generated via CDSS use algorithms derived from rules that are informed by clinical guidelines and published medical research

---

122 CHART was established with the support of the Ministry of Health and the Singapore Economic Development Board.
123 CHART's twin objectives are to enable (a) "Hospitals of the future" (using robots to provide precision care and medicine in hospitals and also in community hospitals, nursing homes and day residential care); and (b) "Hospital to Home" (using robots to assist in providing care and for the aged at home with equipment for consumer use).
124 "Assistive Technologies to Improve Healthcare quality, productivity" MIS Today, 27 Feb 2016.
125 "Charting the way to hospitals of the future" 23 January 2018 at https://www.edb.gov.sg/en/news-and-events/insights/innovation/charting-the-way-to-hospitals-of-the-future.html.

(Lysaght et al. 2019). Natural language processing is used to analyse EHR data comprising the doctors' personal notes and narrations of symptoms. The data regarding the various symptoms of a disease may be labelled in advance and imputed into a system using supervised machine learning in order to diagnose the patient's condition. Deep learning algorithms are currently used in radiography, mammography for breast cancer detection and in MRI to detect brain tumours. AI may also be used to conduct predictive analysis from aggregated data from various sources of medical information.

The Singapore Personal Data Protection Commission (PDPC) in its Model AI Governance Framework (Second Edition) (Jan 2020)[126] suggests that, depending on whether the harms from AI use are likely and/or severe, the "Human-in-the-loop" approach (*ie*, where "human oversight is active and involved, with the human retaining full control and the AI only providing recommendations or input") should be employed. In such an approach, whilst the doctor utilises AI to identify possible diagnoses and treatments of a patient's condition, he makes the final decision on the diagnosis and the corresponding treatment. This is on the assumption the AI provides sufficient information for the human doctor to make an informed decision.

The use of artificial intelligence in medical diagnoses or treatment also raises the question as to whether the doctor may be liable in medical negligence in the event of patient injuries resulting from an AI error. Under the *Bolam* test, the mere fact that the doctor's use of medical AI deviates from existing medical practice does not necessarily amount to negligence. Otherwise, it would not be feasible at all to introduce any medical innovations in clinical practice. We have already alluded above to such a position in *Rathanamalah d/o Shunmugam v Chia Kok Hoong*.[127] Further, a strict reliance on the *Bolam* test – which is used to assess standard of care in diagnosis and treatment when there are genuine differences of medical expert opinion – may not be justified for assessing the standard of care in the use of medical AI since doctors do not for the moment possess similar expertise in medical AI. In any event, courts should have the leeway to look at standard factors such as risks of harm, extent of harm and costs of taking precautions instead of being tied only to the *Bolam* and *Bolitho* tests for assessing the reasonableness of the doctor's conduct in using medical AI.[128]

Software including artificial intelligence may be utilised in connection with medical devices as stipulated in the Health Products Act to assist in diagnosis, treatment or to monitor patients' health conditions. The HSA's 2019 Regulatory Guidelines govern the use of various software medical devices: software embedded in medical devices (*eg*, imaging software in ultrasound system), standalone software (*eg*, imaging processing software), standalone mobile applications (*eg*, mobile apps to remotely monitor patient's vital signs) and web-based software (*eg*, a software application accessed through a web browser for users to upload

---

126 https://www.pdpc.gov.sg/-/media/files/pdpc/pdf-files/resource-for-organisation/ai/sgmodelai-govframework2.pdf, para 3.14-3.16 (there may be other factors involved eg, nature of harm and (ir)reversibility of harm).

127 [2018] 4 SLR 159 at [127], *per* Aedit Abdullah JC. Cf *Hepworth v Kerr* [1995] 6 Med LR 139 (defendant anaesthetist was negligent in experimenting with new hypotensive anaesthetic technique which exposed patient to excessive risk).

128 *Hii Chii Kok v Ooi Peng Jin London Lucien and another* [2017] 2 SLR 492.

patient images for diagnostic purposes). They cover the various stages of product development and use: the implementation of Quality Management Systems for software medical devices to ensure their "safety, quality and effectiveness",[129] pre-market product registration requirements[130], licensing and controls over the manufacturers and distributors of the devices, the management of changes to the registered software, post-market management of the devices, and cybersecurity concerns (including patient privacy and the confidentiality of patient data).

With respect to Artificial Intelligence Medical Devices (AI-MD) in particular, pre-market registration will require information relating to: (i) the input data and features such as the patient's historical records, diagnostic images and medication records; (ii) source, size and attribution of training, validation and test datasets; (iii) the AI model selection; (iv) the test protocol and report for verification and validation of the AI-MD; (v) the performance of AI-MD in terms of accuracy, specificity and sensitivity of the device; (vi) the clinical association between AI-MD's output and clinical conditions; (vii) the device workflow including how the output result should be used (*eg*, whether it is human-in-the-loop) and others. For AI-MD with continuous learning capabilities, there are additional process controls and validations to monitor the learning and evolving performances of the device.

An interesting issue is whether the medical doctor or hospital may reasonably *rely* on the approving authorities and thereby absolve themselves from negligence liability. According to the Singapore case of *TV Media Pte Ltd v De Cruz Andrea Heidi*,[131] the defendant (distributor of pills) cannot absolve negligence liability by placing "unquestionable reliance" on a health approving authority with respect to certain pills that caused the plaintiff's injuries. In that case, there were suspicious circumstances arising from tests conducted on the pills. If this argument were to be used in the context of AI, the doctor would have to show that he had reasonably relied on the AI as opposed to mere unquestioning reliance on the authorities which approved the AI use. To determine the reasonableness or otherwise of reliance on medical AI which has been approved as a medical device, it is argued that we should consider the authority's scope of approval, the review process before granting approvals and the knowledge of the medical doctor regarding such processes.

> **Box 12.2 – Doctor's obligation to utilise medical AI?**
>
> Do you think medical doctors should be liable to a patient who suffers injury as a result of the doctor's *omission* to use AI? For example, when an AI-driven knowledge interface such as Watson is available to the doctor, and the doctor failed to consider the AI results derived from the AI's review of millions of patterns of a disease, and misdiagnosed the patient's illness, can we say that he has fallen below the reasonable standard of a doctor?

---

129 HSA (2019) Guidelines, at p. 5.
130 This relates to the safety and performance of the devices, labelling requirements, design verification and validation and clinical evaluation of the devices, risk management and cybersecurity.
131 [2004] 3 SLR(R) 543.

Another problem is that biased training data (*eg*, disproportionately significant positive results for a particular ethnic group within the population) may lead to inaccurate AI outputs. Further, the opacity of the AI model and the unpredictability of machine learning may prevent the users from obtaining a proper explanation of the output in human-interpretable terms. The question of where the loss lies in the event of an AI mistake would need to take account of a number of policy considerations such as fairness to the doctor, adequate protection for the welfare of the patients and the assessments of the benefits and risks of embracing technological innovations such as medical AI.

12.5 Conclusion

Singapore has put in place a fairly stringent set of legal rules and ethical principles to ensure that human biomedical research is conducted properly with due regard for the safety of research subjects. The legislation delineates the scope of human biomedical research including prohibited and restricted research. The onus of ensuring proper conduct in human biomedical research falls largely on research institutions and their researchers with supervision and approvals to be obtained from IRBs, the Director of Medical Services and/or the Ministry for Health. Authorisations are required for clinical trials of medicinal and therapeutic products with strict reporting requirements for sponsors and investigators. The autonomy of research and clinical trial subjects is respected through the imposition of strict requirements for consent to be obtained and detailed explanations to be given by researchers as to the purpose, procedures and risks pertaining to the research or trial. Medical innovations such as novel treatments and untested practices are not discouraged in Singapore provided patient welfare is safeguarded. The use of information technology in healthcare including the digitalised collation and interoperability of patient electronic data under the NEHR initiative is gathering pace. Telemedicine and telehealth products based on HSA's regulatory guidelines seek to provide medical services to patients remotely without compromising the standards of medical services and patient safety. Whilst there is no special legislation for the use of robotics and artificial intelligence as yet, regulatory guidelines on the use of AI-medical devices serve to prevent or mitigate the risks of AI errors. The existing law on negligence can be adapted and harnessed to accommodate important considerations such as the promotion of technological innovations, fairness to parties and the safety of patients.

References

Ang, C.L. (2016). "Singapore General Hospital" in Lee C. E. & Satku, K. (eds) *Singapore's Health Care System: What 50 years have achieved* (World Scientific: Singapore), pp. 221–227.
BAC (Bioethics Advisory Committee) (2004). *Research Involving Human Subject Guidelines for IRBs*.
BAC (2010). *Human-Animal Combinations in Stem Cell Research—A Report* (September).
BAC (2015). *Ethics Guidelines for Human Biomedical Research* in June 2015 at https://www.bioethics-singapore.org/files/publications/reports/ethics-guidelines-for-human-biomedical-research-full-report.pdf.
Chan, T.E. (2008). "Minors and Biomedical Research in Singapore" 28 *Legal Studies* 396.
Chan, T.E. (2010). "The Challenge of Regulating Human Biomedical Research" 22 *Singapore Academy of Law Journal* 958.
Chan, T.E. (2013). "Legal and Regulatory Responses to Innovative Treatment" 21 *Medical Law Review* 92.

Cowan, DH (1985). "Innovative Therapy versus Experimentation" 21 *Torts & Ins LJ* 619.
Health Sciences Authority (2019). *Regulatory Guidelines for Software Medical Devices – A Lifecycle Approach* (December).
Ho, M. & Chang, M.P. (2019). "Singapore", chapter 25 in Kingham, R. (ed), *The Life Sciences Law Review* 8th Ed (Law Business Research) pp. 347–365.
Ienca, M. & Andorno, R. (2017). "Towards New Human Rights in the Age of Neuroscience and Neurotechnology" 13 *Life Sciences, Society and Policy* 5.
Kaan, S.H.T. (2004). "Medical Research" in Yeo Khee Quan (ed) *Essentials of Medical Law* (Sweet & Maxwell Asia), ch 9.
Lysaght, T., Lim, H.Y., Xafis, V. et al. (2019). "AI-Assisted Decision Making in Healthcare: The Application of an Ethics Framework for Big Data in Health and Research" 11(3) *Asian Bioethics Review* 299–314. https://doi.org/10.1007/s41649-019-00096-0.
Labude, M.K. (2016). "A New Framework for Self-Regulation: Human Biomedical Research Act 2015" *Singapore Journal of Legal Studies* 194–208.
McHale, J. (2010). "Law, Regulation and Public Health Research: A Case for Fundamental Reform" in Letsas, G. & O'Cinneide, C. (eds) *Current Legal Problems*, Vol 63 (Oxford University Press: Oxford), pp. 475–510.
McHale, J. (2017). "Clinical Research" in Laing, J. & McHale, J. (eds) *Principles of Medical Law*, Fourth Edition (Oxford University Press: Oxford), pp. 712–751.
National Medical Ethics Committee (NMEC) (1997). *Ethical Guidelines on Research Involving Human Subjects*.
Sim, J. (2016). "National University Hospital" in Lee C.E. & Satku, K. (eds) *Singapore's Health Care System: What 50 years have achieved* (World Scientific: Singapore), pp. 247–256.
van Wynsberghe, A. (2013). "Designing Robots for Care: Care Centered Value-Sensitive Design" 19 *Science and Engineering Ethics* 407–433.

INDEX

Note: *Page numbers followed by "n" denote footnotes.*

abortion: decision-making 77; ethics 43, 80, 190-192; foetus' right 104, 190-192; law 188-190; mother's right 191-192
act-omission distinction 220, 229
adoption 196, 197-198
advanced care planning 209
advanced medical directive (AMD) 147, 213-217, 224-225, 229
Agency for Integrated Care (AIC) 4, 4n13, 113, 151n88, 209
allied healthcare professionals 8, 10
alternative medicine 11, 46, 164, 164n1, 176
artificial intelligence 24, 276-279
automatism 123, 132-133
autonomy 29, 31, 45; and beneficence 38; and biomedical research 257n12, 260, 265n74, 266, 279; and confidentiality 145, 160; and Confucianism 31; consent to treatment 94, 96, 97, 102, 103-104, 106, 108-109, 135; and end of life 37-38, 215, 217-218, 225, 229-230; and human dignity 40; and negligence 53, 65, 74; principlism 34-37; relational autonomy 36-37; and reproduction 191, 194, 204-206; and robots 276; types of 36

BAC Ethics Guidelines for Human Biomedical Research 264, 266
bailment 247-248, 251
battery 23, 84, 94-95, 97, 98n19, 101, 106, 131, 175
Belmont Report 265, 266n75

beneficence 34-35, 38, 45-46; and best interests 102; and biomedical research 265n74; and treatment 107; procreative beneficence 201; and reproduction 203
best interests: biomedical research 254n6, 263; and confidentiality 140n5, 154, 158-159; of donors 119; emergency 111; end of life 218-222, 226; medical innovations 271; mentally incapable persons 38, 98-99, 100, 101-103, 104-105, 109-110, 112, 118n33, 122, 137; minors 112, 140n5, 186; no consent 104; of patients 44-45, 94, 102, 105, 109-110, 166; and reproduction 187, 207; and substituted judgement 102; and TCM practitioners 172
Bioethics Advisory Committee (BAC) 26-27, 34n6, 157, 199-201, 203, 207, 233, 255, 257, 271n104
blood: Code of Ethics for Blood Donation and Transfusion 242; donation 234, 240, 242-243; Health Sciences Authority 12, 242; sale and supply 240-242, 247, 253; samples and tests 142, 152; transfusion 104, 106-107
breach of confidence 23, 141-146, 155, 162
breach of statutory duty 23, 85, 162

capabilities approach 30, 33-34, 37-38
care ethics 31-32, 94, 276
children: abuse 57; best interests 218; consent to treatment 97, 186; decision-making 36; disabilities 34n6, 54-55, 80, 189n41, 192,

Index

204, 207; medical expenses 6; organs and tissues 248-249; rationality 39; standard of care 133; *see also* adoption; conjoined twins; reproduction

civil liabilities: defences to civil liabilities 23, 49, 72, 145; medical practitioners 23-24, 118; TCM practitioners 175-178; *see also* breach of confidence; contract; tort law

cloning 201-202, 207, 255, 264

complementary medicine 2, 60, 164, 165n9

confidentiality: assisted reproduction 193; biomedical research 254n6, 263, 265n73, 266n75, 266n76; duties generally 45, 136, 139-140; ethical guidelines 159-160; genetic information 37, 155-157; software medical devices 278; statutory duties 146-149; surrogacy 197; surveillance 160; TCM practitioners 172-173; telemedicine 273; tissues and organs 233, 236, 240; *see also* breach of confidence; personal data and privacy

Confucianism 31, 40, 46

conjoined twins 103, 221-224, 231

consent: abortion 188-189; assisted reproduction 193, 194; biomedical research 251, 254-255, 258-263, 265, 267-268, 279; deemed consent 140, 149-151; to disclosure of confidential information 140, 147-151, 154, 156-160, 162, 172, 190; by donee of LPA 101; by donors 194, 234-236, 240, 252; end of life 216-217, 221, 224, 226; informed consent 65-66, 74, 108, 172, 206, 249-250; meaning and scope 94-98, 135; to nutrition 107; parental consent 103, 189; presumed consent 238, 245; surrogacy 196; telemedicine 273; to treatment 68-69, 105-106, 110-112, 175; validity of 95-98; withdrawal of 107; *see also* mental capacity, *volenti non fit injuria*

consequentialism 27-29

contraceptives 185-188

contract: breach of 23, 186, 248; duty/obligation 52, 142, 145, 152, 161; liability 86; prohibited contracts 202-203, 236-237, 240-242

conversion 246, 249-251

corpse 244-246

criminal liabilities 120-122, 149, 236-237, 241-243, 253; defences to crime 22, 122-127, 133, 137; medical practitioners 22-23, 118, 187, 214, 225, 251; TCM practitioners 173-174, 183; *see also* defences; *ex turpi causa*

damage: assessment of damages for negligence 86-88; battery 106; breach of confidence 144; causation 72-78; egg-shell-skull rule 78-79; loss of chance 80-83; remoteness of damage 78; scope of duty 80; types of damage (personal injuries, psychiatric harms) 54-55

death and dying: assisted dying 227-228; cardiac and brain death 201-203; death certificate 210; dignified death 230; doctrine of double effect 221, 223; imminent death 104, 213, 225; mortality rate 1; palliative care 38, 209, 213, 221, 225, 231; quality of death 209; *see also* AMD; conjoined twins; euthanasia

Declaration of Helsinki 265, 269n93

defences: contributory negligence 84-86; *ex turpi causa* 83; necessity 103, 222-224, 227; no exemption of liability 86; *volenti non fit injuria* 83-84; *see also* criminal liabilities

dementia 1, 113, 115-116, 135-136

dentists 7-9, 22, 24, 84n73, 121n52, 262-263

deontology 29-30, 35, 46

detention: of persons with mental disorder 83, 103, 116-117, 134

diagnostic and statistical manual of mental disorders (DSM) 100n36, 115-116

diminished responsibility 83, 122, 125-127, 137, 155

Director of Medical Services 11-13, 117, 146-148, 189, 239-240, 244, 261, 279

disability or disabilities 33-34, 79, 92, 114, 116, 121, 126, 132-133, 224, 226, 230, 264n72; insurance coverage 5-6; mental or intellectual 122, 128-129, 257; rights of persons with 42, 114; TCM practitioner 169-170; *see also* children

discipline: dental practitioners 22; ethical guidelines 46, 110; medical practitioners 43, 65, 108-109, 140, 157-160, 162, 214-215, 269-272; process 2, 8, 14-19, 24; sentencing 20-22; TCM practitioners 170-171, 178-180, 183

doctrine of double effect 42-43, 221, 223

duty of care: contraceptives 186; doctor-patient relationship 52; duty to third parties 136; general principles 45, 49-51; hospital administration 59; human organs and tissues 248-249; medical emergency 53; medical examinations and reports 57-58; patient's genetic information 155-157; personal injuries 54; psychiatric harm 54-57; telemedicine 273; wrongful life 207; wrongful prolongation of life 216

emergencies 11, 23, 52-53, 59, 64, 66-68, 71, 103, 106, 108, 111, 150, 158, 171, 257n12, 263, 275
ethics: abortion 190-192; biomedical research 264-268; confidentiality 159-160; design of care robots 276; ethics bodies and committees 11, 26-27, 194, 240, 255, 270; euthanasia 228-231; principlism 34-39; TCM practitioners 178-180; theories 27-34
euthanasia 29, 220; conscientious objection 30; physician-assisted 37, 215, 224-231

fairness: biomedical research 266; charging of medical fees 17n108, 43; conjoined twins 222; disciplinary process and sentencing 21-22, 24; duty of care 51; egg-shell skull rule 79; expropriation of human tissues 250; general concept 32-33; human embryo research 203; information technologies 279; non-delegable duty 89; organ transplant 239-240; resource allocation 39; standard of care of mentally disordered defendants 132; TCM practitioner 176-177; to patients 45; see also justice

genetics: cloning 201-202, 207, 255, 264; genetic information 37, 59, 155-157, 162; genetic testing 142; human dignity 40; mitochondrial donation 200; see also reproduction
good Samaritan law 53-54

health: health products 12, 61, 146n52, 150, 257, 262, 264, 274, 277, 279; health promotion 1, 3, 13; health surveillance 160; meaning 2-3; public health 1, 8, 11-12, 143n25, 148, 153, 234n5, 257, 272; see also mental health
Health Sciences Authority (HSA) 12-13, 61, 181-183, 242, 255, 262, 264n70, 272n109
healthcare: costs 5-7; medical education and training 7-8; services 4, 10-11; team-based 68-69; see also regulation, healthcare professionals and healthcare institutions
Hippocratic Oath 37, 44, 139, 230-231
HIV patients 143n24, 144, 147-148, 153, 156n127, 193, 242-243
human biomedical research: clinical trials 261-264; definition and scope 256-258; ethical guidelines 264-268; framework 254-255; law and regulations 233-234, 260-261

human body and parts 243; property rights 244-252
human dignity 29, 31, 40, 44-46, 74, 95, 139, 144-145, 171, 229, 266n76
human organs and tissues: bioprinting 252-253; donations 236, 239-240, 243-244; sale and supply 236-238, 240-243; transplants 238-240

Institute of Mental Health (IMH) 114-115, 158
institutional review boards (IRBs) 236, 255, 258-261, 264, 267, 270, 279
insurance: biomedical research and clinical trials 263, 268; long-term care 6; medical insurance system 5-6; for medical practitioners 9; processing by third party administrators 46; TCM expenses coverage 167
intoxication 124-125, 137

justice 34, 45, 59, 265n74, 266; capabilities approach 33; miscarriage of 19; principlism 34-35, 38-39; sentencing in disciplinary process 21; see also fairness

licensing terms and conditions for assisted reproduction services 2020 (LTC-ARS 2020) 192-194, 196, 200
life: quality of 4, 33, 37, 41, 46, 136, 218, 222, 225, 229, 231; sanctity of 41, 206, 219, 222, 225, 229-231; see also rights, to life
life-sustaining treatment 101, 213, 214, 219; refusal of 226; withholding or withdrawal of 30, 214, 215, 226, 229, 231
limitation periods 91-93

mandatory treatment order 129-130
medical: medical bodies and institutions 13-14; medical negligence protocols 90-91; medical profession 3, 18, 20, 26, 30, 44-46, 61, 66, 69, 82, 106, 160, 162, 218, 225-226, 230-231
mental capacity: assessment of 97-100, 116, 217; autonomy 36; code of practice 118; consent 136, 235-236, 259, 267; court deputies 119-120; ethical guidelines 108-109, 111-112; lasting power of attorney 118-119; limitation period 92; professional donees and deputies 120, 137
mental disorder: assessment of 3, 99, 114-115; care and treatment of persons with mental disorder 116-119; medical advice to persons with mental

disorder 135; sentencing of offenders with mental disorder 127-130; tort liabilities of persons with mental disorder 130-134
mental health: abortion 188-189; in community 113-114; meaning 116; see also mental capacity; mental disorder
Ministry of Health (MOH) 4-8, 11, 13, 22, 68, 113-114, 153, 159, 166-167, 190, 196, 255, 276n122
moral relativism 34

nanobiotechnology 268
National Medical Ethics Committee (NMEC) 26-27, 157, 215, 254n1, 255
negligence 23, 46, 49-51
neurotechnology 268-269
non-delegable duties 72, 88-90
non-maleficence 34-35, 37-38, 45-46, 107
Norwich Pharmacal order 161
Nuremberg Code 41, 264
nurses 8, 10, 68, 94, 106, 114, 117, 120n47, 121n52, 143n25, 217, 238

Office of Public Guardian (OPG) 121

palliative care 38, 209, 213-214, 221, 225, 231
parent: parental consent 186, 189; parental right 97, 200-201; parenthood 198, 204-205, 208n171
PDPC Advisory Guidelines for Healthcare Sector 150, 152n98, 155
persistent vegetative state (PVS) patients 206, 211n7, 212, 217, 219-220, 225-226, 229, 231
personal data: access and ownership 154-155; consent 149-150; data intermediary 152-153; protection 23, 140, 146, 149, 151, 273; purpose 149-151
personhood 29, 32; human dignity 40; rationality 39; sentience 40
pharmacists 8, 10, 22, 121n52, 146n52, 154-155, 186, 275
principlism 34-39, 45-46
privacy 36, 40, 46, 128n91, 140, 153, 155, 160-162, 257n12, 265n73, 266n76, 268-269, 278; anonymised information 140, 148, 155, 160, 257n12; meaning and scope 144-146; tort of misuse of private information 23, 142, 145, 153
psychiatric: care and/or treatment 83, 88, 113, 117, 127, 130, 134, 137; condition 3, 96, 126, 130, 158;
harm or injuries 50, 54-57, 79, 86, 247-249; institution 116-117, 130, 134, 137

regulation: healthcare institutions 11-12, 147-148; healthcare professionals 8-10; private hospitals and medical clinics 146-147, 151, 193n62
religion and/or religious views: Buddhism 230; Catholic 103, 203, 221; Christianity 230; Hinduism 230; Jewish 203; Islam or Muslim 107n72, 203, 215, 230, 238, 243
reproduction: assisted 37, 192-194, 197, 199, 206-207; in vitro fertilisation (IVF) 185, 192, 193-195, 197, 199, 205, 251; procreative beneficence 201; sex selection 200; wrongful birth 204-207, 216; wrongful life 206-208; see also cloning; genetics
res ipsa loquitur 69-70
rights: basic liberties 32, to health 41-42; to life 41, 190-191, 206, 222, 226, 229
robotics 255, 268-269, 273-274, 276, 279

Singapore Medical Council (SMC) 2, 17, 19, 21, 46, 158, 165-166, 272
SMC Ethical Code and Ethical Guidelines (ECEG) (2002) 68, 108, 159, 269-270
SMC Ethical Code and Ethical Guidelines (ECEG) (2016) 18, 44-46, 65, 68-69, 108-112, 159-160, 162, 218, 269-270, 273
SMC Handbook on Medical Ethics 45, 109, 159, 164-165
SMC Physician's Pledge 44
social egg-freezing 194
standard of care: of medical practitioners 59-66, 134-136; of mentally disordered defendants 130-134; of TCM practitioners 175-177
statistical evidence 73, 81, 83, 270
sterilisation 52n15, 77, 99, 186-188, 207
substituted judgement 102, 105, 225-226
surrogacy 37, 196-199, 207

technology: electronic health records (EHR) 275-277, 279; information technology 269, 279; innovative medicinal product 147; innovative treatments 269, 271-272; see also artificial intelligence; telehealth and telemedicine
telehealth 274-275, 279
telemedicine 46, 272-274, 279

tort law *see* battery; breach of statutory duty; conversion; negligence; privacy, tort of misuse of private information
traditional Chinese medicine (TCM): Chinese proprietary medicine 180-181, 183, 262; TCM practitioners 10, 22, 165-180; TCMPB Ethical Code and Ethical Guidelines 170-173, 177-179
traditional Indian medicine 182-183
traditional Malay medicine 181-182
transplant ethics committee (TEC) 240-241

UNESCO Declaration of Human Rights and the Human Genome 40
UNESCO Universal Declaration on Bioethics and Human Rights 266

unsoundness of mind or unsound mind 122-124, 126, 131, 137
utilitarianism 28-30, 33, 35, 38-40, 139, 223, 228-229, 248

vicarious liability 88-89
virtue ethics and virtues 28, 30-31, 35-36, 46, 230
volenti non fit injuria 83-84, 177
vulnerable adults 121-122

will: disposition by 251; statutory wills 122
World Health Organization (WHO) 2, 164n1, 266n75